Bayesian Methods for Interaction and Design

Intended for researchers and practitioners in interaction design, this book shows how Bayesian models can be brought to bear on problems of interface design and user modelling. It introduces and motivates Bayesian modelling and illustrates how powerful these ideas can be in thinking about human–computer interaction, especially in representing and manipulating uncertainty. Bayesian methods are increasingly practical as computational tools to implement them become more widely available, and offer a principled foundation to reason about interaction design.

The book opens with a self-contained tutorial on Bayesian concepts and their practical implementation, tailored for the background and needs of interaction designers. The contributed chapters cover the use of Bayesian probabilistic modelling in a diverse set of applications, including improving pointing-based interfaces, efficient text entry using modern language models, advanced interface design using cutting-edge techniques in Bayesian optimisation, and Bayesian approaches to modelling the cognitive processes of users.

JOHN H. WILLIAMSON is Senior Lecturer in Computing Science at the University of Glasgow.

ANTTI OULASVIRTA is Professor of Electrical Engineering and leads the User Interfaces research group at Aalto University and the Interactive AI research program at the Finnish Center for AI.

PER OLA KRISTENSSON is Professor of Interactive Systems Engineering in the Department of Engineering at the University of Cambridge and a Fellow of Trinity College, Cambridge.

NIKOLA BANOVIC is Assistant Professor of Electrical Engineering and Computer Science at the University of Michigan–Ann Arbor.

Bayesian Methods for Interaction and Design

Edited by

JOHN H. WILLIAMSON
University of Glasgow

ANTTI OULASVIRTA
Aalto University

PER OLA KRISTENSSON
University of Cambridge

NIKOLA BANOVIC
University of Michigan–Ann Arbor

CAMBRIDGE
UNIVERSITY PRESS

University Printing House, Cambridge CB2 8BS, United Kingdom

One Liberty Plaza, 20th Floor, New York, NY 10006, USA

477 Williamstown Road, Port Melbourne, VIC 3207, Australia

314–321, 3rd Floor, Plot 3, Splendor Forum, Jasola District Centre,
New Delhi – 110025, India

103 Penang Road, #05–06/07, Visioncrest Commercial, Singapore 238467

Cambridge University Press is part of the University of Cambridge.

It furthers the University's mission by disseminating knowledge in the pursuit of
education, learning, and research at the highest international levels of excellence.

www.cambridge.org
Information on this title: www.cambridge.org/9781108834995
DOI: 10.1017/9781108874830

First published 2022

A catalogue record for this publication is available from the British Library.

Library of Congress Cataloging-in-Publication Data
Names: Williamson, John H., 1980- editor. | Oulasvirta, Antti, 1979– editor. |
Kristensson, Per Ola, 1982- editor. | Banovic, Nikola, editor.
Title: Bayesian methods for interaction and design edited by John H. Williamson,
University of Glasgow, Antti Oulasvirta, Aalto University, Finland, Per Ola Kristensson,
University of Cambridge, Nikola Banovic, University of Michigan, Ann Arbor.
Description: First edition. | Cambridge, United Kingdom ; New York, NY, USA :
Cambridge University Press, 2022. | Includes bibliographical references.
Identifiers: LCCN 2022016991 (print) | LCCN 2022016992 (ebook) |
ISBN 9781108834995 (hardback) | ISBN 9781108792707 (paperback) |
ISBN 9781108874830 (epub)
Subjects: LCSH: Human-machine systems–Mathematical models. | Human
engineering–Mathematics. | User interfaces (Computer systems) | Bayesian statistical
decision theory. | BISAC: COMPUTERS / Social Aspects
Classification: LCC TA167 .B39 2022 (print) | LCC TA167 (ebook) |
DDC 620.8/2–dc23/eng/20220602
LC record available at https://lccn.loc.gov/2022016991
LC ebook record available at https://lccn.loc.gov/2022016992

ISBN 978-1-108-83499-5 Hardback
ISBN 978-1-108-79270-7 Paperback

Contents

8   Preferential Bayesian Optimisation for Visual Design
     Y. Koyama, T. Chong and T. Igarashi   239

9   Bayesian Optimisation of Interface Features   *J. Dudley*
     and P. O. Kristensson   259

Part IV   Bayesian Cognitive Modelling   285

10 Cue Integration in Input Performance   *B. Lee*   287

11 Bayesian Parameter Inference for Cognitive Simulators
     J. Jokinen, U. Remes, T. Kujala and J. Corander   308

     Appendix: Mathematical Background and Notation
     J. H. Williamson   335

Contributors

Nikola Banovic   *Electrical Engineering and Computer Science, University of Michigan, Ann Arbor, Michigan, USA*

Michel Beaudouin-Lafon   *CNRS, Inria, LISN, Paris-Saclay University, France*

Xiaojun Bi   *Department of Computer Science, Stony Brook University, Stony Brook, New York, USA*

Daniel Buschek   *Department of Computer Science, University of Bayreuth, Germany*

Toby Chong   *Department of Creative Informatics, Graduate School of Information Science and Technology, The University of Tokyo, Tokyo, Japan*

Jukka Corander   *Department of Mathematics and Statistics, University of Helsinki, Helsinki, Finland*

Alan Dix   *Computational Foundry, Swansea University, Swansea, Wales*

John Dudley   *Engineering Design Centre, University of Cambridge, Cambridge, UK*

Xiangmin Fan   *Institute of Software, Chinese Academy of Sciences, Beijing, China*

Dylan Gaines   *Department of Computer Science, Michigan Technological University, Houghton, Michigan, USA*

Takeo Igarashi   *Department of Creative Informatics, Graduate School of Information Science and Technology, The University of Tokyo, Tokyo, Japan*

Jussi P. P. Jokinen   *Department of Computer Science/Finnish Center for Artificial Intelligence (FCAI), University of Helsinki, Helsinki, Finland*

Per Ola Kristensson   *Engineering Design Centre, Department of Engineering, University of Cambridge, Cambridge, UK*

Yuki Koyama   *National Institute of Advanced Industrial Science and Technology (AIST), Ibaraki, Japan*

Tuomo Kujala   *Cognitive Science, University of Jyväskylä, Jyväskylä, Finland*

Byungjoo Lee   *Department of Computer Science, Yonsei University, Seoul, Korea*

Wanyu Liu   *STMS IRCAM-CNRS-Sorbonne Université, Paris, France*

Roderick Murray-Smith   *School of Computing Science, University of Glasgow, Glasgow, UK*

Antti Oulasvirta   *Finnish Center for Artificial Intelligence FCAI, Department of Communications and Networking, Aalto University, Helsinki, Finland*

Ulpu Remes   *Department of Computer Science, University of Helsinki, Helsinki, Finland*

Olivier Rioul   *ComElec, Télécom ParisTech, Paris, France*

Feng Tian   *Institute of Software, Chinese Academy of Sciences, Beijing, China*

Francesco Tonolini   *School of Computing Science, University of Glasgow, Glasgow, UK*

Keith Vertanen   *Department of Computer Science, Michigan Technological University, Houghton, Michigan, USA*

John H. Williamson   *School of Computing Science, University of Glasgow, Glasgow, UK*

Suwen Zhu   *Grammarly, Inc., San Francisco, California, USA*

Preface

Motivation

This edited book synthesises recent progress in applications of probabilistic methods in the area of human–computer interaction (HCI). HCI is a field concerned with the design and study of computing systems for human use. Most design efforts in HCI follow a human-centred (also known as user-centred) approach that considers the context of use and the abilities and needs of stakeholders. However, most existing human-centred methods prescribe resource-intensive design and evaluation methods. The prevailing paradigm relies extensively on trial and error and expensive empirical measurements.

HCI has recently revived its interest in using algorithmic approaches to drive design and evaluation [17]. *Computational interaction* is a topic area that studies algorithmic methods to optimise designs, adapt user interfaces, automate evaluation, and even explain and describe interaction through simulation of user interfaces and prediction of user actions on those interfaces. However, traditional computational modelling approaches in HCI [1], such as model human processor (MHP) [5], GOMS [11] and Fitts' law [15], ignore uncertainty. Statistical analysis methods commonly used in HCI tend towards a frequentist treatment of probability with its known shortcomings [3, 13].

This book aims to fill a gap in the literature and promote research on Bayesian methods in HCI. Bayesian methods, such as *Bayesian statistical analysis* [9] (statistics that use Bayesian interpretation of probability of events) and *uncertainty quantification (UQ)* [10] (the characterisation and computation of uncertainty and confidence for models and data in a principled statistical manner), have been adopted across a wide range of scientific and engineering research disciplines and fields (e.g. physics [16], nuclear safety and management [18], astronautical engineering [6], medicine and healthcare [2]). However, despite there being Bayesian approaches to a variety of related problems in science and engineering, applications in HCI are still nascent. Although there are already some examples of successful use of Bayesian methods in interaction design (e.g. supporting user modelling [4, 12], probabilistic interfaces [44], novel interactions [20, 21], design optimisation [8, 14], evaluation and statistical analysis [7, 13]), such methods are not yet widely adopted in the broader HCI community.

Outline

The chapters in this book expose the reader to Bayesian methods for interaction design and teach them how to apply such principled methods to their own research and practice. One of the main goals of this book is to bridge the gap between literature on theoretical Bayesian methods and practical applications in interaction and design and make Bayesian methods accessible to a broader HCI audience.

This book does so through a series of chapters split in four parts, beginning with an introduction to Bayesian methods and Bayesian statistics, followed by a section that illustrates applications of Bayesian inference to infer user intents in probabilistic interfaces. This is followed by a collection of chapters on Bayesian optimisation in the design of interfaces. The final section illustrates use of Bayesian methods in cognitive and user performance modelling and simulation.

Part I of this book explains the Bayesian treatment of probability and uncertainty through two chapters. Chapter 1 makes a case for Bayesian modelling and illustrates principles and applications of Bayesian inference on simple, tutorial-like examples relevant to interactive design. Chapter 2 explains Bayesian statistics and its application to interactive design evaluation. After reading Part I, the reader will have the foundational knowledge on how to apply the Bayesian method to interactive design with a road map for how to explore related, more advanced topics further.

Part II illustrates how to design user interfaces that can reduce the uncertainty about the user's goals and intentions using Bayesian inference. Chapters 3–6 show how to infer user goals and intentions for four different, fundamental interaction types: information search, pointing target selection, command selection and text entry. Chapter 7 then discusses how to combine forward (traditional ML) models with inverse (Bayesian) modelling in the context of touch sensing. Having read Part II, the reader will know how to implement probabilistic user interfaces that can reason about and act in response to inherently uncertain user behaviours.

The next part of the book, Part III, illustrates Bayesian optimisation approaches to design user interfaces that optimise for user preferences and abilities. User preferences for particular features of an interface or the interface as a whole are notoriously difficult to elicit and often require repeated, costly empirical user studies. The chapters in this part detail how to use Bayesian optimisation to efficiently reduce the search space of all possible interfaces to a few user-desired options. The methods covered in this section will give the reader new tools to optimise their user interface design in a principled way that goes beyond trial and error.

Finally, Part IV illustrates applications of Bayesian approaches to computational cognitive models that simulate human decision-making and physical actions. Such approaches provide a theoretical and methodological update to traditional computational modelling approaches in HCI. After reading these final chapters, the reader will be able to apply a probabilistic lens onto the user's decision-making and how their cognitive plans result in physical action.

References

[1] N. Banovic, A. Oulasvirta and P. O. Kristensson. 2019. Computational modeling in human–computer interaction. Page 1–7, Paper No. W26 of: *Extended Abstracts of the 2019 CHI Conference on Human Factors in Computing Systems*. CHI EA '19. Association for Computing Machinery.

[2] E. Begoli, T. Bhattacharya and D. Kusnezov. 2019. The need for uncertainty quantification in machine-assisted medical decision making. *Nature Machine Intelligence*, **1**(1), 20–23.

[3] L. Besançon and P. Dragicevic. 2019. The continued prevalence of dichotomous inferences at CHI. Pages 1–11 of: *Extended Abstracts of the 2019 CHI Conference on Human Factors in Computing Systems*. Association for Computing Machinery.

[4] X. Bi and S. Zhai. 2013. Bayesian touch: a statistical criterion of Target selection with finger touch. Pages 51–60 of: *Proceedings of the 26th Annual ACM Symposium on User Interface Software and Technology*. UIST '13. Association for Computing Machinery.

[5] S. K. Card, A. Newell and T. P. Moran. 1983. *The Psychology of Human–Computer Interaction*. L. Erlbaum Associates Inc.

[6] L. G. Crespo, S. P. Kenny and D. P. Giesy. 2014. The NASA Langley multidisciplinary uncertainty quantification challenge. In: *16th AIAA Non-Deterministic Approaches Conference*. American Institute of Aeronautics and Astronautics.

[7] P. Dragicevic, Y. Jansen, A. Sarma, M. Kay and F. Chevalier. 2019. Increasing the transparency of research papers with explorable multiverse analyses. Pages 1–15, Paper No. 65 of: *Proceedings of the 2019 CHI Conference on Human Factors in Computing Systems*. CHI '19. Association for Computing Machinery.

[8] J. J. Dudley, J. T. Jacques and P. O. Kristensson. 2019. Crowdsourcing interface feature design with Bayesian optimization. Pages 1–12, Paper No. 252 of: *Proceedings of the 2019 CHI Conference on Human Factors in Computing Systems.* CHI '19. Association for Computing Machinery.

[9] A. Gelman, J. B. Carlin, H. S. Stern and D. B. Rubin. 2004. *Bayesian Data Analysis*, 2nd ed. Chapman and Hall/CRC.

[10] R. Ghanem, D. Higdon and H. Owhadi, eds. 2017. *Handbook of Uncertainty Quantification.* Springer International Publishing.

[11] B. E. John and D. E. Kieras. 1996. The GOMS family of user interface analysis techniques: comparison and contrast. *ACM Transactions on Computer–Human Interaction*, **3**(4), 320–351.

[12] A. Kangasrääsiö, J. P. P. Jokinen, A. Oulasvirta, A. Howes and S. Kaski. 2019. Parameter inference for computational cognitive models with approximate Bayesian computation. *Cognitive Science*, **43**(6), e12738.

[13] M. Kay, G. L. Nelson and E. B. Hekler. 2016. Researcher-centered design of statistics: why Bayesian statistics better fit the culture and incentives of HCI. Pages 4521–4532 of: *Proceedings of the 2016 CHI Conference on Human Factors in Computing Systems.* CHI '16. Association for Computing Machinery.

[14] J. D. Lomas, J. Forlizzi, N. Poonwala, P. Patel, S. Shodhan, K. Patel, K. Koedinger and E. Brunskill. 2016. Interface design optimization as a multi-armed bandit problem. Pages 4142–4153 of: *Proceedings of the 2016 CHI Conference on Human Factors in Computing Systems.* CHI '16. Association for Computing Machinery.

[15] I. S. MacKenzie. 1992. Fitts' law as a research and design tool in human–computer interaction. *Human–Computer Interaction*, **7**(1), 91–139.

[16] W. L. Oberkampf, T. G. Trucano and C. Hirsch. 2004. Verification, validation, and predictive capability in computational engineering and physics. *Applied Mechanics Reviews*, **57**(5), 345–384.

[17] A. Oulasvirta, X. Bi and A. Howes. 2018. *Computational Interaction.* Oxford University Press.

[18] M. Pilch, T. G. Trucano and J. C. Helton. 2006. *Ideas Underlying Quantification of Margins and Uncertainties (QMU): A White Paper.* Technical report, Sandia National Laboratories.

[44] J. Schwarz, J. Mankoff and S. Hudson. 2011. Monte Carlo methods for managing interactive state, action and feedback under uncertainty. Pages 235–244 of: *Proceedings of the 24th Annual ACM Symposium on User Interface Software and Technology.* UIST '11. Association for Computing Machinery.

[20] A. Spielberg, A. Sample, S. E. Hudson, J. Mankoff and J. McCann. 2016. RapID: a framework for fabricating low-latency interactive objects with RFID tags. Pages 5897–5908 of: *Proceedings of the 2016 CHI Conference on Human Factors in Computing Systems.* CHI '16. Association for Computing Machinery.

[21] E. Zhang and N. Banovic. 2021. Method for exploring generative adversarial networks (GANs) via automatically generated image galleries. In: *Proceedings of the 2021 CHI Conference on Human Factors in Computing Systems.* CHI '21. Association for Computing Machinery.

Part I

Introduction to Bayesian Methods

1

An Introduction to Bayesian Methods for Interaction Design

John H. Williamson

Abstract

Bayesian modelling has much to offer those working in human–computer interaction, but many of the concepts are alien. This chapter introduces Bayesian modelling in interaction design. The chapter outlines the philosophical stance that sets Bayesian approaches apart, as well as a light introduction to the nomenclature and computational and mathematical machinery. We discuss specific models of relevance to interaction, including probabilistic filtering, non-parametric Bayesian inference, approximate Bayesian computation and belief networks. We include a worked example of a Fitts' law modelling task from a Bayesian perspective, applying Bayesian linear regression via a probabilistic program. We identify five distinct facets of Bayesian interaction: probabilistic interaction in the control loop; Bayesian optimisation at design time; analysis of empirical results with Bayesian statistics; visualisation and interaction with Bayesian models; and Bayesian cognitive modelling of users. We conclude with a discussion of the pros and cons of Bayesian approaches, the ethical implications therein and suggestions for further reading.

1.1 Introduction

We assume that most readers will be coming to this text from an interaction design background and are looking to expand their knowledge of Bayesian approaches, and we started from this framing when structuring this chapter. Some readers may be coming the other way, from a Bayesian statistics background to interaction design. These readers will find interesting problems and applications of statistical methods in interaction design.

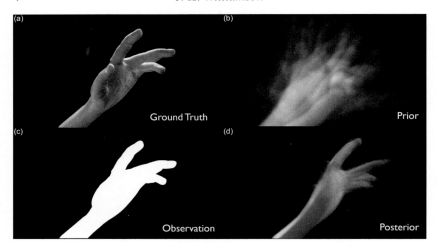

Figure 1.1 Which hand pose, generated the silhouette (c)? We cannot resolve a unique answer from this **observation**. Instead, we can start from a **prior** set (b) of viable hand poses and infer the distribution of *likely* poses given the observed silhouette (the **posterior** belief about poses) (d). **Uncertainty** about the pose is represented in the prior and reduced (but still present) in the posterior, inferred after observing the silhouette.

This book discusses how Bayesian approaches can be used to build models of human interactions with machines. Modelling is the cornerstone of good science, and actionable computational models of interactive systems are the basis of *computational interaction* [42]. A Bayesian approach makes *uncertainty* a first-class element of a model and provides the technical means to reason about uncertain beliefs computationally.

Human–computer interaction is rife with uncertainty. Explicitly modelling uncertainty is a bountiful path to better models and ultimately better interactive systems. The Bayesian world view gives an elegant and compelling basis to reason about the problems we face in interaction, and it comes with a superbly equipped wardrobe of computational tools to apply the theory. Bayesian approaches can be engaged across the whole spectrum of interaction, from the most fine-grained, pixel-level modelling of a pointer to questions about the social impact of always-on augmented reality. Everyone involved in interaction design, at every level, can benefit from these ideas. Thinking about interaction in Bayesian terms can be a refreshing perspective to re-examine old problems.

And, as this book illustrates, it can also be transformational in practically delivering the human–computer interactions of the future.

A Note on This Chapter
This chapter is intended to be a high-level look at Bayesian approaches *from the point of view of an interaction designer.* Where possible, I have omitted mathematical terminology; the Appendix of the book gives a short introduction to standard terminology and notation. In some places I have provided skeleton code in Python. This is not intended to be executable, but to be a readable way to formalise the concepts for a computer scientist audience, and should be interpretable even if you are not familiar with Python. All data and examples are synthetic.

The chapter is structured as follows:

- A short introduction to Bayesian inference for the unfamiliar.
- A high-level discussion of the distinctive aspects of Bayesian modelling.
- A detailed worked example of Bayesian modelling in an HCI problem.
- A short summary of Bayesian algorithms and techniques particularly relevant to interaction, including approximate Bayesian computation, Bayesian optimisation and probabilistic filtering.
- A discussion of the important facets of Bayesian interaction design.
- Finally, a reflection on the implications of these ideas as well as recommendations for further reading.

1.1.1 What Are Bayesian Methods?

Bayesian methods is a broad term. In this book, the ideas are linked by the fundamental property of representing *uncertain belief* using probability distributions, and updating those beliefs with evidence. The underpinning of probability theory puts this on a firm theoretical basis, but the concept is simple: we represent what we know about the specific aspects of the world with a **distribution** that tells us how likely possible configurations of the world are, and then refine belief about these possibilities with data. We can repeat this process as required, accumulating evidence and reducing our uncertainty. In its simplest form, this boils down to simply counting potential configurations of the world, then adjusting those counts to be compatible with some observed data. This idea has been become vastly more practical as computational power has surged, making the efficient 'counting of possibilities' a feasible task for complex problems.

Why Model at All?

'I am never content until I have constructed a mechanical model of the subject I am studying. If I succeed in making one, I understand, otherwise I do not.' – Lord Kelvin, *Baltimore Lectures on Molecular Dynamics and the Wave Theory of Light.* 1884
For the twenty-first century, replace 'mechanical' with 'computational'.

Modelling creates a simplified version of a problem that we can more easily manipulate, and could be mathematical, computational or physical in nature. Good science depends on good models. Models can be shared, criticised and re-used. Fields of study where there is healthy exchange of models can 'ratchet' constructively, one investigation feeding into the next. In interaction design, modelling has been relatively weak. When models have been used, they have often been descriptive in nature rather than causal. One of the motivations for a Bayesian approach is in the adoption of statistical models that are less about describing or predicting the superficial future state of the world and more about predicting the underlying state of the world. The other motivation is to build and work with models that properly account for uncertainty.

We can consider the relative virtues of models, in terms of their authenticity to the real-world phenomena, their complexity or their mathematical convenience. However, for the purposes of human–computer interaction, several virtues are especially relevant:

- Models that are *generative* and can be executed in a computer simulation to produce synthetic data.
- Models that are *computational* and can be manipulated, transformed and validated algorithmically; for example, written as programs.
- Models that are conveniently *parameterisable* and ideally have parameters that are meaningful and interpretable.
- Models that are *causal* and describe the underlying origins of phenomena rather than predict the manifestations of phenomena.
- Models that preserve and propagate *uncertainty*.
- Models that fit well with software engineering practices to deploy them, whether embedded in an interaction loop, in design tools or in analyses of evaluations.

1.1.2 What Is Distinctive about *Bayesian* Modelling?

Bayesian modelling has several salient consequences:

- We can often directly use *simulators* of the process we believe to be generating the world that we observe, instead of relying on abstract, fixed models that can be difficult to shoehorn into interaction problems. For example, we might be able to use a detailed, agent-based simulation of pedestrian movement rather than a standard regression model.
- We reason from belief to evidence, not the other way around. This subtle difference means that we have a way to easily fuse information from many sources. This can range from sensor fusion in an inertial measuring unit to meta-reviews of surveys in the literature.
- We have a *universal* approach to solving problems that gives us a simple and consistent way to formulate questions and reason our way to answers.
- We also have a *universal* language with which to exchange and combine information: the probability distribution. Want to plug a language model into a gesture recogniser? No problem – exchange probability distributions.
- That same freedom and flexibility to model, and the need to represent distributions rather than values, implies technical difficulties. The devil is in the details.

1.1.3 How Is This Relevant to Interaction Design?

Everything we do with interactive systems has substantial *uncertainty* inherent in it. We don't know who our users are. We don't know what they want, or how they behave, or even how they tend to move. We don't know where they are, or in what context they are operating. The evidence that we *can* acquire is typically weakly informative and often indirectly related to problems we wish to address. This extends across all levels, from tightly closed control loops to design-time questions or retrospective evaluations. For example:

- Do a user's pointing movements indicate an intention to press button A or B?
- Is now a good moment to pop up a dialog?
- How many touch interaction events will happen in the next 500 ms?
- How tired is the user right now?
- Is it better to allocate a shorter keyboard shortcut to Save or for Refresh?
- Does adding spring-back to a scrolling menu increase or decrease user stress?
- Which volatility visualisation strategy helps users make more rational decisions?
- Is this interactive system more or less likely to polarise society?

We typically have at least partial models of how the human world works: from psychology, physiology, sociology or physics. Good interaction design behooves us to take advantage of all the modelling we can derive from the research of others. Being able to slot together models from disparate fields is essential to advance science. The Bayesian approach of formally incorporating knowledge as priors can make this a consistent and reasonable thing to do.

We are in the business of interacting with computers – so computational methods are universally available to us. We care little about methods that are efficient to be hand-solved algebraically. The blossoming field of *computational* Bayesian statistics means that we can realistically embed Bayesian models in interactive systems or use them to design and analyse empirical studies at the push of a button. We have problems where it is important to pool and fuse information, whether in low-level fusion of sensor streams or in combining survey data from multiple studies. We have fast CPUs and GPUs and software libraries that subsume the fiddly details of inference.

1.1.4 What Does This Give Us?

Why might we consider Bayesian approaches?

- Taming uncertainty by representing and manipulating it grants us robustness, whether this is robustness within a control loop or in the interpretation of the evaluation of a system. Represented uncertainty *regularises* predictions and avoids making extreme inferences based on limited data.
- We explicitly and precisely model *prior beliefs*. This allows knowledge to be encoded, inspected and shared, whether among software components or among researchers.
- A focus on generative models leads us to model constructively, to build models that synthesise what we expect to observe. These models can be strikingly more insightful than models that seek to summarise or describe what we have observed.
- Bayesian inference makes it realistic to fuse information from many sources without ad hoc tricks, and a principled way to deal with missing data and imputation.

Most of all, Bayesian approaches give us a new perspective from which to garner insight into problems of interaction, supported by a bedrock of mathematical and computational tools.

1.1.5 Is This Just for Statistical Analysis?

Bayesian methods are a powerful tool for empirical analysis, and historically Bayesian methods have been used for statistical analyses of the type familiar to HCI researchers in user evaluations. But that is not their only role in interaction design, and arguably not even the most important role they can play. Bayesian methods can be used directly within the control loop as a way of robustly tracking states (for example, using probabilistic filtering). Bayesian optimisation makes it possible to optimise systems that are hard and expensive to measure, such as subjective responses to UI layouts. Bayesian ideas can change the way we think about how users make sense of interfaces, how we should represent uncertainty to them and how we should predict users' cognitive processes.

1.2 A Short Tutorial

Terminology We will use a number of specific terms in the rest of the chapter:

- **model** a simplified representation of a problem that has some parts that can vary. Our models will always be implemented as computer programs.
- **parameter** one variable in a model that partially determines how a model operates.
- **configuration** a collection of parameter values that fully specifies a specific instantiation of a model.
- **observations** values which we observe, i.e. data.
- **probability** a number between 0 and 1 representing how much we believe something.
- **distribution** an assignment of probabilities to possible configurations, defining how likely each is.
- **sample** a specific value, drawn at random according to a probability distribution.
- **prior** a belief about the world before observing data, as a distribution over configurations.
- **posterior** a belief about the world after observing data, as a distribution over configurations.
- **likelihood** a belief about how likely observations are, given a configuration, as a distribution over possible observations.

We will also use the following notation for probability:

- $P(A)$ the probability that event A occurs.
- $P(A, B)$ the probability that both event A and event B occur together.
- $P(A|B)$ the probability that event A occurs, if we *know* that B occurs.

See the Appendix of this book for a more thorough explanation.

1.2.1 An Example of Bayesian Inference

Imagine we have three app variants deployed to a group of users, A, B and C. App A has two buttons on the splash screen, App B has four, and App C has nine. We get a log event that indicates that '3' in the splash screen was pressed, but not which app generated it. Which app was the user using, given this information (Figure 1.2)?

We have an unobserved **parameter** (which app is being used) and observed **evidence** (button 3 was pressed). Let us further assume there are 10 test users using the app: five using A, two using B and three using C. This gives us a **prior** belief about which app is being used (for example, if we knew nothing about the interaction, we expect it is 50% more likely that App C is being used than App B). We also need to assume a *model* of behaviour. We might assume a very simple model that users are equally likely to press any button – the **likelihood** of choosing any button is equal.

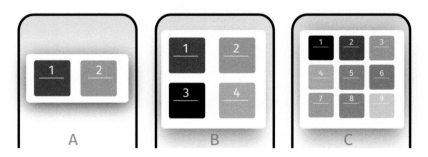

Figure 1.2 Which app was used? We know button 3 was pressed, but not on which app.

This is a problem of Bayesian updating (Figure 1.3); how to move from a prior probability distribution over apps to a posterior distribution over apps, having observed some evidence in the form of a button press.

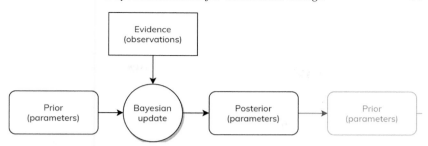

Figure 1.3 Bayesian inference takes a prior probability distribution, which represents beliefs about parameters, incorporates observed evidence and produces a posterior distribution which captures those beliefs that are compatible with the evidence. The posterior from one inference step can form the prior of a subsequent update.

How do we compute this? In this case, we can just count up the possibilities for each app, as shown in Figure 1.4.

We know that button 3 was logged, so:

- There is no possibility that the user was using App A, which has only two buttons.
- If they were using App B, 1/4 of the time they would press 3; and 1/9 of the time if using App C.

These numbers come directly from our assumption that buttons are pressed with equal likelihood, and so the **likelihoods** of seeing button 3 for each app are (A = 0, B = 1/4, C = 1/9). Given our prior knowledge about the number of apps in use, we can multiply these likelihoods by how likely we thought the particular app was *before* observing the '3'. This **prior** was (A = 5/10, B = 2/10, C = 3/10). This gives us: (A = 0 * 5/10, B = 1/4 * 2/10, C = 1/9 * 3/10) = (0, 1/20, 1/30). We can normalise this so it sums to 1 to make it a proper probability distribution: (0, 3/5, 2/5). This is the **posterior** distribution, the probability distribution revised to be compatible with the evidence. We *now* believe there is a 60% chance that App B was used and a 40% chance App C was used.

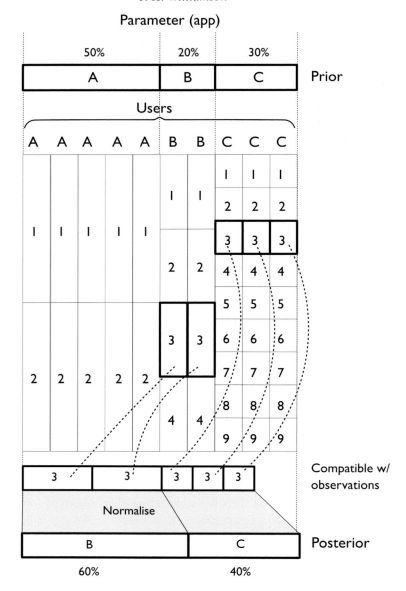

Figure 1.4 A table showing the parameters and the likelihood of each possible option (top). By selecting those compatible with the evidence, we can work out the division of possibilities that gives us the posterior probability distribution (bottom).

A2 B2 B1 C5 B4 A2 B2 C5 A2 C5 C6 C5 C1 A2 A1 B2 B4 A2 A2 C2 C5 **C3** **B3** **C3** C7 B1 C8 A1 A2 A1 C8 A1
A1 C6 A1 A1 C2 C7 A1 A2 A2 C9 A2 A1 C1 B4 A2 A1 A1 A1 A2 A1 C5 C1 C4 A2 A2 A1 C7 C9 C4 C4 B2 C1
B2 B2 B2 B4 A2 B4 C8 C2 A1 A2 A2 A1 A1 A1 **B3** A1 C4 A1 C1 A1 A2 A1 A1 C1 A2 B1 C5 A2 C8 A2 **B3** C5
A1 B1 C2 A1 A1 B4 A1 C9 C2 **B3** A1 A2 B4 B4 C2 C5 C5 C6 C1 C4 B1 C9 A1 B4 B2 B1 B2 A1 A1 **B3** B1 A1
A2 A2 C7 B1 A2 C7 C9 **B3** C6 A1 A1 C5 C7 B2 A1 C6 A1 C5 C4 C9 A1 A2 C6 C2 A1 B2 A1 B2 A1 B2 **C3** C5
B2 A1 A1 C1 C8 A2 B1 A2 C2 A1 **B3** C5 B1 A2 B1 B4 A2 **B3** C8 C9 A2 C7 A1 **B3** B1 A1 A1 C4 B2 A2 A2 A2
C5 C5 A1 A1 C1 **B3** A1 A1 A2 A1 B4 A1 A1 B2 A2 C7 C4 A1 C6 **C3** B4 C8 C7 A2 A1 A1 A2 A2 A2 A1 A1 **C3**
C1 C1 B2 A1 **C3** C1 A1 A2 A2 A2 C4 A1 C8 A1 A2 C9 A2 C2 A2 B4 A1 C8 C4 C6 A2 A1 **B3** C4 A1 C9 C1 **B3**

Figure 1.5 Simulating the predictive model and highlighting elements where button 3 is pressed.

A1 A1 A1 A1 A1 A1 A1 A1 A1 A1 A1 A1 A1 A1 A1 A1 A1 A1 A1 A1 A1 A1 A1 A1 A1 A1 A1 A1 A1 A1 A1 A1
A1 A1 A1 A1 A1 A1 A1 A1 A1 A1 A1 A1 A1 A1 A1 A1 A1 A1 A1 A1 A1 A1 A1 A1 A1 A1 A1 A1 A1 A1 A1 A1
A1 B1 B1 B1 B1 B1 B1 B1 B1 B1 B1 B1 C1 C1 C1 C1 C1 C1 C1 C1 C1 C1 C1 C1 C1 A2 A2 A2 A2 A2 A2 A2
A2 A2 A2 A2 A2 A2 A2 A2 A2 A2 A2 A2 A2 A2 A2 A2 A2 A2 A2 A2 A2 A2 A2 A2 A2 A2 A2 A2 A2 A2 A2 A2
A2 A2 A2 A2 A2 A2 A2 A2 B2 B2 B2 B2 B2 B2 B2 B2 B2 B2 B2 B2 B2 B2 B2 B2 B2 C2 C2 C2 C2 C2 C2
C2 C2 C2 **B3 B3 B3 B3 B3 B3 B3 B3 B3 B3 B3 B3** **C3 C3 C3 C3 C3 C3** B4 B4 B4 B4 B4 B4 B4 B4 B4 B4
B4 B4 C4 C4 C4 C4 C4 C4 C4 C4 C4 C4 C5 C5 C5 C5 C5 C5 C5 C5 C5 C5 C5 C5 C5 C5 C5 C5 C6 C6 C6
C6 C6 C6 C6 C6 C7 C7 C7 C7 C7 C7 C7 C7 C7 C8 C8 C8 C8 C8 C8 C8 C8 C9 C9 C9 C9 C9 C9 C9 C9

Figure 1.6 There are 12 Bs and 6 Cs in this random sample; a 66%/33% split close to the expected 60%/40% split.

This is easy to verify if we simulate this model to generate synthetic data.

```python
import random

def simulate_app():
    # simulate a random user with a random app
    app = random.choice("AAAAABBCCC")
    if app=='A':
        button = random.choice([1,2])
    if app=='B':
        button = random.choice([1,2,3,4])
    if app=='C':
        button = random.choice([1,2,3,4,5,6,7,8,9])
    return app, button
```

If we run this simulation, and highlight the events where `button=3`, we get output as in Figure 1.5.

Sorting the selected events and shading them shows the clear pattern that B is favoured over C (Figure 1.6).

There are two key insights. First, the result of Bayesian inference is not always intuitively obvious, but if we can consider all possible configurations and count the compatible ones, we will correctly infer a probability distribution. Secondly, having a clear understanding of a model in terms of how it generates observations from unobserved parameters – to be able to simulate the model process – is a useful way to understand models and to verify their behaviour.

Another Observation

A Bayesian update transforms a probability distribution (over apps, in this case) to another probability distribution. What happens if we see *another* observation? For example, we might next observe that the user next pressed the '2' button on the same app. How does this affect our belief? *We use the posterior from the previous step (A = 0, B = 0.6, C = 0.4) as the new prior*, and repeat the exact same process to get a new posterior. We can do this process over and over again, as new observations arrive.

- New prior (old posterior): (A = 0, B = 0.6, C = 0.4)
- Observation: '2'
- Likelihood: (A = 1/2, B = 1/4, C = 1/9)
- Unnormalised posterior: (A = 1/2 * 0 = 0, B = 1/4 * 0.6 = 0.15, C = 1/9 * 0.4 = 0.044...)
- Posterior, after normalising: (A = 0, B = 0.77, C = 0.23)

We are now slightly more confident that the app being used is B, but with reasonable uncertainty between B and C. If the second button observed had instead been '6', the posterior would have assigned all probability to C and zero to all the other apps – because no other app could have generated a button press with label '6'.

Continuous Variables

When we want to deal with continuous variables and cannot exhaustively enumerate values, there are technical snags in extending the idea of counting. But modern inference software makes it easy to extend to a continuous world with little effort. These basic Bayesian concepts put very little restriction on the kinds of problems that we can tackle.

A continuous example When might we encounter continuous variables? Imagine we have an app that can show social media feeds at different font sizes. We might have a hypothesis that reading speed changes with font size. If we measure how long a user spent reading a message, what font size were they using (Figure 1.7)?

We cannot enumerate all possible reading times or font sizes, but we can still apply the same approach by assuming that these have distributions defined by functions which we can manipulate. A single measurement will in this case give us very little information because the inter-subject variability in reading time drowns out the useful signal; but sufficient measurements can be combined to update our belief.

Figure 1.7 Can we work out what font size someone is using from how long they spend reading a message?

1.2.2 A Bayesian Machine

At the heart of a Bayesian inference problem, we can imagine a *probabilistic simulator* as a device like Figure 1.8. This is a simulator that is designed to mimic some aspect of the world. The behaviour of the simulator is adjusted by *parameters*, which specify what the simulator will do. We can imagine these are dials that we can set to change the behaviour simulation. This simulator can (usually) take a real-world observation and pronounce its *likelihood*: how likely this observation was to have been generated by the simulator *given the current settings of the parameters*. It can typically also produce *samples*: example runs from the simulator with those parameter settings. This simulator is *stochastic*. One setting of the parameters will give different samples on different runs, because we simulate the random variation of the world. We assume that we have a probability distribution over possible parameter settings – some are more likely than others.

Here is the basic generative model, sketched in Python:

```python
class Simulator:

    def samples(self, parameters, n):
        # return n random observations given parameters
        # (this corresponds to the output on the right)

    def likelihood(self, parameters, observations):
        # return the likelihood of some observation
        # *given the parameters* (i.e. dial settings)
        # (this corresponds to the input on the left)
```

Inference Engine

An inference engine can take a simulator like this and manage the distributions over the parameters. This involves setting prior distributions over the parameters and performing inference to compute posterior distributions using the likelihood given by the simulator. Parameter values drawn from the prior or posterior can be translated into synthetic observations by feeding them into the simulator,

J. H. Williamson

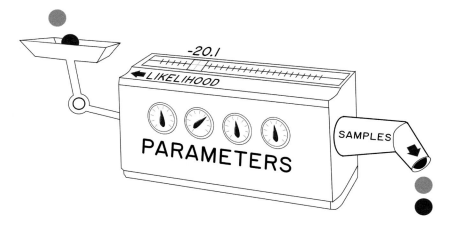

Figure 1.8 A cartoon of a probabilistic simulator, which encodes a model of the world. Parameters (dials, top) change the simulation. Distributions are maintained over possible dial settings. The simulator can synthesise samples (right spigot) or take real-world observations and determine how likely they are *under the current parameter settings* (left arm).

generating samples from the distribution known as the **posterior** (or prior) **predictive**. We can also compute summary results using **expectations**. To compute an expectation, we pass a function, and the inference engine computes the average value of that function evaluated at all possible parameters, weighted by how likely that parameter setting is.

The inference engine *inverts* the simulator. Given observations, it updates the likely settings of parameters.

A Reading Time Simulator

For example, we might model the reading time of the user based on font size, as in the example in the subsection 'Continuous Variables'. The simulator might have three 'dials' to adjust (parameters): the average reading time, the change in reading time per point of font size, and the typical random variation in reading time. This is a very simplistic cartoon of reading time, but enough that we can use it to model something about the world. By tweaking these parameters, we can set up different simulation scenarios.

```
import scipy.stats as st
import numpy as np

class ReadingTimeMachine:
    # store the initial parameters
    def __init__(self, mean_time,
```

```
                    font_time, std_time):
    self.mean_time = mean_time
    self.font_time = font_time
    self.std_time = std_time


# given a font_size, generate
# n random simulations by drawing from
# a normal distribution
def simulate(self, n, font_size):
    model = st.norm(self.mean_time +
                    self.font_time * font_size,
                    std_time)

    return model.rvs(n)

# given a list of reading times and font sizes
# compute how likely a
# (reading_time, font_size) pair is
# under the current parameters. Return the sum
# of the log likelihood. The log is only used
# to make computations more numerically stable.
def log_likelihood(self, reading_times,
                         font_sizes):
    llik = 0
    for time, size in zip(reading_times, font_sizes):
        model = st.norm(self.mean_time +
                        self.font_time * size,
                        self.std_time)
        llik += model.logpdf(time)
    return llik
```

If we set the dials to 'average time = 500ms, font time = 10ms/pt, variation = +/−100ms' and cranked the sample output with font size set to 12 (i.e. called `simulate(n, font_size=12)`), the machine would spit out times: 600.9 ms, 553.3 ms, 649.2 ms, etc.

If we fed the machine an observation, say 300 ms and font size 8, it would give a (log-)likelihood (e.g. via `log_likelihood([300], [9]) = -9.7` for the settings above). Given another observation, say 1800 ms, it would give a much smaller value (−72.7, in this example), as such an observation is very unlikely given the settings of the machine.

Inference

One traditional, non-Bayesian approach to using this machine would be to feed a bunch of data into the likelihood inlet, and then iteratively adjust the parameters until the data was 'as likely as possible' – *maximum likelihood estimation* (MLE). This optimisation approach would tweak the dials to best approximate the world (a model can never *reproduce* the world, but we can align its behaviour with the world).

> We'd usually not tweak the dials randomly until things got better, but use information about the slope or curvature of the likelihood function to quickly find the best setting, which is often done with automatic differentiation libraries. Traditionally, derivatives of likelihood functions were worked out and used for the optimisation process. This MLE approach is the basis of most machine learning, even if not always stated in these terms.

Bayesian inference instead puts prior distributions on the parameters, describing likely configurations of these parameters. Then, given the data, it computes how likely *every* possible combination of the parameters is by multiplying the prior by the likelihood of each sample. This gives us a new set of distributions for the parameters which is more tightly concentrated around settings that more closely correspond to the evidence.

What's the difference? In the optimisation (MLE) case, imagine we are using the reading time machine, and we only have an observation from one user, of 50 000 ms at font size 12. What is the most likely setting of the machine given this data? It will be a very unrealistic average time, a very large font size time, or an extremely large variation; any combination is possible.

> In practice, no one would use maximum likelihood in such a naive way, and instead would use some process to *regularise* the estimates that would have been used. However, this could be seen as a roundabout way of specifying a prior that implicitly favours certain parameterisations.

A Bayesian model would have specified likely distributions of the parameters in advance. A single data point would move these relatively little, especially one so unlikely under the prior distributions. We'd have to see *lots* of observations to be convinced that we'd really encountered a population of users who took 50 seconds to read a sentence.

Data space and parameter space In Bayesian modelling, it is important to distinguish the **data space** of observations and the **parameter space** of parameters in the model. These are usually quite distinct. In the example above, the observations are in a data space of reading times, which are just single scalar values. Each model configuration is a point in a three-dimensional parameter space (`mean_time, font_time, std_time`). Both the prior and the posterior are distributions over parameter space. Bayesian inference uses values in observation space to constrain the possible values in parameter space to move from the prior to the posterior. When we discuss the results of inference, we talk about the *posterior* distribution, which is the distribution over the parameters (dial settings on our machine).

The *posterior predictive* is the result of transforming the parameter space back into distribution of simulated observations *in the data space*. We could imagine getting these samples by repeatedly randomly setting the parameters according to the posterior distribution, then cranking the sample generation handle to simulate outputs. The *observations* would be measured reading times. The *prior* and *posterior* of the reaction times would be a distribution over (mean_time, font_time, std_time). The *posterior predictive* would again be a distribution over reading times.

Types of Uncertainty: Aleatoric and Epistemic

This brings up a subtlety in Bayesian modelling. We have uncertainty about values, because the simulator, and the world it simulates, is stochastic; given a set of fixed parameters, it generates plausible values which have random variation. But we *also* have uncertainty about the settings of the parameters, which is what we are updating during the inference process. The inference process is indirect in this sense; it updates the 'hidden' or 'latent' parameters that we postulate are controlling the generative process. For example, even if we fix the parameters of our reading-time simulator, it will emit a range of plausible values. But we don't *know* the value of the parameters (such as font time), and so there is a distribution over these as well.

We can classify uncertainties: *aleatoric* uncertainty, arising from random variations, that cannot be eliminated by better modelling; and *epistemic* uncertainty, arising from our uncertainty about the model itself. In most computational Bayesian inference, we also have a third source of uncertainty: *approximation* uncertainty. This arises because most methods for performing Bayesian inference do not compute exact posterior distributions, and this introduces an independent source of variation. For example, many standard inference algorithms that applied the same model and same data twice would yield two different approximate posteriors, assuming the random seed was not fixed. The approximation error should be slight for well-behaved models but can be important, particularly for large and complex models where few samples can be obtained for computational reasons.

- **aleatoric** random noise in observations (e.g. random reading times given fixed parameters); modelled by the likelihood.

- **epistemic** the unknown state of parameters or model structure, modelled by the parameter distribution.
- **approximation** error in parameter estimates due to computational approximations, e.g. as introduced by Monte Carlo sampling.

1.3 Bayesian Approaches

1.3.1 What Are the Key Ideas in Bayesian Approaches?

There are some distinctive aspects of Bayesian approaches that distinguish them from other ways of solving problems in interaction design. We summarise these briefly, to give a flavour of how thinking and computation change as we move to a Bayesian perspective.

> We will refer to individuals applying Bayesian principles and adopting a Bayesian world view as 'Bayesians'. No one is really ever a 'true Bayesian', but it is a useful shorthand to delineate the Bayesian perspective from the non-Bayesian perspective. There are many subsets of Bayesian thought with slightly different assumptions and approaches; see Weisberg [57] for an in-depth discussion of the philosophical and technical distinctions of these varieties.

Beliefs Are Probabilities

A Bayesian represents *all* beliefs as probabilities. A belief is a measure of how likely a configuration of a system is. A probability is a real number between 0 and 1. Larger numbers indicate a higher degree of certainty. Manipulation of belief comes down to reassigning probabilities in the light of evidence.

For example, we might have a belief that two versions, A and B, of a website have different 'comprehension' scores, but we have no idea which is better, if any. We could represent this as a probability distribution, perhaps a 50/50 split in the absence of any further information: $A_{\text{better}} = 0.5$, $B_{\text{better}} = 0.5$. We could make observations, by running a user trial and gathering data, and form a new belief $A_{\text{better}} = 0.8$, $B_{\text{better}} = 0.2$. Whether version A or B is better is not a knowable fact (there isn't any possible route to precisely determine it), nor is it the result of some long sequence of identical experiments. Instead it is just a quantified belief. We used to believe that version A was as likely to be as good as B; we now believe that A is probably better (Figure 1.9).

If we went further, we might quantify *how much* better A was than B on some scale of relative comprehension and represent that as a probability distribution.

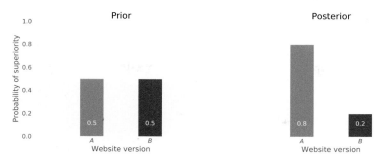

Figure 1.9 Belief that version A or B is the superior website for comprehension, represented as probabilities.

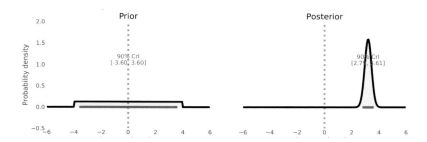

Figure 1.10 Distribution over relative change in reading comprehension contracts from prior to posterior.

Perhaps we'd assume that A could be anywhere from $[-4, 4]$ units of comprehension better than B. After doing an experiment, this might be concentrated with 90% of the probability now in the range $[2.7, 3.6]$ (Figure 1.10).

Representing a full distribution like this can be much more enlightening than a dichotomous approach that only considers the relative superiority of one belief above another. For example, we might know that each unit of increased comprehension is 'worth' 10 extra repeat visits to our website. We can now make concrete statements like 'we expect around 32 additional return visits with version B' directly from the posterior distribution. Representing distributions over many hypotheses can make *decisions* much easier to reason about.

Distributions, Not Points

To be Bayesian, we work not with definite values but with *distributions* over possible values. For example, we would not write code to find the best estimate of how long a user takes to notice a popup, or optimise to find the geometrical

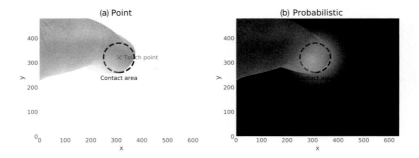

Figure 1.11 Imagine a touchscreen inferring a finger contact point from a contact blob (dashed circle). A standard approach would find the single point that best represents the intended touch (a). A Bayesian approach would form a probability distribution over possible touches, given an input (b).

configuration of the hand pose that is most compatible with a camera image. That is not congruent with a Bayesian world view which deals exclusively with beliefs about configurations. Instead, we would consider a distribution over *all possible* times, or *all possible* poses (Figure 1.11). After we update this with evidence (e.g. by running a user evaluation and showing many popups), we expect our distribution to have contracted around likely configurations. Wherever possible, we *keep* our beliefs as full distributions and avoid at all times reducing them to point estimates, such as the most likely configuration.

The fundamental principle: If we don't know something for sure, we preserve the whole distribution over possible configurations.

This has several consequences:

- We always explicitly have a representation of uncertainty.
- We have a universal language (or data type) with which we reason – the probability distribution.
- The probability distribution is a data type that is hard to work with, and consequently we often have to rely on approximations to do computations.
- We need to be able to summarise and visualise distributions to report them.

It is hard to communicate directly about distributions, so they are often reported using summary statistics, like the mean and standard deviation, or visualised with histograms or Box plots. Bayesian posterior distributions are

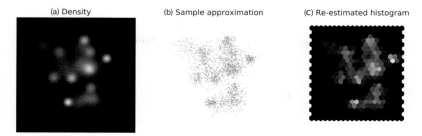

Figure 1.12 A complex density (a) can be approximated with a collection of samples (b) – definite values – which are easy to transform algorithmically. They can be transformed back into an approximate distribution, e.g. with a histogram (c).

often summarised in terms of **credible intervals** (CrI). These are intervals which cover a certain percentage of the probability mass or density. For example, a 90% credible interval defines an interval in which we believe that an unknown parameter lies with 90% certainty (given the priors).

Approximation Is King

Probability distributions are hard to work with. As a consequence, almost all practical Bayesian inference relies on approximations. Much of the traditional complexity of Bayesian methods comes from the contortions required to do manipulate distributions. This has become much less tricky now that there are software tools that can apply approximations to almost any model at the press of a button.

There are several important approximations used in practice, and they can largely be separated into two major classes: variational inference, where we represent a complex distribution with the 'best-fitting' distribution of a simpler one; and sample-based methods, where we represent distributions as collections of samples; definite points in parameter space (Figure 1.12).

Approximations can sometimes confound the use of Bayesian models. The obvious, pure way to solve a problem may not mesh well with the approximations available, and this may motivate changes in the model to satisfy the limitations of computational engines. This problem is lessening as 'plug and play' inference engines become more flexible, but it is often an unfortunate necessity to think about how a model will be approximated.

Integrate, Don't Optimise

As a consequence of the choice to represent belief as distribution, our techniques for solving problems are typically to *integrate* over possible configurations, rather than to optimise to find a precisely identified solution.

> *Integrate* is used here in the mathematical sense of 'summing over all possible values'.

For example, imagine a virtual keyboard that was interpreting a touch point as a keypress. We might model each key as being likely to be generated by some spatial distribution of touch points *given the size of the user's finger*, or more precisely the screen contact area of the finger pad. Depending on how big we believe the user's finger to be, our estimate of which key might have been intended will be different: a fat finger will be less precise.

How do we identify the key pressed, as Bayesians? We do *not* identify the most likely (or even worse, a fixed default) finger size and use that to infer the distribution over possible key presses. Instead, we would integrate over *all possible* finger sizes from a finger size distribution, and consider all likely possibilities. If we become more informed about the user's finger pad size, perhaps from a pressure sensor or from some calibration process, we can use that information immediately, by refining this finger size distribution (Figure 1.13).

This comes at a cost. As we increase the number of dimensions – the number of parameters we have – the volume of the parameter space to be considered increases exponentially. If we had to integrate over all possible finger sizes, all possible finger orientations, all possible skin textures and so on, this 'true' space of possibilities becomes enormous. This makes exhaustive integration computationally infeasible as models become more complex. The reason Bayesian methods work in practice is that approximations allow us to efficiently integrate 'where it matters' and ignore the rest of the parameter volume.

Expectations

The focus on integrating means that we often work with **expectations**, the expected *value* averaging over all possible configurations weighted by how likely they are. This assumes we attach some *value* to configurations. This could be a simple number, such as a dollar cost or a time penalty, or it could be a vector or matrix or any value which we can weight and add together.

In a touch keyboard example, we might have a correction penalty for a mis-typed key, the cost of correcting a mistake; say in units of time. What is the expected correction penalty once we observe a touch point? We can compute this given a posterior distribution over keys, and a per-key correction cost.

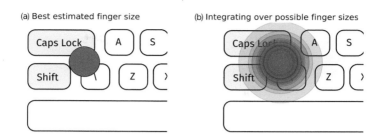

Figure 1.13 What key was intended to be pressed? This varies depending on what finger size we think the user has. We need to integrate over the possibilities, weighted by how likely they are, to get a correct distribution over possibilities. (a) A naive distribution using a single finger size splits the probability evenly between | and Caps Lock and zero elsewhere; (b) integrating over possible finger sizes indicates there is some small probability of Shift, and even A or Z.

Assume the key actuated is the key with highest probability, k_1. For each of the *other* keys, $k_2, \ldots, k_n$, we can multiply the probability that key k_i was intended by the penalty time it would take to correct k_1 to k_i. It is then trivial to consider the expected correction cost if some keys are more expensive than others (perhaps backspace has a high penalty, but shift has no penalty).

In an empirical analysis, we might model how an interactive exhibit in a museum affects reported subjective engagement versus a static exhibit. We might also have a model that predicts increase in time spent looking at an exhibit given a reported engagement. Following a survey, we could form a posterior distribution over subjective engagement, pass it through the time prediction model and compute the expected increase in dwell time that interaction brings (e.g. 49.2s additional dwell time).

Bayes' Rule

Bayesian inference updates beliefs using Bayes' rule. Bayes' rule is stated, mathematically, as follows:

$$P(A|B) = \frac{P(A)P(B|A)}{P(B)},$$

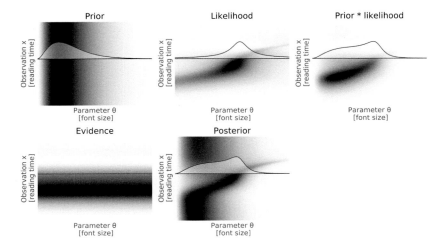

Figure 1.14 Bayesian inference. Consider a simple model with one parameter θ (say, font size) and one observed variable x (say, reading time). Assume we want to infer font size used given an observed reading time. The **prior** distribution weights possible values of θ in advance of seeing data, and does not depend on x. A **likelihood** function is defined by the model so that it maps every possible input x to a distribution over θ. If we observe a specific x (black horizontal line), one likelihood is 'selected' (light-shaded regions). This is multiplied by the prior, and then normalised by the **evidence** (which depends on x but not θ) to produce a proper **posterior** distribution over θ. The posterior can be used as the prior in a future inference of the same type (as in probabilistic filtering) or fed into another inference process.

or in words,

$$\text{posterior} = \frac{\text{prior} \times \text{likelihood}}{\text{evidence}},$$

or often simplified to

$$\text{posterior} \propto \text{prior} \times \text{likelihood}$$

This means that reasoning moves from a **prior** belief (what we believed before), to a **posterior** belief (what we now believe), by computing the **likelihood** of the data we have for every possible configuration of the model. We combine simply by multiplying the probability from the prior and the likelihood **over every possible configuration** (Figure 1.14).

To simplify our representations, and limit what we mean by 'every possible configuration', we assume that our models have some 'moving parts' – parameters, traditionally collected into a single vector θ – that describe specific configurations, in some space of possible configurations. All Bayes' rule tells us is that the probability of each possible θ can be updated from some initial prior belief (quantified by a real number assigned to each configuration of θ, a probability) via a likelihood (giving us another number) and then normalising the result (the evidence) so that the probabilities of each configuration still add up to 1.

Priors

As a consequence of Bayes' rule, it is necessary for all Bayesian inference to have **priors**. That is, we must quantify, precisely, what we believe about every parameter before we observe data. This is analogous to traditional logic; we require **axioms**, which we can manipulate with logic to reach conclusions. It is not possible to reason logically without axioms, nor is it possible to perform Bayesian inference without priors. This is a powerful and flexible way of explicitly encoding beliefs. It has been curiously controversial in statistics, where it is has been criticised as *subjective*. We will leave the gory details of this debate to others.

Priors are defined by assigning probability distributions to the parameters. Priors can be chosen to enforce hard constraints (e.g. a negative reaction time to a visual stimulus is impossible unless we believe in precognition, so a prior on that parameter could reasonably have probability zero assigned to all negative times), but typically they are chosen so as to be *weakly informative* – they represent a reasonable bound on what we expect but do not rigidly constrain the possible posterior beliefs. Priors are an explicit way of encoding inductive bias, and the ability to specify a prior that captures domain knowledge grants Bayesian methods its great strength in small data regimes. When we have few data points, we can still make reasonable predictions if supported by an informative prior. Eliciting appropriate priors requires thought and engagement with domain experts.

Latent Variables

Bayesian approaches involve inference; the process of determining what is hidden from what is seen. We *assume* that there are some parameters that explain what we observe but whose value is not known. These are **hidden** or **latent** parameters.

For example, if we are building a computer vision-based finger pose tracker, we might *presume* a set of latent variables (parameters) that describe joint angles of the hand, and describe the images that we observe as states generated from the (unknown) true joint angle parameters. Inference refines our estimates of these joint angles following the observation of an image and allows us to establish what hand poses are compatible with the observed imagery – not *which* hand pose, but what poses are likely. We never identify latent variables; we only refine our belief about plausible values.

Latent variables sometimes have to be accounted for in an inference, even though they are not what we are directly interested in. These are *nuisance variables*. For example, in the hand tracker, the *useful* parameters are the joint angles of the hand. But in a practical hand tracker, we might have to account for the lighting of the scene, or the camera lens parameters, or the skin tone. We are not interested in inferring these nuisance variables, but we may have to estimate them to reliably estimate the joint angles.

In a simpler scenario, we might predict how much time a user spends reading a news article on a mobile device as a function of the font size used, and *assume* that this follows some linear trend, characterised by a slope β_1 and a constant offset β_0:

$$\text{read time s} = \beta_1 * \text{font size pt} + \beta_0 + \text{noise}.$$

β_1, β_0 are latent variables that describe all possible forms of this line. By observing pairs of `read_time` and `font_size` we can narrow down our distribution over the latent variables β_0, β_1. Obviously, this simplistic model is not a true description of how reading works; but it is still a useful approximation.

In many scientific models there are many more latent variables than observed variables. Imagine inferring the complex genetic pathways in a biological system from a few sparse measurements of metabolite masses – there are many latent parameters and low-dimensional observations. In interaction, we sometimes have this problem: for example, modelling social dynamics with many unknown parameters from very sparse measurements. Often, however, we have the opposite problem, particularly when dealing with inference in the control loop: we have a large number of observed variables (e.g. pixels from an image from camera) which are generated from a much smaller small set of latent parameters (e.g. which menu option the user wants).

Simulations and Generative Models

Bayesian methods were historically called the 'method of inverse probability'. This is because we build Bayesian models by writing down *what we expect to observe given some unobserved parameters*, and **not** *what unobserved parameters we have given some observation*. In other words, we write *forward models* that have some assumed underlying mechanics, governed by values we do not know. These are often not particularly realistic ways of representing the way the world works, but they are useful approximations that can lead to insight. We can run these models forward to produce synthetic observations and update our belief about the unobserved (latent) parameters. This is a **generative** approach to modelling; we build models that ought to generate what we observe.

Forward and inverse We can characterise Bayesian approaches as using generative, **forward** models, from parameters to observations. Approaches common in machine learning, like training a classifier to label images, are **inverse** models. These map from observations to hidden variables. A Bayesian image modelling approach would map labels $\rightarrow$ images; an inverse model would map images $\rightarrow$ labels. One major advantage of the generative approach is that it is easy to fuse other sources of information. For example, we might augment a vision system with an audio input. A Bayesian model would now map labels $\rightarrow$ images, sounds – two distinct manifestations of some common phenomena, with evidence from either being easily combined. An inverse model can be trained to learn sounds $\rightarrow$ labels, but it is harder to combine this with an existing images $\rightarrow$ labels model.

In practice, we usually use a combination of forward models and inverse models to make inference computationally efficient. For example, imagine we are tracking a cursor using an eye tracker. We want to know what on-screen spatial target a user is fixating on, given a camera feed from the eyes. A 'pure' Bayesian approach would generate *eye images* given targets; synthesise actual pixel images of eyes and compare them with observations to update a belief over targets (or be able to compute the likelihood of an image given a parameter setting).

This is theoretically possible but practically difficult, both for computational reasons (images are high-dimensional) and because of the need to integrate over a vast range of irrelevant variables (size of the user's pupils, colour of the viscera, etc.). A typical compromise solution would be to use an inverse model, such as traditional signal processing and machine learning, to extract a pupil contour from the image. Then, the Bayesian side could infer a distribution over parameterised contours given a target, and use that to identify targets.

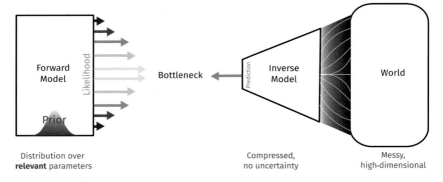

Figure 1.15 An inverse model which does not represent uncertainty but is efficient can be used to compress observations so that Bayesian inference can be used to maintain uncertainty over states that matter.

This is a common pattern: the **inverse model bottleneck**, where some early parts of the model are implemented in forward mode and inferred in a Bayesian fashion; but these are compared against results from an inverse model that has compressed the messy and high-dimensional raw observations into a form where Bayesian inference is practical (Figure 1.15). Combinations of modern non-Bayesian machine learning methods with Bayesian models can be extremely powerful. A deep network, for example, can be used to compress images into a lower-dimensional space to be fed into a Bayesian model. This can turn theoretically correct but computationally impractical pure Bayesian models into workable solutions.

Decision Rules and Utilities

Bayesian methods in their narrowest sense are concerned only with updating probabilities of different possible configurations. This, on its own, is insufficient to make **decisions**. In an HCI context, we often have to make irreversible state changes.

For example, in a probabilistic user interface, at some point, we have to perform actions, that is, make a decision about which action to perform. Similar issues come up when deciding whether interface A is more usable than interface B; we might well have *both* a probability of superiority of A over B, and a value gained by choosing A over B. Whenever we have to go from a distribution to a state change, we need a decision rule, and this usually implies that we also have a *utility function* $U(x)$ that ascribes values to outcomes.

In a probabilistic user interface, we might have just updated the distribution over the possible options based on a voice command, $P(\text{option}|\text{voice})$ from a

Action	P(A|speech)	P(A|language)	P(A|speech,language)	U(Right)	U(Wrong)	Exp. U
reply all	0.28	0.38	0.65	1	−10	−2.90
reply Paul	0.03	0.38	0.06	1	−1	−0.87
delete Paul	0.56	0.04	0.13	1	−5	−4.23
delete all	0.14	0.19	0.16	1	−100	−83.71

Figure 1.16 An example of utility in decision making. This table shows possible voice commands that could be compatible with an utterance recorded. The speech recogniser gives some probability to different actions A according to the acoustics $P(A|\text{speech})$. This is combined with a prior from a language model that assigns probability to different commands based on prior usage $P(A|\text{language})$. These are combined into a posterior probability $P(A|\text{speech, language})$. For each action, there is also a possible benefit to the user $U(Right)$ (in this case they are all equal) and a possible cost $U(Wrong)$, which might capture the work required to undo the action if it were triggered in error. Given this table, the *least likely* option is 'reply Paul' but it is the option with highest *expected utility* (**Exp. U**) – the rational choice.

speech recogniser. Which option should be actuated? The probabilities don't tell us. We also need a **decision rule**, which will typically involve attribution of **utility** (goodness, danger, etc.) to those options.

The decision rule will combine the probability and the utility to identify which (if any) option should be actuated. A simple model is maximum expected utility: choose the action that maximises the average product of the probability and utility. This is a rational way to make decisions: choose the decision that is most likely to maximise the 'return' (or minimise the 'loss') in the long run. But many decision rules are possible which will be appropriate in different situations, such as:

- The option with the highest posterior probability (sometimes called the *maximum a posteriori* (MAP) estimate), if no utility function is known or appropriate. However, this ignores the fact that the outcomes might have different values ('reply all' is potentially more destructive than 'reply Paul').
- The option with the highest expected value, which is the product of the probability and the utility. In a probabilistic interface, this automatically makes useful actions easier to select and dangerous ones hard to select; we need to be more certain that an action is intended if it is less desirable.
- The option which minimises regret, which would also capture the lost utility of not selecting particularly valuable actions. This might be particularly relevant in time-constrained interactions, where actions may not be freely available in the future.

Any time we have to take action based on a Bayesian model, we need to define a decision rule to turn probabilities into choices. This almost always requires some form of utility function. Utility functions can be hard to define and may require careful thought and justification.

1.3.2 What about Machine Learning? Is It Just the Same Thing?

Modern machine learning uses a wide range of methods, but the dominant approach at the time of writing is distinctly optimisation focused, as opposed to Bayesian. A neural network, for example, is trained by adjusting parameters to find the **best** parameter setting that minimises a prediction error and so makes the best predictions (or some other loss function). A Bayesian approach to do the same task would find the distribution over parameters (network weights) most compatible with the observations, and not a single best estimate. There are extensive Bayesian machine learning models, from simple Bayesian logistic regression to sophisticated multi-layer Gaussian processes and Bayesian neural networks, but these are currently less widespread.

Most ML systems also try to map from some observation (like an image of a hand) to a hidden state (which hand pose is this?), learning the inverse problem directly, from outputs to inputs. This can be very powerful and is computation-ally efficient, but it is hard to fuse with other information. Bayesian models map from hidden states to observations, and adding new 'channels' of inputs to fuse together is straightforward – just combine the probability distributions.

Bayesian methods are most obviously applicable when uncertainty is relevant, and where the parameters that are being inferred are interpretable elements of a generative model. Bayesian neural networks, for example, provide some measure of uncertainty, but because the parameters of a neural network are relatively inscrutable, some of the potential benefit of a Bayesian approach is lost. Distributions over parameters are less directly useful in a black box context. All Bayesian machine learning methods retain the advantage of robustness in prediction that comes from representing uncertainty. They are less vulnerable to the specific details of the selection of the optimal parameter setting and may be able to degrade more gracefully when predictions are required from inputs far from the training data.

Bayesian machine learning methods have sometimes been seen as more computationally demanding, though this is perhaps less relevant in the era of billion-parameter-deep learning models. The ideal Bayesian method integrates over all possibilities, and so the problem complexity grows exponentially with dimension unless clever shortcuts can be used. Machine learning approaches like deep networks rely on (automatic) differentiation rather than exhaustive integration, and more easily scale to large numbers of parameters. This is why we see deep networks with a billion parameters, but rarely Bayesian models with more than tens of thousands of parameters. However, many human–computer interaction problems have only a handful of parameters and are much more constrained by limited data than the flexibility of modelling. Bayesian methods are powerful in this domain.

Prediction and Explanation

Much of machine learning is focused on solving the *prediction* problem, learning to make predictions from data. Bayesian methods address predictions but can be especially powerful in solving the *explanation* problem; identifying what is generating or causing some observations. In an interaction context, perhaps we wish to *predict* the reading speed of a user looking at tweets as a function of the font size used; we could build a Bayesian model to do this. But we might alternatively wish to determine which changes in font size and changes in typeface choice (e.g. serif and sans-serif) might best *explain* changes in reading speed observed from a large in-the-wild study. Modelling uncertainty in this task is critical, as is the ability to incorporate established models of written language comprehension. Bayesian methods excel at this.

1.3.3 How Would I Do These Computations?

We have so far spoken in very high-level terms about Bayesian models. How are these executed in practice? This is typically via some form of approximation (Figure 1.17).

Exact Methods

In some very special cases, we can directly compute posterior distributions in closed form. This typically restricts us to represent our models with very specific distribution types. Much of traditional Bayesian statistics is concerned with these methods, but except for the few cases where they can be exceptionally computationally efficient, they are too limiting for most interaction problems.

An Exact Example: Beta-Binomial Models

A classic example where exact inference is possible is a beta-binomial model, where we observe counts of binary outcomes (0 or 1) and want to estimate the distribution of the parameter that biases the outcomes to be zeros rather than 1s. If we *assume* that we can represent the distribution over this parameter using a *beta distribution* (a fairly flexible way of representing distributions over values bounded in the range $[0, 1]$), then we can write a prior as beta distribution,

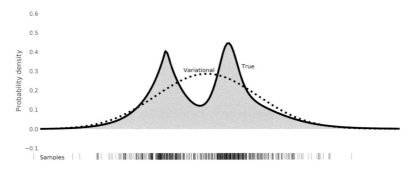

Figure 1.17 Most approximation methods represent complex distributions (solid line) using either Monte Carlo approaches which use random samples to approximate distributions (samples illustrated as vertical ticks in the lower strip), or variational methods which represent complex distributions with simple and easily paramaterised distributions optimised to best fit the true distribution (dashed curve).

observe some 0s and 1s and write a new posterior beta distribution down exactly, following some simple computations.

For example, we might model whether or not a user opens an app on their phone each morning. What can we say about the distribution of the *tendency* to open the app? For example, it is not reasonable to believe that a user will *never* open an app if they don't open it the first day, so we need a prior to regularise our computations. We can then make observations and compute posteriors exactly, as long as we are happy that a beta distribution is flexible enough to capture our belief. Because Bayesian updating moves just from one distribution to another, we can update these distributions in any order, in batches or singly, *assuming* that the observations are independent of each other.

Monte Carlo Approximation

The most promising and most general approach to Bayesian inference is **sample-based** approaches that sidestep manipulation of distributions by approximating them as collections of samples. To perform computations, we draw *random* samples from distributions, apply operations to the *samples* and then re-estimate statistics we are interested in. In Bayesian applications, we draw random samples from the posterior distribution to perform inference. This makes operations computationally trivial. Instead of working with tricky analytical solutions, we can select, summarise or transform samples just as we would ordinary tables of data. These methods normally operate by randomly sampling realisations from a distribution and are known as **Monte Carlo** approximations.

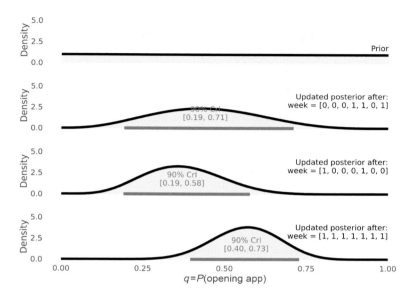

Figure 1.18 Beta-binomial exact inference. We want to model the propensity for a user to open an app on a given day. We can see the user activity as a process that has a bias q to produce a 0 (no open) over a 1 (open). If we think a beta distribution captures our uncertainty about this parameter q, we can exactly update the posterior distribution over q following batches of binary observations x. In each row, the distribution over q is shown after one new week of observations (right on each panel) is observed. Each distribution becomes the prior for the successive one beneath. '90% CrI', the 90% credible interval, (grey horizontal line) indicates a range of parameters where the propensity lies with 90% probability, given the priors and model we have chosen.

Markov chain Monte Carlo (MCMC) is a specific class of algorithms which can be used to obtain Monte Carlo approximations to distributions from which it is hard to sample. In particular, MCMC makes it easy to sample from the product of a prior and likelihood, and thus draw samples from the posterior distribution. MCMC sets up a 'process' that walks through the space of the distribution, making local steps to find new samples. There are many ways of implementing this, but under relatively weak assumptions this can be shown to *eventually* draw samples from any posterior.

Interested readers are invited to view the interactive gallery of MCMC algorithms by Feng [17] to get a deeper understanding of how MCMC sampling works in practice.

MCMC is very powerful and general, but there are a number of MCMC algorithms available, and each has its own parameters to tweak that affect the inference results. This is undesirable: our posterior distributions should depend only on the prior and the evidence we have, not on settings like the 'step size' in an MCMC algorithm. In practice, MCMC is often a bit like running a hot rod car: there's a lot of tuning to get smooth performance, and if you don't know what you are doing, it might blow up. There is an art to tuning a MCMC algorithm to make them tick over smoothly, and many diagnostics to verify that the sampling process is behaving itself.

Monte Carlo approaches generate samples from posterior distributions, but we often want to represent and report results in terms of distributions. This requires a conversion step back from samples into summaries of the approximated distributions. Common approaches to do this include histograms or kernel density estimates (e.g. for visualisation). Alternatively, summary statistics, such as means, medians or credible intervals, can be computed directly from the samples themselves. All MCMC methods have approximation error. This error reduces as the number of samples increases, but slowly (the Monte Carlo error decreases as $O(\sqrt{N})$, *assuming* the sampling is working correctly).

Variational Approximation

Variational methods approximate posteriors with distributions of a simple, constrained form which are easy to manipulate. The approximating distributions are optimised to best fit the posterior. One common approach, for example, is to represent the posterior with a normal distribution, which can be completely represented by a mean vector (location) and covariance matrix (scale/spread).

Variational approximations have benefits and drawbacks:

- They are typically *extremely* efficient. When they are applicable, they can be orders-of-magnitude faster than Monte Carlo approximations for the same level of accuracy.
- They often have relatively few parameters of their own to tweak, so less tuning and tweaking is required to get good results than is common in Monte Carlo approaches.
- They are relatively rigid in the posterior forms that can be represented. This depends on the approximation used, but, for example, a variational approximation with a normal distribution cannot represent multiple modes (peaks in the probability density), which may be important.

- Variational methods typically need to be specifically derived for a particular class of models. Most variational methods cannot simply be slotted into a probabilistic program and instead need expert skills to construct.

Some modern methods, such as automatic differentiation variational inference (**ADVI**), *can* be used without custom derivations and can be plugged into virtually any Bayesian inference models with continuous parameters. ADVI can be used in a wide range of modelling problems, but it has a limited ability to represent complex posteriors.

In interaction problems, variational methods are an excellent choice *if* an existing variational method is a good fit to the problem at hand *and* the form of posterior expected is compatible with the approximating distribution. They can be particularly valuable when low-latency response is required, for example, when embedded in the interaction loop.

Probabilistic Programming

A rapidly developing field for Bayesian inference is **probabilistic programming**, where we write down probabilistic models in an augmented programming language. This transforms modelling from a mysterious art of statisticians to an ordinary programming problem. In probabilistic programming languages, *random variables* are first class values that represent distributions rather than definite values. We can set priors for these variables and then 'expose' the program to observed data to infer distributions over variables. Inference becomes a matter of selecting an algorithm to run. This is often a MCMC based approach (e.g. in Stan [12]), but other tools allow variational methods to be plugged in as well (as in pymc3 [48]). Probabilistic programs can encode complex simulators and are easy and familiar for computer scientists to use. Probabilistic programming languages still need tuning and diagnostics of their underlying inference engines, but otherwise are plug-and-play inference machines. As an example, the following pymc3 code implements the model of reading time as a linear relationship.

This code implements the simple linear reading time example
as a probabilistic program in pymc3

```
with pm.Model():
    # prior on slopes;
    # probably around 0, not much more
    # than 10-20 in magnitude
    b1 = pm.Normal(0, 10)

    # prior on constant reading time;
    # positive and probably
```

```
# less than 30-60 seconds
b0 = pm.HalfNormal(30.0)

# prior on measurement noise;
# positive and not likely to
# be much more than 10-20
measurement_noise = pm.HalfNormal(10.0)

# font_size is observed.
# We set ba uniform prior here to
# allow simulation without data
font_size = pm.Uniform("font_size", 2,
                        32, observed=font_size)

# estimated average reading
# time is a linear function
mean_read_time = b1 * font_size + b0

# and the reading time is observed
read_time = pm.Normal("read_time",
                        mu=mean_read_time,
                        sigma=measurement_noise,
                        observed=read_time)
```

Observing a table of pairs of the observed variables `read_time` and `font_size` would let us infer distributions over `b0` and `b1` and `measurement_noise` – more precisely, an MCMC sampler would draw a sequence of random samples approximately from the posterior distribution, and return a table of posterior parameter distributions. This sample sequence from an MCMC process is known as a **trace**. Traces can be visualised directly or represented via summary statistics.

1.4 Can You Give Me an Example?

Let's work through a worked example of Bayesian analysis. We'll examine a problem familiar to many interaction designers: Fitts' law [19]. This 'law' is an approximate model of pointing behaviour that predicts time to acquire a target as a function of how wide a target is and how far away it is (Figure 1.19). It is a well-established model in the HCI literature [39].

1.4.1 Model

The Fitts' law model is often stated in the form:

$$MT = a + b \log_2 \left(\frac{d}{w} + 1 \right).$$

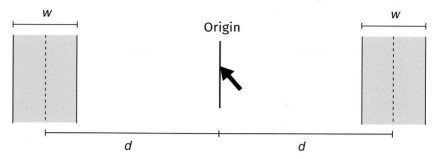

Figure 1.19 Fitts' law pointing task. The distance d and width w determine time to acquire the target. However, there are unknown parameters a and b that parameterise this relationship for different input devices.

This tells us that we predict that MT (the movement time to acquire a target) will be determined by the logarithm of the ratio of the target distance d and target size w. This is a crude but surprisingly robust predictive model. The two parameters a and b are constants that vary according to the input device used. In statistical terminology, this is a generalised linear model with a log link function. It can be easier to see the linear nature of the model by writing $ID = \log_2(\frac{d}{w} + 1)$ and the model is then just $MT = a + bID$ – i.e. a straight-line relationship between MT and ID defined by a, b. The term ID is often given in units of *bits*; the justification for doing so comes from information theory. A higher ID indicates a larger space of distinguishable targets, and thus more information communicated by a pointing action.

How might we approach modelling a new pointing device in a Bayesian manner? Let's assume we run an experiment with various settings of ID (by asking users to select targets with some preset distances and sizes). This fixes ID; it is an independent variable. We measure MT, the dependent variable. We are therefore interested in modelling the latent parameters a and b, which we cannot observe directly. We *know* that our measurements are noisy. Running the same trial with the same ID will not give the exact same MT. So we must model the expected noise, which we will notate as ϵ. Perhaps we expect it to be normally distributed, and we can write our model down:

$$MT = a + bID + \epsilon,$$

$$MT = a + bID + \mathcal{N}(0, \sigma^2).$$

The notation

$$\mathcal{N}(0, \sigma^2)$$

indicates normally distributed random noise with a standard deviation of σ. Its presence indicates that even if we knew a and b and ID, there would be random variation in MT – and we are assuming that this is normally distributed with some scale σ.

We don't know what σ is, so it becomes another latent parameter to infer. Unlike in, say, least square regression, we don't *have* to assume that our noise is normally distributed, but it is a reasonable and simple assumption for this problem. For a justification, see Section A.3.1 in the Appendix, subsection on the normal distribution.

In code, our generative model is something like:

```python
class FittsSimulator:

    def __init__(self, a, b):
        self.a, self.b = a, b


    def simulate(self, n, d, w):
        # compute ID
        ID = np.log2(d / w + 1)

        # generate random samples
        mu = a + b * ID
        return scipy.stats.norm(mu, sigma).rvs(n)

    def log_likelihood(self, ds, ws, mts):
        # compute IDs
        IDs = np.log2(ds / ws + 1)
        mu = a + b * IDs

        # compute how likely these movement times
        # given a collection of matching d, w pairs
        return np.sum(scipy.stats.norm(mu, sigma).logpdf(mts))
```

Priors

To do Bayesian inference, we must set priors on our latent parameters. These represent what we believe about the world. Let's measure MT in seconds, and ID in bits, to give us units to work with. Now we can assume some priors on a, b and σ. Reviewing our variables:

- **MT** is the dependent variable and is observed.
- **ID** is the independent variable and is also observed.

- **a** is the 'offset' and is unobserved. We might assume it has a normal prior distribution, perhaps mean 0, standard deviation 1.
- **b** is the 'slope' and is unobserved. We might again assume a normal prior distribution, perhaps mean 0, standard deviation 2.
- σ is the noise level and is also unobserved. Here, we need a positive value. We might choose a 'half-normal' with standard deviation 1.

These priors are *weakly informative*. These are our conservative rough guesses as plausible values (it is not likely that we have a 3-second constant offset a, but it's not *impossible*). There is nothing special about this choice of normal distributions. It is simply a convenient way to encode our rough initial belief.

> A common question:
>
> - Q: Did we not just **choose** the answer? Couldn't we set the prior to whatever we want to get the answer we want to see?
> - A: **No, we did not**, and this argument is ill-founded. We *could* write down a prior that specified the answer. For example, we could set a prior that puts all probability density on the possibility b = 0.0. This is possible, but obviously the evidence will never change this belief. It is equivalent to logical reasoning that started with the *axiom* 'all apples are red', then followed a process of reasoning. The final result would be 'apples are red', because we *assumed* that to start the reasoning process! Likewise, a prior specifies our assumptions explicitly. This is both a reasonable thing to do, and a valuable one – it requires us to be explicit in stating our assumptions, and in a form that we can then *test and inspect*, with ideas like prior predictive checks.

Prior Predictive Checks

What do these priors imply? One major advantage of a Bayesian model is that we can draw samples from the prior and see if they look plausible. It's most useful to see these as the lines MT, ID space that a, b imply, even though we are sampling from a, b, σ. Transforming from the prior distribution over parameters to the observed variables gives us *prior predictive* samples. We can see that the prior chosen can represent many lines, a much more diverse set than what we are likely to encounter (Figure 1.20), and can conclude that our priors are not unreasonably restrictive. Here we are just eyeballing the visualisations as a basic check; in other situations, we might compute summary statistics and

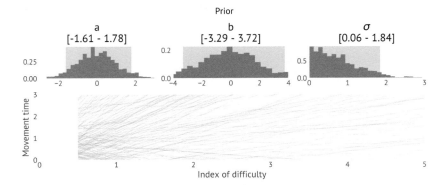

Figure 1.20 Prior predictive visualisation for the priors we set above. At the top, histograms showing the distribution of the hidden parameters; numbers indicate the (centred) 90% credible interval – a region in which we believe the true parameter is 90% likely to lie within. Below are those parameters used to draw possible lines compatible with the prior model. We see that there are very many linear models compatible with our model. Our prior distributions are at least flexible enough to be compatible with our genuine prior beliefs.

validate them numerically (e.g. testing that known positive values are positive in the prior predictive).

Inference

Now imagine we run a pointing experiment with users and capture MT, ID pairs and that are plotted in Figure 1.21.

Our model outputs the likelihood of seeing a set of MT, ID pairs for any possible a, b, σ. **Note: our model does not predict a, b, σ given MT, ID, but tells us how likely an MT, ID pair is under a setting of a, b, σ!** An inference engine can approximate the posterior distribution following the observations. Figure 1.22 shows how the posterior and posterior predictive change as more observations are made (typically, we'd only visualise the posterior after observing all the data, in this case $6 \times 18 = 108$ data points). The posterior distribution contracts as additional data points constrain the possible hypotheses.

Analysis

What is the value of a and b for this input device? A Bayesian analysis gives us distributions, not numbers; we can summarise these distributions with statistics. After the $N = 108$ observations, the 90% credible intervals are $a = [-0.05, 0.13]$ seconds and $b = [0.5, 0.57]$ bits/second. What about σ? The 90% CrI is $[0.25, 0.31]$ seconds. This gives us a sense of how noisy our predictions are;

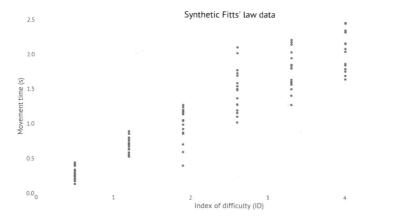

Figure 1.21 The raw data for the Fitts' law problem – 18 replicates of 6 different values for ID and corresponding movement times. All of these data are synthetic.

small σ indicates a clear relationship; big σ indicates weak relationship. What we *cannot* do from this is separate aleatoric measurement noise (e.g. human variability) from epistemic modelling noise (e.g. perhaps Fitts' law is too crude to model the motions we see).

Alternative priors What if we had chosen weaker priors? The inference is essentially unchanged even if we use very broad priors, as in Figure 1.23. If we had reason to choose tighter priors, perhaps being informed by other studies, we'd also get very similar results, as shown in Figure 1.24. Note the effect on the predictions when we use only 5 data points – we have much more realistic fits with the stronger priors in the small data case. It's important to note that these are alternative hypotheses we might have made *before* we observed the data. If we adjust priors after seeing the results of inference, the inference may be polluted by this 'unnatural foresight'. P-hacking-like approaches where priors are iteratively adjusted to falsely construct a posterior are just as possible in Bayesian inference as in frequentist approaches, although perhaps easier to detect. Alternative priors could be postulated *if* they arose from external independent knowledge; e.g. another expert in Fitts' law suggests some more realistic bounds.

A New Dataset

Perhaps we observe another dataset. In this case we have 40 MT, ID measurements from an in-the-wild, unstructured capture from an unknown

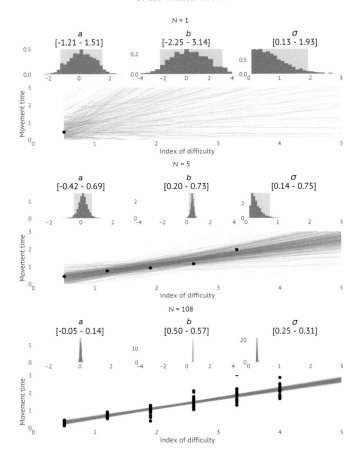

Figure 1.22 Bayesian inference for the Fitts' law task as data are acquired; N indicates the number of data points included. The space of plausible models contracts as more data points are included. Each block shows histograms for a, b, σ (the posterior) as well as the posterior predictive (the lines in the MT, ID space.) Shaded areas of the histogram, and the numbers $[a, b]$ above indicate centred 90% credible intervals.

pointing device (Figure 1.25). **How likely is it that the b parameter is different in this dataset?**

This question might be a suitable proxy for whether these 40 measurements are from the same pointing device or distinct pointing device. We can fit our model to these data (independently of the first model) and then compute the distribution of $b_1 - b_2$, the change in b across the two datasets (b_1 being the

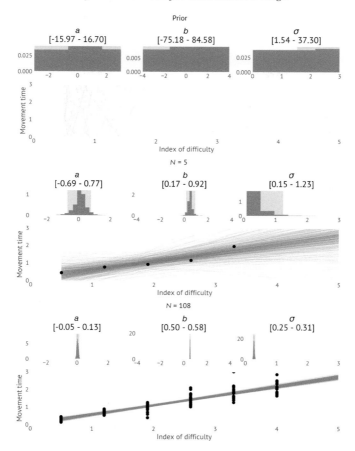

Figure 1.23 Much broader priors have essentially no effect on the inference with the full dataset ($N = 108$, lower), though have higher uncertainty if we only observe a few data points ($N = 5$, upper).

original and b_2 the new, in-the-wild dataset). This gives us a distribution (Figure 1.26), from which we can be *relatively* confident that the b value is different, and we are probably dealing with data collected from another device.

Since we have a predictive model, we can easily compute derived values. For example, we could ask the concrete question: how much longer would it take to select a width 2 distance 5 target using this second device than the first device. We can push this through our model and obtain the distribution shown in Figure 1.27.

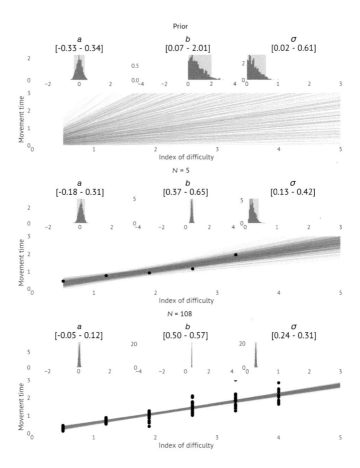

Figure 1.24 Tighter priors also have little effect with the full dataset ($N = 108$, lower), but the informed priors constrains the belief more effectively when there are only a few data points ($N = 5$, upper).

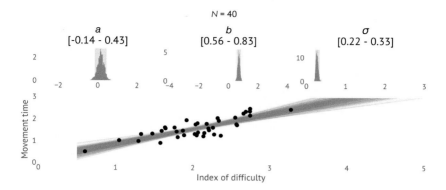

Figure 1.25 A new dataset, from uncontrolled observational studies of an unknown pointing device. We can refit the Bayesian model and estimate the parameters as before.

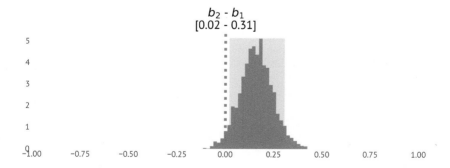

Figure 1.26 The change in distribution of b going from the posterior fitted on the original data to the posterior on the new data. The 90% CrI does not overlap 0, but it is close. So it is likely that there is a real difference in b, but the evidence is relatively weak.

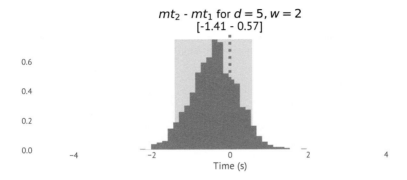

Figure 1.27 The predicted change in movement time to acquire a width 2 target 5 units away when switching from the first pointing device to the second. We expect the second device to take about 1 second longer to acquire this target, but there is reasonably large uncertainty.

What's the Point?

Why did we do this? What benefits did a Bayesian approach give us?

- **Uncertainty:** For one, we have realistic and useful uncertainty in our parameters. The credible intervals for our parameters are easy to interpret (there *is* a 90% chance that a lies in $[-0.05, 0.13]$, given our model, priors and observations).
- **Priors:** It is very easy for us to incorporate domain knowledge. If we had done studies before, we might have justified tighter priors. Even without other Fitts' law studies, we could have formed more informative priors than we did based on basic scientific knowledge; we'd expect that b has to be positive, and we'd also expect that the human motor system cannot generate more than 30 bits/second. We can *directly* use this information in the inference. Or perhaps another researcher is sceptical of these priors and prefers to be less cautious. We can re-run the inference and get new results; we'll find in this case that the priors have very little effect on the results with this much data.
- **Flexibility of modelling:** One advantage is that it is simple to write alternative models. When writing such models in a probabilistic programming language, the following modifications are one or two lines of extra code:
  - We might assume that noise is actually Gamma distributed (or any other noise model) so $MT = a + bID + \Gamma(\alpha, \beta)$. We'd just put priors on α and β and run the inference again.
  - We might assume there is some small quadratic term, perhaps $MT = a + bID + cID^2 + \mathcal{N}(0, \sigma)$. We'd put a prior on c that would suppose it to be small, because we know the relationship is *roughly* linear, and re-run the inference.
  - Perhaps we assume that Fitts' law holds for between some range of IDs, but becomes increasingly linear in distance after targets get a certain distance away. We can write this as a model and infer the unknown crossover point between Fitts' and linear behaviour: $MT = a + bID + \max(k(w - m), 0) + \mathcal{N}(0, \sigma)$, adding two new parameters k and m
  - We might instead assume that the parameters vary *per participant*, so $MT = a_i + b_i ID + \sigma_i$, and infer the parameter vectors $a_1, a_2, \dots$. In this case, the user ID i is observed.
  - As a more sophisticated approach, we might assume that parameters vary per participant, but that the participants' parameters come from some common distribution (that generates a_i, b_i, σ_i.). This is a 'partially pooled' model and encodes our belief that humans vary but have similar characteristics, and can be a powerful way to efficiently model populations.

- **Relevant hypotheses:** There is a distinct absence of statements about null hypotheses. These *might* be relevant, and we could analyse the data with frequentist methods to answer them. But they probably aren't what really interests us in this specific problem. Instead, we have relative likelihoods of hypotheses that *do* matter. For example, if we are interested in comparing our two input devices, we can make statements like 'acquiring a $(w = 2, d = 5)$ target has a 90% chance of taking [0.57, 1.41] seconds longer when using the second device'. Compare this to the statement 'if we repeatedly ran this exact experiment, there is a less than 5% chance that we'd see differences equal to or bigger than this if the differences were purely random'.

Is This Generative Modelling?

Fitts' law isn't a particularly *generative* way to think about pointing motions. Fitts' law describes the data, but it is not a strong explanation of underlying causes. A more sophisticated model might, for example, simulate the pointer trajectories observed during pointing. We could, for example, infer the parameters of a controller we suppose is approximating how humans acquire targets, generating spatial trajectories. Bayesian inference could be applied, but now we would be able to make richer predictions about pointing (for example, predicting error rates instead of just time to acquire, or properly accounting for very close or very distant targets).

What is the difference between generative and descriptive modelling? These distinctions lie on a spectrum between 'what happens' and 'why does this happen', and there is no shining line that divides them. Consider an example:

- Observation: The cat meows around 22:30 each night.
- To build a **descriptive model**, we could measure the time of each meow on a sequence of nights, and build a model by estimating a distribution giving probability of a meow given clock time. This would give us some ability to predict meowing episodes in the future. It describes the observations statistically and can be used for prediction, but it is a weak *explanation*.
- A more **generative** model would be built using expert knowledge to extract causal factors. The cat meows because it is hungry and it anticipates treats. Treats are administered when the humans go to bed. The humans go to bed around 22:30. We can now build a more detailed causal model that links $clock \implies bedtime \implies anticipation \implies meow \impliedby hunger$. This might not make better predictions of the next night than a descriptive model, but it does give us insight in counterfactual scenarios. If the hour changes due to daylight saving time, we'd expect the meowing to follow, because humans use clock time to schedule their lives. If the cat is well fed before bedtime, the meowing will be suppressed. If the cat is alone, it won't meow.

1.4.2 Bayesian Workflows

This worked example outlined the main steps in Bayesian modelling for this example. In general, how should we go about building Bayesian models in an interactive systems context? What do we need to define? How do we know if we have been successful? How do we communicate results? *Workflows* for Bayesian modelling are an active area of research [25, 49]. A high-level summary of the general process is as follows:

- **Define a model.** Ideally, we want a *generative* model that describes how we believe the world works, governed by a set of *parameters* that can vary. For example, say we were modelling the effect of frame rate variation on VR sickness. We would want to create a model that when fed a sequence of frame timings would output a probability of induced nausea. It would be possible but less desirable to use a general model like logistic regression. A better model would be constructed based on psychological and physiological models with parameters in meaningful units that represents our best knowledge of how the process truly works.

- **Construct priors.** We need to specify priors for every parameter in the model. We seek to find priors that are as informative as possible (and thus give us the most precise inferences with the least data) without introducing undue bias. Priors should be elicited from expert knowledge; from previous studies or published literature; or, if nothing else, informed guesses with clear justifications. Priors should **not** be established by looking at the specific data under consideration! 'Fitting' priors to data and then running inference with the same data inevitably biases the results.

- **Test priors.** Bayesian models are executable and we can sample possible simulated observations before doing any inference – sampling from the *prior predictive*. We can and must check that the priors look sensible. This can range from a quick eyeballing of histograms to more in-depth analysis of summary statistics of the prior simulations. Verifying prior predictives with domain experts can save a great deal of pain later. These simulations are most valuable if the model is easy to interpret generatively. Simulating from the prior also lets us test the rest of the analysis pipeline *in advance of observing any data* and verify that visualisations and summary statistics will be computed as we want.

- **Fit model.** With our model and priors set, and our data acquired, we can perform inference. This will eventually produce an estimate of the posterior distribution, often in the form of a **trace** from an MCMC process – a sequence of samples approximately drawn from the posterior.

- **Tune and diagnose.** The inference process can go wrong. Poorly specified priors or models with awkward parameterisations can make inference engines go haywire. This may result in bad approximations or excessive computation time. Inference engines themselves have many settings that can be adjusted that affect the approximation process. It is essential to perform at least some diagnostics to verify that posteriors are being approximated accurately. Many standard packages will compute basic diagnostics automatically. Any problematic results will need to be corrected and re-run until diagnostics 'run clean'.

- **Test the posterior predictive.** Posterior distributions should be run through the generative model to generate synthetic observations from the *posterior predictive*. These should indicate a close match between the true observations and the generated samples from the fitted model; certainly better than samples from the prior predictive. This might be established by comparing expectations (like the mean and standard deviation) of the posterior predictive against the observations, or verifying that the observations would lie in sensible quantiles of the posterior predictive (e.g. not way out in the tails). More thorough testing might involve re-fitting the model, using the posterior predictive as synthetic observations, and verifying that the posterior distributions are not substantially altered.

- **Visualise and form summary statistics for the posteriors (and posterior predictive).** The posterior distributions need to be visualised in some way to communicate an overall picture of the results. This is often challenging, because a model with many parameters can have many joint interactions that cannot all be seen. Reporting and visualisation should represent all uncertainty. This could range from showing a blurred contour onscreen (in an online probabilistic tracking scenario) to rendering histograms, Box plots, cumulative distribution functions, dot quantile plots [18] or violin plots (in a paper reporting on an empirical study). If necessary, summary statistics like means and standard deviations or credible intervals can be used to compress results into a few numbers. If decisions need to be made, then utility functions need to be defined and then combined with posterior distributions.

This workflow is presented from the perspective of performing an empirical analysis. The principles transfer to other uses of Bayesian models in interaction. For example, if we were building a probabilistic filter to track a user's head orientation, we would:

- build a model that predicted head dynamics (e.g. based on biophysics);
- define priors over likely poses;
- test to confirm that these did not look silly (e.g. by rendering them as head poses of a computer graphics character);
- estimate the model online from sensor inputs (e.g. using a particle filter);
- use diagnostics to make sure the particle filter is tracking (e.g. effective sample size);
- render a point cloud visualisation of the posterior distribution for the user.

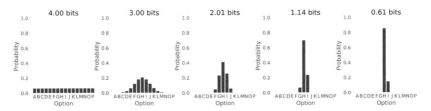

Figure 1.28 A sequence of distributions being updated with evidence, each distribution becoming the prior in the next round. There are 16 possible choices, and initially all are equally likely (an entropy of 4 bits). As information is acquired, the entropy drops towards zero.

1.5 Topics of Special Relevance to Interaction Design

1.5.1 The Relation to Information Theory

Interaction can be seen as the *flow of information* between entities. In human–computer interaction, for example, information flows from users to systems to indicate intent, and information flows back via the display. **Information theory**, as pioneered by Shannon [52], is closely linked to probability theory and integrates cleanly with Bayesian approaches. In particular, we can measure, mathematically, the information required to change one distribution into another. This corresponds directly to how much information we need to pass through a communication channel, such as a human–computer interface, to specify a new distribution.

The key concept is that of *entropy*, the measure of uncertainty in a distribution, sometimes characterised as a measure of the 'surprise' samples from a distribution would have. Entropy is a single number that quantifies how uncertain a distribution is. It is often measured in units of *bits* and tells us how much additional information must be provided to uniquely determine the outcome from a distribution. For example, a distribution with an entropy of 4.3 bits requires knowledge of a little more than four definite yes-or-no questions to completely identify its value. A distribution with zero bits of entropy concentrates all probability mass on a single outcome, so there is no surprise and no additional information needed to resolve the value.

> Entropy is less straightforward when dealing with distributions over continuous values. Instead of an absolute measure of entropy, we talk about the *relative entropy*: the information required to move from one distribution to another, which is also called the *Kullback–Leibler* (KL) divergence.

Entropy is essential in determining how much information must be communicated through a channel to identify (select, in an interaction context) a specific outcome. When we perform a Bayesian update, we will move from a prior to a posterior in light of evidence. If the evidence has constrained the space of possibilities – that is, we have learned something from it – then we will have a precisely quantifiable reduction in entropy as a consequence. Interaction can be seen as a sequential update of probabilities to reduce a system's entropy about intended actions, as in Figure 1.28.

For example, in a pointing task, like operating a calculator app, we might have space divided into a 4×4 grid of buttons. Pressing one of the calculator's buttons selects one of 16 options. If we wish do so without error, this necessarily communicates 4 bits of information, as $\log_2(16) = 4$. Whatever input we use, we need 4 bits of information to unambiguously choose an option. But this information does not have to come from the same source. If we *know* that the + key is pushed much more often than the $\sqrt{}$ key, then we have pre-existing information. This prior belief would *reduce* the information required to operate the calculator by pointing, because there are effectively fewer options – less information is required because the selection is in a sense already partway completed. We can represent more commonly used keys with fewer bits and less frequently used keys with more bits. We could, for example, permit sloppier pointing without increasing the error rate by interpreting pointing actions differently (e.g. by varying the effective size of the buttons). This is a process of decoding intent from uncertain input.

In the scenario of a user-system interaction, we can view the user as 'bit-store' of state, which encodes an intention with respect to the system (for example, 'please cancel this calendar appointment'). The user has to squeeze this intention through the communication channel of the interface to contract the distribution the system has over possible actions so that specific state change happens. Questions about how much information has to flow, and how quickly a decision is being made, are most naturally framed in terms of entropy (Figure 1.29).

As a concrete example, a pointing device which follows Fitts' law [19] might generate a maximum k bits/second for a given user, pointing device and interface layout. If there are n options, with equal prior probability, it will take at least $\lceil (\log_2 n)/k \rceil$ pointing actions to reliably acquire a target. If there is a prior distribution over targets with entropy h, then it takes at least $\lceil h/k \rceil$ pointing actions if we somehow interpret pointing actions more efficiently.

One of the earliest foundational papers incorporating Bayesian methods into an interaction loop is Dasher [56], a text entry system that directly links probabilistic language models to a dynamic target layout. Dasher implements

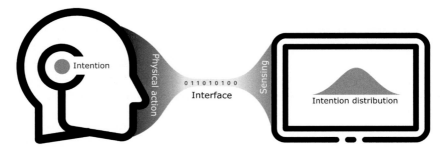

Figure 1.29 A human–computer interface is limited in terms of how quickly information can flow from a user to a system to reduce the entropy of the system's belief distribution. Modelling entropy is essential in understanding the limitations of an interaction method.

an elegant link between information–theoretic approaches and the problem of optimal selection via 1D pointing.

1.5.2 What Is 'Approximate Bayesian Computation'?

Approximate Bayesian Computation (ABC) is a **likelihood-free** way of performing inference. It is useful in the case where we have a simulator, but there is no likelihood 'inlet' – no way of directly computing the likelihood of an observation given a parameter setting (imagine the `Simulator` class from earlier with the `likelihood` method deleted).

Instead, ABC approaches synthesise samples under different parameter configurations and compare these synthetic samples with observations to update distributions over parameters; in the simplest case, just rejecting parameter settings that result in simulation runs too different from the real observations. This approximation comes at a significant cost in terms of computational resources (large numbers of synthetic samples are needed) and inferential power (it is harder to infer parameters reliably). The huge advantage is that if we *only* have a simulator that can generate samples, even if it is not or could not be written in a probabilistic manner, then we can still perform Bayesian inference with it. This means that we can, for example, retro-fit 'legacy' simulators that know nothing of likelihood. Alternatively, we can build Bayesian models for problems when it is conceptually challenging to even define what a likelihood function would look like.

For example, we might have a simulator that can generate likely arm trajectories in a target acquisition task, based on a biomechanical simulation of muscle activations. Given some arm trajectories from a motion tracker, and some priors over muscle activation patterns, how can we get a posterior distribution over muscle activations? The ABC approach would involve simulating many synthetic arm trajectories given the prior over muscle activations, selecting or weighting those samples that are close to the observed trajectories, and updating the distribution using the corresponding, *known* muscle activations that go with each synthetic trajectory. By averaging over many examples this can be used to infer an approximate posterior.

1.5.3 How Do 'Bayesian Networks' Relate?

Bayesian networks, Bayes nets, or **belief networks** are ways of representing relationships between variables in a probabilistic model. They are a compact way of representing and managing uncertainty and have many applications in user interfaces. In most interaction contexts, Bayes nets are used to model relationships between discrete variables, as in the example below with binary outcomes. Models are represented as directed acyclic graphs (DAG) which specifies dependencies between variables. Variables are represented as nodes, and dependencies as edges. Variables may be observed or unobserved (latent). This representation makes it easy to factor the model into independent elements, and the directionality of edges captures the causal relation between variables. The relationship between variables is captured by *conditional probability tables* (CPTs) that specify distributions for outcomes of child variables given all possible states of their parents. There are various implementation strategies to efficiently encode conditional probability tables to avoid exhaustive specification of every possible combination.

Inference is a process of updating the distributions on unknown variables when some variables are known. In small networks, with discrete nodes, this can often be done exactly. Approximations such as Monte Carlo methods can be applied for more complex models.

The example in Figure 1.30 shows a simple Bayes net with Boolean-valued variables (binary outcomes) that models focus change in a desktop user interface, its effect on user frustration and the effect of this frustration on heart rate and the probability of a user making an immediate error in typing. Focus changes can be induced either by the Alt-Tab hotkey or by a dialog stealing focus. Changes in focus affect frustration depending on their source. Changes in frustration can increase heart rate and/or make typing errors more likely. Given observations of *some* of these variables, and the DAG and conditional probability tables, we can answer questions like:

- What is the probability the user is annoyed, given that focus changed and heart rate increased? $P(UA|FC, HR) \approx 0.56$.
- What is the probability of a heart rate increase, given Alt-Tab was pressed and focus did *not* change? $P(HR|AT, \overline{FC}) \approx 0.18$.
- What is the probability that Alt-Tab was pressed, given that we did not observe a heart rate increase? $P(AT|\overline{HR}) \approx 0.38$.
- What is the probability that there was a typing error, given that we observed a heart rate increase? $P(TE|HR) \approx 0.16$.
- What is the probability that there was a typing error but no change in heart rate, given that a dialog did not steal focus? $P(TE, \overline{HR}|\overline{DF}) \approx 0.046$.

It is important to realise that the directions of the arrows specify causal relations. The model describes the probability distribution of variables as consequences of the states of their parents. Inference about the state of variables can progress in *either* direction.

Bayesian networks have a long history in human–computer interaction. As well as inferring specific probabilities in a network, it is also possible to *learn* conditional probability tables from observations and thus 'fit' a belief network with a given graph structure to observations. For example, in the scenario above we might log focus change events, heart rate and other factors in a set of user trials, and then use the event co-occurrences to update the conditional probability tables. This can be done in a Bayesian manner by setting priors on the CPTs and conducting ordinary Bayesian inference. In certain cases it is further possible, though computationally challenging, to infer the structure of the networks themselves from observations, i.e. to learn the graph structure as well as the conditional probability tables.

> **Note:** Somewhat confusingly, Bayes nets are probabilistic models, but *not* necessarily Bayesian in the sense we are using in this chapter. It *is* possible to do Bayesian inference on Bayes nets, but many applications of Bayes nets do not do so and use standard frequentist estimation. However, as probabilistic models with wide application in interaction design, it makes sense to include them here.

Belief networks can be extended to model sequences of observations over time, **dynamic belief networks** (DBNs). This includes models like the Hidden Markov Model (HMM), traditionally used in speech and gesture recognition. These models have dependency graphs that include state at the previous time step as parents and are powerful in modelling sequential processes. Hidden Markov Models, for example, are used to infer unobserved sequences of discrete

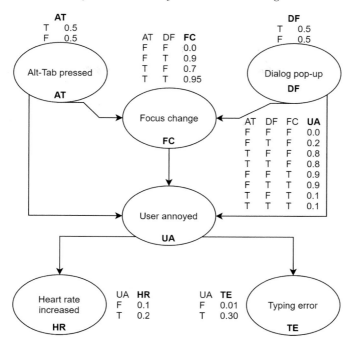

Figure 1.30 An example Bayes net in an interaction context. In this case, all variables (ellipses) are Boolean and have possible outcomes True (T) or False (F). Arrows indicate causal relations between variables. Conditional probability tables (text next to ellipses) show the probability of a variable taking on the True state (right column) given all possible configurations of its immediate parents (left columns). This simple Bayes net models the relationship between focus changes in a window manager and user frustration.

states that are believed to be 'causing' observations. An HMM for speech recognition might be used to infer a sequence of phonemes (unobserved states) from a sequence of acoustic features (observations), where the underlying model is that an phoneme sequence (i.e. spoken language) is being generated by a human speaker and 'causing' the acoustic observations. The HMM can then be used to decode a probability distribution over possible phoneme sequences; this can be combined with a probabilistic language model to further refine the recognition process. Dynamic belief nets are closely related to **probabilistic filtering**, the online (i.e. inference during a process) estimation of states. Probabilistic filters encompass DBNs, but the probabilistic filtering approach is typically identified with problems with continuous multi-dimensional

J. H. Williamson

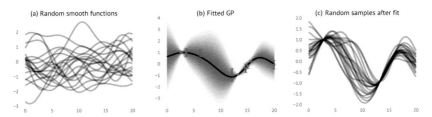

Figure 1.31 Gaussian process models form probability distributions over functions themselves. (a) Random functions drawn from a distribution over functions with a particular smoothness. (b) Observations have constrained the distribution, but note that the uncertainty is preserved (shaded area) and measurement uncertainty on each point (error bars) is taken into account. (c) Random samples from this distribution over functions compatible with the observations are shown.

unobserved states; whereas DBN approaches like Hidden Markov Models are typically applied in problems with discrete unobserved states.

1.5.4 What about 'Bayesian Non-Parametrics'?

We have presumed, so far, that our models have a fixed set of parameters that define a configuration – a few moving parts that can be adjusted. Bayesian non-parametric methods do not assume a parametric form, and instead form distributions over *possible functions* that could have generated data. These models are constructed by defining a class of functions, such as a particular space of functions of variable smoothness, and then forming a prior distribution over all possible functions of this class. This prior is updated with observations to produce a new distribution over functions which are compatible with the data. In the simplest case, this might be distribution over all functions which pass through some data points, a distribution over interpolating functions of a specific smoothness.

The most important of these approaches is the Gaussian process (GP), an exceptionally flexible modelling tool. The details of the GP are beyond this book, but it allows the definition of a space of functions via *kernels* that define how nearby observations co-vary; this becomes a restriction on the smoothness of functions. GPs are a powerful way to interpolate and extrapolate functions from observed samples (Figure 1.31), with appropriate uncertainty, and have a huge range of uses in interaction design.

In the simplest cases, non-parametric models like GPs can be used as smooth interpolators which maintain uncertainty, for example, to predict expected

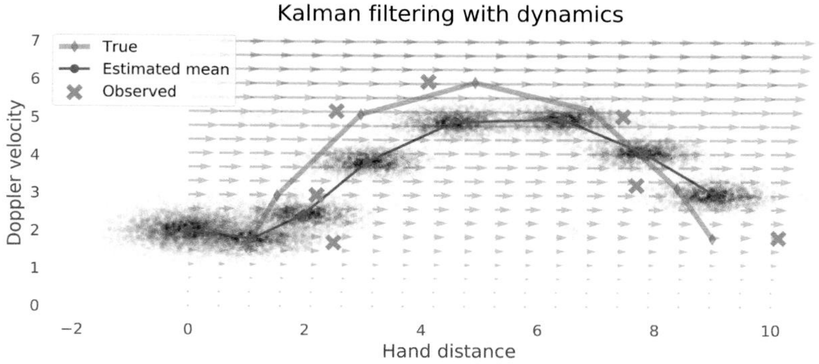

Figure 1.32 Probabilistic filtering in a hand tracking problem. We estimate a distribution over the distance and velocity of a hand, which are measured separately by a sensor. Noisy observations update the inference. Dynamics (arrows showing vector field) transform posterior distributions (shown as point clouds) to form the priors at the next step. Even with heavy noise in the position estimate, the dynamic model can make reliable predictions (posterior mean shown as a solid line).

offsets between actual touch and intended touch [11]. One important use in interaction design is as **proxy objective functions** in Bayesian optimisation. GPs are often used to represent an unknown function mapping properties of an interface to some quantitative measure, such as reported satisfaction or response time. By sequentially updating the distribution over functions, optimisation can be performed *at the same time* as learning about the function. This can be an efficient way to optimise interface designs with humans in the loop.

1.5.5 What Are Probabilistic Filters?

Probabilistic filtering is sequential Bayesian inference and is used to estimate parameters that vary over time. This is particularly salient in interaction problems where we often have an ongoing interaction *process* and want to infer states as they are happening.

This means we move from a prior to a posterior on a series of time steps, at each step having an estimate of some unknown state. Probabilistic filters are of wide use in the interaction loop, particularly in problems like estimating a stable cursor from noisy sensing, or fusing together multiple sensors, perhaps running at different sampling rates. For example, we might be tracking the distance and movement of a user's hand to a mobile device screen, based on a Doppler return from an ultrasonic sensor. This sensor might give us *both* crude and noisy estimates of distance but reasonably accurate velocity estimates. How can we fuse this information to obtain reliable estimates of hand distance? This involves a predictive model over time.

We can treat the true position of the hand as an unobserved parameter and estimate it from sensor data using Bayesian inference. A simple probabilistic filter uses posteriors from the previous time step to form the prior in the following step. To account for the passage of time, *dynamics* are applied to the posterior before it becomes the next prior (Figure 1.32). These dynamics are a predictive model that moves the distribution forward in time. The dynamics can often be very simple and can involve parameters that are also simultaneously inferred. For example, we might assume that hand position changes by the current estimated hand velocity over a fixed time interval. We can update both position and velocity using ordinary Bayesian inference, then apply the velocity to the posterior distribution of positions and feed this forward to the next time step.

Techniques like (unscented [55]) Kalman filters [1] and particle filters (also called sequential Monte Carlo filtering) make implementing probabilistic filters in interaction problems straightforward – once the modelling is done – and reasonably computationally efficient.

1.6 Facets of Bayesian Methods for Interaction Design

Bayesian approaches intersect with interaction problems in several ways. Five of these facets are outlined in the sections below:

1. Bayesian inference at **interaction time**, inferring the intention of a user in the control loop.
2. Bayesian optimisation at **design time**, efficiently optimising designs with humans in the design process.
3. Bayesian analysis at **evaluation time**, analysing the outcomes of an empirical interaction work.

4. Interaction to support Bayesian modelling, through visualisation, workflow support and interactive model construction and exploration.
5. Bayesian models as an approximation for human cognition, to guide the design of interactive systems with well-founded predictions of user behaviour.

1.6.1 Optimal Mind-Reading: How Can Bayesian Methods Work Out What a User Wants to Do?

Bayesian methods can be used to represent the problem of interaction itself – how does information flow from human to computer? This can be used to derive robust models based around inference of intention. Strong prior models of what we expect users to do allow us to extract maximum value from input and preserve uncertainty about user intent. If we already know what intentions are *likely* to be expressed, we do not need as much information to reliably determine the true intention. This is a model of interaction founded in the idea of the interface as a concentrator of belief, whose mechanics are driven by the logic of probability. Such an interface represents, manipulates and displays uncertainty as a first-class value [50, 51]. This can extend throughout the interaction loop, from low-level inference about user state from sensors [47], interpretation of pointing actions [27], probabilistic GUIs [10], text entry [56], error-tolerant interfaces [58], motion correlation [54] and 2D selection [37].

We can conceive of an interface as a system that tries to *infer* what the user wants. We formulate a distribution over possible outcomes (e.g. over items on a menu), and an associated prior (e.g. from historical frequencies of interaction). We then update this probability distribution using observed inputs (e.g. the sequence of motion events from a pointing device).

> Note that this involves building a model that simulates the sequence of motion events *given* the menu item: a forward model that predicts for all possible menu items what the observed pointer movements would be! This is the opposite of the typical way of thinking about this problem.

Bayesian probabilistic interfaces let us formulate the intent inference problem in this way. This has some interesting effects:

• We can consistently introduce priors to imbue our interfaces with 'intelligence', without special ad hoc hacks;

  – these priors can include static, historical models,
  – or they can come from other input streams ('sensor fusion'),

– or they can come from preceding states to fuse together information over time ('probabilistic filtering').

• We can simulate into the future and predict likely future actions (and, e.g., pre-cache likely responses).
• We can incorporate models of how interaction will unfold (e.g. what does a pointing movement look like) directly into our interface.
• We can provide feedback and display uncertainty to the user and make the behaviour of an interface more interpretable and predictable.
• We have a distribution over outcomes, and we can choose appropriate decision rules to actuate events. This can incorporate utility functions to account for different values that events might have.

This view on interaction sees user intentions as **unknown values** which are partially observed through inputs. The time series of inputs from the user give a partial, noisy, incomplete view of intention inside the user's head, along with a great deal of superfluous information. This is equivalent to the information–theoretic viewpoint of an interface as a noisy channel through which intention flows.

We try to infer a *generative model*, which is a simplified representation of intention and how it is mediated and transformed by the world. The stronger the model we have available, the more effectively we can infer intention. In this view, improving interaction (or at least *input*) comes down to more efficiently concentrating probability density where a user wants it to go. A better pointing device reduces uncertainty faster; a better display helps a user understand how best to target future actions to concentrate belief as desired; a better model of the user intentions concentrates belief with less explicit effort on the part of a user.

1.6.2 Fast Tuning in a Noisy World: How Can Bayesian Approaches Be Used to Optimise User Interfaces?

In an optimisation problem we have one or more *objective functions* (each a single numerical measure of goodness or badness), which depend upon some *parameters*, which we are interested in adjusting to minimise the objective function, usually bounded by some *constraints*. Many design problems can be framed in these terms. As an example, we might want to improve an aspect of a user interface, such as the scrolling speed of a photo viewer. This has an adjustable parameter (speed), bounded by some maximum and minimum speed (constraints), and we could derive a measure of performance, like the reported subjective satisfaction, as our objective function.

Numerical optimisation is an extremely powerful tool to solve these types of problems, but it developed in engineering contexts like the design of aeroplane wings, where strong mathematical models were well established and precise measurements were practical. Objective functions, however, are not always known, as is very often the case in interaction design. We would *not* expect to have any good model of satisfaction as a function of scroll speed, and it would be impractical to imagine deriving one from first principles. We may instead have a situation where we can only measure the value of the objective function at a few *definite* parameter settings, perhaps with significant measurement noise. In the scrolling example, we are free to sample different scroll speeds and ask users how they like it. Acquiring measurement points like this is expensive if humans are in the loop, so it is important to be parsimonious in sampling possible parameter settings. Humans are expensive to measure, noisy in their actions and not governed by simple mathematical formulae.

These issues motivate the use of a *proxy objective function*, a model that we learn from data that approximates the functional relationship between the parameters and the response (Figure 1.33). We now have to deal with two problems: Which specific example parameters (speeds, in the example) should we test with users? And how should we deal with the fact that the measurements we make may be noisy? We certainly don't expect to be able to repeat an experiment with a fixed scrolling speed and get the same satisfaction level. These are problems well solved by **Bayesian optimisation**, where we form a distribution over possible proxy objective functions, update these from measurements and can sequentially optimally select the most *informative* next test to make, taking into account the (epistemic) uncertainty of our model and the (aleatoric) uncertainty of our measurements.

This can range from simple Bayesian A/B testing to sophisticated modelling of user behaviour at a fine level of granularity. Bayesian optimisation can be applied to a huge range of problems with expensive or noisy functions, from inferring subjective preferences [9] and effective interface design [16] to optimising touch sensor configurations. Proxy objective function models like Gaussian processes [46] are well-supported by software packages and can often be slotted straight into a HCI problem. We can still combine these proxy objective functions with strong priors. As we incrementally improve our priors, our optimisation automatically becomes more informed and the sampling of measurements becomes more efficient.

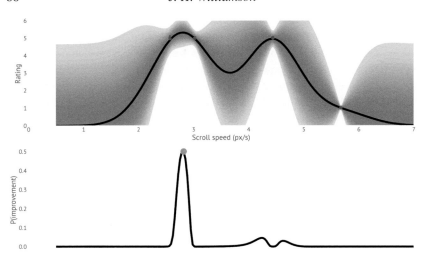

Figure 1.33 A mock example of Bayesian optimisation, using a proxy function to estimate user satisfaction (each point representing averaged scores from many participants on a 1- to 5-point scale) as the speed of a scrolling photo viewer is adjusted. Which speed should we test next to most quickly tune the photo browser? The uncertainty in the proxy function gives informed strategies to do so. The upper pane shows a Gaussian process proxy function fitted to four noisy satisfaction score measurements. The lower panel shows the probability of improvement across the space of scroll speeds. By selecting the point with maximal probability of improvement (marked with a circle), we define a strategy to find the next scroll speed to try out with users.

1.6.3 Evaluating with Uncertainty and Limited Data: How Can Bayesian Methods Be Used to Analyse the Results of Human–Computer Experiments?

Human–computer interaction, by its very nature, depends heavily on the evaluation of interactive systems with users. Empirical evaluations are a basic and near universal aspect of HCI research and practice.

Bayesian approaches offer a potentially superior way of analysing some kinds of quantitative experimental work that arise in HCI. Experiments of all types result in numbers, but we know that the interpretation of these are subject to uncertainty; this is why we have statistics. Statistics is divided into two schools of thought: *frequentist* statistics, which encompasses classical approaches such as null hypothesis testing widely used in HCI; and *Bayesian* statistics, which involves quite distinct principles of inference, reasoning from a prior to a posterior. These two schools of thought remain bitterly divided over the correct way to interpret data. Kay et al. [31] motivate the use of Bayesian statistics in the evaluation of HCI experiments and put forward the case that Bayesian statistics are a better fit to the research practices in HCI, particularly in the re-usability of analyses from previous work and dealing with small sample sizes and weak effects. The awkward fit of 'dichotomous inference' (does this effect exist or not?) that is the focus of frequentist methods to interaction design has also come under criticism [3].

It is important to note that both frequentist and Bayesian methods are valid ways of interpreting data, but they answer different questions and have distinct trade-offs. For historical reasons, empirical research in psychology-adjacent fields such as HCI has focused almost exclusively on frequentist methods, particularly null hypothesis testing (NHST). While powerful and well-understood, they are not always well suited to answer the questions that we wish to investigate in HCI, and in the worst cases degrade into cargo cult statistics ('just slap a t-test on it and hope for p < 0.05'). Bayesian methods are no less susceptible to poor research practices, but they do require a more explicit consideration of the problem.

From an interaction design perspective, Bayesian approaches can directly answer questions of interest and can incorporate first-principles models from domain experts. They are well suited to problems where there is small data, where large controlled studies may not be practical or desirable. Bayesian statistical models make it easy to incorporate complex models, such as hierarchical regression. There are opportunities for novel and efficient experimental designs (e.g. online Bayesian experimental design) and practical meta-analyses. The advance of easy-to-use packages for Bayesian inference (e.g. stan, pymc3, brms, pyro) makes powerful Bayesian inference models reachable for non-specialist researchers. *Statistical Rethinking* [40] is recommended reading as a non-HCI introduction to Bayesian data analysis. Phelan et al. [44] give some guidance for the application of Bayesian models specifcally in human–computer interaction.

We cannot adequately describe the distinction between the two statistical schools of thought in this chapter. We refer interested readers to the recommended reading at the end of the chapter. A brief summary of the distinctive aspects of Bayesian approaches to designing and interpreting empirical work for interaction designers is summarised below:

- Bayesian methods require *priors* to be defined. Frequentist methods do not. This has several consequences:

  – we *have* to be able to come up with justifiable priors, which may be hard;
  – but if we do have them, we can use them (and frequentist methods cannot);

- our priors force us to 'lay our cards on the table' and make our assumptions explicit;
- priors are actionable and scrutable, in that we can visualise or otherwise explore their consequences.

- Bayesian methods answer questions about the specific evidence in this instance, given the priors. Frequentist methods answer questions about long-run behaviour, without regard to priors. In HCI, we often only *can* ever have one experiment and may be less concerned about objective statements about the long-run behaviour.
- Frequentist methods are ideal to establish if an effect exists (as opposed to a random occurence), in the context of randomised controlled trial. This is, for example, vitally important in medical contexts. In HCI, such problems do occur, but there are other research investigations of interest that do not fit into this dichotomous mode of thinking, or for which randomised controlled trials are not feasible or meaningful. In these cases, a Bayesian approach may be more flexible.

  - Bayesian methods *can* be used for dichotomous analyses, using **Bayes factors** to compare the relative likelihood of two competing hypotheses with the same evidence. However, this is sensitive to the choice of priors and therefore requires particular caution.

- Bayesian methods are flexible regarding combining evidence acquired at any time, from any source. It is possible to run a Bayesian design where experiments are run until a result is established with a certain degree of confidence. This is harder to do correctly with a frequentist approach. Likewise, it is easier to combine multiple studies in a Bayesian framework than it is to conduct a meta-analysis of studies in a frequentist framework. A Bayesian framework can feed the results of previous studies in *directly* as priors.
- Many frequentist methods have to be applied very carefully to preserve their validity (for example, it is essential to apply corrections to preserve false positive resistance in the presence of multiple tests on the same data). Bayesian methods still require care in application but often break in more obvious ways.
- All modelling involves a bias–variance trade-off. A more complex model with more parameters will require more evidence to be constrained than a simpler model with fewer parameters. In a Bayesian framework, this is usually easy to inspect; the posterior distribution will tell us how informed the parameters of our model are. This can be harder to reason about in frequentist models.

- Bayesian methods can use models of essentially any form that can be computed, including complex simulators. Frequentist methods require a more limited class of models.

  - Bayesian models require the statistical model to be defined in detail (e.g. as a program), which may require more work, but this model is a free choice. Frequentist methods can devolve into picking an approach from a zoo of tests and procedures, which may be an awkward fit.
  - It is easy in Bayesian approaches to build *hierarchical models*, where the parameters at one 'layer' depend on another 'layer'. For example, we might model reaction time as coming from a distribution that is distinct for each user; and the distribution of user distributions might be governed by a common population model. This is a flexible way of gradually introducing more sophisticated models.

- Frequentist methods can often be computed in a closed-form directly, exactly and efficiently. This is rarer in Bayesian methods, where approximate and computationally intensive methods are used (such as MCMC).

  - Frequentist methods are rarely troubled by computational problems. Because Bayesian methods depend on computational approximations, it is often necessary to tweak models so that the computation works efficiently (e.g. reparameterisation to make MCMC sample well). This is a clear case of the tail wagging the dog! Approximations can also go wrong and produce dubious results. This requires vigilance in monitoring diagnostics and can involve tricky 'debugging'.

- Bayesian methods give results in terms of the likelihood of different hypotheses. This is often the question we want to answer, and means we can use the statistics to work the argument we want to make, rather than having the statistics define the argument we are able to make:

  - **Bayesian:** 'The 95% credible interval for increase in reading speed from version A to version B is [1.7, 2.1]', meaning that we are 95% sure that the reading speed improvement is in that range, given our priors.
  - **Frequentist:** 'The 95% confidence interval for increase in reading speed is [1.7, 2.1]', meaning we expect that if we ran this experiment repeatedly, the interval we computed would capture the true reading speed 95% of the time (but this specific interval might not!).

  - **Bayesian:** 'Given our priors, the expected increase in tweets read per day is +2.9, and a decrease in tweets read has a probability of less than 5%', meaning exactly what it says.

- **Frequentist:** 'We find a mean increase of 2.9 tweets/day, and [following an appropriate test] we reject the null hypothesis with $p < 0.05$', meaning that if we ran this experiment repeatedly, and the null hypothesis was true and variation in tweets was purely random, then we would expect to see results as extreme or more extreme than this less than 5% of the time. Is this a question we are interested in knowing the answer to?
- In all cases, these statements depend on the assumptions made. In the Bayesian case, these are the models and the priors. In the frequentist case, we have no priors to worry about, but we have a restricted class of models and distributions available, and we must make sure that these are appropriate for the problem. Many common frequentist models are *normal linear models* and are powerful if these assumptions hold but problematic if not.

1.6.4 Bayesian Interaction: How Can We Visualise and Interact with Bayesian Models?

One notable problem with Bayesian models is that they can be hard to understand, particularly for non-experts and particularly when couched in the traditional technical language. The results of Bayesian inference can be rich – and therefore hard to summarise and superficially non-intuitive. Building Bayesian models and verifying they are doing what is expected is a task that can be error-prone. This is a problem that human–computer interaction is well placed to solve.

Bayesian interaction is the problem of how to display, explain, explore, construct and criticise probabilistic Bayesian models: how and where to put users in the loop in Bayesian modelling. This involves supporting users in making rational and informed decisions, like assessment of risk or of expected value, in comprehending the structure of Bayesian models and the interpretation of their parameters, and in aiding the development of new models and debugging and criticising them. User interaction with Bayesian models has a few important aspects:

- **Visualisation of uncertainty:** Distributions are the basis of Bayesian modelling, and so the representation of distributions to users is important, particularly the visualisation of uncertainty [28, 43]. People have a hard time understanding distributions and their implications, and this is exacerbated when distributions are over a high-dimensional parameter space. Visualising and summarising distributions in ways that preserve uncertainty are significant challenges in HCI. Even in simpler problems there can be user-facing uncertainty that should not be elided. Interacting with noisy sensors, like a brain–computer interface, results in an uncertain interface state. Reflecting this uncertainty to users could improve interaction, but requires new interface techniques such as uncertain cursors.

- **Interactive exploration of Bayesian models:** Early work in Bayesian visualisation has focused on static summaries of posteriors. There are many open research questions in user interfaces that support dynamic interaction. Interactive systems to explore possible configurations is the most promising way to communicate large Bayesian models. The ability to slice, brush or tour posterior distributions can reveal structured correlations in the results of inference [53].

- **Prior elicitation and Bayesian workflow support:** Bayesian models depend upon suitable priors. There are open research questions around the best interfaces to elicit priors from experts, and to test and verify their validity (e.g. via interactive prior predictive checks). This ties into the problem of **Bayesian workflow** research: how to support users in building, running and verifying Bayesian models, such as visualisation in Bayesian workflows [22] and interactive prior elicitation [30]. This might range from debugging tools to diagnose poor parameterisations or misbehaving MCMC samplers, to defining wider processes to construct and revise models within a scientific team.

1.6.5 A Higher Perspective: How Can Bayesian Ideas Help Us Understand Human Cognition?

There is a school of thought that interprets the thought processes of humans and other living beings as an approximate form of Bayesian inference. This 'Bayesian brain' hypothesis [20, 21] implies that we are all engaged in some form of approximate Bayesian inference, from low-level sensory perception through to higher-level cognition. It posits a model of cognition where organisms form predictive models of the world [26] and revise them in light of sensory evidence in a manner compatible with Bayesian belief updates. This framework gives a structure by which causal origins of perceptual stimuli can be inferred by organisms, and by links to information-theoretic models of behaviour and perception [29].

This is a controversial hypothesis, and one that is hard to gather definitive evidence for or against. However, it can be a powerful lens through which to examine how we will react and behave with interactive systems. Regardless of its biological 'truth', Bayesian cognitive models are amenable to computation and can provoke new thoughts on how to engineer interactions. As a concrete example, Rao [45] models visual cue integration as a Kalman filter, a recursive Bayesian update process. This form of model postulates that living beings combine predictive models of how the world is expected to evolve and evaluate this against evidence from sensory channels. In human–computer interaction, research on understanding how users interpret data visualisations [32, 59] can be modelled by representing users with a Bayesian cognition and the consequent belief updates they would perform under this model.

1.7 Bayesian Pasts and Futures

1.7.1 How Did These Ideas Come About?

Bayesian ideas of probability were first stated in a limited form by Thomas Bayes, in the eighteenth century, in notes that were unpublished until after his death [2]. The ideas were extended by Pierre Simon Laplace in France in the early nineteenth century [35].

Bayesian interpretations fell out of favour, and for many decades these approaches were ignored, either because they could not practically be used for lack of computational power, or on philosophical grounds. Vigorous and bitter debates about validity of Bayesian ideas in the first half of the twentieth century left Bayesian modelling as a niche subject until the end of the twentieth century. We leave the details to others; McGrayne [41] is an accessible history of this conflict.

1.7.2 Why Is This Suddenly Relevant Now?

From the 1980s onwards, computational power became available that made Bayesian statistics suddenly practical. The development of tools like BUGS in the early 1990s, and the subsequent development of efficient Markov chain Monte Carlo samplers interfaced to probabilistic programming languages, brought these modelling tools to specialists who did not have to implement the micro-details of numerical inference. These two factors make large Bayesian models tractable, and reduce the need for clever algebraic manipulations. An increasing number of accessible texts on Bayesian modelling has ignited interest among new audiences.

There is also an increasing realisation that traditional statistical methods are not always well suited to the problems that are encountered in interaction design, and alternative methodologies can be more insightful. Some Bayesian methods, such as Kalman filtering, have long been known in HCI, but as a kind of 'magical' special-case algorithm, rather than what is a fairly ordinary use of Bayesian modelling.

1.7.3 Does Uncertainty = Bayesian?

Our primary motivation for applying Bayesian modelling is to properly account for uncertainty. Uncertainty in Bayesian models is represented with probability. Probability is *not* the only way to represent uncertainty, but it is arguably the *right* way to represent it [36]. Probability has a simple, rigorous axiomatic basis [13]. It can further be shown that any non-probabilistic representation in a situation with uncertain outcomes of different values, as in a betting game, is inferior to a probabilistic representation, in terms of expected return [14]. However, there are other models of uncertainty which may be computationally or philosophically more convenient to apply; a review of alternatives is given by Zio and Pedroni [60].

We can also use probability without applying Bayesian ideas, as in frequentist models. Frequentism strictly limits the elements about which we may be uncertain, limiting probability to represent the uncertain outcomes of repeatable experiments (or draws from some distribution). At the same time, this avoids the troubles of subjective probability, and the well-developed mathematical theory for frequentist models means that many quantities of interest can be computed quickly and without resort to approximation. Many useful probabilistic models in human–computer interaction, such as Hidden Markov Models for sequence recognition, are often implemented from a frequentist perspective.

1.7.4 Ethics of Bayesian Interaction

Modelling choices are *not* ethically neutral, even at this highest of abstraction levels. Placed as we are at the junction between computer science and the human world, interaction designers and HCI researchers have a particular role in evaluating the ethical implications of our modelling choices and advancing ethical research practices.

- **Uncertainty:** Above all else, failure to represent uncertainty can be an ethical failing. Bayesian methods are not the only way to work with and represent with uncertainty, but they put uncertainty at the heart of all computation. Discarding or eliding uncertainty can be deception (for example, in reporting of empirical work), or can present direct risks of harm (for example, in safety critical systems). Uncertainty must be accounted for, preserved and represented. Bayesian methods are the most straightforward way to do so; some would argue, the *only* correct way to do so.
- **Priors:** Bayesian methods need priors. On one hand, the requirement that assumptions are always laid out in the open as fully defined priors invites inspection and transparency. This is important if the outcome of inference

affects people's lives; these explicit priors can be reviewed, challenged or modified. On the other hand, malevolent manipulation of priors can be used to produce any result at all. This implies a duty and responsibility to document and justify priors, and to publish models that allow inference to be conducted under alternative priors. Reproducibility is important for all science, but especially for Bayesian models.

- **Small data** Bayesian models can often make useful inferences with very small datasets, by using informative priors. This is typical, for example, in astronomical tasks like identifying exoplanets – there is simply very little data to work with. In interaction, human responses are *valuable*. It costs money and time to run experiments with users. Wasteful experimental designs or analyses are unethical. Bayesian methods have two advantages: they can work well in the small data domain; and *active learning* approaches can be used to adapt experiments online to precisely control the uncertainty remaining.

1.7.5 Disadvantages, Cons and Caveats

Why isn't *everything* Bayesian? We've seen how much Bayesian approaches offer, and yet it currently has a tiny foothold in human–computer interaction. Even in other disciplines like astronomy, where it is better established, it is still a minority approach. Part of the reason Bayesian approaches in interaction can appear so appealing is because of the vacuum of general ideas in interaction [33] and the in-rush of enlightenment that these approaches bring lays bare much low-hanging fruit.

A great deal of the slow uptake is historical, stemming from the rancorous debates over the validity of Bayesian ideas in statistics and the absence of workable solutions to perform inference. However, there are real issues with Bayesian approaches that need to be understood.

- **Computational resources:** Bayesian methods can require extensive computational resources, certainly compared with common frequentist experimental analyses. In real-time settings with a human-in-the-loop, Bayesian inference may be difficult to compute quickly enough to maintain responsiveness. In large, complex offline analyses with hundreds of parameters, inference can be extremely time consuming. In cases where uncertainty is not especially relevant, or good priors are not available, other approaches may be much more practical. Non-Bayesian machine learning or statistical approaches will likely outperform Bayesian methods in such cases.
- **Approximations:** Computational approaches to Bayesian inference almost invariably rely on approximations. Approximations can be hard to configure.

They can go wrong and produce meaningless results. They can be hard to debug. Diagnostics are available, but they are not perfect indicators of flaws. Care must be taken in formulating problems to get a form that is both conceptually correct and practical to approximate. Users of Bayesian methods need to be diligent in verifying the quality of approximations, and reporting carefully exactly how inference was performed and any relevant diagnostic measures.

- **Communication and understanding:** Bayesian methods may be harder to communicate to audiences unfamiliar with them. This presents a barrier to dissemination. There are venues where reviewers expect to see an ANOVA and a p-value and will be uncomfortable if these are absent. On the other hand, Bayesian models and results are often easier to correctly interpret once understood. Credible intervals and posterior histograms coincide more closely with human intuitions than confidence intervals or other frequentist summaries. There is not always a standard way to represent the results of inference. Bespoke visualisations or summary statistics may be needed.

- **Formulation of problems:** Bayesian approaches are extremely general. This also implies that there is a lot of work in correctly specifying a Bayesian approach. The real difficulty is in formulating problems in terms of probabilistic models. This is a difficult skill to acquire and takes a change in perspective that is unfamiliar to most researchers and practitioners. Bayesian models can be much more sophisticated than standard statistical methods. This offers power, but it can often be hard to explain something like a hierarchical Bayesian model, and particularly to give meaningful names and interpretations to high-level parameters ('the mean of the variance of the distribution of variances over variances'). Bayesian models will be specific to the problem under consideration, and not an 'off-the-shelf' statistical model like a t-test or ANOVA. This means that these models *have* to be communicated clearly and rigorously.

- **Subjectivity:** Bayesian methods are typically applied in a *subjective* fashion (there is such a thing as objective Bayesian statistics, but this is perhaps best left alone). It only answers questions that relate to how belief changes from a prior in the light of evidence. Most of the time, this is what we want, and subjectivity is a desirable quality. Subjective beliefs, however, require justification and explanation. Documenting how results are arrived requires care and thought.

1.8 Where Do I Go from Here?

1.8.1 Introductory Texts on Bayesian Statistics

- For those looking for a first introduction to Bayesian statistics, we particularly recommend McElreath's *Statistical Rethinking* [40], which provides a thorough and highly readable grounding in Bayesian modelling without assuming any background.
- *Think Bayes* (second edition) by Allen Downey [15] is a slender and accessible text on Bayesian statistics with extensive worked examples in Python.
- We also recommend Lambert's *A Student's Guide to Bayesian Statistics* [34], which has excellent supporting video material.
- McGrayne's *The Theory that Would Not Die* [41] is a very accessible popular science account of the history of Bayesian reasoning and is enlightening in establishing the context in which Bayesian methods are discussed and used in the statistical world.
- For a more mathematically rigorous discussion, the series of online articles by Michael Betancourt are self-contained, rigorous and beautifully illustrated. In particular, *Foundations of Probability Theory* [5], *Conditional Probability Theory for Scientists and Engineers* [4], *Probabilistic Computation* [6], *Modeling and Inference* [7] and *Towards a Principled Bayesian Workflow* [8] are approachable for computer scientists with some background in mathematics.

More Advanced Texts

- *Bayesian Data Analysis* by Gelman et al. [23] is the standard book on Bayesian approaches to data analysis. It requires significantly more mathematical background than the introductory texts listed above, but it is a comprehensive resource.
- *Regression and Other Stories* by Gelman, Hill and Vehtari [24] is a thorough introduction to Bayesian regression modelling and encompasses both the how and the why of regression modelling.
- A more adventurous text that links together information theory, machine learning and Bayesian approaches is *Information Theory, Inference and Learning Algorithms* [38], by MacKay (who, in the HCI world, introduced the *Dasher* probabilistic text entry system [56]). This is a more mathematically challenging text, but the perspective that it provides is particularly useful for human–computer interaction, where flows of information interact with inference engines.

References

[1] T. Babb. 2015. *How a Kalman Filter Works, in Pictures.* Bzarg. www.bzarg.com/ p/how-a-kalman-filter-works-in-pictures/.

[2] T. Bayes, Thomas. 1763. LII. An essay towards solving a problem in the doctrine of chances. By the late Rev. Mr. Bayes, FRS communicated by Mr. Price, in a letter to John Canton, AMFR S. *Philosophical Transactions of the Royal Society of London*, 370–418.

[3] L. Besançon and P. Dragicevic, Pierre. 2019. The continued prevalence of dichotomous inferences at CHI. Pages 1–11 of: *Extended Abstracts of the 2019 CHI Conference on Human Factors in Computing Systems.* CHI EA '19. Association for Computing Machinery.

[4] M. Betancourt. 2018 (Oct.). *Conditional Probability Theory (For Scientists and Engineers).* https://betanalpha.github.io/assets/case_studies/conditional_ probability_theory.html.

[5] M. Betancourt. 2018 (Oct.). *Probability Theory (for Scientists and Engineers).* https://betanalpha.github.io/assets/case_studies/probability_theory.html.

[6] M. Betancourt. 2019 (June). *Probabilistic Computation.* https://betanalpha.github .io/assets/case_studies/probabilistic_computation.html.

[7] M. Betancourt. 2019 (Mar.). *Probabilistic Modeling and Statistical Inference.* https://betanalpha.github.io/assets/case_studies/modeling_and_inference.html.

[8] M. Betancourt. 2020 (Apr.). *Towards a Principled Bayesian Workflow.* https:// betanalpha.github.io/assets/case_studies/principled_bayesian_workflow.html.

[9] E. Brochu, T. Brochu and N. de Freitas. 2010. A Bayesian interactive optimization approach to procedural animation design. Pages 103–112 of: *Proceedings of the 2010 ACM SIGGRAPH/Eurographics Symposium on Computer Animation.* SCA '10. Eurographics Association.

[10] D. Buschek, Daniel, and F. Alt. 2017. ProbUI: generalising touch target representations to enable declarative gesture definition for probabilistic GUIs. Pages 4640–4653 of: *Proceedings of the 2017 CHI Conference on Human Factors in Computing Systems.* CHI '17. Association for Computing Machinery.

[11] D. Buschek, S. Rogers and R. Murray-Smith. 2013. User-specific touch models in a cross-device context. Pages 382–391 of: *Proceedings of the 15th International Conference on Human-Computer Interaction with Mobile Devices and Services.* Association for Computing Machinery.

[12] B. Carpenter, A. Gelman, M.D. Hoffman, D. Lee, B. Goodrich, M. Betancourt, M. A. Brubaker, J. Guo, P. Li and A. Riddell. 2017. Stan: a probabilistic programming language. *Grantee Submission*, **76**(1), 1–32.

[13] R. T. Cox. 1946. Probability, frequency and reasonable expectation. *American journal of physics*, **14**(1), 1–13.

[14] B. De Finetti. 1975. *Theory of Probability: A Critical Introductory Treatment*, Vol. 6. John Wiley & Sons.

[15] A. B. Downey. 2021. *Think Bayes.* O'Reilly Media, Inc.

[16] J. J. Dudley, J. T. Jacques and P. O. Kristensson. 2019. Crowdsourcing interface feature design with Bayesian optimization. Pages 1–12 of: *Proceedings of the 2019 CHI Conference on Human Factors in Computing Systems.* Association for Computing Machinery.

[17] C. Feng. *MCMC Interactive Gallery*. https://chi-feng.github.io/mcmc-demo/app.html.

[18] M. Fernandes, L. Walls, S. Munson, J. Hullman and M. Kay. 2018. Uncertainty displays using quantile dotplots or CDFs improve transit decision-making. Pages 1–12 of: *Proceedings of the 2018 CHI Conference on Human Factors in Computing Systems*. Association for Computing Machinery.

[19] P. M. Fitts. 1954. The information capacity of the human motor system in controlling the amplitude of movement. *Journal of experimental psychology*, **47**(6), 381.

[20] K. Friston. 2010. The free-energy principle: a unified brain theory? *Nature Reviews Neuroscience*, **11**(2), 127–138.

[21] K. Friston. 2012. The history of the future of the Bayesian brain. *Neuroimage*, **62-248**(2), 1230–1233.

[22] J. Gabry, D. Simpson, A. Vehtari, M. Betancourt and A. Gelman, Andrew. 2019. Visualization in Bayesian workflow. *Journal of the Royal Statistical Society: Series A (Statistics in Society)*, **182**(2), 389–402.

[23] A. Gelman, J. B. Carlin, H. S. Stern, D. B. Dunson, A. Vehtari and D. B. Rubin. 2013. *Bayesian Data Analysis*. CRC Press.

[24] A. Gelman, J. Hill, and A. Vehtari. 2020. *Regression and Other Stories*. Cambridge University Press.

[25] A. Gelman, A. Vehtari, D. Simpson, C. C. Margossian, B. Carpenter, Y. Yao, L. Kennedy, J. Gabry, P.-C. Bürkner and M. Modrák. 2020. Bayesian Workflow. *arXiv preprint arXiv:2011.01808*.

[26] T. L. Griffiths, and J. B. Tenenbaum. 2006. Optimal predictions in everyday cognition. *Psychological Science*, **17**(9), 767–773.

[27] T. Grossman, and R. Balakrishnan. 2005. A probabilistic approach to modeling two-dimensional pointing. *ACM Transactions on Computer–Human Interaction*, **12**(3), 435–459.

[28] J. Hullman, X. Qiao, M. Correll, A. Kale and M. Kay. 2018. In pursuit of error: a survey of uncertainty visualization evaluation. *IEEE Transactions on Visualization and Computer Graphics*, **25**(1), 903–913.

[29] G. Jensen, R. D. Ward and P. D. Balsam. 2013. Information: theory, brain, and behavior. *Journal of the Experimental Analysis of Behavior*, **100**(3), 408–431.

[30] G. Jones and W. O. Johnson, Wesley O. 2014. Prior elicitation: interactive spreadsheet graphics with sliders can be fun, and informative. *The American Statistician*, **68**(1), 42–51.

[31] M. Kay, G. L. Nelson and E. B. Hekler. 2016. Researcher-centered design of statistics: why Bayesian statistics better fit the culture and incentives of HCI. Pages 4521–4532 of: *Proceedings of the 2016 CHI Conference on Human Factors in Computing Systems*. Association for Computing Machinery.

[32] Y.-S. Kim, L. A. Walls, P. Krafft and J. Hullman. 2019. A Bayesian cognition approach to improve data visualization. Pages 1–14 of: *Proceedings of the 2019 CHI Conference on Human Factors in Computing Systems*. CHI '19. Association for Computing Machinery.

[33] V. Kostakos. 2015. The big hole in HCI research. *Interactions*, **22**(2), 48–51.

[34] B. Lambert. 2018. *A Student's Guide to Bayesian Statistics*. Sage.

[35] P.-S.Laplace. 1812. *Théorie Analytique Des Probabilités*. Courcier.

[36] D. V. Lindley. 1987. The probability approach to the treatment of uncertainty in artificial intelligence and expert systems. *Statistical Science*, **2**(1), 17–24.

[37] W. Liu, d'Oliveira, M. Beaudouin-Lafon and O. Rioul, Olivier. 2017. Bignav: Bayesian information gain for guiding multiscale navigation. Pages 5869–5880 of: *Proceedings of the 2017 CHI Conference on Human Factors in Computing Systems*. Association for Computing Machinery.

[38] D. J. C. MacKay. 2003. *Information Theory, Inference and Learning Algorithms*. Cambridge University Press.

[39] I. S. MacKenzie. 1992. Fitts' law as a research and design tool in human–computer interaction. *Human-Computer Interaction*, **7**(1), 91–139.

[40] R. McElreath. 2018. *Statistical Rethinking: A Bayesian Course with Examples in R and Stan*. Chapman and Hall/CRC.

[41] S. B. McGrayne. 2011. *The Theory That Would Not Die: How Bayes' Rule Cracked the Enigma Code, Hunted Down Russian Submarines, and Emerged Triumphant from Two Centuries of C*. Yale University Press.

[42] A. Oulasvirta, X. Bi and A. Howes. 2018. *Computational Interaction*. Oxford University Press.

[43] L. Padilla, M. Kay, and J. Hullman. 2020. *Uncertainty Visualization*. https://psyarxiv.com/ebd6r

[44] C. Phelan, J. Hullman, M. Kay and P. Resnick. 2019. Some prior(s) experience necessary: templates for getting started with Bayesian analysis. Pages 1–12 of: *Proceedings of the 2019 CHI Conference on Human Factors in Computing Systems*. Association for Computing Machinery.

[45] R. P. N. Rao and D. H. Ballard. 1997. Dynamic model of visual recognition predicts neural response properties in the visual cortex. *Neural Computation*, **9**(4), 721–763.

[46] C. E. Rasmussen. 2003. Gaussian processes in machine learning. Pages 63–71 of: O. Bousquet, U. von Luxberg and G. Rätsch, eds., *Advanced Lectures on Machine Learning*. Springer.

[47] S. Rogers, J. Williamson, C. Stewart and R. Murray-Smith. 2011. AnglePose: robust, precise capacitive touch tracking via 3D orientation estimation. Page 2575 of: *Proceedings of the 2011 Annual Conference on Human Factors in Computing Systems – CHI '11*. ACM Press.

[48] J. Salvatier, T. V. Wiecki and C. Fonnesbeck. 2016. Probabilistic programming in Python using PyMC3. *PeerJ Computer Science*, **2**(Apr.), e55.

[49] D. J. Schad, M. Betancourt and S. Vasishth. 2020. Toward a principled Bayesian workflow in cognitive science. *Psychological Methods*, **26**(1), 103–126.

[50] J. Schwarz, S. Hudson, J. Mankoff and A. D. Wilson. 2010. A framework for robust and flexible handling of inputs with uncertainty. Pages 47–56 of: *Proceedings of the 23nd Annual ACM Symposium on User Interface Software and Technology*. Association for Computing Machinery.

[51] J. Schwarz, J. Mankoff and S. Hudson. 2011. Monte Carlo methods for managing interactive state, action and feedback under uncertainty. Pages 235–244 of: *Proceedings of the 24th Annual ACM Symposium on User Interface Software and Technology*. Association for Computing Machinery.

[52] C. E. Shannon. 1948. A Mathematical Theory of Communication. *The Bell System Technical Journal*, **27**(3), 379–423.

[53] E. Taka, S. Stein and J. H. Williamson. 2020. Increasing interpretability of Bayesian probabilistic programming models through interactive visualizations. *Frontiers in Computer Science*, **2**. https://doi.org/10.3389/fcomp.2020.567344.

[54] E. Velloso and C. H. Morimoto. 2021. A probabilistic interpretation of motion correlation selection techniques. Pages 1–13 of: *Proceedings of the 2021 CHI Conference on Human Factors in Computing Systems*. Association for Computing Machinery.

[55] E. A. Wan and R. Van Der Merwe. 2000. The unscented Kalman filter for nonlinear estimation. Pages 153–158 of: *Proceedings of the IEEE 2000 Adaptive Systems for Signal Processing, Communications, and Control Symposium (Cat. No. 00EX373)*. IEEE.

[56] D. J. Ward, A. F. Blackwell and D. J. C. MacKay. 2000. Dasher—a data entry interface using continuous gestures and language models. Pages 129–137 of: *Proceedings of the 13th Annual ACM Symposium on User Interface Software and Technology*. Association for Computing Machinery.

[57] J. Weisberg. 2011. Varieties of Bayesianism. *Inductive Logic*, **10**, 477–551.

[58] J. H. Williamson, M. Quek, I. Popescu, A. Ramsay and R. Murray-Smith. 2020. Efficient human-machine control with asymmetric marginal reliability input devices. *PLOS One*, **15**(6), e0233603.

[59] W. Wu, L. Xu, R. Chang and E. Wu. 2017. Towards a Bayesian model of data visualization cognition. In: *IEEE Visualization Workshop on Dealing with Cognitive Biases in Visualisations (DECISIVe)*. IEEE.

[60] E. Zio and N. Pedroni. 2013. Literature review of methods for representing uncertainty. *FonCSI*, **2013-03**(ISSN 2100-3874).

2

Bayesian Statistics

Alan Dix

Abstract

Bayesian statistics is not just the application of Bayes' theorem within statistics, which is ubiquitous anyway. Rather, it is a whole style of thinking that leads to different forms of statistical testing and estimation. This chapter examines the 'job of statistics': obtaining uncertain understanding of the unknown world through probabilistic measurements. We see how traditional statistics and Bayesian statistics address this fundamental uncertainty in different ways; in particular, Bayesian statistics fundamentally reasons about our beliefs encoded as if they were probabilities. This can be incredibly powerful, but, like driving a Porsche, also potentially dangerous. The chapter introduces you to some of the techniques of Bayesian statistics for testing hypotheses, estimating values, and creating credible intervals as ways of expressing range of uncertainty. It also aims to help you dispel some of the hype, avoid some of the pitfalls, and learn when it is the right tool for the job.

2.1 What Is Bayesian Statistics?

Bayes' theorem is used extensively in both probability theory and practical statistics. *Bayesian statistics* is not just the application of Bayes' theorem within statistics, that is ubiquitous anyway. Rather, it is a whole style of thinking that leads to different forms of statistical testing and estimation. We'll see in this chapter how this different approach can be applied to offer alternative ways to address common statistical questions: comparing alternative hypotheses, estimating values, and creating intervals to express the uncertainty of knowledge.

Whereas traditional statistics takes a 'know nothing' approach and tries to obtain worst-case solutions, Bayesian methods try to take on board your existing knowledge and build these into calculations as a prior 'probability'. This approach has both strengths and risks, and understanding these can help to ensure that you can make appropriate choices as to when to use Bayesian statistics, and that you can avoid the pitfalls when you do.

As an example, consider an experiment where you are worried that a coin is biased towards heads. You toss it five times and it comes up heads every time. The (one-tail) probability of this given the coin is unbiased is 1/32 ($\sim$0.031). With traditional statistics this passes the (albeit low) 5% band for statistical significance, so you might conclude that the coin is biased.

In Bayesian statistics one would need to know a little more about the alternative, not simply 'biased towards heads'. Let's say we'll compare with the possibility that the biased coin has exactly a 0.9 probability of landing heads. Given this alternative theory, the probability of 5 heads is 0.95 ($\sim$0.59). This is then compared to the probability of the observation given the unbiased coin, giving an *odds ratio* of 0.59:0.031. That is, the observation is nearly 20 times more likely given the biased coin than it is if the coin is biased. This is quite strong evidence towards bias.

This evidence is then combined with one's initial beliefs about the relative likelihood of the biased vs unbiased coin. If the coin has just come from the Royal Mint, this might be different from the coin used by a stage magician. If we assume that the probability of the coin being biased (prior) is 1 in 1,000, then the evidence means we might now revise that to about 1 in 50, which is still unlikely, but more likely than before seeing the evidence. However, if (say with the stage magician) we think the odds before are 50–50 of the coin being biased, then afterwards this will be about 20 to 1.

Notice here the *power* of Bayesian statistics to include one's knowledge of the world (Royal Mint vs stage magician), but also the potential for *confirmation bias* in assessing the probabilities to attach to prior beliefs – is one in a thousand a good estimate of bias in freshly minted coins?

2.2 Cinderella of Statistics

The use of Bayesian statistics has become more common in recent years, not least because of a growing unease about traditional statistics and in particular *NHST* (null hypothesis significance testing), sometimes termed the *statistical crisis* [1, 3]. Indeed, if you kept abreast of some of the epidemiological modelling and medical literature during the Covid crisis, you may have seen quite frequent references to *credible intervals*, the Bayesian version of confidence intervals.

Bayesian statistical methods date back more than 80 years and have been applied widely in specific areas, in particular decision theory. However, the more general use of Bayesian statistics has been largely eschewed amongst professional statisticians with a small number of fervent followers, viewed almost like cultists! Although now given higher prominence, as recently as 2010, the Royal Statistical Society's mini-guide for non-statisticians, *Making Sense of Statistics*, did not mention Bayesian statistics at all [14].

There have been two reasons for this reticence to adopt Bayesian statistics:

- **Practical and computational:** While traditional statistical tests can often be calculated with paper and pencil (with the aid of pre-computed tables), many calculations in Bayesian statistics require extensive computations including numerical integration.
- **Methodological and epistemological:** These are fundamental issues about the assumptions made in Bayesian methods and the way these are interpreted.

To see why the first is a problem, think back to the initial example. In reality we won't be comparing with a specific probability for a biased coin, but instead it may be any biased value. To use Bayesian statistics, we need to have some sort of assumed distribution over potential bias, say a uniform distribution. To calculate the odds ratio, one has to integrate over these values.

While the calculations are still necessary, increasing computational power has effectively eradicated this as a barrier. This, together with the problems noted in traditional statistics, has led to the rapid recent growth in Bayeisan methods.

Bayesian statistics has a conceptual simplicity and apparent mathematical purity that can make it beguiling. However, while it is a powerful technique, it also has potential pitfalls.

Crucially, it is not a magic bullet to solve the problems identified in the statistical crisis. Many of the same problems arise with both traditional and Bayesian techniques including *reporting bias* (only taking notice of the results that you agree with), *cherry-picking* (choosing the few impressive results out of many that show nothing), and the *file drawer effect* (only publishing positive effects, leaving the unsuccessful experiments 'in the filing cabinet'). There are ways to deal with the systemic misapplication of statistics, for example pre-registration of studies [3], and better statistical education [2, 6, 13]. However, these need to be applied equally, whatever kind of statistics you choose to apply.

To understand these issues, and hence to understand how to use or interpret Bayesian appropriately, it is helpful to consider different kinds of knowledge in the role of statistics.

2.3 The Job of Statistics

In a book about the use of Bayesian methods more generally, the reader will undoubtedly have a good understanding already of the use of probability theory. However, whilst statistics uses probability theory, it has somewhat different aims.

Statistics covers a wide range of techniques, but most of these are about attempting to reason backwards (inductively) from observations to understanding about the world. For example, we test two alternatives of a piece of software with 40 users, 20 using variant A, 20 using variant B. Of those using variant A, 10 have problems, whereas only 5 people have problems using software B. These are our observations. What we really want to know is whether this corresponds to software A being generally more usable (if millions of people use it), or whether it is simply a fluke of the 40 people we happened to choose.

2.3.1 Types of Knowing

There are various kinds of knowledge and lack of knowledge at play here:

- **Known:** The things we have a degree of certainty about, for example, the behaviour of the software when particular actions are taken
- **Probabilistic:** The likelihood that if 15 of the people in the study are simply less good at using software that these might end up divided 10:5 between the groups
- **Unknown:** How good the software actually is.

In practice, these are not totally hard categories – for example, if there are obscure intermittent bugs in the software (shifting *known* to *probabilistic* or *unknown*), or if, as with the coins, we have a feeling that one thing is more likely than another, but we cannot put a figure on it.

In most statistical techniques we require some probabilistic knowledge. This is usually a *conditional probability*, which tells us the probability of an outcome *given* the (potentially unknown) state of the world. For example, if the coin is unbiased, then the probability of getting five heads out of five tosses is 1/32.

2.3.2 Reasoning with Probability

Sometimes the state of the world can be seen as a probabilistic phenomenon, for example, if we've not opened the curtains yet, one might make a probabilistic assessment of the weather based on the time of year and recent weather.

In such cases one can operate entirely within probability theory; in particular, if one has additional observations, such as a puddle seeping under the back door, Bayes' theorem can be used to produce a posterior probability for the weather (see Box 2.1)

Box 2.1 Applying Bayes' Theorem When All Probabilities Are Known

Prior probability (given time of year, etc.):
heavy rain $P_{\mathrm{pr}}(HR) = 0.3$,
little or no rain $P_{\mathrm{pr}}(LR) = 0.7$.
Conditional probability of puddle under door:
given heavy rain (door not closed securely)
$P(P|HR) = 0.6$,
given little or no rain (local dog peeing on door)
$P(P|LR) = 0.1$.
Apply Bayes' theorem:
probability heavy rain given puddle

$$P(HR|P) = \frac{P(P|HR)P_{\mathrm{pr}}(HR)}{(P(P|HR)P_{\mathrm{pr}}(HR)+P(P|LR)P_{\mathrm{pr}}(LR))}$$
$$= \frac{0.6\times0.3}{(0.6\times0.3+0.1\times0.7)}$$
$$= 0.18/0.25$$
$$= 0.72,$$

probability little or no rain given puddle

$$P(LR|P) = \frac{P(P|LR)P_{\mathrm{pr}}(LR)}{(P(P|HR)P_{\mathrm{pr}}(HR)+P(P|LR)P_{\mathrm{pr}}(LR))}$$
$$= \frac{0.1\times0.7}{(0.6\times0.3+0.1\times0.7)}$$
$$= 0.07/0.25$$
$$= 0.28$$
$$= 1 - P(HR|P).$$

Often however, the state of the world is unknown – for example, whether neutrinos can travel faster than light, whether a vaccine is effective or whether a radical new interface concept makes things easier or more difficult for a user.

This is the key place where traditional forms of statistical inference are used. In various ways they use *counter-factual reasoning* (Figure 2.1). We have probabilistic knowledge of the outcomes *given* the state of the world. This is then used, topsy-turvy, to obtain some form of estimate or to make decisions about the *unknown* state of the world given the actual observations. Of course, all such methods are, by necessity, uncertain.

A. Dix

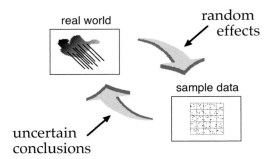

Figure 2.1 The job of statistics: counter-factual reasoning from observations to uncertain conclusions about the world.

2.3.3 Dealing with Uncertainty

Many of the traditional statistical methods, notably hypothesis testing and confidence intervals, take the conditional probability of the observed outcome as a metric over the possible states of the world, called a *likelihood function*. For example, suppose we were interested in comparing two pieces of software, A and B. We would like to test the (null) hypothesis that there is no difference. Suppose 9 out of 10 users say they prefer software A. We calculate the probability of this (or more extreme), given a null hypothesis of no difference ($\sim$1% one-tailed; $\sim$2% two-tailed). If this is less than 0.05 ($p < 0.05$), we reject the null hypothesis at the 5% significance level and therefore assume there is a real difference.

Note that this treats the actual state of the world (which software is better) as *entirely unknown*. In practice, one demands higher levels of evidence in terms of the 'p value' if the alternatives seem highly unusual (e.g. faster than light neutrino), or the results are very critical (e.g. medical use), but the methods themselves make no such judgement.

In practice, one often does have some belief that one option is more likely to be true. *Bayesian statistics* asks us to make an assessment of our level of belief in the alternatives and then treat this as if it were 'prior probability'. Perhaps we think our new software will be better, so we code that as:

    prior(software B better)   = 0.7,
    prior(software A the same or better) = 0.3.

Once *your beliefs* have been expressed as if they were probabilities, one can apply the mechanics of Bayes' theorem, just as we did in Box 2.1 when the state of the world was truly probabilistic.

2.3.4 Ontological Understandings of Probability

Sometimes when comparing traditional statistics with Bayesian statistics, you'll hear the term *frequentist* applied to the former. This is a bit of a misnomer, as one can have frequentist understanding of Bayesian techniques. In reality, it is more about the way one understands what probability means. For example, when one says the probability that a coin comes up heads is 0.5, do you mean:

- **Frequentist:** If you toss the coin lots and lots of times, eventually on average one-half will be heads.
- **Formalist:** 'Do you mean' is a meaningless question. We'll write p(H) = 0.5, and so long as we use the axioms of probability, we will be fine.
- **Platonist:** There is a deep but quantifiable uncertainty to tossing the coin that is 50:50, and the actual frequency and probability rules are consequences of this.

Most (mathematical) statisticians are probably Platonists at heart, who use formalism to do proofs and calculations and use frequentist language for explanations! Crucially, one can use frequentist analysis of Bayes' theorem and Bayesian statistics, and one can use formalism to reason about traditional statistics.

In practice, this rather abstract ontological distinction is compounded by epistemological concerns – what do you actually know? For example, one might believe that a coin has a well-defined probabilistic behaviour, but be uncertain about its bias.

2.4 Comparing Alternatives

One of the standard uses of statistics is to help us decide between alternatives: Is software A better than B? Is the coin biased? This is where significance testing is used in traditional statistics. Bayesian statistics instead uses the *Bayes Factor*, which is the ratio of the posterior probabilities of competing theories given the observations.

Bayes Factor $= Prob(\text{ theory } 1 \,|\, \text{evidence}) \,/\, Prob(\text{ theory } 2 \,|\, \text{evidence})$.

Crucially, because this is based on the posterior, the prior probabilities (or levels of belief) feed into this calculation.

Just as various levels of significance (5%, 1%, 0.1%) are used to help assess broad bands of strength of evidence in traditional statistics, there are broad bands of Bayes factors that are often used to give descriptors (see Table 2.1). There are good reasons to avoid any such labelling and instead simply quote

Table 2.1 Bayes Factor as strength of evidence.

Factor	Descriptor
3–10	substantial
10–100	strong
>100	decisive

Source: Kass and Raftery [9], based on Jeffreys [8].

the measure of evidence, whether in terms of a p value or Bayes Factor [16]. However, these are widely used, so you will almost certainly end up seeing them and needing to interpret them. Certainly, in your own work, if your statistical software has given you an exact value, do report this as well as any descriptor.

We'll work through some examples by hand, but don't worry if you get lost. In practice, the software package you are using will do all the heavy work if you are doing a standard comparison,

2.4.1 Simple Comparisons

We have already seen an example of Bayesian statistics at the beginning of this chapter. Let's look at it again in a little more detail.

We were comparing two competing theories:

Theory 1: biased towards heads with prob 0.9 of being a head
Theory 2: coin is unbiased

We assumed we had performed an experiment and all five coin tosses were heads and calculated the probability of the observation given the alternatives (the likelihood):

$P(5 \text{ heads}|\text{biased}) = 0.59,$
$P(5 \text{ heads}|\text{unbiased}) = 0.031.$

This gave a raw odds ratio of 0.58:0.031, which is a measure of strength of the evidence towards the biased alternative (about 20:1). However, we then weighted this by our beliefs of the prior probability of the two alternatives.

Box 2.2 Coins from the Royal Mint

Prior

$P_{\mathrm{pr}}(\text{biased}) \quad = 0.001,$

$P_{\mathrm{pr}}(\text{unbiased}) = 0.999.$

Posterior

$P(\text{biased} \mid 5 \text{ heads})$

$= 0.001 \times 0.59/(0.001 \times 0.59 + 0.999 \times 0.031)$

$\sim 0.02,$

$P(\text{unbiased} \mid 5 \text{ heads})$

$= 0.999 \times 0.031/(0.001 \times 0.59 + 0.999 \times 0.031)$

$\sim 0.98.$

Box 2.2 shows the calculations assuming the coin was from the Royal Mint with a prior probability of it being biased on one in a thousand. After taking into account the evidence from the five coin tosses, the posterior probability that the coin is biased is 0.02, and the Bayes Factor, the ratio of probability of biased to unbiased is about 1:50. For this, we would conclude it is unlikely to be a biased coin, but our beliefs are certainly shifted by this evidence. This accords with our intuitions and, we need a lot of evidence before we accept that an officially minted coin is substantially biased.

Note that the denominator in the calculations of the Bayes Factor is the same for both terms, so, if one were doing this by hand, one would typically not bother and simply calculate the ratio:

$$(0.001 \times 0.59) : (0.999 \times 0.031) = 0.00059{:}0.031.$$

This is not simply a fluke of the numbers, but always true.

Given two alternatives A and B and evidence E, the posterior probabilities are given by:

$P(A|E) = P(A \text{ and } E)/P(E) = P(E|A)P_{\mathrm{pr}}(A)/P(E),$

$P(B|E) = P(B \text{ and } E)/P(E) = P(E|B)P_{\mathrm{pr}}(B)/P(E).$

In each case the denominator is the same:

$P(E) = P(A \text{ and } E) + P(B \text{ and } E)$

$\quad = (P(E|A)P_{\mathrm{pr}}(A) + P(E|B)P_{\mathrm{pr}}(B))$

and the Bayes Factor is:

$$P(A|E){:}P(B|E) = P(E|A)P_{\mathrm{pr}}(A){:}P(E|B)P_{\mathrm{pr}}(B).$$

The two values $P(E|A)P(A)$ and $P(E|B)P(B)$ are the relative values of the posterior probability, and we can use this to simplify the calculations for the stage magician in Box 2.3. We could convert the relative probabilities into a precise posterior by dividing by their sum (0.315), but they are sufficient to work out the Bayes Factor of 0.3:0.015 or 20:1. This would class as *strong evidence* based on Table 2.1; hence, one might conclude that the coin is indeed biased.

Box 2.3 Coins from the Stage Magician

Prior
$$P_{\mathrm{pr}}(biased) \quad = 0.5,$$
$$P_{\mathrm{pr}}(unbiased) = 0.5.$$
Posterior (*relative*)
$$P_{\mathrm{rel}}(\text{ biased} \mid 5 \text{ heads }) \quad = 0.5 \times 0.59$$
$$\sim 0.3,$$
$$P_{\mathrm{rel}}(\text{ unbiased} \mid 5 \text{ heads }) = 0.5 \times 0.031$$
$$\sim 0.015.$$

2.4.2 Multiple Alternatives and Continuous Distributions

Often alternatives are not simply one exact value versus another.

It is easy to extend the Bayes Factor above to multiple alternatives. Say we have three alternatives:

A – coin is unbiased
B – coin is head biased with prob 0.9 of head
C – coin is tail biased with prob 0.1 of head

Given some evidence (coin tossing), we can calculate the posterior probability of each and either compare specific alternatives, say unbiased vs head biased; that is the Bayes Factor for A vs B:

$$= P(A|E){:}P(B|E).$$

Or compare one against the unbiased against both biased alternatives; that is the Bayes Factor for A vs B or C:

$$= P(A|E){:}(P(B|E) + P(B|E)).$$

In general, if there are many alternatives, we can compute the Bayes Factor for A vs everything:

$$= P(A|E){:}(P(B_1|E) + P(B_2|E) + P(B_3|E) + \cdots).$$

However, when we think of a biased coin in general, it might have any level of bias. Similarly, when we considered the experiment comparing software A and B, how much better is B than – it is probably not one fixed alternative amount better.

Let's measure how much better software is by the proportion of people who prefer A to B. It will be a number between 0 and 1, let's call it $pref(A, B)$. When we say 'software B is better', we mean $pref(A, B) < 0.5$; and when we say 'software A is the same or better', we mean $pref(A, B) \geq 0.5$.

Assuming we selected our 10 users at random, the probability that a user will prefer A is $pref(A,B)$, so this is very much like a coin toss. We can therefore work out the likelihood of the outcome (9 out of 10 users prefer software A), for any preference level:

$$P(9 \text{ out of } 10 \text{ prefer A} \mid pref(A, B) = p) = 10 \times p^9 \times (1 - p).$$

In traditional statistical testing, one typically looks at the likelihood that 9 *or more* people asked say they prefer software A. That is, one looks at the exact results or things that are more extreme. For traditional statistics, it is pretty much essential that you do this; for Bayesian statistics, this is more of a choice one can make. In this case it makes very little difference, so we'll stick to the single value.

When we first saw this example, we suggested a prior:

prior(software B better) $= 0.7$ $\quad - pref(A, B) < 0.5$,
prior(software A the same or better) $= 0.3$ $\quad - pref(A, B) \geq 0.5$.

But what does this mean when there are lots of values for the preference metric *pref(A,B)*? As well as making this gross level measure of beliefs in the prior, we also have to look at a finer level and distribute the 0.7 amongst potential *pref(A,B)* values less than 0.5 and distribute the 0.3 over values greater than 0.5.

Let's say, as it is easiest, that it is spread evenly over the values. That is, all values of *pref(A,B)* less than one-half are equally probable and add up to 0.7 and all those greater than one-half are equally probable and add up to 0.3. This is a probability distribution.

Figure 2.2 shows this, where the area under the curve represents the prior probability that *pref(A,B)* is in a particular range. Formally, the distribution is:

priordist ($pref(A, B) = p$) $= 1.4$ $\quad - pref(A, B) < 0.5$,
priordist ($pref(A, B) = p$) $= 0.6$ $\quad - pref(A, B) \geq 0.5$.

Note, we've written this as 'priordist' rather than 'prior' to remind us it is a *probability density distribution*. For example, probability that p is somewhere in the range [0.1, 0.3] is $1.4 \times 0.2 = 0.28$.

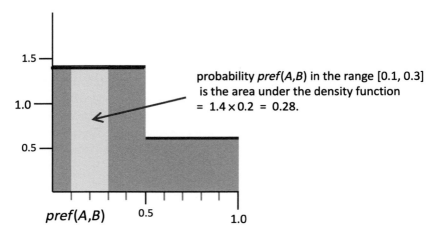

Figure 2.2 Prior as probability density function.

To make the sums easier, let's just imagine a trivial user study with just one user, and that the single user preferred software A. The likelihood is then simple:

$P(\text{single user prefers A} \mid pref(A, B) = p) = p.$

We multiply this by the prior probability to get the relative posterior probability density:

$P_{\text{dist}}(pref(A, B) = p \mid \text{single user prefers A}) = 1.4\,p,$

$P_{\text{dist}}(pref(A, B) = p \mid \text{single user prefers B}) = 0.6\,p.$

We can use this on its own to create Bayes Factors to compare single values, but we really want to compare 'software B is better' vs 'software A is the same or better'. For this we have to integrate the (relative) posterior probability density over the relevant ranges to obtain the (relative) posterior probabilities of the alternatives.

$$
\begin{aligned}
P_{\text{rel}}(\text{B better}|E) &= \int_{p=0}^{0.5} 1.4p \\
&= 1.4[\tfrac{1}{2}p^2]_0^{0.5} \\
&= 1.4 \times (0.125 - 0) = 0.175,
\end{aligned}
$$

$$
\begin{aligned}
P_{\text{rel}}(\text{A better}|E) &= \int_{p=0.5}^{1} 0.6p \\
&= 0.6[\tfrac{1}{2}p^2]_{0.5}^{1} \\
&= 0.6 \times (0.5 - 0.125) = 0.225.
\end{aligned}
$$

Then finally from this, we get the Bayes Factor comparing A being better vs B being better:

Bayes Factor A vs B $= 0.225:0.125 = 1.8:1.$

As a reader of this book you will have encountered similar calculations before, but still it is evident that these rapidly get hard to calculate, even with a spreadsheet. For some cases one can use closed formulae, but often some form of numerical integration is required.

Happily, all of this will be managed by whatever statistical software you use, but it does help explain the difficulty of applying this kind of method until relatively recently.

2.5 Priors, Belief and Uncertainty

As is evident, the choice of priors makes a huge difference to the results. This is part of the strength of Bayesian statistics compared with traditional statistics. The latter treats all situations equally; it is left to the analyst to take into account their subjective understanding of the different situations as they interpret the results (is $p = 0.01$ good enough?). In contrast, Bayesian statistics builds this *subjective understanding* of the situation up front into the prior, which is explicit and can be questioned and discussed. After that, the rest of the process is rigorous and objective.

However, this strength inevitably comes with costs. First, you have to codify your subjective assessment, which may not be easy. (Is the likelihood of a biased Royal Mint coin one in a thousand, or one in a million?) Once codified, the subjectivity of the initial prior can easily be forgotten leading to an unwarranted confidence in the mathematically derived outcomes (*automation bias* [12]). In addition, we have seen that the posterior is sensitive to the choice of prior – indeed, this is often the reason you are using Bayesian statistics in the first place. However, there is a danger that your final results merely reflect your prior assumptions (*confirmation bias*). These are not reasons to avoid Bayesian methods, but they are reasons to do so with as much care as you would if you were using other forms of statistics.

When you have a strong idea of the relative probabilities of different states of the world, the prior is precisely your best estimate of these probabilities. This might be based on past data, such as weather data or the past performance of a designer in creating better software. Sometimes however, you have no real idea. It is precisely the *unknown* situations that traditional statistics is designed to deal with.

One option at this point is to return to using traditional significance testing and leave Bayesian statistics for those cases where there is a well-defined prior. However, Bayesian statistics has some additional tricks up its sleeves to deal with this!

2.5.1 Uniform Priors: Bounded Values

When the prior is unknown, the usual technique in Bayesian statistics is to choose a prior that embodies as few assumptions as possible. In the case of a finite range, this is usually a uniform prior, that is, where the prior probability of every situation is regarded as equal.

$prior(A) = K$ – a constant for all alternatives A.

In the discrete case of a finite set of N alternative theories $A_1 \ldots A_N$, this 1/N:

$prior(A_1) = prior(A_2) = \cdots = prior(A_N) = \frac{1}{N}$.

In the continuous cases where there is an unknown value in a range, this is the density function with height 1/W where W is the width of the range.

Note that we have already partially applied this in the distribution in Figure 2.2. This is not an overall uniform distribution, but as we only had belief about the overall probability of *pref(A,B)* below and above 0.5, we used a uniform probability density above and below this value. If we wanted to express (as well as is possible with this representation) no knowledge at all, we would have a completely flat distribution:

$prior(pref(A, B) = p) = 1 \qquad \forall p \in [0, 1]$.

When we use a uniform prior in Bayes' theorem, we get a relative posterior that exactly mirrors the likelihood function (see also Figure 2.3):

$posterior(A_i) = P(A_i|E) = P(E|A_i) \times prior(A_i) = P(E|A_i) \times K$.

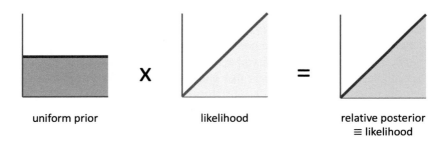

uniform prior   X   likelihood   =   relative posterior ≡ likelihood

Figure 2.3 Uniform prior combined with likelihood.

In many ways this ends up being very similar to traditional statistics, which is often based directly on the likelihood function. However, the use of the likelihood function is subtly different. Traditional statistical methods tend to focus on points of this function, either a particular point of interest (such as $pref(A, B) = 0.5$) or at one extreme of a range of interest (e.g. the values where $pref(A, B) < 0.5$). This is effectively taking 'worst case' over the null hypothesis and seeing how unlikely the observed outcome is. In contrast, Bayesian methods usually integrate under this curve (or sum in the case of a finite set of theories), to obtain an overall probability of the outcomes and compare these (see also Figure 2.4).

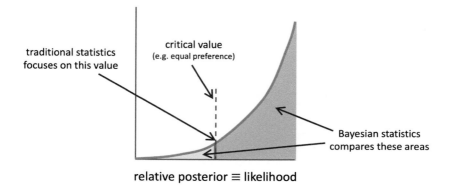

Figure 2.4 Different uses of the likelihood function.

Box 2.4 recalculates the relative posterior and Bayes Factor given a totally uniform prior. The resulting Bayes Factor of 3 is on the lower edge of 'substantial' evidence according to the Kass and Raftery [9] descriptors in Table 2.1. Personally, I would look for far more evidence than observing a single user to regard it as being 'substantial', so I would take these descriptors with a sizeable pinch of salt.

Box 2.4 User Study with Uniform Prior

Recall we imagined a trivial study with just one user who preferred Software A, and in this example we will assume a uniform prior:

$$prior(pref(A, B) = p) = 1$$

and the likelihood function is linear (as Figure 2.3):

$$P(\text{single user prefers A}|pref(A, B) = p) = p.$$

This then leads to a relative posterior that is also linear:

$P(pref(A, B) = p \,|\, \text{single user prefers A})$
$= P(\text{single user prefers A} \,|\, pref(A, B) = p) \times prior(pref(A, B) = p)$
$= p.$

We can then then work out the probability of the two alternatives we'd like to compare

$$P_{\text{rel}}(B \text{ better} \,|\, E) = \int_{p=0}^{0.5} p$$
$$= [\tfrac{1}{2}p^2]_0^{0.5}$$
$$= (0.125 - 0) = 0.125,$$

$$P_{\text{rel}}(A \text{ better} \,|\, E) = \int_{p=0.5}^{1} p$$
$$= [\tfrac{1}{2}p^2]_{0.5}^{1}$$
$$= (0.5 - 0.125) = 0.375.$$

This then gives a Bayes Factor comparing A being better vs B being better:

$$= 0.375{:}0.125 = 3{:}1.$$

This would be on the edge of 'substantial' evidence given the descriptors in Table 2.1.

2.5.2 Don't Cherry-Pick!

In this case the traditional statistics are far more conservative than the Bayesian statistics. However, there are examples where the opposite is true. For example, Wetzels et al. [17] examined a large number of cases and found that there was, by and large, agreement between the two, but that within the examples they studied, the Bayesian tests they used were slightly more conservative.

Beware, it can be tempting to 'shop around' different statistical techniques until one 'works', indeed, there have even been articles that suggest using Bayesian statistics if traditional statistics doesn't yield significant results [5]. I recall reading one paper, where all of the analysis was done using traditional hypothesis testing, and then one central experiment was analysed using a Bayesian method. Both were reasonable to do, but there was no explanation for the swap between techniques; I strongly suspect it was because the traditional test had failed to find a significant result, so the researchers tried a Bayesian test and it 'worked'. The same could equally well happen the other way round.

It is hard to overstate how dangerous this malpractice can be; it is a form of cherry-picking, looking at many things and choosing the 'good ones'. At best this weakens the results, as you should devalue the metrics (significance by Bonferroni correction, Bayes Factor by similar technique) by the number of tests – not just those you tried, but also those you *might have considered trying* until you got the 'right' result. Of course, few researchers do this calculation. Hence, there is a real danger: first, that the results themselves are misleading or completely wrong; and, more important still, if the practice is common, that the whole scientific discipline is undermined.

2.5.3 Dealing with Unbounded Values

The uniform prior works only if the range of values is bounded, but this is not always the case. For example, if we are considering the difference between task completion times for two systems, there is no particular limit positive or negative on how big the difference can be. We could choose some 'sufficiently big' value – say, eight hours – but this effectively spreads probability so thin that it may not be possible to obtain meaningful results.

In such circumstances the Cauchy distribution is a frequent choice, which is essentially a form of $\frac{1}{1+x^2}$ positioned and scaled in different ways. Figure 2.5 shows various examples with different centre points (x_0) and spread parameters (γ). Note that the upper and lower quartiles are at $x_0 \pm \gamma$; the spread parameter has a very easy interpretation.

At first this looks rather like the bell curve of the Normal distribution; however, the Cauchy distribution has 'fatter' tails – that is, it has more of its probability in values further from its centre point. This is one of the reasons it is chosen as it is closer to being uniformly spread, albeit, by necessity, clumped somewhere.

As the Cauchy has a spread and central parameter, you need to choose these.

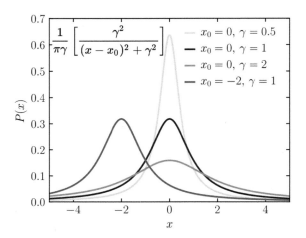

Figure 2.5 Cauchy distribution with different centre and spread parameters. (Skbkekas, CC BY 3.0 via Wikimedia Commons https://commons.wikimedia.org/wiki/File:Cauchy_pdf.svg).

The central parameter is often (but not always) obvious, as there may be a clear 'all things are equal' point. For example, in the case of a difference of task completion times between two systems, zero is the obvious centre point, neither being more or less likely to be faster to use than the other.

The spread is more problematic, and for this one has to rely on experience of similar situations, standard values used in the literature for the measure, or informed guesswork. For example, for task completion times I might choose γ at about 10–20% of my estimated task completion time, as a gain of this order would seem a good, but not amazingly large, improvement for an interface change.

In the case where the values are unbounded in one direction only, for example a response time itself, which cannot be negative, a split Cauchy is often used; that is, a Cauchy simply chopped off at the lower bound and then re-scaled accordingly. However, there are many distributions that can be used in specialised situations depending on what is known, or not known, about the phenomenon.

2.5.4 Natural Scales?

Another choice that is critical when choosing uniform or uniform-like distributions is the natural scale of the measure. For example, when dealing with sound in an interface, do you measure it using a decibel scale or in terms of Watts of output? The decibel scale is a logarithmic scale, so a uniform scale over a range will have a different shape depending on whether you take this over the decibel or Watt scales. Similarly, if you are looking at the colour in an interface you can use wavelength, frequency or location on the colour wheel – each will give a different 'uniform' distribution.

Sometimes there will be a 'right' answer, although it is not always obvious at first (see Box 2.5). For example, time is typically measured in seconds, minutes or hours – all are linearly related to one another, so they give the same uniform distribution; this seems straightforward. However, rather like decibels for sound, a logarithmic transform of times often works better with statistical analysis. This is because variations often scale. If a task takes twice as long to complete, then variability tends to be proportionate; people tend to be 20% faster or slower, not a particular number of seconds or minutes. Note that even when I suggested an appropriate spread parameter (γ) for task completion times, I suggested about 10–20% of estimated task completion time – that is a proportionate amount.

Box 2.5 The Newcomb–Benford Law

A fun example of an unexpected natural scale is the Newcomb–Benford law. If you look at physical constants, share prices on the stock exchange, or the first number mentioned on a newspaper page, the leading digit is more likely to be 1 than 2, more likely to be 2 than 3, etc. If you think of ranges of numbers [1,10), [10,100), [100,1000) and randomly choose a number over a uniform distribution, then the first digits will all come out equally likely. However, if you look at numbers using a logarithmic scale, you end up with precisely the observed frequencies. One explanation for this is that the absolute scale used is often arbitrary (e.g. centigrade vs Fahrenheit for temperature) and a logarithmic scale is *invariant* under transformations of scale.

2.5.5 More Choices, More Opportunities to Cherry Pick!

As is evident, there are various choices you make even when attempting to have a 'least knowledge' solution: which distribution of prior to use, central and spread parameters for the Cauchy, natural scale for the measurements. Sometimes these will be obvious, sometimes given by past data or disciplinary norms. However, often you need to make the choices yourself, and the choices you make affect the outcomes leading to two dangers:

1. First, this can add further to the potential of *confirmation bias*. If you opt for a uniform-like distribution, this is less obvious than when you fully encode your beliefs in a custom prior; however, your personal bias can influence parameter choice, so it is important to be explicit to yourself about the reasons for your choices.
2. Second, this offers yet more opportunities for *cherry-picking* if, say, you experiment with several alternatives for the parameters of a Cauchy distribution until you find ones that 'work'.

When you report results, make sure you fully list all of the priors used, the parameters used in them and the *reason for the choices*. There may be differences in opinion on this, but by being open with what you have chosen, you make it easier for others to replicate, re-interpret or critique your work and also make it easier for subsequent meta-analysis [15].

2.6 Combining Evidence

In the last section we imagined a trivial experiment with just one user. We could repeat the same analysis for the original case of an experiment with 10 users, 9 of whom preferred software A. We would end up integrating p^{10}, and then do some arithmetic on $1/11\ p^{11}$. It isn't quite as scary as it sounds, as the computer would do all the work. However, with Bayes' theorem, it is possible to treat each user as separate evidence. One simply takes the posterior from the first user and treats this as the prior for the next.

Assuming the evidence is independent, it doesn't matter if one takes all the evidence together and applies Bayes with it all, or if one takes each piece of evidence individually and applies Bayes sequentially in order. Furthermore, the order in which the evidence is supplied doesn't matter (see Box 2.6 for informal proof).

Box 2.6 (Informal) Proof that Independent Evidence Can Be Applied Sequentially

To verify this, it is easiest just to think about relative probabilities again, that is, it is sufficient to think 3:1 and not convert this into 0.75:0.25.

Imagine we have two alternative theories A and B, and have two pieces of evidence E_1 and E_2, and a (possibly relative) prior: $P_{\text{pr}}(A), P_{\text{pr}}(B)$. The (relative) posteriors taking both evidence into account is:

$$P_{\text{rel}}(A|E_1 \text{ and } E_2) = P(E_1 \text{ and } E_2|A)P_{\text{pr}}(A),$$
$$P_{\text{rel}}(B|E_1 \text{ and } E_2) = P(E_1 \text{ and } E_2|B)P_{\text{pr}}(B).$$

If the items of evidence are independent, the conditional probability of E_1 and E_2 is simply the product of the individual conditional probabilities:

$$P(E_1 \text{ and } E_2 \mid A) = P(E_1|A)P(E_2|A).$$

So these formulae both become simple products:

$$P_{\text{rel}}(A|E_1 \text{ and } E_2) = P(E_1|A)P(E_2|A)P_{\text{pr}}(A),$$
$$P_{\text{rel}}(B|E_1 \text{ and } E_2) = P(E_1|B)P(E_2|B)P_{\text{pr}}(B).$$

Now imagine we first apply evidence E_1. The relative posterior after considering E_1 is:

$$P_{\text{rel}}(A|E_1) = P(E_1|A)P_{\text{pr}}(A),$$
$$P_{\text{rel}}(B|E_1) = P(E_1|B)P_{\text{pr}}(B).$$

Take this as the prior and apply evidence E_2. The relative posterior after considering E_2 is:

$$\begin{aligned} P_{\text{rel}}(A|E_2|E_1) &= P(E_2|A)P_{\text{rel}}(A|E_1) \\ &= P(E_2|A)P(E_1|A)P_{\text{pr}}(A), \end{aligned}$$

$$\begin{aligned} P_{\text{rel}}(B|E_2|E_1) &= P(E_2|B)P_{\text{rel}}(B|E_1) \\ &= P(E_2|B)P(E_1|B)P_{\text{pr}}(B). \end{aligned}$$

It is evident both that the order doesn't matter and that this is precisely the same as applying both pieces of evidence simultaneously.

However, this only holds if the items of evidence are *independent*.

This is particularly powerful when performing meta-analysis, building on the results of several, possibly individually inconclusive, experiments to provide a more definitive overall result. It is possible to combine p values from traditional statistical tests, but the methods are complex and p values are not fundamentally designed to facilitate this. In contrast Bayes' theorem is all about combining new evidence with old.

It is also possible to apply a sort of dynamic meta-analysis when multiple experiments use posterior probabilities from earlier experiments as their priors. Indeed, Kay et al. [10] suggest that this is a good reason why Bayesian statistics would be preferable in the HCI domain. For example, suppose an experiment studied whether iris colour affected reading and found a final Bayes Factor of 1.8 in favour. This would in itself be inconclusive. Then imagine someone else then does an experiment, that, perhaps as part of studying other things, also includes aspects of this. The value of 1.8 could be fed into the formulation of the prior, and then the paper could publish its own update on the Bayes Factor in favour of the notion.

However, while this sounds appealing, it can be potentally dangerous advice, as it all comes with that caveat *'assuming the evidence is independent'*.

In some ways this is a standard issue in all kinds of statistics. For example, imagine you have collected users' completion times for a task comparing systems A and B. You might apply a T-test to compare the average completion time of systems A and B. However, this is only valid if each time measurement is independent. This is not always the case: Perhaps there was noisy building work happening throughout one set of runs that may have affected them all, or perhaps the tasks were carried out sequentially by the same person and hence the possibility of a practice effect, so that completing one task successfully made the next more likely to be successful too. In these cases, applying the T-test without some sort of correction would lead to misleading results.

In some ways the problems for Bayesian statistics are similar, and if you are aware of non-independent evidence, it is possible to account for it in Bayesian analysis. However, extra care has to be taken when applying Bayesian methods sequentially or performing meta-analysis, as it is easy to lose track of common evidence, particularly shared priors.

Imagine there is a foundational paper in an area that creates results R1. Imagine now two research groups independently build on this and produce results R2 and R3 about the same phenomena, maybe additional information on whether iris colour impacts readability of screens. Note this may be direct, with both explicitly using R1 as a prior in their Bayesian analysis, or maybe implicit in that the knowledge of R1 is so pervasive in their discipline it is part of the common knowledge they build into their apparently individual priors. In both cases any attempt to combine R2 and R3 must account for the shared information; otherwise it will 'double count', a bit like accidentally transcribing the data from one run of an experiment twice into a dataset.

It is clear that in Bayesian statistics, as in all of science, it is crucial that you keep track of and document all the sources that lead into the analysis. In the case of simple discrete comparisons, you can ensure you always publish the raw odds ratio before multiplying by the prior as well as the final Bayes Factor. However, this becomes more complicated for continuous distributions as this is not a simple number but a whole function!

In fact, the best way to ensure others can use you work in subsequent meta-analysis is to ensure that your data are openly available and well documented, this will allow reproducibility of your results as well as alternative analyses, including combining it with other's work.

2.7 Estimation

One of the most common things one does with data is to estimate values; for example, simply taking the average height of a sample of people as a way of estimating the overall mean height of a population. This can sometimes be more complicated, for example the $\sqrt{(n-1)}$ that keeps popping up in estimates of the standard deviation.

Happily, this is particularly easy with Bayesian statistics. You simply take the posterior distribution, treat that as a probability distribution, and then work out the expected value of whatever value you are interested in.

In our running example of comparing user preferences for systems A and B, let's take the relative posterior based on the uniform prior in Box 2.4:

$$P_{\text{rel}}(\,pref(A, B) = p\,|\,\text{single user prefers A}\,) = p.$$

To work out an expected value from this, we will need to normalise this to make it a true probability distribution. We do this by dividing by its integral, in this case the integral of p between 0 and 1 is $\frac{1}{2}$, so the proper probability density function is:

$$P_{\text{true}}(\,pref(A, B) = p\,|\,\text{single user prefers A}\,) = 2p.$$

We can then work out expected values of anything we like:

$$
\begin{aligned}
E(p) &= \int p \times 2p \\
&= [\tfrac{2}{3}p^3]_0^1 = 0.67, \\
E(p^2) &= \int p^2 \times 2p \\
&= [\tfrac{2}{4}p^4]_0^1 = 0.5, \\
E(\tfrac{1}{p}) &= \int \tfrac{1}{p} \times 2p \\
&= [2]_0^1 = 2.
\end{aligned}
$$

These are all examples where we can do the integrals using school maths, but in practice, real Bayesian statistics will involve numerical integration. However, the principle is the same no matter how complex the distributions.

2.8 Quantifying Bounds: Credible Intervals

The final common element in traditional statistics is the confidence interval. At least while writing 'common', these are less commonly used than they should be!

There are two uses of confidence intervals:

1. To quantify how similar things are when testing reveals no significant difference.
2. To give bounds on estimates of parameter values (e.g. mean).

The first of these is far less necessary in Bayesian statistics as the Bayes Factor gives evidence for all alternatives anyway.

Say we are comparing systems A and B. With significance testing one really looks only at the null hypothesis, usually the thing you hope isn't true, such as your new system being no better than the old one. If the probability of the results given this is low, one takes that as evidence that it is false and hence that the alternative is true (your new system really *is* better). However, obtaining a non-significant result is interpreted as 'not sufficient evidence', and one cannot conclude that the null is true. The use of confidence intervals here is to give some bounds on how similar they are.

In contrast the posterior distribution gives probabilities for all outcomes. If the probability that software A is 'the same or better' is low and the probability that software B is better is high, then we can conclude that B really is an improvement over A. However, equally if the probability for software A being 'the same or better' is high, we can use this as evidence for it. Only if the probabilities are 'in between' for both do we need to say 'insufficient evidence'. Indeed, this two-way nature of the Bayes Factor is often cited as a key advantage of Bayesian statistics.

The second use of confidence intervals, giving some form of bounds on an estimate, has a Bayesian equivalent called a credible interval. The 95% credible interval is created by finding the range by selecting a range on the posterior that (i) has the points with highest probability and (ii) has a total probability of 0.95 (see Figure 2.6).

In contrast, the confidence interval, used in traditional statistics, is based on individual points and their likelihood, and the 95% interval is the range of

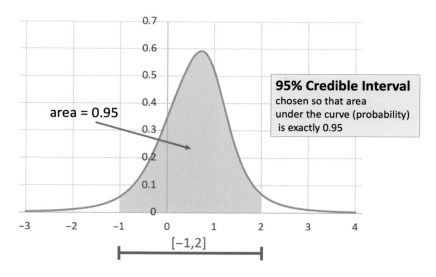

Figure 2.6 Posterior distribution with credible interval calculated from the area under the curve.

values where all the points within have individual likelihood greater than 0.05 (see Figure 2.7).

There is an interesting case when using a uniform prior, as in this case the posterior has exactly the same shape as the likelihood but is scaled to make it a valid probability (area under the curve is one). In this case the function being used is effectively the same, but the scaling and different method of calculation yield different intervals.

Figure 2.8 shows a posterior distribution based on the likelihood in Figure 2.7 and a uniform prior over the range. Note how the different method of calculation yields a 95% credible interval of [−1.4,3.4], whereas the confidence interval is [−2,4]. In this case the traditional statistics are slightly more conservative. This is not surprising; if the prior is accurate, Bayesian statistics 'knows' more about the situation than traditional statistics. However, as with testing between alternatives, this is not always the case.

The different assumptions (or lack of assumptions) between traditional and Bayesian techniques mean that the two kinds of intervals come with different 'guarantees'. For confidence intervals we can be sure that if we calculate 95% confidence intervals, then, in the long run, at least 95% of the time the real value lies within the range, but we cannot say anything about the probability of the particular result we are looking at. For credible intervals, *assuming the*

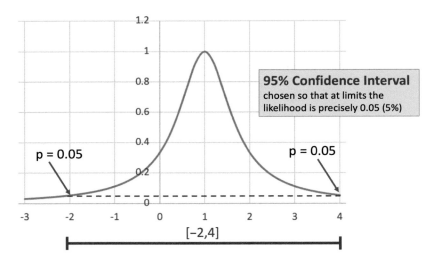

Figure 2.7 Likelihood with confidence interval calculated from the height of
the curve.

prior is accurate, we can say that the probability that the result lies in the range
is 0.95. The difference is subtle, but the confidence interval statement is about
you as a researcher engaging in experiments and studies, whereas the credible
interval speaks to the current study.

Most commonly, the prior is about your belief, not 'true' probability. So it
would be most accurate to say that so long as the prior faithfully captures your
beliefs about the world, then if you follow through your beliefs logically, you
should have 95% belief that the true value lies within the credible interval.

Table 2.2 summarises the similarities and differences between the confidence
interval and credible interval.

2.9 Final Discussion

We have seen that Bayesian statistics comes with a range of techniques that
sometimes act as like-for-like alternatives to traditional statistics. There are
some extra complications with using Bayesian statistics, not least the choice of
prior and the reliance on heavy computation. However, once these have been
overcome, many issues become easier as they are 'just' a normal application of
probability theory.

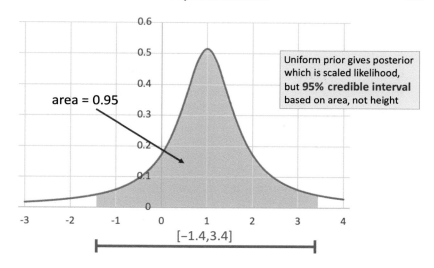

area = 0.95

Uniform prior gives posterior
which is scaled likelihood,
but **95% credible interval**
based on area, not height

[−1.4,3.4]

Figure 2.8 Uniform prior gives posterior with exactly the same shape as the likelihood, but the credible interval is calculated from the area under the curve.

It can be hard to enter into a dispassionate discussion about Bayesian statistics as they often arouse near religious zeal amongst adherents. Indeed, there are few academic topics where a mainstream journal would publish an article entitled 'Bayesian versus Orthodox Statistics: Which Side Are You On?' [4].

Han and Wasserman [11] talk about four kinds of Bayesian statistician:

Subjective Bayesians interpret probability strictly as personal degrees of belief. Objective Bayesians try to find prior distributions that formally express ignorance with the hope that the resulting posterior is, in some sense, objective. Empirical Bayesians estimate the prior distribution from the data. Frequentist Bayesians are those who use Bayesian methods only when the resulting posterior has good frequency behavior. [11, p. 301]

Taking away the personalities, we can think about this as 'ways of using Bayesian statistics', which can be adopted by anyone, not just a card-carrying Bayesian! Largely, the latter two are about situations where we do have some probabilistic knowledge about the world, the former two where we are dealing with the unknown, albeit in the first case with some subjective views about it.

2.9.1 Quantified Belief

For the times when everything has well-defined and known probabilities, Bayesian reasoning yields precise and mathematically valid probabilistic

Table 2.2 Comparing confidence intervals and credible intervals.

	Confidence Interval	Credible Interval
Genre	traditional	Bayesian
Base distribution	on likelihood alone (probability of outcome given parameter values)	posterior (likelihood × prior)
Chosen values	largest in likelihood	largest in posterior
Choice criterion	point value $> 0.05, 0.01$, etc.	overall probability (integral) $= 0.95, 0.99$, etc.
What you can say	in the long run, at least 95% of times you calculate the confidence interval the true result will be in the range	*if your prior is an accurate reflection of probability*, then there is exactly 95% probability that the true result lies within the credible interval
With the caveat	*... but you never know which times it is!—*	*... but if not*, then the results may be valueless or misleading

outcomes. This is the case with many of the application areas in this book. However, as we have discussed, statistics often has to deal with the unknown as well as the probabilistic.

In these cases, Bayesian statistics asks us to encode our beliefs in terms of numeric probabilities. Sometimes this is termed *plausibility* rather than probability to emphasise it is about degrees of belief, but crucially these numbers can be manipulated as if they were probabilities.

There are strengths to this. I often use as an example walking down the street and meeting a person with two large antennae. Approaching this a traditional hypothesis testing, we can formulate this as (i) a null hypothesis (H_0) that the person is a human being and (ii) an alternative hypothesis (H_1) that it is a Martian. We know it is highly unlikely (say less than one in a million) that a human being has antennae, so this would be statistically significant at $p < 0.01\%$, and so we would reject the null hypothesis and call in the Men in Black.

Clearly, something is not right here. Traditional statistics, within its formal calculations, does not take into any account whether the alternative hypothesis is reasonable or utterly absurd, perhaps unbiased and objective to the point of potentially becoming ridiculous. In fact, things are not this bad. As noted previously, in practice, we tend to look for stronger significance figures for unexpected outcomes, but this is part of post hoc interpretation, not part of the formal process.

Happily, Bayesian statistics helps us here; our prior probability of finding a Martian walking down the high street will have a lot of leading zeros after the decimal point! Even multiplying by the unlikelihood of a human with antennae, we would still come to the conclusion that this was human and then look for alternative explanations for the antennae. That is, the formal Bayesian approach accords with intuition.

However, the encoding of belief as probabilities has attendant problems, even if our beliefs are somewhat vague, we are forced to turn them into hard numbers (just how unlikely is that Martian?). Even more difficult are the situations when one has no idea and so has to use the various forms of uniform and uniform-like distributions for the prior.

In principle, one could choose several priors that express one's uncertainty about the 'probabilities' and ensure that the results are robust to these alternatives, just as one might do in other forms of mathematical modelling. In practice, I have not seen this form of sensitivity analysis reported with Bayesian statistics.

The most crucial thing is to ensure that, when the use of Bayesian statistics is based on belief, you do not forget this during the analysis phases. The proper understanding of Bayesian statistics in these cases is conditional:

> If I start with belief encode numerically as the prior,
> then my belief after seeing the evidence should be as encoded in the posterior.

The results in such cases are not probabilities themselves, but statements about *reasonable beliefs given evidence*.

2.9.2 Phenomena and Researchers

Statistics has a habit of turning deep metaphysical issues into practical problems that need to be addressed. One example is the meaning (or meaninglessness) of a prior for natural laws whether physical (can neutrinos travel faster than light?) or psychological (does iris colour affect reading?). On the one hand, these are either true or not, any assignment of probability to them is meaningless. On the other hand, one has some sense of the likelihood (interpreted informally) that they are true.

One way that I have found to help make sense of these paradoxes is based on some of the earliest work on confidence intervals and shifts the focus from the phenomena themselves to the researchers/analysts looking at them.

We have already seen this for confidence intervals:

If you calculate a 95% confidence interval, then (on average) at least 95% of the times you do this (as a researcher/analyst) the true value will lie within the range.

This does not say anything about the probability of the particular phenomenon you are studying this time, but is a strong statement about your research career.

One can make a similar statement about a traditional NHST significance tests:

If you calculate that a result is statistically significant at 5% and treat this as meaning the null hypothesis is false, then (on average) at least 95% of the times you do this (as a researcher/analyst) you will be right.

Again, this is over your career as a researcher (Figure 2.9); there will be the odd Martian that proves you wrong, but on average no more than 1 time in 20!

For Bayesian statistics, we can look at subjective priors in a similar way – and use this to calibrate our subjective assessment. Assume one has two alternatives A and B and gives them prior probabilities of 0.75 and 0.25 respectively before considering further evidence. When eventually you discover definitively which is true (not just based on your Bayesian analysis using the prior!), how often does it happen that the alternative to which you assigned the 0.75 prior is true? If this is $\frac{3}{4}$ of the time, then you have an accurate assessment of your scientific beliefs.

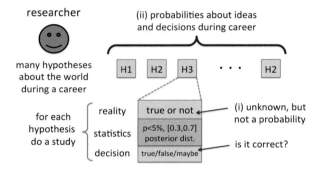

Figure 2.9 Strong probabilities about research career or discipline, uncertain ones about each study.

If your personal judgement is accurate in this sense, then Bayesian statistics can give you even stronger guarantees:

If the prior is an accurate assessment of the researcher's accuracy, then the Bayes Factor gives the exact probability (on average) of the relevant outcomes.

The 'on average' here means that if you do studies where the Bayes Factor is 2:1 and you later find out definitely which of the outcomes in each is right, then two times out of three it will be the alternative that was the 2:1 winner.

Similarly, for the credible interval, we can restate the entry in Table 2.2 with more precision:

> *If your prior is an accurate reflection of probability (as in the probability of the accuracy of your judgement as a researcher)*, then there is exactly 95% probability that the true result lies within the credible interval.

Again, these are all probability statements about your research career or that of your lab, discipline, etc., not about the specific phenomenon.

It is also critical that these are true only if you consider every statistical test formal or informal (no peeking at the figures and then deciding to do formal statistics only on the things that look good!). If you publish only the results that look promising, or if the journals in your discipline do not accept papers about methodologically well-founded studies with negative results, then the published literature has been cherry-picked. Because of this, you will typically see far more positive results, in terms of both highly significant p values and strong-evidence Bayes Factors, than should be the case.

2.9.3 Not a Golden Bullet

As is evident, Bayesian statistics can be a powerful technique, but it is not a magic bullet to solve the statistical problems that have been cited in the literature. Crucially if they are adopted with naive optimism, they can make problems far worse.

In particular, there are several common misconceptions:

- *The statistical crisis (P-hacking, file drawer effect, etc.) is solely a problem for traditional statistics.* This is not the case. you can cherry-pick good results as much with Bayesian techniques, including 'careful' choices of parameters for priors. For both of these are rarely deliberate malpractice, but are inadvertent or well-meaning attempts to present the 'best' results.
- *Corrections for multiple tests (e.g. Bonferroni) are not needed for Bayesian statistics.* They are! As noted, it is as easy to cherry-pick the best Bayes Factor as it is for a p value. There are Bayesian corrections, which are not dissimilar to Bonferroni, effectively dividing 'positive' results by the number of tests [7], albeit a little more complex.
- *It is safe with Bayesian statistics to perform sequential tests and stop when you get a sufficiently high Bayes Factor.* Again, this is not true; you equally need to use special techniques for this using Bayesian techniques when performing sequential tests.

- *Bayesian statistics gives you precise probabilities for phenomena.* Hopefully, by now you can answer this yourself. While this can be true in some cases, more commonly, Bayesian methods gives precise measures of belief relative to, and only as accurate as, the initial belief encoded in the prior.

Note that none of these are fundamental 'problems' with Bayesian statistics, and all but the last are effectively parallels of similar issues with traditional statistics. The problem lies when the use of Bayesian statistics promotes a sense of false security.

2.9.4 When to Use and How to Read Bayesian Statistics

By this stage the answers have become evident. If you have reliable priors, then Bayesian statistics gives you *the* correct answer. If not, then it does become more a matter of taste, Bayesian statistics involves more assumptions and more choices of parameters, but can yield more precise (although not necessarily more accurate) results. Traditional methods are more risk-averse and more nuanced, embracing the unknown. The choice will also be driven in part by different evolving disciplinary cultures.

Currently there is less understanding of Bayesian techniques, and this can lead to misapplication or misinterpretation of results. This has been driven in part by excessive hype. Hopefully this will improve over time.

Crucially, when you publish any statistics, remember to report *all* of the relevant decisions and alternative studies or analysis that were performed, even if they are not being presented in full – this is to avoid the *file drawer effect*. For Bayesian statistics this needs to include all the priors and parameters used, and why they were chosen. In all cases too, where possible given privacy, make all data available so that others can build on your work through re-analysis or meta-analysis.

When reading Bayesian statistics, do not be seduced by the apparent mathematical definitiveness of the results, but examine carefully the assumptions and priors used. Watch especially for accidental combination of non-independent evidence, including shared priors. If you do not agree with the assumptions embodied in priors, you may need to rework the results, perhaps to remove the authors' confirmation bias, and as you do so you will undoubtedly learn lessons on how to report your own results so that others can do the same for your own bias!

Like a Porsche, Bayesian statistics is powerful, but dangerous. Use it well.

References

[1] M. Baker. 2016. Statisticians issue warning over misuse of *P* values. *Nature*, **531**, 151. https://doi.org/10.1038/nature.2016.19503.

[2] P. Cairns. 2019. *Doing Better Statistics in Human-Computer Interaction.* Cambridge University Press. https://doi.org/10.1017/9781108685139.

[3] A. Cockburn, C. Gutwin and A. Dix 2018. HARK no more: on the preregistration of CHI experiments. In *CHI '18: Proceedings of the 2018 CHI Conference on Human Factors in Computing Systems,* Montreal, Canada. CHI Best Paper Award. https://doi.org/10.1145/3173574.3173715

[4] Z. Dienes. 2011. Bayesian versus orthodox statistics: which side are you on? *Perspectives on Psychological Science,* **6**(3), 274290. https://doi.org/10.1177/1745691611406920

[5] Z. Dienes. 2014. Using Bayes to get the most out of non-significant results. *Frontiers in Psychology,* **5**(781). https://doi.org/10.3389/fpsyg.2014.00781

[6] A. Dix. 2020. *Statistics for HCI: Making Sense of Quantitative Data.* Morgan & Claypool, April. https://alandix.com/statistics/book/

[7] M. Guo, and D. F. Heitjan. 2010. Multiplicity-calibrated Bayesian hypothesis tests. *Biostatistics,* **11**(3), 473483. Oxford. https://doi.org/10.1093/biostatistics/kxq012.

[8] H. Jeffreys. 1939. *The Theory of Probability.* Oxford. University Press

[9] R. E. Kass and A. E. Raftery. 1995. Bayes factors. *Journal of the American Statistical Association,* **90**(430), 791. https://doi.org/10.2307/2291091

[10] M. Kay, G. Nelson and E. Hekler. 2016. Researcher-centered design of statistics: why Bayesian statistics better fit the culture and incentives of HCI. Pages 4521–4532 of: *Proceedings of the 2016 CHI Conference on Human Factors in Computing Systems.* CHI '16. Association for Computing Machinery. https://doi.org/10.1145/2858036.2858465

[11] H. Liu and L. Wasserman. 2014. Bayesian inference. Chapter 12 in *Statistical Machine Learning.* www.stat.cmu.edu/ larry/=sml/Bayes.pdf

[12] K. L. Mosier and L. J. Skitka. 1999. Automation use and automation bias. Pages 344–348 of *Proceedings of the Human Factors and Ergonomics Society Annual Meeting,* vol. 43. Sage Publications.

[13] J. Robertson and M. Kaptein, eds. 2016. *Modern Statistical Methods for HCI,* Springer. https://doi.org/10.1007/978-3-319-26633-6.

[14] SaS+RSS 2010. *Making Sense of Statistics.* Sense about Science. In collaboration with the Royal Statistical Society, 29 April. http://senseaboutscience.org/activities/making-sense-of-statistics/

[15] *Transparent Statistics in HumanComputer Interaction* (2020). Accessed 18 December 2020. https://transparentstatistics.org/

[16] R. L. Wasserstein, A. L. Schirm and N. A. Lazar. 2019. Moving to a world beyond "p < 0.05". *The American Statistician,* **73**(sup1), 1–19. https://doi.org/10.1080/00031305.2019.1583913

[17] R. Wetzels, D. Matzke, M. D. Lee, J. N. Rouder, G. J. Iverson and E.-J. Wagenmakers. 2011. Statistical evidence in experimental psychology. *Perspectives on Psychological Science,* **6**, 291. https://doi.org/10.1177/1745691611406923.

Part II

Probabilistic Interfaces and Inference of Intent

3

Bayesian Information Gain to Design Interaction

Wanyu Liu, Olivier Rioul and Michel Beaudouin-Lafon

Abstract

This chapter discusses a perspective on designing interaction by quantifying information that reduces the computer's uncertainty about the user's goal. We begin with how to quantify *uncertainty* and *information* using Shannon's information-theoretic terms and how to optimise decisions under uncertainty using an expected utility function with Bayesian Experimental Design. We then describe the BIG framework – Bayesian Information Gain – where the computer 'runs experiments' on the user by sending feedback that maximises the expected gain of information by the computer, and uses the users' subsequent input to update its knowledge as interaction progresses. We demonstrate a BIG application to multiscale navigation, discuss some limitations of the BIG framework and conclude with future possibilities.

3.1 Introduction

Imagine Alice and Bob are playing the 20 questions game.[1] Alice has a number between 1 and 100 in mind, and Bob can ask up to 20 questions to which Alice can reply only 'yes' or 'no' to guess that number. To maximise his chances of winning, Bob asks questions that give him maximum information at each step. He starts with, 'Is it between 1 and 50'? Alice replies, 'No'. Bob continues with, 'Is it between 51 and 75'? Alice says, 'Yes'. And the game continues until Bob guesses the correct number. Rather than asking less informative questions, such as 'Is it between 1 and 10?', which would leave Bob with a range between 11 and 100, he optimises the questions to reduce his uncertainty about the number in Alice's head.

---

[1] https://en.wikipedia.org/wiki/Twenty_Questions

Twenty questions is a common spoken parlour game, but how is it related to our interaction with computers? We are familiar with the notion that we give inputs (or commands) to the computer which in return executes these commands in a predetermined way. For example, when looking for a particular item on the web, we click on links to navigate the pages, and the computer simply displays the pages. What if it could be more active by asking more informative questions to find out which item we are looking for?

In this chapter, we discuss an information-driven approach to design interaction. Information is defined in terms of the computer's knowledge about what the user wants. At the beginning of the interaction, the user (the role of Alice) has certain goals in mind, e.g. looking for a particular item on a website or typing a particular word on the keyboard. The computer (the role of Bob) has some uncertainty about the user's goal. This uncertainty is represented by the computer's prior knowledge, expressed in a Bayesian probabilistic model. When receiving input from the user, the computer updates its knowledge about what the user is looking for. Therefore, the information carried by the user input is the knowledge gained by the computer to discover the user's goal. We call this framework the Bayesian Information Gain (BIG) framework; it is based on Bayesian Experimental Design [5], using the criterion of information gain, also known as mutual information in information theory [2].

One can simply use BIG to measure the information sent by the user to the computer. However, by manipulating the feedback to maximise or leverage the expected information gain from the user's subsequent input, the computer can increase the information gain from the user, improving interaction efficiency.

3.2 Bayesian Information Gain Framework

The key concepts of the BIG framework are *uncertainty* and *information* on one hand, and *experimental design* on the other. We first go through these two concepts, described in information-theoretic terms (Section 3.2.1) and in Bayesian probability-theoretic terms (Section 3.2.2). This will help clarify the notion of 'making optimal decisions under uncertainty'. Finally, we put it all together in the BIG framework (Section 3.2.3).

3.2.1 Uncertainty and Information

Entropy as a Measure of Uncertainty

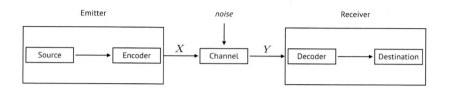

Figure 3.1 Shannon's communication scheme.

Information theory was originally proposed by Claude Shannon [9] using a communication paradigm (Figure 3.1): A *source* produces messages, which are adapted by an *encoder* before being sent over a *channel*, and then decoded by a *decoder* to the final *destination*. The pair of source and encoder is called the *emitter*, and the pair of decoder and destination is the *receiver*.

The emitter inputs X to the channel and the channel outputs Y to the receiver. Since there might be *noise* in the channel, output Y does not always equal input X. The semantic aspect of communication is not relevant to the engineering process of transmitting a source message through a channel [9]. Here the significant aspect of communication is only related to the probability of each possible outcome. Therefore, X and Y refer to random variables[2] with respective probability distributions $p(x)$ and $p(y)$, and the channel is completely described by the probability distribution of Y conditional on X, denoted by $p(y|x)$.

The receiver has a certain uncertainty on the encoded source message X, a random variable that can take several values. This uncertainty is captured by the *entropy* $H(X)$, a function of the distribution $p(x)$ defined as

$$H(X) = -\sum_x p(x) \log_2 p(x). \tag{3.1}$$

Because the logarithm is taken to base 2, the entropy is measured in bits (binary units).

The higher the entropy, the more uncertain the outcome, the harder the prediction. If N denotes the number of possible values of X, the entropy is bounded by $0 \leq H(X) \leq \log_2 N$:

---

[2] To simplify, we consider only discrete random variables taking a finite number of possible values.

- Minimum entropy is zero when X is deterministic:

$$H(X) = 0 \qquad \text{if} \qquad p(x) = 0 \text{ or } 1.$$

- Entropy is maximal when X is uniformly distributed, with N equiprobable values:

$$H(X) = \log_2 N \qquad \text{if} \qquad p(x) = \frac{1}{N}.$$

Taking the Alice and Bob example, if Bob (the receiver) has no idea which number Alice (the emitter) has in mind, he assumes a uniform distribution over the numbers from 1 to 100 and uncertainty is highest: $H(X) = \log_2 100 = 6.6$ bits. On the other extreme, if Bob somehow knows that Alice has the number 56 in mind, uncertainty is 0. All other cases will fall between 0 and 6.6.

Information as a Measure of Uncertainty Reduction

After asking the first question $Y =$ 'Is it between 1 and 50?', Bob reduces his uncertainty by receiving Alice's answer 'No'. Now the answer is reduced to 51 to 100, which is half of the original set. In other words, knowing the specific answer $Y = y$ ('No') has reduced the uncertainty about X: The remaining uncertainty is naturally captured by the entropy of X conditional on Alice's answer $Y = y$:

$$H(X|Y = y) = -\sum_x p(x|y) \log_2 p(x|y). \qquad (3.2)$$

Knowing Alice's answer, the distribution over the remaining numbers is still uniform; the new uncertainty can be calculated as $H(X|Y = y) = \log_2 50 = 5.6$ bits. So in this round, he gained exactly $H(X) - H(X|Y = y) = 6.6 - 5.6 = 1$ bit of information. Had Bob asked the question $Y' =$ 'Is it between 1 and 10?' and had Alice reply 'No', he would have gained only $H(X) - H(X|Y' = y) = 6.6 - \log_2 90 = 0.1$ bits of information. That is why we consider this question less informative.

Note that 1 bit of information gain is here the maximum possible since Bob's question can be answered only by the binary alternative 'yes' or 'no'.

Knowing the answer $Y = y$ from Alice decreased Bob's uncertainty (increased Bob's knowledge) about X. This specific case provides a certain amount of information, given by $H(X) - H(X|Y = y)$. The expected remaining uncertainty (averaged over all possible values y) is known as the *conditional entropy*:

$$H(X|Y) = \sum_y p(y)H(X|Y = y) = -\sum_y \sum_x p(x, y) \log_2 p(x|y), \qquad (3.3)$$

where $p(x, y)$ denotes the joint probability distribution of X and Y. The expected average information gain is then given by $H(X) - H(X|Y)$, which is the *mutual information* between the two random variables X and Y:

$$I(X;Y) = H(X) - H(X|Y) = \sum_y \sum_x p(x,y) \log \frac{p(x,y)}{p(x)p(y)}. \qquad (3.4)$$

In the latter expression we have used the formula $p(x, y) = p(x|y)p(y)$ relating joint, conditional and marginal probability distributions. It can be shown that $I(X;Y)$ is always non-negative [9]; hence, *on average*, knowledge of Y always reduces uncertainty about X.

It is also commonly considered that information is transmitted over a noisy channel; therefore some information might get lost: Alice may not hear the question correctly and thus gives the wrong answer, or Bob might not hear the answer correctly. Mutual information $I(X;Y)$ captures the *actually* transmitted information over the channel (Figure 3.1). Mutual information is also bounded by two quantities: $0 \leq I(X;Y) \leq H(X)$:

- If no message gets transmitted correctly from the source to the receiver (because the channel is too noisy), mutual information drops to its minimum 0.
- If all messages get transmitted perfectly from the source to the receiver, then the remaining uncertainty is $H(X|Y) = 0$ and mutual information is maximised, equal to the source entropy $H(X)$.

3.2.2 Bayesian Experimental Design

So how does Bob choose which question to ask? In other words, if he wants to guess the right number as efficiently as possible, how does he optimise the questions? This can be a rather complex problem depending on how Bob perceives Alice's behaviour and on his previous knowledge of how she is inclined to choose a specific number. Perhaps Bob knows that Alice's lucky number is 13, and she would rather pick her lucky number than any other number such as 56. Or perhaps Alice is mathematically inclined and is known to prefer prime numbers to composite ones, and so on.

This can be given a probability-theoretic framework as an instance of a *parameter estimation problem*: Bob wants to estimate parameter θ, an unknown value that Alice is thinking about. To estimate θ, Bob has at his disposal some set of observations on Alice, or some measured data $Y = y$. Bob assumes some statistical model of Alice's behaviour as a probability distribution $p_\theta(y)$.

In a *Bayesian* setting, Bob assumes a prior distribution $p(\theta)$ of the unknown value that may help his estimation. Without any prior knowledge, he can simply assume that θ is uniformly distributed as in the 20 questions example described above. But if Bob has some prior knowledge about Alice, $p(\theta)$ may be more informative. Since θ is now the outcome of a random variable Θ, the statistical model can then be seen as a conditional distribution $p_\theta(y) = p(y|\theta)$ of Y given Θ. Using this, Bob can then update (hopefully improve) his knowledge by applying Bayes' rule to compute the *posterior* distribution of θ given his observations:

$$p(\theta|y) = \frac{p(y|\theta)p(\theta)}{p(y)}.$$

The theory of Bayesian experimental design [1] was originally proposed by Lindley [5], inspired by Shannon's work [9]. In this framework, Bob designs an experiment $X = x$ to challenge Alice and receives an observation Y from Alice that depends on X and, of course, also on the parameter θ that she is thinking about. Alice's behaviour model is now given by the conditional distribution $p(y|x, \theta)$, and Bob tries to optimise the experiment outcome $X = x$ using some utility function $U(x)$ before updating the posterior distribution using Bayes' rule:

$$p(\theta|x, y) = \frac{p(y|x, \theta)p(\theta)}{p(y|x)}, \tag{3.5}$$

where

$$p(y|x) = \sum_\theta p(y|x, \theta)p(\theta)$$

is an average conditional distribution which can be seen as a 'communication channel' between Bob and Alice. Here we have used that $p(\theta|x) = p(\theta)$ because the parameter Θ unknown to Bob is *a priori* independent from the experimental design X.

The utility $U(x)$ is computed from the prior and posterior distributions and is averaged over all possible Alice's outcomes y (*expected* utility). It can be defined as the information gained about the random variable [5], or the financial or other cost of performing the experiment. Maximising $U(x)$ provides the *optimal decision under uncertainty* (with respect to the given utility function). In other words, when designing an experiment, the goal is to maximise the expected utility of the experiment's outcome.

Interaction between Alice and Bob can further be modelled as a *sequence of experiments*: Each question Bob asks is an 'experiment' on Alice, and the criterion for choice of the experiment then becomes to maximise the expected utility between the current prior and posterior distributions. At every step, the old posterior becomes the new prior and is further updated from the new experiment. Ideally the process continues until no uncertainty remains, which means that θ is perfectly known. This corresponds to a deterministic $\Theta = \theta$ given all previous experiments.

3.2.3 Putting It Together: Bayesian Information Gain

BIG is a general framework to design interaction (Figure 3.2). We consider the user Alice and the computer Bob. Here the goal of the computer is to ask 'clever' questions guided by a utility function to find out what the user wants. The computer does so by 'running experiments' on the user through the feedback $X = x$ that it provides, and using the user's subsequent input $Y = y$ as the outcome of the experiment to update its knowledge about the user's goal $\Theta = \theta$.

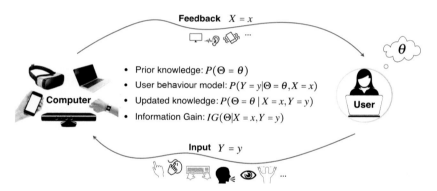

Figure 3.2 The BIG framework. There are three key random variables: the potential targets Θ, system feedback X and user input Y. The computer also has some prior knowledge about the user's intended target $p(\theta) = P(\Theta = \theta)$ and a user behaviour function expressing what the user would do, $p(y|x, \theta) = P(Y = y|\Theta = \theta, X = x)$. After sending the feedback $X = x$ and receiving the user input $Y = y$, the computer updates its knowledge about the user's goal and calculates the information gain from the user input. In order to play a more active role, the computer can try to maximise the expected information gain or leverage it for better interaction by manipulating the feedback.

BIG uses the following notations that are common for Bayesian Experimental Design [5]:

1. The random variable Θ represents the possible intended targets in the user's mind.

2. Its probability distribution, $p(\theta)$ (given for all values of θ) is the prior distribution of targets, which expresses the computer's prior knowledge about Θ. This distribution can be uniform if no data about the user's interests is available, or it can be based on external data sources or interaction history.

3. X represents any possible feedback provided by the computer, and $X = x$ is a particular feedback sent to the user.

4. Y represents any particular command y issued by the user.

5. $p(y|x, \theta)$ is the probability of the user giving an input command $Y = y$ when they want $\Theta = \theta$ and sees $X = x$. This can be modelled from the interaction history, or by user calibration, and can be user-independent or user-dependent.

6. $p(\theta|x, y)$ is the computer's updated knowledge about the user's goal after showing the user $X = x$ and receiving the input $Y = y$ from the user. This is the posterior distribution calculated through Bayes' theorem, as in Equation (3.5).

7. $I(\Theta; Y|X = x)$ is the mutual information between what the user wants and what she provides as input when seeing $X = x$. As explained above, it is the difference between the entropy and the conditional entropy:

$$I(\Theta; Y|X = x) = H(\Theta) - H(\Theta|X = x, Y). \qquad (3.6)$$

Here, for a given $X = x$, knowing Y decreases uncertainty about Θ, by a quantity which is precisely the mutual information $I(\Theta; Y|X = x)$.

We use $U(x) = I(\Theta; Y|X = x)$ as the expected utility function in the Bayesian experimental design: It can be interpreted as the *expected information gain*, and as such is always positive. To calculate this, we use Bayes' theorem for entropy [2] to convert Equation (3.6) to:

$$I(\Theta; Y|X = x) = H(Y|X = x) - H(Y|\Theta, X = x), \qquad (3.7)$$

where the first term is given by $-\sum_y p(y|x) \log_2 p(y|x)$ as in Equation (3.2), and the second term is $-\sum_{y,\theta} p(\theta)p(y|x, \theta) \log_2 p(y|x, \theta)$ as in Equation (3.3).

8. $IG(\Theta|X = x, Y = y)$ is the difference between the computer's previous knowledge $H(\Theta)$ and current knowledge $H(\Theta|X = x, Y = y)$ about the user's goal, representing the *actual information gain* carried by the user input:

$$IG(\Theta|X = x, Y = y) = H(\Theta) - H(\Theta|X = x, Y = y). \qquad (3.8)$$

Information gain might be negative if the user makes an error, for example, but is positive on average since

$$\sum_y p(y)IG(\Theta|X = x, Y = y) = I(\Theta; Y|X = x) \geq 0.$$

Table 3.1 summarises the notations in Bayesian Experimental Design and Bayesian Information Gain respectively.

	BED	*BIG*
θ	Parameter to be determined	Intended target in the user's mind
y	Observation	User input
x	Experimental design	System feedback
$p(y\|\theta, x)$	Model for making observation y, given θ and x	Model for user providing input y, given θ and x
$p(\theta)$	Prior	System's prior knowledge about the user's goal
$p(\theta\|y, x)$	Posterior	Updated knowledge
$I(\Theta; Y\|X = x)$	Utility of the design x	Utility of the feedback x
$IG(\Theta\|X = x, Y = y)$	Utility of the experiment outcome after observation y with design x	Utility of the outcome after user input y with system feedback x

Table 3.1 Notations in Bayesian Experimental Design (BED) and in Bayesian Information Gain (BIG) respectively.

One can always calculate the actual information gain, or the information carried by the user input informing the computer what she wants with Equation (3.8) – 'Running a normal experiment'. By manipulating the feedback with Equation (3.6), e.g. finding the $X = x$ that maximises or leverages the expected information gain, the system 'redesigns the experiment', or 'runs a better experiment' on the user in order to gain more information about the user's goal, i.e. the intended target. The computer then plays a more active role and therefore increases interaction efficiency.

3.3 Application

BIG is a general approach that can be applied to a wide range of interaction tasks. In this section, we describe BIGnav, an application of BIG to multiscale navigation [6].

Multiscale interfaces are a powerful way to represent large datasets such as maps, documents and high-resolution images. The canonical navigation commands in this type of interface are pan and zoom (as seen in many applications such as Google Maps[3]): Panning lets users change the position of the view, while zooming lets them modify the magnification of the viewport [3, 4].

---

[3] www.google.com/maps

3.3.1 BIGnav Implementation

First we define the three key random variables in the BIG framework Θ, X and Y for the multiscale navigation scenario:

- Θ represents any point of interest in the multiscale space. For each target θ, the probability that it is the actual intended target is $p(\theta)$. These probabilities constitute the a priori knowledge that the system has about the user's interest, and is updated as the user navigates.
- X represents any possible view provided by the system. $X = x$ is a particular view shown to the user. Note that the number of possible views is potentially very large.
- Y represents any particular command y issued by the user. The possible input commands are: move in one of the eight cardinal directions, zoom in or click on the target when it is big enough to be clickable. Note that zooming out is not implemented in BIGnav. If the target is out of view, the user should indicate in which direction it is rather than zoom out.

1. *Interpreting user input:* Given the view x shown to the user and the user's intended target θ, $p(y|x, \theta)$ is the probability that the user provides an input command $Y = y$ given θ and $X = x$. This probability distribution is the system's interpretation of the user's intention when giving this command. For example, if city A is to the left of the user, what is the probability of the user giving the left command when knowing that city A is located to her left, provided she can only go left or right? $p($*go left $\mid$ city A is located to the left of the current view, city A is the intended target*$) = 1$ if the user is completely confident about what she is doing. But maybe the user is not accurate all the time. If, say, she is correct only 95% of time, then we need to consider that she makes errors: $p($*go left $\mid$ city A is located to the left of the current view, city A is the intended target*$) = 0.95$ and $p($*go right $\mid$ city A is located to the left of the current view, city A is the intended target*$) = 0.05$. Probability $p(y|x, \theta)$ is a priori knowledge that must be given to the system.

2. *Updating system's knowledge:* Given the view x shown to the user and the user reaction y to that view, the system can update its estimate $p(\theta|x, y)$ of the user's interest with Equation (3.5). If the system has no prior knowledge about the user's intended target, e.g. at the beginning, each θ has the same probability of being the target and $p(\theta)$ is uniform. As the user issues commands, the system gains knowledge about the likelihood that each point of interest be the target, reflected by the changes to the probability distribution. This is done, for each point of interest, by taking its previous probability, multiplying by the above user input function $p(y|x, \theta)$, and

normalising it so that the sum of the new probabilities over all the points of interest equals one.

3. *Navigating to a new view:* With the new probability distribution after receiving user input, BIGnav then goes over each view $X = x$, calculates its expected information gain with Equation (3.7) and picks the view for which it is maximal. To maximise Equation (3.7), BIGnav looks for a trade-off between two entropies. To maximise the first term, the view should be such that all user commands given that view are equally probable (for the system). To minimise the second term, the view should provide the user with meaningful information about the points of interest. Maximising a difference does not necessarily mean to maximise the first term and minimise the second, so the maximum information gain is a trade-off between these two goals. For example, showing only ocean will increase the first term but will also increase the second term. After locating the view with maximal information gain, BIGnav navigates there and waits for the user's next input.

An interactive 1D version of this implementation can be found in a Jupyter notebook,[4] and a video is available on YouTube.[5]

3.3.2 Comparison with Standard Navigation

In order to compare BIGnav with standard pan-and-zoom navigation (STDnav), we implemented a 2D version [6]. In this more realistic setting, we face a computational challenge because the system feedback X can have a huge number of possible views. With BIGnav, we need to calculate the information gain corresponding to every single view $X = x$, which would incur an enormous computational cost if views could be centred at any pixel and have any size. We therefore discretise the set of views by using tiles and discrete zoom factors. This is similar to some pan-and-zoom applications where users can pan in four directions by fixed amounts, and zoom in and out by fixed amounts. We therefore reduce the set of commands to make computation tractable in our prototype. We slice the view into nine regions representing eight panning directions and a central zooming region (Figure 3.3). The eight panning regions have a 45° angle, and the zooming region is half the size of the view. Furthermore, we model user behaviour with a calibration session. The results (Table 3.2) show that 90% of panning commands are correct and 4% are in one of the adjacent directions (Figure 3.3). For zooming commands, 95% of the commands are correct, while for clicking on the target, 100% of the commands are correct.

---

[4] https://github.com/wanyuliu/5thComputationalInteraction/blob/master/BIGMap.ipynb
[5] www.youtube.com/watch?v=N2P-LFh1oLk

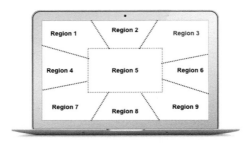

Figure 3.3 Nine regions representing user input, delimited by dotted lines. Panning regions also include the space outside the current view.

Command	Main Region	Adjacent Regions	Other Regions
Pan	0.90	0.04	0.0033
Zoom	0.95	0.00625	0.00625
Click	1	0	0

Table 3.2 Calibration results used as prior knowledge about the user behaviour $p(y|x, \theta)$.

Based on this setup, we ran a controlled experiment and found that BIGnav was up to 40% faster than STDnav. Figure 3.4 shows the number of navigation steps required (x-axis) to reach the target in STDnav and BIGnav, as well as how uncertainty and information gain evolve over time. We can see that with STDnav, sometimes a command does not make a difference in uncertainty, i.e. the information gain is null. This is typically the case when the system is certain of what the user is going to do. For example, when completely zoomed out, users must zoom in. Similarly, if a view contains 99% of the probability distribution, users will almost certainly zoom in. Therefore such feedback is not an 'intelligent' question. On the contrary, BIGnav optimises the feedback at each step to gain a maximum amount of information and reduce the computer's uncertainty.

However, despite being more efficient, BIGnav incurs a higher cognitive load (Figure 3.5). Instead of executing users' panning and zooming commands, BIGnav returns the feedback that maximises the expected information gain from the user's subsequent input. This new feedback might be far away from the current view, and therefore, the user has to interpret what the system has just done and reorient themselves before inputting the next command, whereas with STDnav the user can anticipate the system response. A subsequent version

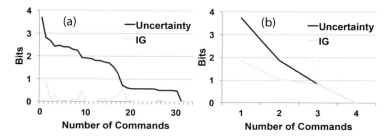

Figure 3.4 Uncertainty and information gain (IG) for each successive command in (a) STDnav and (b) BIGnav.

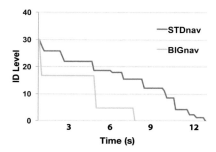

Figure 3.5 Time plot of the decrease in index of difficulty (ID) in the STDnav and BIGnav conditions, for two trials with the same other conditions.

of BIGnav uses animation during the transitions between views to help users orient themselves and anticipate their next action.

3.3.3 Other Applications

BIG is a general framework that can be applied to a wide range of interaction tasks. Once the potential targets Θ and their probability distribution $p(\theta)$, system feedback X, user input Y and user behaviour $p(y|x, \theta)$ are modelled, one can compute the actual information gain, or the information carried by the user input informing the computer of what she wants. We have applied this approach to two other areas: file retrieval [7] and collective music-making [8].

BIGFile [7] is an interaction technique for fast hierarchical file retrieval that leverages the expected information gain. Unlike BIGnav, BIGFile features a split adaptive interface that combines a traditional file navigation interface with an adaptive part that displays the shortcuts selected by BIG. Users can use any shortcut in the adaptive area or simply navigate the hierarchy as usual. BIGFile uses an approximate but efficient algorithm to select shortcuts, and was shown to be up to 40% faster than standard file navigation.

Entrain [8] is an intelligent agent for encouraging social interaction in collective music-making. Here BIG is used to adapt a probabilistic model of individual user behaviour, which is calculated based on user activity and rhythmic periodicity, and modulates music creation at both individual and collective levels via visual and auditory feedback.

We encourage readers to think about their own interaction scenario in a 'BIG' way: How much uncertainty and information are there in the interaction loop? Is the current interaction information efficient? How can one have the computer play a more active role by demanding more information?

3.4 Discussion

In this section, we discuss some limitations of the BIG approach and propose potential solutions as well as future possibilities.

3.4.1 Approximation of Prior Distribution

When no prior information is available, a common practice is to assume a uniform distribution. Then the computer continuously updates its knowledge when receiving user input via Bayes' rule. The approximation of prior distribution can be derived from external data. For example, for a map navigation, it could be based on a large dataset representing the general population, such as the popularity of tourist destinations. It could also be based on the user's own interaction history, such as 'my favourite top destinations'. In BIGnav [6], we showed that even with a uniform prior distribution, BIGnav is more efficient than the standard pan-and-zoom navigation. The more precise the approximation of the prior distribution, the better BIG works.

3.4.2 Dynamic User Behaviour Model

The user behaviour model is the computer's belief about which command the user will issue given what she wants and what she sees. In Bayesian Experimental Design's terms, it is the probability of observing an outcome given the parameter of nature and the experiment. Similar to the approximation of the prior distribution, the better we model it, the better BIG works. We collected user behaviour from a calibration session in BIGnav [6] and from the literature in BIGFile [7]. In both cases this model stays constant for all participants throughout the session. However, we know that users' behaviour changes over time. Novices' behaviour is different from that of experts; people have individual differences; one's behaviour might change given a particular environment. Therefore, a better solution is to have a dynamic user behaviour model, tailored to a specific user whose behaviour changes due to time or her interaction with the environment. This can be done by logging user's interaction over time and constructing the user behaviour model from real data.

3.4.3 Computational Cost

A crucial aspect of interaction is to provide immediate system feedback to users' actions. The BIG method is computationally costly since the calculation of mutual information requires the sum of all possibilities: The overall computational cost is $N_\Theta \times N_X \times N_Y$ (N is the number of possible values). In BIGnav, we discretised system feedback and user input to achieve real-time feedback by the system. In BIGFile we introduced an efficient but approximate algorithm to reduce the computing cost [7].

Other approaches are worth exploring. For example, instead of searching the entire information space (exhaustive search), we could regularise the search to compute the locally maximal expected information gain. We could also use a timer to provide a first, coarse response in, e.g., 0.1s, and refine the search if the user does not provide input. The actual optimisation depends on the exact context of use.

3.4.4 Other Utility Functions

While information alone can be used as the expected utility function for an 'informative experiment' to reduce uncertainty as efficiently as possible, other measures can be considered. For example, we can add a cost to the utility function for the estimated user's cognitive load, so that an optimal feedback needs to be both informative and comfortable. In BIGnav, this cost could be a function of the estimated time for the user to get reoriented after the new feedback.

Other utility functions might include, for example, successful completion of a task, such as success rate, or the time to correct errors if some errors are more severe than others, or dwell time over areas of interest in an eye-tracking experiment. The optimal system feedback, i.e. the experiments the computer runs on the users, depends on the chosen utility criterion.

3.4.5 Future Challenges

We started this chapter with an example of Alice having a number between 1 and 100 in her head and Bob trying to guess that number by asking informative questions. Similarly, we assumed that there is a finite set of potential targets, that the user has a single intended target in her head, and that this target does not change until it is found. BIG is a goal-oriented framework: It does not support pure exploration, when the user has no intended target. How to incorporate these situations, i.e. a changing target, no target or more than one target is an interesting challenge for future work.

3.5 Conclusion

In this chapter we introduced Bayesian Information Gain, a general framework that can be applied to many interaction tasks. In order to compute *information*, one needs to model Θ, the set of potential targets; $p(\theta)$, the computer's prior knowledge about the user's goal; X, the possible system feedback; Y, the possible user input, and $p(y|x, \theta)$, which models the user behaviour. BIG can then calculate how much information there is in the user input to reduce the computer's uncertainty, and optimise interaction efficiency by having the computer extract more information at each step by manipulating the system feedback.

BIG is an example of a probabilistic interface. Similar to other probabilistic interface architectures that treat user input as an uncertain process, BIG uses a user behaviour model to represent the ambiguity of user input for the computer. In conventional settings, there is no information-theoretic uncertainty for the user regarding the computer's behaviour. However, when presenting feedback to the user, the computer is uncertain about what the user will do. From the user's perspective, BIG presents non-deterministic system feedback that challenges the user by leveraging a Bayesian model in order to maximise information gain. It opens the door to a wide range of 'BIG' applications and a new era of probabilistic interaction.

References

[1] K. Chaloner, and I. Verdinelli. 1995. Bayesian experimental design: a review. *Statistical Science*, **10**(3), 273–304.

[2] T. M. Cover and J. A. Thomas. 2012. *Elements of Information Theory*. John Wiley & Sons.

[3] G. W. Furnas, and B. B. Bederson. 1995. Space-scale diagrams: understanding multiscale interfaces. Pages 234–241 of: *Proceedings of the SIGCHI Conference on Human Factors in Computing Systems*. CHI '95. New York, NY, USA: ACM Press/Addison-Wesley Publishing Co.

[4] Y. Guiard and M. Beaudouin-Lafon. 2004. Target acquisition in multiscale electronic worlds. *International Journal of Human-Computer Studies*, **61**(6), 875–905.

[5] D. V. Lindley. 1956. On a measure of the information provided by an experiment. *The Annals of Mathematical Statistics*, **27**(4), 986–1005.

[6] W. Liu, R. L. DOliveira, M. Beaudouin-Lafon and O. Rioul. 2017. BIGnav: Bayesian information gain for guiding multiscale navigation. Pages 5869–5880 of: *Proceedings of the 2017 CHI Conference on Human Factors in Computing Systems*. CHI 17. Association for Computing Machinery.

[7] W. Liu, O. Rioul, J. McGrenere, W. E. Mackay and M. Beaudouin-Lafon. 2018. BIGFile: Bayesian information gain for fast file retrieval. In: *Proceedings of the 2018 CHI Conference on Human Factors in Computing Systems*. CHI 18. Association for Computing Machinery.

[8] H. Scurto, W. Liu, B. Matuszewski, F. Bevilacqua, J.-L. Frechin, U. Petrevski and N. Schnell. 2019. Entrain: encouraging social interaction in collective music making. In: *ACM SIGGRAPH 2019 Studio*. SIGGRAPH 19. Association for Computing Machinery.

[9] Shannon, Claude E. 1948. A mathematical theory of communication. *Bell System Technical Journal*, **27**(3), 379–423.

4

Bayesian Command Selection

Suwen Zhu, Xiangmin Fan, Feng Tian and Xiaojun Bi

Abstract

Command selection – selecting a command from a set of candidates based on input signals – is one of the most basic and common tasks in human–computer interaction. The existing command selection interfaces such as grid menus often adopt a deterministic mapping principle to decide the selection target, which is unsuitable to handle the noises and uncertainty in input signals (e.g. ambiguity in finger touch input). This chapter formalises Bayes' theorem as a generic guiding principle for deciding targets in command selection. Compared with the common deterministic approach, the Bayesian method is better at handling the uncertainty in the input signals and equipped with the ability to model the command selection history.

4.1 Introduction and Background

Command input is essential to human–computer interaction. There is no exception in the era of mobile and wearable computing, where people regularly issue commands on touchscreens with finger touch or gesture [1, 17, 37, 41]. These input modalities are natural to use, but they inevitably introduce uncertainty. For example, touch input is known as notoriously noisy and imprecise due to occlusion and the uncertainty of converting a 'fat' contact region into a single touchpoint [25, 31, 32, 62–64]; a recogniser in a gestural command input system may yield erroneous output if the input gestures deviate from the predefined templates [42, 70].

Despite the wide existence of uncertainty, the existing command input methods are ill-positioned for handling it: they often adopt a deterministic principle to decide which command will be issued. For example, to trigger a command with finger touch, the user needs to land the touchpoint within the target boundaries precisely; to input a command with a gesture, the decoded command name should match the exact command label.

4.1.1 Command Selection with Point-and-Click Input

Using finger touch to select a target among a set of candidates (point-and-click input) is one of the most basic and frequently performed command selection tasks. However, it also suffers from the obvious 'fat finger' problem. It lacks the necessary precision to hit the intended target every time, especially for smaller targets on the screen.

There has been extensive research on understanding and improving touch-pointing accuracy. On a capacitive touchscreen, a touchpoint is converted from the finger's contact region with noise and uncertainty in the converting process. Factors such as hand posture [14, 25], finger angle [31, 32] and body movement [24, 54] may affect the size and shape of the contact region, unintentionally altering the touch position. The lack of feedback on where the finger lands due to occlusion further exacerbates the issue [31, 32, 62–64].

Previous research has explored various approaches to improve touch accuracy. Examples include compensating for the offset caused by different finger input angles [31, 32] or location on screens [30], displaying the touch location in a non-occluded area [63] and using the back of the device for selection [67, 68]. Others also explored using various finger gestures to assist target selection, including crossing [2, 15, 50, 51, 57], sliding [14, 53, 71, 72], rubbing [56, 58], circling [33] and multi-touch gestures [8].

Probabilistic frameworks have also been proposed to deal with the uncertainty in input processes, such as considering the input as a continuous control process in which the system continuously infers a distribution over potential user goals [13, 66, 69], or carrying the uncertainty of input forward all the way through the interaction [60, 61]. For example, Weir et al. [66] proposed mapping the raw sensor data or the touch location reported by the device to the intended touchpoint based on the historical touch behaviour of a specific user. These techniques improve the touch accuracy by various degrees. Other examples include Dasher [65], which used probabilistic models to adapt screen layouts, and Semantic pointing [12], which adapted the control-to-display ratio according to cursor distance to nearby targets. Bayes' theorem has also been adopted to reduce uncertainty in interaction, such as the statistical decoding algorithm of soft keyboards [26], and the Bayesian Information Gain (BIG) framework [44, 45].

4.1.2 Command Selection with Word-Gesture Input

Gesture input has been widely explored as a command input method on touchscreen devices, thanks to the human's ability to memorise pictorial information [55]. It has been adopted in the marking menu [38–40] and its variants [5, 6, 21, 22, 75, 76], gesture-based interfaces [7, 23, 41, 46–49] and multi-touch gesture frameworks [34, 35].

Word-gesture input [36, 73, 74] allows users to enter text using a continuous gesture stroke to traverse the letters on the keyboard. To assist users in memorising the mappings between commands and gestures, previous researchers have explored using word gestures [36, 74] for command input – entering a command by gliding finger over letters in the command name on a virtual keyboard. Word-gesture was initially invented for text entry on touchscreen devices [36, 74], which was later extended as a method for command input. For example, Command Strokes [37] and CommandBoard [1] support triggering a command by drawing its word-gesture on a soft keyboard, and HotStrokes [17] supports word-gesture command input on a laptop trackpad.

The existing gestural command input systems (e.g. [1, 17, 37]), often adopt a deterministic principle to decide the target command: the decoder matches the input gesture with the predefined gesture template of each command candidate; the candidate with highest matching score is the target command. It has little room for handling uncertainty and would result in errors if the input gesture deviates greatly from the template or some commands share the similar predefined templates.

4.1.3 Handle Command Selection Uncertainty with a Bayesian Framework

Since many command input signals involve uncertainty and noises (e.g. touch input and gesture input), Bayes' theorem becomes a natural choice for handling the uncertainty that occurs in command selection processes. We set out from a probabilistic perspective to interpret the ambiguity in a command selection process: the input signals are viewed as a random variable that carries likelihood information of the target command. The posterior belief is formed accordingly via Bayes' theorem. The candidate with the highest posterior probability should be decided as the target. This information is, in turn, used to update the prior probability model for future command input. In the remainder of the chapter, we explain how to model priors and likelihoods of command input signals, demonstrate how to apply Bayes' theorem to solve uncertainty in command input, and evaluate the proposed Bayesian approaches.

4.2 A Bayesian Perspective on Command Selection

From a Bayesian perspective, a command selection task can be described as follows: Assuming $C = \{c_1, c_2, \ldots, c_n\}$ is a set of n available commands, given the input signal $\mathbf{s}$, the goal of a command input task is to find c^* in C that maximises $P(c|\mathbf{s})$. According to Bayes' theorem, it can be calculated as:

$$c^* = \arg\max_{c \in C} P(c|\mathbf{s}) = \arg\max_{c \in C} \frac{[P(\mathbf{s}|c)P(c)]}{P(\mathbf{s})}. \qquad (4.1)$$

Assuming $P(\mathbf{s})$ is a constant across c (because $\mathbf{s}$ is a fixed value for a given input), we can further simplify Equation (4.1) to:

$$c^* = \arg\max_{c \in C} [P(\mathbf{s}|c)P(c)], \qquad (4.2)$$

where $P(c)$ is the prior probability of c being the intended command without the observation of $\mathbf{s}$, and $P(\mathbf{s}|c)$ describes how probable $\mathbf{s}$ is if the intended target is c (the likelihood). Figure 4.1 shows the overview of this method.

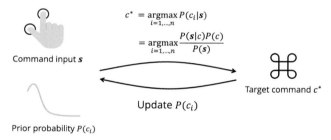

Command input $\mathbf{s}$

$$c^* = \underset{i=1,\ldots,n}{\operatorname{argmax}} P(c_i|\mathbf{s})$$

$$= \underset{i=1,\ldots,n}{\operatorname{argmax}} \frac{P(\mathbf{s}|c)P(c)}{P(\mathbf{s})}$$

Target command c^*

Update $P(c_i)$

Prior probability $P(c_i)$

Figure 4.1 Given an input signal $\mathbf{s}$ and a set of n commands $C = \{c_1, \ldots, c_n\}$, the goal of a command input task is to find $c*$ that maximises $P(c|\mathbf{s})$. We view the input signal $\mathbf{s}$ as a random variable carrying likelihood information, and uses Bayes' theorem to combine it with the prior probability $P(c_i)$ to infer $P(c|\mathbf{s})$. The target command information is then used to update the prior probability model.

To apply Bayes' theorem to general command selection tasks, the key challenge is to obtain the prior probability and the likelihood. While the prior probability is independent of the command input method, the likelihood is closely tied to the specific input method. Next, we explain these components in the text of command selection.

4.2.1 Prior Probability Model

We first show a model that predicts $P(c)$ – the prior probability of the candidate c being the intended target – from the command selection history. Such a prior model is especially valuable in a command selection process where the input signals are noisy. A prior model can be highly informative, compensating for the uncertainty introduced by the noisy command input signals.

In the prior probability model, we assume that the distribution of the intended command among candidates is not entirely random, and the command input history is observable. We formed this assumption based on the findings that the patterns of menu selection [16, 43], command triggering [3, 19] and smartphone app launching [52] are not random and often follow certain distributions (e.g. *Zipfian* distributions). These are all scenarios involving frequent command input.

Before deriving the model, we define two criteria that the model should satisfy:

1. Without observing any selection history, each candidate is equally probable as the target.
2. With a large number of observations, $P(c)$ approximates the frequency that the candidate c was selected as the target in the past.

We propose the frequency model as follows. We view the outcome of a command selection task as a random variable x which follows a categorical distribution with N categories (the N target candidates). The core parameter of this random variable x is the parameter vector $p = (P(c_1), P(c_2), \ldots, P(c_N))$, which describes the probability of each category. As a common practice in Bayesian inference, we also view this parameter vector p as a random variable and give it a prior distribution, using the Dirichlet distribution.

According to the properties of Dirichlet distributions, after each target selection trial we can update the expected value of the posterior p as follows:

$$P(c_i) = \frac{k + t_i}{k \cdot N + \sum_{j=1}^{N} t_j}, \qquad (4.3)$$

where N is the number of available commands (e.g. the number of items in a menu), t_i is the number of times the candidate has been selected and k is the pseudocount of the Dirichlet prior, a hyper-parameter of the distribution. The parameter k can also be viewed as the update rate, which is a positive constant that controls how fast $P(c_i)$ are updated.

The proposed model (Equation (4.3)) satisfies the aforementioned criteria (1) and (2). If no selection history is observed – i.e. $t_i = 0, i \in [1, n]$ – Equation (4.3) shows $P(c_i) = \frac{1}{n}$. It indicates that each candidate is equally probable as the target. On the other hand, if we have a large number of observations on selection history (i.e. $t_i \gg k \cdot n$ and $t_i \gg k, i \in [1, n]$)),

Equation (4.3) shows $P(c_i) \approx \frac{t_i}{\sum_{i=1}^{n} t_i}$, which is the frequency of c_i being the target in the past.

The update rate k in the model controls the balance between two extreme views on calculating $P(c_i)$:

1. $P(c_i)$ is identical to the frequency of c_i being the target in the past.
2. All the candidates are equally probable as the target.

If $k = 0$, $P(c_i) = \frac{t_i}{\sum_{i=1}^{n} t_i}$, which is the view (A). If $k \rightarrow +\infty$, $P(c_i) \approx \frac{1}{n}$, which is the view (B). A positive k controls the weights between these two views. Later we explain how we used a simulation-based approach to determine an optimal k in our applications.

4.2.2 Likelihood Models

Unlike $P(c)$ which is independent of the input signal s, a likelihood model which calculates $P(s|c)$ is tightly connected to the specific command input method. We show how to establish them for two command selection tasks separately.

Dual-Gaussian Likelihood Model for Point-and-Click Input
We adopted a dual-Gaussian likelihood model to calculate $P(s|c)$, assuming that the touchpoints approximately follow a Gaussian distribution [4, 30, 31]. Assuming for a 2-dimensional target we observe a touchpoint s as (s_x, s_y), $P(s|c)$ can be calculated as:

$$P(s|c) = \frac{1}{2\pi\sigma_x\sigma_y} \exp\left[-\frac{z}{2(1 - \rho_i^2)}\right], \qquad (4.4)$$

where

$$z \equiv \frac{(s_x - \mu_x)^2}{\sigma_x^2} - \frac{2\rho(s_x - \mu_x)(s_y - \mu_y)}{\sigma_x\sigma_y} + \frac{(s_y - \mu_y)^2}{\sigma_y^2}. \qquad (4.5)$$

Here (μ_x, μ_y) is the target centre, σ_x and σ_y are the standard deviations of users' touchpoints and ρ is the correlation coefficient between x and y. We followed the next two steps to estimate the parameters of Equations (4.4) and (4.5).

First, we assumed that the centre of touchpoint distribution (μ_x, μ_y) co-locates with the centre of the target. Previous research showed that (μ_x, μ_y) has only a small offset from the target centre, and the magnitude and direction of the offset are affected by various factors including the target position on the screen, users' postures and finger angle [4, 30, 31, 66, 77]. Without further knowledge on these factors, we assume (μ_x, μ_y) is located at the target centre. Similarly, previous research also showed the correlation coefficient (ρ) between x and y largely depends on a variety of factors such as on-screen location, hand posture, and finger angle. Similar to the approach adopted in Bi and Zhai [11], we assume $\rho \approx 0$ without further knowledge of these factors.

Second, we adopted the dual Gaussian distribution hypothesis [9, 10] to estimate σ_x and σ_y. Based on the hypothesis, the distribution of a touchpoint (X) for a target can be seen as the sum of two independent Gaussian distributions X_r and X_α:

$$X = X_r + X_\alpha \sim N(\mu, \sigma^2),$$
$$\mu = \mu_r + \mu_\alpha, \qquad (4.6)$$
$$\sigma^2 = \sigma_r^2 + \sigma_\alpha^2,$$

where X_r is relative to target properties, especially the target size. X_α is intrinsic to the motor control system, reflecting the absolute precision of the inputting device. For point-and-click input, the dual distribution hypothesis [9, 10] states that the variance of touchpoints (σ) has a linear relationship to d^2:

$$\sigma^2 = \sigma_r^2 + \sigma_\alpha^2 = \alpha \times d^2 + \sigma_\alpha^2, \qquad (4.7)$$

where α and σ_a are empirically determined parameters, and d is the target size.

Two-Step Likelihood Model for Word-Gesture Command Input

For word-gesture command input, a user enters a command by drawing the word-gesture [36, 74] of the command name. To develop the corresponding likelihood model, we first view the decoding process, i.e. the procedure of mapping an input gesture s to a command c as a two-step process:

1. s is first decoded into a word w by a gesture decoder (e.g. $SHARK^2$ [36, 74] or i'sFree decoder [78]).
2. w is mapped to a specific command c. Note that a user may trigger a command with different words. For example, to launch a clock application, users could input *clock*, *time*, *timer* or *watch*.

If we view s, w and c as random variables, the graphical model in Figure 4.2 describes their dependencies. The two-step likelihood model is developed based on this graphical model.

Conditional dependencies:

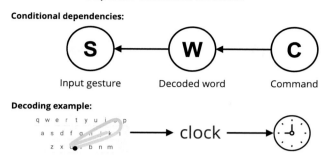

Figure 4.2 A graphical model showing the conditional dependencies between the input gesture **s**, decoded word w and command c. The example shows the process of triggering the command 'clock' with a word-gesture. The word-gesture is entered on a keyboard, and the black dot illustrates the start of the gesture.

According to the law of total probability, we can get $P(\mathbf{s}|c)$ as:

$$P(\mathbf{s}|c) = \sum_{i=1}^{N} P(\mathbf{s}, w_i|c) = \sum_{i=1}^{N} P(\mathbf{s}|w_i, c)P(w_i|c), \qquad (4.8)$$

where **s** is the input gesture, w_i is a decoded word candidate from a gesture typing decoder, N is the total number of decoded word candidates and c is a command candidate.

The graphical model (Figure 4.2) suggests that c and **s** are conditional independent given w. Therefore, Equation (4.8) can be further expressed as:

$$P(\mathbf{s}|c) = \sum_{i=1}^{N} P(\mathbf{s}|w_i, c)P(w_i|c) = \sum_{i=1}^{N} P(\mathbf{s}|w_i)P(w_i|c). \qquad (4.9)$$

Equation (4.9) is our two-step likelihood model. As shown, the key of using this model is to obtain $P(\mathbf{s}|w_i)$ and $P(w_i|c)$. These two terms can be calculated as follows.

The term $P(\mathbf{s}|w_i)$ represents the probability of observing the input gesture **s** if w_i is the target word. From a gesture typing decoder's perspective, it is the spatial score of w_i given **s** is the input gesture [36, 74].

The term $P(w_i|c)$ represents the probability of inputting the word w_i if the c is the intended command. Since a command might be triggered by different words (e.g. launching a clock with *clock*, *timer* or *watch*), we calculate $P(w_i|c)$ as follows. For a given command c, we first form a set of words corresponding to it: $M = \{m_0, m_1, m_2, ..., m_K\}$ from a thesaurus (e.g. thesaurus.com), where m_i is a valid word for triggering c. If a decoded word candidate w_i does not belong to this set, we assume $P(w_i|c) = 0$. Otherwise, $P(w_i|c) = \frac{1}{K}$, assuming that each word in this thesaurus has equal probability for triggering command c.

4.2.3 Combine Prior and Likelihood Model to Obtain Posterior

After obtaining the prior probability and the likelihood, we can apply Bayes' theorem to calculate the posterior probability (Equation (4.2)) to decide the target command. Algorithm 4.1 shows how the principle works.

Algorithm 4.1

1: **Input**: s – the input signal s,
2:              C – a set of command candidates $\{c_1, \cdots, c_n\}$
3: **Output**: the target command $c*$
4: **for** $i = 1, 2, \cdots, n$ **do**
5:     obtain prior probability $P(c_i)$ from Equation (4.3)
6:     calculate $P(s|c_i)$ from the likelihood model
7: **end for**
8: select $c* = \arg \max P(s|c_i)P(c_i)$ as the target command
9: update prior probability $P(c_i)$ for each c_i based on Equation (4.3),
     given that $c*$ is the selected command.

4.3 A Bayesian Framework for Command Selection

In this section, we show how to use the Bayesian framework for command selection. By integrating the prior and likelihood models, the Bayesian framework computes the posterior distribution of the intended command among a set of candidates. The computed posterior distribution can be further integrated into a probabilistic framework or combined with other input events (e.g. [59, 60]) to infer a user's interaction intention, or be combined with the utility of each command to select the command with highest expected utility.

We first show the general recipe of applying the Bayesian framework as a principle to select commands, and then use two examples to demonstrate how to apply the recipe. In the two examples, we assume that the expected utility of a command is equal across all candidates. Therefore, searching for the command with the the highest expected utility is equivalent to finding the candidate with the highest posterior. In a real-world application, if the utilities of commands can be estimated from empirical data, they should be integrated with the posterior distribution to select the command with highest expected utility. Nevertheless, our investigation shows that the simplified Bayesian approach (i.e. assuming equal utility across commands) improves the command selection accuracy over a deterministic approach (e.g. using visual boundaries) and the maximum likelihood approach which has no update on prior distributions.

4.3.1 Recipe of Using the Bayesian Framework as a Principle to Select a Command

How to Build the Prior Model from Command Selection History

As shown in Algorithm 4.1, the prior probability $P(t_i)$ will be updated from the command selection history. We can use accumulated command selection frequencies to build the prior model. If no such history exists, we can assume all commands are equally probable and update the prior model as the system observes more data.

How to Obtain the Likelihood Model from the Input Data

The likelihood model should be established according to the input modality, as shown in Sections 4.2.2 and 4.2.2. We can also run user studies to understand the command selection behaviour to build the likelihood model.

How to Combine Prior and Likelihood to Obtain Posterior and Then Decide the Target Command

After obtaining the prior and likelihood, we can compute the product of two (Equation (4.2)) to get the posterior probability $P(c|s)$. The command with the highest posterior should be selected as the target command.

How to Update the Prior and Likelihood Based on the Selection

After the user confirms the selected command, we can use the selected command (i) to update the prior model, i.e. the command selection history following Equation (4.3). We can also use the input information (e.g. the touchpoint coordinates for point-and-click command selection, or the gesture trajectory for word-gesture command) to refine the likelihood model.

4.3.2 Examples of Applying the Recipe

Example 1: Visually Guided Command Selection on a Grid Menu

We first applied the Bayesian framework on a touch-based point-and-click interface: triggering a command by touchpointing the corresponding icon, button, or menu item.

Parameterise the likelihood model: Following the procedure reported in the previous research [10], we conducted a target acquisition study to obtain α and σ_a values for Equation (4.7).

We recruited 36 participants (12 female) aged between 19 and 37 (average 25.4 $\pm$ 4.2). Each participant was instructed to naturally select a circular target, which randomly appeared on a Nexus 5X touchscreen device. The study included four levels of target size (diameter): 8, 12, 16 and 20 mm, each with 20 trials. To avoid over-fitting, we randomly divided the data into two sets: 29 ($\sim$ 80%) participants as the training set and the rest as the test set. Both datasets included a mix of two postures (index finger, thumb).

We established the touch model of the training set following the procedure described in [10]. More specifically, we first calculated the mean and standard deviation of the touchpoints relative to the target centre. As conventional in Android and iOS, we assume the positive x-direction is right, and the positive y-direction is down. Table 4.1 shows the touch model parameters (in mm) of the training set data.

d	μ_x	μ_y	σ_x	σ_y
8	0.472	0.327	1.372	1.598
12	0.648	0.348	1.756	2.010
16	0.628	0.411	1.843	2.350
20	0.973	0.348	2.138	2.451

Table 4.1 Touchpoint distribution for different target sizes. All units are in mm. The target centre is (0,0). d is the diameter of the target. μ_x, μ_y are the mean of the touchpoints. σ_x and σ_x are the standard deviations of the touchpoints.

We then ran linear regression for the variance of x and y directions against d^2. The estimations are shown in Figure 4.3. The α and σ_a values serve as the parameters for Equation (4.7). To verify the trained parameters, we tested them on the σ values on the test dataset. The mean (SD) RMSE were 0.10 (0.11) mm on σ_x and 0.12 (0.04) mm on σ_y across different d. This confirmed the validity of the model.

Build the prior model: Next, we investigated how fast the prior probability $P(t_i)$ will be updated from the selection history. In other words, we decided the optimal k value in Equation (4.3) via a simulation study.

The simulation worked as follows. We first designed a 6 $\times$ 4 touchscreen grid layout for command selection (see Figure 4.4). Each cell in the grid corresponded to a command candidate. We then implemented Algorithm 4.1

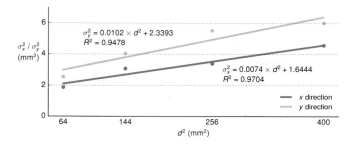

Figure 4.3 Regression between the variance in x directions (σ_x^2) / y direction (σ_y^2) and the target width (d^2).

as the principle for deciding the target on this grid interface. We implemented a set of conditions with different k values in the prior probability models. We used the touch models of test set users to generate the touchpoints, fed the touchpoints into this grid layout and evaluated the accuracy of different prior models to determine which k value led to optimal performance.

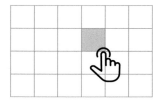

Figure 4.4 The grid layout used in the simulation. The shaded block shows the simulated target. The finger illustrates the simulated touchpoint.

We ran the simulation using the data collected in Section 4.3.2. We used the training set to train a touch model which served as the likelihood model (Figure 4.3). We developed independent touch models for each user in the test set to generate the touchpoints for testing.

On this grid layout, we assumed the target frequency follows the Zipfian distribution [79]:

$$f(l; s, N) = \frac{1/l^s}{\sum_{n=1}^{N}(1/n^s)}, \tag{4.10}$$

where N is the number of elements, $l \in \{1, 2, \ldots, N\}$ is the rank of the element, and s is the value of the exponent characterising the distribution. We randomly picked 12 square targets from a grid layout (Figure 4.4) and simulated two different distributions with exponent $s = 1$ and $s = 2$, based on 600 total selections. The generated frequencies were (216, 106, 98, 79, 52, 25, 7, 6, 4, 4, 2, 1) for $s = 1$ and (430, 142, 14, 3, 2, 2, 2, 1, 1, 1, 1, 1) for $s = 2$. We assumed these 12 frequencies showed how frequently a target would be the intended command, and assigned these 12 frequencies to the selected 12 targets.

Seven target sizes (4, 5, 6, 7, 8, 9 and 10mm) were tested. We ran the simulation for every user in the test set separately. The target order was randomised. In each simulation trial, we picked one candidate as the target and generated a touchpoint for selecting this target following the test user's individual touch model. Given the touchpoint location, we then determined the selected target using Algorithm 4.1 with different k values in the prior probability models. We repeated the procedure five times.

In total, the simulation included: 2 Zipfian distributions × 7 target sizes × 7 test users × 600 trials × 5 repetitions = 294,000 simulation trials.

To determine which k should be used in the prior probability model, we compared the following k values:

1. optimal k. We searched for the optimal k in the prior probability model by initialising k to 0.1 and increasing it to 20 with a step length of 0.1. The k that led to the highest accuracy was optimal.
2. $k = 1$. We used $k = 1$ across users and conditions. We discovered that $k = 1$ performed well in pilot simulation runs and would like to see if it could be generalised.

We calculated the target acquisition accuracy of each repetition as the total number of correct selections divided by the total number of selections averaged across the users in the test set. Figure 4.5 shows the average accuracy over the five repetitions.

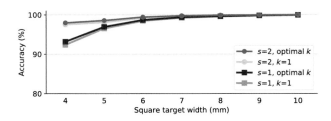

Figure 4.5 Average target acquisition accuracy by target size for different target frequency (Zipfian distribution with $s = 1$ or $s = 2$) and k.

The optimal value of k varied across different runs, but it generally fell within the range of $[0.5, 3]$. As shown in Figure 4.5, when $k = 1$, the average accuracy was close to the optimal accuracy. Therefore, we chose $k = 1$ in the prior probability model (Equation (4.3)) and used this value for implementation. Note that the choice of k is specific to our particular application. Different values should be selected depending on the actual scenario.

After determining the update rate (i.e. the k parameter), we conducted a study to evaluate the Bayesian framework for point-and-click command selection.

Experiment I: Apply the Bayesian Framework for Visually Guided Command Selection

Participants and Apparatus: Eighteen adults (4 females) aged between 21 and 35 (average 27.3 ± 3.3) participated in the study. Of these, 16 participants were right-handed. The self-reported average usage time of mobile phones was 24.5 hours per week. We used a Ticwatch S Smartwatch with a 45mm diameter screen in the study (Figure 4.6a).

Experiment Setup: The study was a within-subject design. There were 2 independent variables: target size and target-deciding principle. We evaluated two target sizes: 3mm and 4mm square targets on a 4-by-6 grid layout. The target deciding principles included three levels:

- *Bayesian framework:* We used Equation (4.3) as the prior probability model and Equation (4.7) (Figure 4.3 for parameters) to obtain the likelihood value. We chose $k = 1$ in the prior probability model according to the previously described simulation study. We refer to this condition as BayesianCommand.
- *BTC* [10]: BTC uses only the likelihood function to decide the target command. BTC also used the dual Gaussian distribution hypothesis [9, 10] to obtain the likelihood value.
- *Boundary criterion:* This is the commonly adopted criterion that decides the target command by examining whether the touchpoint falls within the target boundaries. It served as a baseline in our experiment.

In the first two conditions, we used the same touch model obtained from Section 4.3.2 in the likelihood model. Except for the form factor, the two devices used capacitive touch screens and were both running Android OS, i.e. the underlying mechanism to convert the finger touch to a touchpoint was the same. We assumed the previously developed touch model was valid on our testing device.

We designed a point-and-click command input task. The item corresponding to the target command was highlighted in yellow. Participants were instructed to select the target item as fast and accurately as possible. When a selection was made, the selected item would be highlighted with a blue background. A trial was completed if the selection was correct or three failed attempts were made.

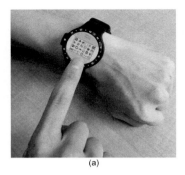 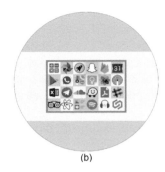

      (a)   (b)

Figure 4.6 The setup of Experiment I: (a) shows a participant selecting a 4mm target, and (b) shows the application with 3mm square targets. The shaded ones were the targets tested in the experiment.

We randomly selected 12 items as targets. We used the same set of targets across participants and conditions. The target positions were fixed, as shown in Figure 4.6(b). Target item frequencies were generated according to Zipfian distribution with exponent $s = 1$ based on 30 selections. The generated frequencies – i.e. the number of occurrences – were (7, 5, 4, 4, 2, 2, 1, 1, 1, 1, 1, 1). The frequency assignments were randomised across participants and conditions. Participants were not informed of the frequency distribution of the items or the position of the most frequent items.

We balanced the frequency assignments on the target items across all participants and conditions. Each target item was assigned to each frequency an equal number of times to ensure that the same total number of selections was collected for each target. The order of the targets within each block was randomised. A similar strategy was used in [3, 27].

Before the formal study, participants were introduced to the task and performed a warm-up session of 5 trials. Each condition contained two blocks, each with 30 trials. Every participant performed the task three times in a row, using a different target-deciding principle each time. The order of the three principles was fully counterbalanced across the 18 participants. In total, the study included: 18 participants × 3 principles × 2 target sizes × 60 trials = 6,480 trials.

Results: Error rates measure the ratio of the number of incorrect selections over the total number of trials. The average error rates by target-deciding principle are shown in Figure 4.7. BayesianCommand reduced the error rates: on 4mm targets, it reduced the error rate by 37.2% and 39.3% compared to the boundary criterion and BTC; on 3mm targets, the error rate

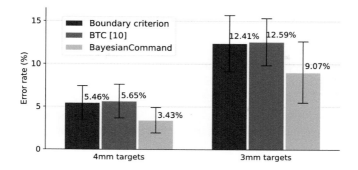

Figure 4.7 Average error rates (95% confidence interval) of the three target-deciding principles on 3mm and 4mm targets.

reduction was 26.9% and 28.0% respectively. ANOVA showed there was a significant main effect of the target-deciding principle on the error rates ($F_{2,34} = 7.98, p < .005$). Pairwise comparisons with Bonferroni adjustment showed that the difference was significant between BayesianCommand and BTC ($p = .004$) and between BayesianCommand and boundary criterion ($p = .017$). The 4mm targets were less error-prone and easier to select than the 3mm targets. ANOVA showed the differences were significant for target size ($F_{1,17} = 39.93, p < .005$). We did not observe a significant interaction effect of target-deciding principle $\times$ target size ($F_{2,34} = 0.33$, $p = .72$).

We compared the average target acquisition time, which was the elapsed time from a target being highlighted on the screen to the time the participant made the first selection. We considered only the first attempt in every trial, regardless of whether it was correct or not.

Target size	Boundary criterion	BTC [10]	BayesianCommand
4mm	0.74 ± 0.25	0.78 ± 0.26	0.71 ± 0.15
3mm	0.86 ± 0.26	0.88 ± 0.24	0.94 ± 0.44

Table 4.2 Average target acquisition time in seconds.

The target size had a main effect on the target acquisition time ($F_{1,17} = 6.98, p = .017$). We did not observe a main effect of the target-deciding principle ($F_{2,34} = 0.30, p = .75$) or any interaction effect ($F_{2,34} = 1.45, p = .25$). As shown in Table 4.2, using different target-deciding principles had little effect on the target acquisition time.

We used a subset of NASA-TLX [29] questions to measure the perceived workload of the task, including mental demand, physical demand and effort. The rating was from 0 to 10. The lower the rating, the better.

For 4mm targets, the median ratings were 4 (mental demand), 3 (physical demand) and 3 (effort) for using BayesianCommand; 3, 4, 4 for the boundary criterion and 3.5, 4, 4 for BTC. For 3mm targets, the median ratings were 4, 5, 5 for using BayesianCommand, 5, 5, 5 for the boundary criterion and 5, 5, 6 for BTC. The Bayesian approach was perceived slightly less mentally demanding than the other two principles on 3mm targets.

Example 2: Recall-Based Command Selection: Gestural Shortcuts on Smartphone

In the second example, we investigated how to apply the Bayesian framework for word-gesture command selection by combining the two-step likelihood model and the prior probability model.

Experiment II: Apply the Bayesian Framework for Word-Gesture Command Selection

Participants and Apparatus: Eighteen adults (4 females) aged between 23 to 31 (average 26.9 ± 2.5) participated in the study. The self-reported average usage time of mobile phones was 30.1 hours per week. Of the participants, 17 were right-handed. The median of self-reported familiarity with the QWERTY layout (1: not familiar at all, 5: very familiar) was 4.5. The median familiarity with gesture typing was 3. A Google Pixel running Android 9.0 was used for the study, as shown in Figure 4.8b.

Experiment Setup: The study was a within-subject design. The independent variable was the command deciding principles with three levels:

- *Bayesian framework:* We used Equation (4.3) to calculate prior probability and the two-step likelihood model in Equation (4.9) to calculate likelihood. Similar to Experiment I, we chose $k = 1$ in the prior probability model. This condition is also referred to as BayesianCommand.
- *Likelihood-only:* The command candidate with the highest likelihood value (the two-step likelihood model in Equation (4.9)) is the intended target. It uses likelihood value only.
- *Deterministic approach:* This is the typical target deciding principle for gestural command input. The gesture decoder used a set of available command names as the dictionary and matched the input gesture with the words in this dictionary. The word with the highest matching score was the intended command.

We used the same gesture decoder [78] across all three conditions. We swapped the language model in the original decoder with the command set used in the study (including all the trigger words for each command in Section 4.4.2). The composition of the command set is explained in detail later.

Before the study, participants were shown the 20 commands and their corresponding graphical representations. Participants needed to memorise $\geq 80\%$ of the commands before they could proceed to the formal study: They had to recall at least one of the trigger words of the commands. This procedure ensured that the results wouldn't be affected by participants' familiarity with the commands, or any external cause other than the three principles.

For each trial, an icon was first displayed on the screen as the target command. The participants then gestured the word in the white space below it to trigger the command. The input command name was shown to the participants after the finger lifted off from the screen, regardless of whether it was the intended command or not, as shown in Figure 4.8a. A trial was completed if the input command was correct or three failed attempts were made. For each condition, participants first performed a warm-up session of two trials, followed by 60 trials divided into two blocks. Participants were allowed to take a short break after the completion of each block. Each participant performed the task three times, with different target-deciding principles each time. The orders of three target-deciding principles were fully counterbalanced across participants.

(a)

(b)

Figure 4.8 (a) The application for Experiment II. The user draws a word-gesture command, then the target command is shown on the screen. (b) Experiment setup.

A subset of 12 commands was picked as the targets. The same set of commands were used across participants. We used the same item frequencies as

calculator	delete	keyboard	rotate
camera	download	mail	search
clock	edit	network	share
copy	file	print	weather
cut	help	recent	zoom

Table 4.3 List of the 20 commands. The underlined commands were tested in the experiment.

in Experiment I, i.e. the number of occurrences for the commands, was (7, 5, 4, 4, 2, 2, 1, 1, 1, 1, 1, 1). Participants were not informed of the frequency distribution of the items. The rest of the experiment design is similar to Experiment I. For each command, a set of 10 additional words for triggering this command was created from [18]. The list of commands is shown in Table 4.3. The command set included 20 commands. Each command has 11 corresponding trigger words (10 synonyms and the command name). The command set includes 220 words in total, which was incorporated into the decoder used in the study.

In total, the study included: 18 participants × 3 principles × 60 trials = 3,240 trials.

Results: Error rates measure the ratio of the number of incorrect gesture inputs over the total number of trials. The average error rates are shown in Figure 4.9.

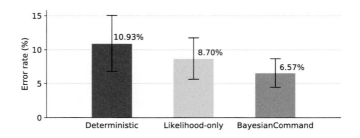

Figure 4.9 Average error rates (95% confidence interval) of the three principles for word-gesture shortcuts.

Using the Bayesian framework lowered the error rate by 39.9% and 24.5% compared to the deterministic and the likelihood-only approaches. ANOVA showed a significant main effect of the command-deciding principle on the error rates ($F_{2,34} = 5.56, p < .01$). Pairwise comparisons with Bonferroni adjustment showed that the difference was significant for BayesianCommand versus deterministic strategy ($p = .01$), but not for BayesianCommand versus likelihood-only ($p = .13$) or likelihood-only versus deterministic strategy ($p = .54$).

We compared the average command triggering time, which was the elapsed time from a target command icon being shown on the screen to the completion of a gesture command. The average command-triggering time was 2.91 ± 1.32 seconds for the deterministic strategy, 2.83 ± 0.98 seconds for the likelihood-only approach, and 2.98 ± 1.35 seconds for using BayesianCommand. We did not observe a main effect of the principle ($F_{2,34} = 0.19, p = .83$). This result also indicates that using different principles had little effect on the overall command triggering time.

We examined the trigger words of each command in the deterministic condition. We counted the number of unique trigger words (i.e. the decoded word from the gesture recogniser) of each command when it was successfully triggered. We excluded the first two conditions as they used probabilistic approaches, and the decoded word did not always correspond to the command label. The average number of trigger words was 2.92 ($SD = 1.38$) across the 12 tested commands. This result supported the validity of the graphical model (Figure 4.2) and our hypothesis that multiple trigger words could be used for a command.

A subset of NASA-TLX [29] questions was used to measure the perceived workload of the task. The range of the ratings was 1 to 10 (the smaller the rating, the better). The median ratings were 4 (mental demand), 2.5 (physical demand) and 3 (effort) for using BayesianCommand; 5, 4, 5 for the deterministic method and 4.5, 4, 5 for likelihood-only. The Bayesian approach was perceived as less demanding than the other two principles in all questions.

4.4 Discussion and Future Work

4.4.1 Discussion

Experiment I showed that the Bayesian approach outperformed the boundary criterion and BTC. Using the Bayesian framework substantially reduced the touchpointing error rate for both large and small menu targets. The reduction was especially remarkable for small targets: around 26% over both boundary criterion and BTC. It also showed that learning the prior probability distribution and combining it with the likelihood function outperforms using the likelihood function alone. Since the approach is algorithmic, these improvements were achieved without altering any UI layout, which was advantageous to frequency-based menu adaptation (e.g. morphing menu [16]), and thus less likely to slow users down or reduce user satisfaction [20].

BTC had almost identical error rates to the boundary criterion. According to the definition of BTC (Equation (1) in [10]), when the target sizes are equal, BTC is equivalent to comparing the distance from the touchpoint to the target centre (touchpoint-to-centre distance). Since the targets were of the same size and were arranged in a grid with no gaps between them in our experiment, BTC was equivalent to boundary criterion: the item whose boundary contains the touchpoint is also the target that has the shortest distance to the touchpoint.

Experiment II also showed that Bayesian framework effectively improved the input accuracy for word-gesture shortcuts. It reduced the command triggering error rate by 39.9% compared to the deterministic method. Notably, it performed better than the deterministic strategy when the gesture decoder failed to distinguish commands in similar shapes. For example, the average input error rate for the command 'cut' was 34.2% for the deterministic method, because its gesture trace was very similar to 'copy' on a QWERTY keyboard. Also, 65% of input for 'cut' was misrecognised to 'copy' for the deterministic method. BayesianCommand reduced the error rate to 16.2%, showing that combining prior and likelihood resolved some ambiguity introduced in the gesture decoding. It also outperformed the likelihood-only approach by 24.5%. The results also substantiated our claim that fully applying the Bayesian framework could be adopted in various applications to deal with the input uncertainty.

Likewise, limiting the number of failed attempts to 3 had minor effects on the results. Nine participants correctly finished all trials in under three tries in all conditions. For the other nine participants, the average percentage of trials that failed three times was $1.30 \pm 1.67\%$ for the deterministic approach, $1.02 \pm 1.53\%$ for likelihood-only and $1.30 \pm 2.78\%$ for BayesianCommand. Compared to the other two conditions, BayesianCommand did not introduce more trials that failed three times or contained inaccessible commands. The percentage increased over Experiment I as gesture input is a more complex procedure with higher cognitive and motor execution demands.

4.4.2 Future Work

How can designers or developers leverage the benefits of the Bayesian approach? Many applications and software have collected usage patterns of menus, buttons and commands – e.g. the command usage frequency of Microsoft Word 2003 [28]. These accumulated frequencies and patterns could serve as the prior probability for adopting the Bayesian framework; the system can then adapt the prior probability as a user is interacting with the system. If no prior command history is available, the system can assume every command is equally probable and learn the distribution probability as more actions are observed. We would also point out that the Bayesian framework works under the assumption that the command input distribution model can be established. It might not show significant benefits for some applications if their command frequency model is not that obvious (e.g. Maps).

While the second example focused on word-gesture command selection, the Bayesian framework could be extended to other gestural command input methods, e.g. Command Strokes [37], CommandBoard [1] or HotStrokes [17]. The prior probability and the likelihood models are independent of the gesture decoder, thus being applicable to other gestural command input methods with minor modification. Investigation on the generalisation and other recall-based methods are interesting future work.

References

[1] J. Alvina, C. F. Griggio, X. Bi and W. E. Mackay. 2017. CommandBoard: creating a general-purpose command gesture input space for soft keyboard. Pages 17–28 of: *Proceedings of the 30th Annual ACM Symposium on User Interface Software and Technology*. UIST '17. Association for Computing Machinery.

[2] G. Apitz, F. Guimbretière and S. Zhai. 2008. Foundations for designing and evaluating user interfaces based on the crossing paradigm. *ACM Transactions on Computer Human–Interaction*, **17**(2), 9:1–9:42.

[3] C. Appert and S. Zhai. 2009. Using strokes as command shortcuts: cognitive benefits and toolkit support. Pages 2289–2298 of: *Proceedings of the SIGCHI Conference on Human Factors in Computing Systems*. CHI '09. Association for Computing Machinery.

[4] S. Azenkot and S. Zhai. 2012. Touch behavior with different postures on soft smartphone keyboards. Pages 251–260 of: *Proceedings of the 14th International Conference on Human-computer Interaction with Mobile Devices and Services*. MobileHCI '12. Association for Computing Machinery.

[5] G. Bailly, E. Lecolinet and L. Nigay. 2007. Wave menus: improving the novice mode of hierarchical marking menus. Pages 475–88 of: *Proceedings of the 11th IFIP TC 13 International Conference on Human–Computer Interaction*. INTERACT'07. Springer-Verlag.

[6] G. Bailly, E. Lecolinet and L. Nigay. 2008. Flower menus: a new type of marking menu with large menu breadth, within groups and efficient expert mode memorization. Pages 15–22 of: *Proceedings of the Working Conference on Advanced Visual Interfaces*. AVI '08. Association for Computing Machinery.

[7] O. Bau and W. E. Mackay. 2008. OctoPocus: a dynamic guide for learning gesture-based command sets. Pages 37–46 of: *Proceedings of the 21st Annual ACM Symposium on User Interface Software and Technology*. UIST '08. Association for Computing Machinery.

[8] H.Benko, A. D. Wilson and P. Baudisch . 2006. Precise selection techniques for multi-touch screens. Pages 1263–1272 of: *Proceedings of the SIGCHI Conference on Human Factors in Computing Systems*. CHI '06. Association for Computing Machinery.

[9] X. Bi, Y. Li and S. Zhai. 2013. FFitts law: modeling finger touch with Fitts' law. Pages 1363–1372 of: *Proceedings of the SIGCHI Conference on Human Factors in Computing Systems*. CHI '13. Association for Computing Machinery.

[10] X. Bi and S. Zhai. 2013. Bayesian touch: a statistical criterion of target selection with finger touch. Pages 51–60 of: *Proceedings of the 26th Annual ACM Symposium on User Interface Software and Technology*. UIST '13. Association for Computing Machinery.

[11] X. Bi and S. Zhai. 2016. Predicting finger-touch accuracy based on the dual Gaussian distribution model. Pages 313–319 of: *Proceedings of the 29th Annual Symposium on User Interface Software and Technology*. UIST '16. Association for Computing Machinery.

[12] R. Blanch, Y. Guiard and M. Beaudouin-Lafon. 2004. Semantic pointing: improving target acquisition with control-Display ratio adaptation. Pages 519–526 of: *Proceedings of the SIGCHI Conference on Human Factors in Computing Systems*. CHI '04. Association for Computing Machinery.

[13] D. Buschek and F. Alt. 2015. TouchML: a machine learning toolkit for modelling spatial touch targeting behaviour. Pages 110–114 of: *Proceedings of the 20th International Conference on Intelligent User Interfaces*. IUI '15. Association for Computing Machinery.

[14] D. Buschek and F. Alt. 2017. ProbUI: generalising touch target representations to enable declarative gesture definition for probabilistic GUIs. Pages 4640–4653 of: *Proceedings of the 2017 CHI Conference on Human Factors in Computing Systems*. CHI '17. Association for Computing Machinery.

[15] E. K. Choe, K. Shinohara, P. K. Chilana, M. Dixon and J. O. Wobbrock. 2009. Exploring the design of accessible goal crossing desktop widgets. Pages 3733–3738 of: *CHI '09 Extended Abstracts on Human Factors in Computing Systems*. CHI EA '09. Association for Computing Machinery.

[16] A. Cockburn, C. Gutwin and S. Greenberg. 2007. A predictive model of menu performance. Pages 627–636 of: *Proceedings of the SIGCHI Conference on Human Factors in Computing Systems*. CHI '07. Association for Computing Machinery.

[17] W. Cui, J. Zheng, B. Lewis, D. Vogel and X. Bi. 2019. HotStrokes: word-gesture shortcuts on a trackpad. Pages 165:1–165:13 of: *Proceedings of the 2019 CHI Conference on Human Factors in Computing Systems*. CHI '19. Association for Computing Machinery.

[18] Dictionary.com. 2019. *Thesaurus.com – Synonyms and Antonyms of Words*. www.thesaurus.com/. Accessed 6 August 2019.

[19] S. R. Ellis and R. J. Hitchcock. 1986. The emergence of Zipf's law: spontaneous encoding optimization by users of a command language. *IEEE Transactions on Systems, Man, and Cybernetics*, **16**(3), 423–427.

[20] L. Findlater and K. Z. Gajos. 2009. Design space and evaluation challenges of adaptive graphical user interfaces. *AI Magazine*, **30**(4), 68.

[21] J. Francone, G. Bailly, E. Lecolinet, N. Mandran and L. Nigay. 2010. Wavelet menus on handheld devices: stacking metaphor for novice mode and eyes-Free selection for expert mode. Pages 173–180 of: *Proceedings of the International Conference on Advanced Visual Interfaces*. AVI '10. Association for Computing Machinery.

[22] J. Francone, G. Bailly, L. Nigay and E. Lecolinet. 2009. Wavelet menus: a stacking metaphor for adapting marking menus to mobile devices. Pages 49:1–49:4 of: *Proceedings of the 11th International Conference on Human-Computer Interaction with Mobile Devices and Services*. MobileHCI '09. Association for Computing Machinery.

[23] B. Fruchard, E. Lecolinet and O. Chapuis. 2017. MarkPad: augmenting touchpads for command selection. Pages 5630–5642 of: *Proceedings of the 2017 CHI Conference on Human Factors in Computing Systems*. CHI '17. Association for Computing Machinery.

[24] M. Goel, L. Findlater and J. Wobbrock. 2012. WalkType: using accelerometer data to accomodate situational impairments in mobile touch screen text entry. Pages 2687–2696 of: *Proceedings of the SIGCHI Conference on Human Factors in Computing Systems*. CHI '12. Association for Computing Machinery.

[25] M. Goel, J. Wobbrock and S. Patel. 2012. GripSense: using built-in sensors to detect hand posture and pressure on commodity mobile phones. Pages 545–554 of: *Proceedings of the 25th Annual ACM Symposium on User Interface Software and Technology*. UIST '12. Association for Computing Machinery.

[26] J. Goodman, G. Venolia, K. Steury and C. Parker. 2002. Language modeling for soft keyboards. Pages 194–195 of: *Proceedings of the 7th International Conference on Intelligent User Interfaces*. IUI '02. Association for Computing Machinery.

[27] T. Grossman, P. Dragicevic and R. Balakrishnan. 2007. Strategies for accelerating on-line learning of hotkeys. Pages 1591–1600 of: *Proceedings of the SIGCHI Conference on Human Factors in Computing Systems*. CHI '07. Association for Computing Machinery.

[28] J. Harris. 2006. *No Distaste for Paste (Why the UI, Part 7)*. https://blogs.msdn.microsoft.com/jensenh/2006/04/07/no-distaste-for-paste-why-the-ui-part-7/. Accessed 19 August 2019.

[29] S. G. Hart and L. E. Staveland. 1988. Development of NASA-TLX (Task Load Index): results of empirical and theoretical research. Pages 139–183 of: *Human Mental Workload. Advances in Psychology*, vol. 52. North-Holland.

[30] N. Henze, E. Rukzio and S. Boll. 2011. 100,000,000 taps: analysis and improvement of touch performance in the large. Pages 133–142 of: *Proceedings of the 13th International Conference on Human Computer Interaction with Mobile Devices and Services*. MobileHCI '11. Association for Computing Machinery.

[31] C. Holz and P, Baudisch. 2010. The generalized perceived input point model and how to double touch accuracy by extracting fingerprints. Pages 581–590 of: *Proceedings of the SIGCHI Conference on Human Factors in Computing Systems*. CHI '10. Association for Computing Machinery.

[32] C. Holz and P. Baudisch. 2011. Understanding touch. Pages 2501–2510 of: *Proceedings of the SIGCHI Conference on Human Factors in Computing Systems*. CHI '11. Association for Computing Machinery.

[33] H. Ka. 2013. Circling interface: an alternative interaction method for on-screen object manipulation. PhD thesis, University of Pittsburgh.

[34] K. Kin, B. Hartmann, T. DeRose and M. Agrawala. 2012. Proton: multitouch gestures as regular expressions. Pages 2885–2894 of: *Proceedings of the SIGCHI Conference on Human Factors in Computing Systems*. CHI '12. Association for Computing Machinery.

[35] K. Kin, B. Hartmann, T. DeRose and M. Agrawala. 2012. Proton++: a customizable declarative multitouch framework. Pages 477–486 of: *Proceedings of the 25th Annual ACM Symposium on User Interface Software and Technology*. UIST '12. Association for Computing Machinery.

[36] P. O. Kristensson and S. Zhai. 2004. SHARK2: a large vocabulary shorthand writing system for pen-Based computers. Pages 43–52 of: *Proceedings of the 17th Annual ACM Symposium on User Interface Software and Technology*. UIST '04. Association for Computing Machinery.

[37] P. O. Kristensson and S. Zhai. 2007. Command strokes with and without preview: using pen gestures on keyboard for command selection. Pages 1137–1146 of: *Proceedings of the SIGCHI Conference on Human Factors in Computing Systems*. CHI '07. Association for Computing Machinery.

[38] G. Kurtenbach and W. Buxton. 1994. User learning and performance with marking menus. Pages 258–264 of: *Proceedings of the SIGCHI Conference on Human Factors in Computing Systems*. CHI '94. Association for Computing Machinery.

[39] G. P. Kurtenbach. 1993. The design and evaluation of marking menus. PhD thesis, University of Toronto. UMI Order No. GAXNN-82896.

[40] G. P. Kurtenbach, A. J. Sellen and W. A. S. Buxton. 1993. An empirical evaluation of some articulatory and cognitive aspects of marking menus. *Human–Computer Interaction*, **8**(1), 1–23.

[41] Y. Li. 2010. Gesture search: a tool for fast mobile data access. Pages 87–96 of: *Proceedings of the 23nd Annual ACM Symposium on User Interface Software and Technology*. UIST '10. Association for Computing Machinery.

[42] Y. Li. 2010. Protractor: a fast and accurate gesture recognizer. Pages 2169–2172 of: *Proceedings of the SIGCHI Conference on Human Factors in Computing Systems*. CHI '10. Association for Computing Machinery.

[43] W. Liu, G. Bailly and A. Howes. 2017. Effects of frequency distribution on linear menu performance. Pages 1307–1312 of: *Proceedings of the 2017 CHI Conference on Human Factors in Computing Systems*. CHI '17. Association for Computing Machinery.

[44] W. Liu, R. L. D'Oliveira, M. Beaudouin-Lafon and O. Rioul. 2017. BIGnav: Bayesian information gain for guiding multiscale navigation. Pages 5869–5880 of: *Proceedings of the 2017 CHI Conference on Human Factors in Computing Systems*. CHI '17. Association for Computing Machinery.

[45] W. Liu, O. Rioul, J. McGrenere, W. E. Mackay and M. Beaudouin-Lafon. 2018. BIGFile: Bayesian information gain for fast file retrieval. Pages 385:1–385:13 of:

Proceedings of the 2018 CHI Conference on Human Factors in Computing Systems. CHI '18. Association for Computing Machinery.

[46] H. Lü, J. A. Fogarty and Y. Li. 2014. Gesture script: recognizing gestures and their structure using rendering scripts and interactively trained parts. Pages 1685–1694 of: *Proceedings of the SIGCHI Conference on Human Factors in Computing Systems.* CHI '14. Association for Computing Machinery.

[47] H. Lü and Y. Li. 2011. Gesture avatar: a technique for operating mobile user interfaces using gestures. Pages 207–16 of: *Proceedings of the SIGCHI Conference on Human Factors in Computing Systems.* CHI '11. Association for Computing Machinery.

[48] H. Lü and Y. Li. 2013. Gesture studio: authoring multi-touch interactions through demonstration and declaration. Pages 257–266 of: *Proceedings of the SIGCHI Conference on Human Factors in Computing Systems.* CHI '13. Association for Computing Machinery.

[49] H. Lü and Y. Li. 2015. Gesture on: enabling always-on touch gestures for fast mobile access from the device standby mode. Pages 3355–3364 of: *Proceedings of the 33rd Annual ACM Conference on Human Factors in Computing Systems.* CHI '15. Association for Computing Machinery.

[50] Y. Luo and D. Vogel. 2014. Crossing-based selection with direct touch input. Pages 2627–2636 of: *Proceedings of the SIGCHI Conference on Human Factors in Computing Systems.* CHI '14. Association for Computing Machinery.

[51] Y. Luo and D. Vogel. 2015. Pin-and-cross: a unimanual multitouch technique combining static touches with crossing selection. Pages 323–332 of: *Proceedings of the 28th Annual ACM Symposium on User Interface Software and Technology.* UIST '15. Association for Computing Machinery.

[52] A. Morrison, X. Xiong, M. Higgs, M. Bell and M. Chalmers. 2018. A large-scale study of iPhone app launch behaviour. Pages 344:1–344:13 of: *Proceedings of the 2018 CHI Conference on Human Factors in Computing Systems.* CHI '18. Association for Computing Machinery.

[53] T. Moscovich. 2009. Contact area interaction with sliding widgets. Pages 13–22 of: *Proceedings of the 22nd Annual ACM Symposium on User Interface Software and Technology.* UIST '09. Association for Computing Machinery.

[54] J. Musić and R. Murray-Smith. 2016. Nomadic input on mobile devices: the influence of touch input technique and walking speed on performance and offset modeling. *Human-Computer Interaction,* **31**(5), 420–71.

[55] D. L. Nelson, V. S. Reed and J. R. Walling. 1976. Pictorial superiority effect. *Journal of Experimental Psychology: Human Learning and Memory,* **2**(5), 523.

[56] A. Olwal, S. Feiner and S. Heyman. 2008. Rubbing and tapping for precise and rapid selection on touch-Screen displays. Pages 295–304 of: *Proceedings of the SIGCHI Conference on Human Factors in Computing Systems.* CHI '08. Association for Computing Machinery.

[57] C. Perin, P. Dragicevic and J.-D. Fekete. 2015. Crossets: manipulating multiple sliders by crossing. Pages 233–240 of: *Proceedings of the 41st Graphics Interface Conference.* GI '15. Canadian Information Processing Society.

[58] A. Roudaut, E. Lecolinet and Y. Guiard. 2009. MicroRolls: expanding touch-Screen input vocabulary by distinguishing rolls vs. slides of the thumb. Pages 927–936 of: *Proceedings of the SIGCHI Conference on Human Factors in Computing Systems.* CHI '09. Association for Computing Machinery.

[59] J. Schwarz. 2010. Towards a unified framework for modeling, dispatching, and interpreting uncertain Input. Pages 367–370 of: *Adjunct Proceedings of the 23rd Annual ACM Symposium on User Interface Software and Technology.* UIST '10. Association for Computing Machinery.

[60] J. Schwarz, S. Hudson, J. Mankoff and A. D. Wilson. 2010. A framework for robust and flexible handling of inputs with uncertainty. Pages 47–56 of: *Proceedings of the 23rd Annual ACM Symposium on User Interface Software and Technology.* UIST '10. Association for Computing Machinery.

[61] J. Schwarz, J. Mankoff and S. Hudson. 2011. Monte Carlo methods for managing interactive state, action and feedback under uncertainty. Pages 235–244 of: *Proceedings of the 24th Annual ACM Symposium on User Interface Software and Technology.* UIST '11. Association for Computing Machinery.

[62] D. Vogel and R. Balakrishnan. 2010. Occlusion-aware interfaces. Pages 263–272 of: *Proceedings of the SIGCHI Conference on Human Factors in Computing Systems.* CHI '10. Association for Computing Machinery.

[63] D. Vogel and P. Baudisch. 2007. Shift: a technique for operating pen-Based interfaces using touch. Pages 657–666 of: *Proceedings of the SIGCHI Conference on Human Factors in Computing Systems.* CHI '07. Association for Computing Machinery.

[64] D. Vogel and G. Casiez. 2012. Hand occlusion on a multi-touch tabletop. Pages 2307–2316 of: *Proceedings of the SIGCHI Conference on Human Factors in Computing Systems.* CHI '12. Association for Computing Machinery.

[65] D. J. Ward, A. F. Blackwell and D. J. C. MacKay. 2000. Dasher – a data entry interface using continuous gestures and language models. Pages 129–137 of: *Proceedings of the 13th Annual ACM Symposium on User Interface Software and Technology.* UIST '00. Association for Computing Machinery.

[66] D. Weir, S. Rogers, R. Murray-Smith and M. Löchtefeld. 2012. A user-Specific machine learning approach for improving touch accuracy on mobile devices. Pages 465–476 of: *Proceedings of the 25th Annual ACM Symposium on User Interface Software and Technology.* UIST '12. Association for Computing Machinery.

[67] D. Wigdor, C. Forlines, P. Baudisch, J. Barnwell and C. Shen. 2007. Lucid touch: a see-through mobile device. Pages 269–278 of: *Proceedings of the 20th Annual ACM Symposium on User Interface Software and Technology.* UIST '07. Association for Computing Machinery.

[68] D. Wigdor, D. Leigh, C. Forlines, S. Shipman, J. Barnwell, R. Balakrishnan and C. Shen. 2006. Under the table interaction. Pages 259–268 of: *Proceedings of the 19th Annual ACM Symposium on User Interface Software and Technology.* UIST '06. Association for Computing Machinery.

[69] J. Williamson. 2006. Continuous uncertain interaction. PhD thesis, University of Glasgow.

[70] J. O. Wobbrock, A. D. Wilson and Y. Li. 2007. Gestures without libraries, toolkits or training: a $1 recognizer for user interface prototypes. Pages 159–68 of:

Proceedings of the 20th Annual ACM Symposium on User Interface Software and Technology. UIST '07. Association for Computing Machinery.

[71] W. Xu, C. Yu and Y. Shi. 2011. RegionalSliding: enhancing target selection on touchscreen-based mobile devices. Pages 1261–1266 of: *CHI '11 Extended Abstracts on Human Factors in Computing Systems*. CHI EA '11. Association for Computing Machinery.

[72] K. Yatani, K. Partridge, M. Bern and M. W. Newman. 2008. Escape: a target selection technique using visually-cued gestures. Pages 285–294 of: *Proceedings of the SIGCHI Conference on Human Factors in Computing Systems*. CHI '08. Association for Computing Machinery.

[73] S. Zhai and P. O. Kristensson. 2003. Shorthand writing on stylus keyboard. Pages 97–104 of: *Proceedings of the SIGCHI Conference on Human Factors in Computing Systems*. CHI '03. Association for Computing Machinery.

[74] S. Zhai and P. O. Kristensson. 2012. The word-gesture keyboard: reimagining keyboard interaction. *Communications of the ACM*, **55**(9), 91–101.

[75] S. Zhao and R. Balakrishnan. 2004. Simple vs. compound mark hierarchical marking menus. Pages 33–42 of: *Proceedings of the 17th Annual ACM Symposium on User Interface Software and Technology*. UIST '04. Association for Computing Machinery.

[76] J. Zheng, X. Bi, K. Li, Y. Li and S. Zhai. 2018. M3 gesture menu: design and experimental analyses of marking menus for touchscreen mobile interaction. Pages 249:1–249:14 of: *Proceedings of the 2018 CHI Conference on Human Factors in Computing Systems*. CHI '18. Association for Computing Machinery.

[77] S. Zhu, T. Luo, X. Bi and S. Zhai. 2018. Typing on an invisible keyboard. Pages 439:1–439:13 of: *Proceedings of the 2018 CHI Conference on Human Factors in Computing Systems*. CHI '18. Association for Computing Machinery.

[78] S. Zhu, J. Zheng, S. Zhai and X. Bi. 2019. i'sFree: eyes-free gesture typing via a touch-enabled remote control. Pages 448:1–448:12 of: *Proceedings of the 2019 CHI Conference on Human Factors in Computing Systems*. CHI '19. Association for Computing Machinery.

[79] G. K. Zipf. 1949. *Human Behavior and the Principle of Least Effort: An Introduction to Human Ecology*. Addison-Wesley Press.

Appendix: Trigger Words of the Commands

Table 4.4 shows the 11 trigger words of the 20 commands in Experiment II. The words in bold were the trigger words used by the participants to trigger the corresponding commands in the deterministic condition. Note that these words represent the decoding output from the gesture recogniser, not necessarily what the participants intended to input.

Command	Trigger words
	calculator, calculators, calculate, calculation, compute, computer, computation, microcomputer, count, appraise, spreadsheet
	camera, **cameras**, camcorder, video, photograph, photographer, **cameraman**, videocamera, tripod, lens, projector
	clock, clocks, timer, time, dial, watch, stopwatch, alarm, tick, seconds, wristwatch
	copy, copying, copyist, replicate, replica, imitate, reproduce, emulate, duplicate, plagiarize, clone
	cut, cutting, slice, trim, reduce, prune, shorten, truncate, curtail, scissors, clippers
	delete, deleting, deleted, **deletes**, deletion, remove, uninstall, eliminate, omit, overwrite, discard
	download, **downloads**, downloadable, upload, redownload, load, **downloader**, browse, access, **file-sharing**, homepage
	edit, **editing**, editor, **edits**, **edited**, annotate, annotated, **essay**, alter, revise, rewrite
	file, files, **filing**, filename, filed, **refile**, **folder**, document, documents, archive, directory
	help, helping, helps, helped, assist, assistance, aid, support, avail, advice, service
	keyboard, **keyboards**, touchpad, trackpad, keypad, qwerty, stylus, numberpad, typewriter, typing, laptop
	mail, mails, **mailbox**, mailing, e-mail, email, spam, letter, postal, post, **mailed**
	network, networks, networked, net, internet, web, cable, channel, connectivity, networking, interconnect
	print, **printing**, **printer**, printed, reprint, handwritten, **photocopy**, **publish**, publication, booklet, distribute
	recent, subsequent, recently, latest, previous, past, earlier, prior, preceding, later, coming
	rotate, rotation, **rotational**, tilted, pivot, tilt, rotating, **rotated**, revolving, swivel, spin
	search, searches, **searching**, retrieve, discover, check, find, look, quest, searcher, scour
	share, shared, sharing, exchange, swap, commonality, pool, combine, express, collect, common
	weather, inclement, meteorological, windy, forecast, forecaster, winter, foggy, thunderstorm, meteorologist, blizzard
	zoom, zoom-in, close-up, enlarge, magnify, magnifier, scroll, augment, enhance, expand, amplify

Table 4.4 The trigger words for the 20 commands used in Experiment II.

5

Probabilistic UI Representation and Reasoning in Touch Interfaces

Daniel Buschek

Abstract

This chapter describes and reflects on the *ProbUI* framework as an example of a probabilistic alternative to the representation of input behaviour in graphical user interfaces (GUIs), in particular for touch: Concretely, *ProbUI* treats touch input as uncertain and decouples the GUI elements' visuals from their internal representation of user behaviour. This opens up three generalisations beyond the current standard of bounding boxes, namely allowing for probabilistic handling of input behaviour, multiple such behaviour representations per GUI element, and sequential models. The chapter reflects on *ProbUI* and more broadly on probabilistic approaches for building GUIs, extracting a generalised perspective of viewing GUIs as a method for structuring signal and noise in an abstract input behaviour space. The chapter concludes with implications for the design of (touch) GUIs to improve usability and user experience, in particular by building adaptive GUIs that reason about, and react to, ongoing user input behaviour.

5.1 Introduction

Touch interfaces and direct manipulation are used daily by millions of people, for example on public displays, terminals and personal mobile devices. Despite this, finger touch also presents several challenges for end users as well as interface designers and developers. For example, the finger has a certain size and softness to it (e.g. compared to a pen/stylus [2, 13]). Moreover, it often occludes its target on the screen at the very moment of impact [46, 47]. These factors make precise targeting tricky, leading to offsets [9, 14, 22, 49]. Users may also use different visual features of their finger to align them with the target (e.g. tip of finger, centre of nail, etc. [24]) – yet there may be a mismatch between this perceived feature and the sensed location [23]. Related, the relative locations of eye and finger and screen can result in a parallax effect, that is, a systematic shift between the expected point of touch and the sensed point [26]. Thus, humans are not pixel-perfectly accurate when operating a touch screen with their fingers. Further uncertainty might arise, for example, from movement [35, 36], or from the target itself (e.g. target changes [41]). In summary, touch input has considerable uncertainty. This insight drives the ideas in this chapter.

5.1.1 Uncertain Inputs Meet Deterministic GUIs

Human finger touch inputs vary and are uncertain [7, 8, 48]. This conclusion in itself may not seem very surprising for many users that have had experiences, for example, with mistyped messages. Nevertheless, most touch interfaces still handle user input *deterministically*. This is the key challenge at the focus of this chapter, for which we motivate, describe and reflect on a Bayesian approach:

> Touch GUIs today use deterministic representations of user input behaviour, which do not account for uncertainty in input intention and enactment.

For example, such deterministic representations are used in many modern mobile GUI frameworks, such as Android,[1] iOS[2] and the mobile web.[3] Concretely, GUI elements in these ecosystems are internally represented as *bounding boxes*, that is, rectangular screen areas. Interpreting user input then becomes a simple point-in-box test with a binary outcome: A GUI element (e.g. a button) is activated if the touchpoint falls within the bounds of the rectangle representing said element. Inversely, nothing happens if the touchpoint does not fall within such a rectangle.

Figure 5.1 illustrates two concrete problems with these deterministic representations: First (a), consider a touch barely missing a button, for example by a few pixels. Users might not even notice that the finger touchpoint was not on the button. Against their expectation, the button is not activated, resulting in a negative user experience, such as perceiving the user interface as not responsive or unreliable. Second (b), consider the related case of a user hitting a button at the edge with another button close by. Here, should the GUI still trigger the button, or maybe ask for confirmation? A deterministic GUI cannot react to such 'corner cases'. In contrast, explicitly considering uncertainty in user

---

[1] http://developer.android.com/guide/practices/ui_guidelines/widget_design.html#anatomy
[2] https://developer.apple.com/library/ios/documentation/UIKit/Reference/UIView_Class/index.html
[3] www.w3.org/TR/CSS21/box.html

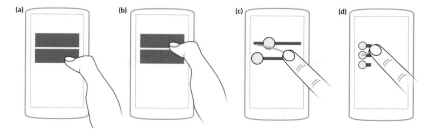

Figure 5.1 Examples of uncertain touch input: (a) Did the user intend to activate the button? (b) Which button did the user intend to activate here? (c) The user trailed off the slider while swiping. Should the system still continue to update the top slider or stop? Or switch to updating the bottom one (cf. [43])? (d) Which toggle should be flipped? Or maybe the user wants to flip two in one go (cf. [34])? Only if a GUI considers uncertainty can it adequately handle these questions. For instance, a deterministic GUI might (inappropriately) trigger a GUI element based on a strictly pixel-perfect interpretation of the touch input, while a probabilistic GUI could try to resolve uncertainty, for instance, through feedforward, adaptations, or by asking for clarification.

input here could inform a 'clarification' step. Finally, the figure shows further examples for uncertainty about the target GUI element as input unfolds over time (slider), and uncertainty from densely placed elements with identical state and thus activation behaviour (toggle buttons).

5.1.2 *ProbUI*: An Example of a Probabilistic Touch GUI Framework

The described mismatch between the uncertain nature of finger touch input and its deterministic treatment in current GUI interfaces motivates the Bayesian approach presented in this chapter. Concretely, we present and reflect on *ProbUI* [10], a probabilistic GUI framework – with 'framework' both in the sense of a set of concepts and a facilitating implementation (Android library).

As its core conceptual contribution, *ProbUI* replaces deterministic target models (bounding boxes) with probabilistic models ('bounding behaviours'). We focus on this conceptual aspect in this chapter. Furthermore, as an implemented library for (Android) developers, *ProbUI* practically demonstrates how such Bayesian concepts could be integrated into GUI development, without requiring developers to become experts in probabilistic modelling. As an overview, *ProbUI* has three goals:

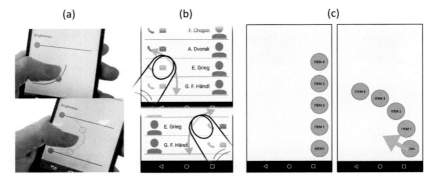

Figure 5.2 Probabilistic GUI elements created with *ProbUI*, which adapt to the user's hand posture. (a) A slider that bends to match the thumb trajectory for improved reachability and ergonomic use. (b) A contact list that flips its left-right alignments of portraits and buttons based on the scrolling trajectory, such that the thumb is always close to the call/email buttons and does not occlude the portrait/name. (c) A menu button which is either openend straight on tap, or in an arc-like arrangement via a short flick.

- *Decoupling view and behaviour model: ProbUI* decouples a GUI element's visuals from its internal representation of usage behaviour.
- *Generalising behaviour representation in GUIs: ProbUI* leads to three generalisations in how (touch) GUIs are modelled, namely allowing for probabilistic models, multiple models per element and sequential models.
- *Improving GUI development and use: ProbUI* opens new opportunities for developers to improve usability and user experience through 'live' inference during interaction (e.g. adaptive GUIs).

Figure 5.2 shows examples of probabilistic GUI elements realised with *ProbUI*. Section 5.3 presents *ProbUI* in more detail. Readers are also invited to refer to the original *ProbUI* paper [10], in particular for further details on supporting developers (e.g. a user study with developers).

5.1.3 Towards a Bayesian View on Touch GUIs

Starting with the concrete case of *ProbUI* in this introduction here, the Bayesian view at the focus of this book is present in the following three aspects:

1. *ProbUI treats touch input as uncertain events* by modelling a touch as a distribution of likely intended locations (2D Gaussian), and touch sequences (e.g. from sliding the finger) as probabilistic transitions (Hidden Markov Model [5, 39] with 2D Gaussian emissions). Thus, *ProbUI* uses probabilities as expressing beliefs (about the user's intended input) with uncertainty.

2. *ProbUI keeps and propagates uncertainty* from input to all GUI elements, instead of resolving it straight away. This means that GUIs can work with multiple 'hypotheses' about user intention as input behaviour unfolds. For example, a GUI might pre-load two content pages as long as the outcome of an ongoing navigation action is uncertain.

3. *ProbUI resolves uncertainty with probabilistic reasoning,* for instance when the user lifts the finger and a reaction by the GUI is expected. For example, here a GUI might implicitly infer the most likely action and trigger it, or present the user with an additional confirmation dialog to resolve uncertainty explicitly.

More broadly, in the context of this book, we take *ProbUI* as an exemplar for realising a Bayesian view for the specification of touch GUIs. Based on this example, we derive and discuss a generalised perspective on the conceptual role of GUIs:

> The key conceptual contribution of this chapter is the idea of viewing (probabilistic) GUI elements as a tool for meaningfully structuring expected behaviour and noise in the 'space' of input behaviour.

This aligns well with the Bayesian view in that it renders explicit the notion of a distribution of possible and likely behaviours, and probabilities as beliefs, rather than focusing on GUI elements as being triggered by discrete, concrete events.

Following this introduction, this chapter first discusses related work (Section 5.2), before describing *ProbUI* in more detail (Section 5.3). Taking this framework as an exemplar of a Bayesian approach to touch GUIs, Section 5.4 then extracts a generalised perspective. This leads to implications for interaction and design of touch GUIs (Section 5.5), before concluding with takeaways and an outlook (Section 5.6).

5.2 Related Work

As outlined in the introduction, input behaviour analyses show that touch input is uncertain [7, 8, 48]. In more detail, these challenges seem all the more acute if we consider that one of the most common uses of touch interfaces is on mobile devices, such as smartphones: Here, precise touch interaction is challenged by the limited screen space, the small target sizes [11], encumbrance [36], form factor and grip shifting [12, 14, 18], multitasking [37], as well as general body motion (e.g. touching while walking, or on a shaky bus ride) [35], and other situational impairments [40].

Mobile touch keyboards are one specific research area where bounding boxes have already been widely abandoned in favour of probabilistic models (e.g. [4, 19, 21, 50]). Concretely, these approaches typically model each key k as a 2D Gaussian that represents the conditional distribution $p(t|k)$, that is, the distribution of 2D touch locations t for that key. Using Bayes' rule, this is combined with a language context l (e.g. the last five words) as a prior over keys $p(k|l)$ [19], leading to a posterior over keys, for a given touch and context $p(k|t, l)$. Thus, the user's intended text can be inferred using both language context and touch behaviour. Similar (Bayesian) approaches have also been explored for touch targeting in general [8], and to model finger touch [7].

Other work explored related probabilistic ideas for *touch GUIs in general*, beyond keyboards or abstract targeting tasks: For example, Schwarz et al. [43] presented a framework for handling touch input with uncertainty. It represents touch input with a probability mass function and mentions further related ideas, such as a 'selection score' for sliders. Moreover, it proposes to send each touch event to *all* interactive GUI elements; thus essentially keeping multiple hypotheses, with probabilities, instead of immediately deciding for an element activation. This is a key part of a Bayesian perspective and also realised in *ProbUI*. They further extended this perspective in later work: This includes sampling-based (i.e. Monte Carlo) inference for handling probabilistic events with deterministic event handlers in GUIs [44], and an architecture for generating feedback in such probabilistic GUIs [45]. The work on *ProbUI* [10] detailed in this chapter builds on these ideas. While the above frameworks mostly assume that an input probability is provided already, *ProbUI* directly integrates a systematic approach for specifying the probabilistic models needed for getting these probabilities.

This leads us to other work on *modelling touch input probabilistically*: Beyond simple taps [7, 8, 48], touch input includes gestures, such as those finger movements on the screen involved in interactions like pan and zoom, yet also concepts such as crossing [3, 38] or encircling [17, 25]. There are tools for generating probabilistic recognition models for these and more complex gestures, including via demonstration (e.g. see [30–33]). In general, probabilistic recognisers provide probabilities for a set of gestures, given (touch) input sensor data (e.g. cf. [1, 6, 16, 31, 32]). *ProbUI* [10] could be extended to include existing gesture models. In its current version, it trades off supported complexity against the need for such external tools: It allows developers to declaratively define gestures, which are mapped to (simple) probabilistic models automatically. However, in this chapter, we focus less on this aspect of supporting developers, and rather on the conceptual core of Bayesian inference using such probabilities.

Nevertheless, *declarative gesture languages* present an alternative to training-data-based recognition: Most notably, *Proton* [28] follows an approach in which gestures are defined with a string of symbols and modifiers similar to regular expressions. However, declarative approaches typically struggle to integrate a notion of uncertainty [27–29, 42]. *Proton++* [29] attempts to remedy this (partly) by supporting the integration of 'confidence calculators' – yet these need to be realised by the developers in some way in the first place. These challenges motivated the new combination of declaration with probabilistic modelling in *ProbUI* [10].

To conclude this overview of the literature, what benefits do probabilistic GUIs provide? To name a few examples: Beyond the motivated handling of uncertain input, probabilistic GUIs are particularly well suited for realising *personalisation* and *adaptation*. For instance, the keyboard work referenced above is often motivated by tailoring the key model to an individual user, and/or other factors, such as the hand posture [50], or dynamic changes thereof [15]. Moreover, Schwarz et al. [45] dynamically generated feedback and confirmation flows, which can also be seen as adaptation. Finally, the example widgets presented in the original *ProbUI* paper [10] infer and adapt to one-handed smartphone use in particular.

5.3 Probabilistic GUI Representations: The Example of *ProbUI*

This section introduces *ProbUI* in terms of (1) its conceptual motivations and generalisations, and (2) its use of probabilistic models of touch and inference using these models. Figure 5.3 shows a development example as a visual overview of using *ProbUI*.

5.3.1 Conceptual Overview of *ProbUI*: From Bounding Boxes to Bounding Behaviours

To introduce the core conceptual ideas of *ProbUI*, we start with the observation that GUI elements today have two aligned representations:

- *Visual:* The 'look', for example, a green button of 120 by 35 pixels.
- *Functional:* A box that defines the button's active screen area. Touches within this box trigger the button.

In this box model, visual and functional representations are aligned: A button is triggered by hitting its visuals. As outlined in the introduction,

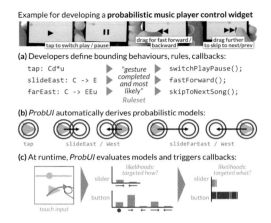

Example for developing a **probabilistic music player control widget**

(a) Developers define bounding behaviours, rules, callbacks:

tap: Cd*u   ▶ "gesture   ▶ switchPlayPause();
slideEast: C -> E   ▶ completed   ▶ fastForward();
                           and most
farEast: C -> EEu   ▶ likely"   ▶ skipToNextSong();
                           Ruleset

(b) *ProbUI* automatically derives probabilistic models:

tap   slideEast / West   slideFarEast / West

(c) At runtime, *ProbUI* evaluates models and triggers callbacks:

touch input   slider ⎰ likelihoods: slider ⎰ likelihoods:
                          targeted how?   targeted what?
                   button   button

Figure 5.3 Developing a probabilistic music player control widget with *ProbUI*: (a) Developers define behaviours (gestures) declaratively, plus rules that trigger callbacks. The used declarative language is not at the focus of this chapter but explained in the paper [10]. (b) Probabilistic gesture models (small HMMs) are derived from these declarations automatically by *ProbUI*. (c) Inference at runtime in two steps: First, *ProbUI* computes a posterior over behaviours per element, given current touch behaviour (i.e. *if used, how?*). Second, it computes a posterior over elements (i.e. *used what?*). This figure is based on the *ProbUI* paper [10].

ProbUI generalises from such traditional *bounding boxes* to what we here call *bounding behaviours*. Concretely, this generalisation manifests in three aspects, as explained in the following subsections. Therein, the idea of 'breaking the box', that is, breaking the one-to-one alignment of visual and functional representation, is at the heart of achieving generalisations, which later lead us to the new perspective on (probabilistic) GUIs described in Section 5.4.

From Rectangles to Sequences

The first issue with bounding boxes is that a box is an inadequate representation for anything other than a click or tap: For example, a point-in-box test can detect that a user tapped on a button yet does not adequately model a slider. For example, what if a phone user clearly slides their finger to the right, yet a bit below the slider's visuals? Nothing happens. The box model does not represent gestures, or generally input that unfolds over time, in particular when this shows variability.

Pragmatically realising a working GUI with boxes is common practice today. However, in the Bayesian view of this book, this results in extremely coarse and 'point-like' models of input behaviour without respecting variability.

This motivates providing a better, probabilistic model for gestures. Concretely, *ProbUI* uses probabilistic sequence models (small Hidden Markov Models) to model behaviour that yields sequences of touch events over time (e.g. a swipe). For intuition, we can roughly think of such models as chains of screen areas, instead of a single box. For instance, 'slide-to-unlock' is a gesture starting at the *left end* of the slider, then moving to the *right end*. Returning to the example above, using such a more general model, the slider can be implemented to stay responsive even if the user's finger happens to wiggle a bit, does not start on the slider or leaves the slider's visuals on the way.

From Deterministic to Probabilistic GUI Elements

The box model imposes a binary event handling: A touch is either in or out of a box. Referring back to the examples from the introduction, nothing happens if the user just barely misses a button: There is no notion of uncertainty, which could be used, for example, to trigger the most likely action or ask the user for clarification.

This motivates probabilistic event handling in a Bayesian view: Concretely, in *ProbUI*, UI designers and developers get a probability that the user intended to interact with a target, for each target, updated with each incoming touch event. This unlocks new design opportunities: For instance, an app may ask the user for clarification in case they pressed inbetween two buttons. Or the app may still trigger a button if the user missed its visuals only by a very small margin.

From 1:1 to 1:N Mappings

The box model imposes a direct mapping of GUI elements and users' input behaviour: Each GUI element can have only one box. Thus, users can trigger each element in only one specific way. For instance, while most users might tap on a button in an app, people with hand tremor might prefer a gesture (e.g. crossing [3, 38], encircling [17, 25]). The box model does not readily account for this. It thus hinders designing for accessibility and generally for more individual input behaviour. This is 'un-Bayesian' in the sense that a point-like solution is expected in the design (one box) and from the user (one implied behaviour).

This motivates a 1:N mapping, as realised in *ProbUI*: Here, each GUI element can react to multiple input behaviours. Instead of a single box, UI designers and developers may specify any number of input behaviours for the same GUI element. This introduces a Bayesian perspective in that designers and developers can account for a range of expectations regarding possible user behaviour. Put even more into Bayesian terms, they specify a prior over a range of possible behaviours. For instance, we might design a button that reacts to both the usual tap as well as to encircling it with the finger. This supports accessibility and individual preferences and input styles.

5.3.2 Technical Overview of *ProbUI*

Here we describe how *ProbUI* realises these conceptual generalisations.

A Basic Probabilistic Touch Model per GUI Element

It is common practice in work on probabilistic touch input to model a touch t for a target GUI element e as a 2D Gaussian $p(t|e)$ (e.g. [19–21, 48, 50]). Formally:

$$p(t|e) = \mathcal{N}(\mu_e, \Sigma_e). \tag{5.1}$$

ProbUI goes two steps further: First, instead of a *single* Gaussian (Equation (5.1)) it uses a graphical model with *multiple* ones, namely a Hidden Markov Model (HMM) [5, 39] with 2D Gaussian emissions. Second, *ProbUI* uses one or *multiple* such HMMs per GUI element, as described in more detail next.

A Composed Probabilistic Touch Model for a Whole GUI

ProbUI represents each touch behaviour (e.g. tap or a gesture) with an HMM. Crucially, multiple HMMs can be attached to a single GUI element (e.g. a button), to account for multiple possible touch behaviours (e.g. a button might react to both being tapped on and being crossed with the finger). Thus, a whole GUI of multiple elements is represented by a *set of sets of HMMs*.

More formally, a touch gesture input t is a sequence (i.e. trajectory) $t = t_1 t_2 \ldots t_n$ of touch locations $t_i = (x, y)^T$ or 'touch events'. Conceptually, 'event' here thus refers to the measurement of the finger's touch location (x, y) at a point in time. Technically, such events are fired regularly by the touchscreen driver (e.g. in Android) while the finger is on the screen.

Moreover, a whole GUI consists of a set of GUI elements $e \in E$, each of which has a set of touch behaviours B_e ('bounding behaviours'). As an overview of the probabilistic GUI model, we can look at the joint distribution as defined by the model's factorisation:

$$p(t, b, e) = p(t|b)p(b|e)p(e). \tag{5.2}$$

First, $p(t|b)$ is the likelihood of the touch sequence t given the defined bounding behaviour b, modelled as an HMM, as described above. In other words, if for example b describes a tap on a certain button, then $p(t|b)$ describes how likely it is that aiming to tap on this button leads to the touch input t.

Moreover, $p(b|e)$ is the probability of the bounding behaviour b defined for the element e. This is an element-specific prior over bounding behaviours. For example, if a button e_1 is set up by the developer to react to both tapping $b_{\text{tap-}e1}$ and crossing $b_{\text{cross-}e1}$, then $p(b_{\text{tap-}e1}|e_1)$ describes how likely it is that the user will tap (as opposed to cross) if they want to interact with this button. This is a prior in the sense that no touch data has been observed yet. Practically, this prior might be simply set as uniform, yet it could also be used, for example, to integrate knowledge about user preferences (e.g. a user might prefer to use elements like e in a certain way b – such as always crossing buttons instead of tapping them, cf. [3, 38]).

Similarly, $p(e)$ is a prior over the GUI's elements before any touch input is observed. Again, one might choose a uniform default, or use this to integrate further knowledge (e.g. consider those GUI elements more likely that trigger the user's most recently or frequently used functionality). For example, a simple choice dialog GUI might have two buttons e_{yes} and e_{no}, and we might know from past interactions that the user presses 'yes' in 90% of the cases. Then, $p(e_{\text{yes}})$ might be set to 0.9 (and $p(e_{\text{no}})$ to 0.1) to reflect this prior knowledge about the user's likely intention for interaction with the elements in this GUI.

Inference in the Probabilistic Touch GUI Model

ProbUI conducts inference 'live' while the user is interacting. It does this in two steps, which evaluate the 'how' and 'what' of the user's intention. The 'how' here means '*Which touch behaviour is the user performing?*', and the 'what' means '*Which GUI element do they want to interact with?*'.

Note that *ProbUI* evaluates the 'how' *before* the 'what': The intuition here is that a GUI element is the more likely intended target the better the bounding behaviours defined for it overall explain the currently observed user behaviour. In other words, *ProbUI* does not aim to refine the 'what' with the 'how', but rather sees the intention for a GUI target as the sum of all the possible ways of activating that target and their likelihood given the currently observed behaviour. Thus, we first evaluate for each GUI element $e \in E$ how likely each of its developer-defined bounding behaviours $b \in B_e$ is (which yields $p(b|t, e)$). Then, the 'what' – that is, $p(e|t)$ – follows by Bayes' rule with summation over all $b \in B_e$. The next two paragraphs describe this in detail.

Behaviour Probabilities ('Used How?') First, *ProbUI* evaluates the likelihood of the current touch input per behaviour via the HMMs – formally:

$$p(t|b) = \text{HMM}_b(t). \tag{5.3}$$

Therein, HMM_b is the HMM's evaluation function ([5, 39]); specifically, that of the HMM that represents the touch behaviour b. The posterior over $b \in B_e$ for e is then obtained with Bayes' rule:

$$p(b|t, e) = \frac{p(t|b)p(b|e)}{\sum\limits_{b_i \in B_e} p(t|b_i)p(b_i|e)}. \qquad (5.4)$$

As a result, in this step, *ProbUI* provides a distribution of user intention over touch behaviours (gestures) for each GUI element e, assuming that e was indeed the target, updated 'live' with each touch event.

GUI Element Probabilities ('Used What?') Building on the previous inference step, *ProbUI* further evaluates the user's intended target GUI element. Formally, it first obtains the likelihood $p(t|e)$ of touch input t given element e via marginalisation, summing over all behaviours $b_i \in B_e$ defined for e (i.e. the denominator of Equation (5.4)):

$$p(t|e) = \sum_{b_i \in B_e} p(t|b_i)p(b_i|e). \qquad (5.5)$$

This realises the intuition that a GUI element is more likely to be the user's intended target if the expected behaviour for this element better matches the user's current touch behaviour. Again, we obtain a posterior with an application of Bayes' rule:

$$p(e|t) = \frac{p(t|e)p(e)}{\sum\limits_{e_i \in E} p(t|e_i)p(e_i)}. \qquad (5.6)$$

As a result, *ProbUI* provides a distribution of user intention over GUI elements, updated 'live' with each touch event.

Computation Example

Consider this illustrating example (see Figure 5.4): This simple GUI has two buttons e_1 and e_2. For each button, we have defined a tapping behaviour and a crossing behaviour, as visualised via the Gaussian emission distributions (sigma ellipses) and HMM transitions (arrows). That is, this GUI has four bounding behaviours: Two for e_1 (i.e. $B_{e_1} = \{b_{\text{tap-e1}}, b_{\text{cross-e1}}\}$) and two for e_2 (i.e. $B_{e_2} = \{b_{\text{tap-e2}}, b_{\text{cross-e2}}\}$). Moreover, we assume uniform priors throughout, that is: $p(b|e) = 0.5$ for the two behaviours $b \in B_e$ per element e; and $p(e) = 0.5$ for both elements e. Now we consider the computations for the shown touch input t.

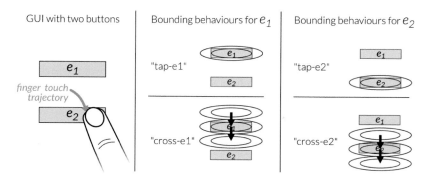

Figure 5.4 Example GUI and touch input, plus visualisations of the defined bounding behaviours, for the computation example in Section 5.3.2.

First Inference Step *ProbUI* first conducts the following computations:

1. Compute $p(t|b)$ for each b (Equation (5.3)). That is, we evaluate the likelihood of the touch input with the four behaviours' HMMs: $p(t|b_{\text{tap-}e1}) = \text{HMM}_{\text{tap-}e1}(t)$, $p(t|b_{\text{cross-}e1}) = \text{HMM}_{\text{cross-}e1}(t)$, $p(t|b_{\text{tap-}e2}) = \text{HMM}_{\text{tap-}e2}(t)$ and $p(t|b_{\text{cross-}e2}) = \text{HMM}_{\text{cross-}e2}(t)$. Concretely, this *evaluation problem* can be solved for HMMs with dynamic programming (the *forward algorithm* or *filtering*) [5, 39].

2. Apply Bayes' rule (Equation (5.4)) to obtain the posterior over behaviours per element; for example (assuming a uniform prior as mentioned above):

$$
\begin{aligned}
p(b_{\text{tap-}e1}|t, e_1) &= \frac{p(t|b_{\text{tap-}e1})p(b_{\text{tap-}e1}|e_1)}{p(t|b_{\text{tap-}e1})p(b_{\text{tap-}e1}|e_1) + p(t|b_{\text{cross-}e1})p(b_{\text{cross-}e1}|e_1)} \\
&= \frac{p(t|b_{\text{tap-}e1})0.5}{p(t|b_{\text{tap-}e1})0.5 + p(t|b_{\text{cross-}e1})0.5} \\
&= \frac{p(t|b_{\text{tap-}e1})}{p(t|b_{\text{tap-}e1}) + p(t|b_{\text{cross-}e1})},
\end{aligned}
\tag{5.7}
$$

and equivalently for $p(b_{\text{cross-}e1}|t, e_1)$, $p(b_{\text{tap-}e2}|t, e_2)$ and $p(b_{\text{cross-}e2}|t, e_2)$.

Second Inference Step Next, *ProbUI* conducts the following computations:

1. Compute $p(t|e)$ for each e (Equation (5.5)); for example:

$$
\begin{aligned}
p(t|e_1) &= p(t|b_{\text{tap-}e1})p(b_{\text{tap-}e1}|e_1) + p(t|b_{\text{cross-}e1})p(b_{\text{cross-}e1}|e_1) \\
&= p(t|b_{\text{tap-}e1})0.5 + p(t|b_{\text{cross-}e1})0.5,
\end{aligned}
\tag{5.8}
$$

and equivalently for $p(t|e_2)$. Note that for each e this is the denominator of the first inference step (Equation (5.7) line 2, i.e. before cancelling the '0.5's).

2. Apply Bayes' rule (Equation (5.6)) to obtain the posterior over elements; for example (again assuming a uniform prior):

$$
\begin{aligned}
p(e_1|t) &= \frac{p(t|e_1)p(e_1)}{p(t|e_1)p(e_1) + p(t|e_2)p(e_2)} \\
&= \frac{p(t|e_1)0.5}{p(t|e_1)0.5 + p(t|e_2)0.5} \\
&= \frac{p(t|e_1)}{p(t|e_1) + p(t|e_2)},
\end{aligned}
\tag{5.9}
$$

and equivalently for $p(e_2|t)$.

To conclude this example, we have now computed the posteriors over bounding behaviours per GUI element, and the posterior over elements. Looking at the concrete touch input in Figure 5.4, numerically here $p(e_2|t)$ will be much higher than $p(e_1|t)$ since the finger has clearly moved onto e_2. That is, both $p(t|b_{\text{tap-e2}})$ and $p(t|b_{\text{cross-e2}})$ are much higher than $p(t|b_{\text{tap-e1}})$ and $p(t|b_{\text{cross-e1}})$.

For a more complex GUI, we might have more complex touch gestures (i.e. HMMs with more states and transitions), more bounding behaviours per GUI element, and/or more GUI elements – yet these computational steps stay the same.

Summary

In the described way, *ProbUI* realises the conceptual generalisations described in Section 5.3.1. As a result, for ongoing touch interactions, *ProbUI* conducts Bayesian reasoning to infer both (1) a posterior distribution over intended touch behaviours (gestures), and (2) a posterior distribution over intended targets in the GUI. Compare this to traditional, deterministic GUIs: These only provide a 'Hit? yes/no' decision for a GUI element at the end of a touch input.

5.4 Generalised Perspective: GUI Elements Structure Signal and Noise in Interaction

Reflecting on the concepts of *ProbUI* and the overarching Bayesian perspective in this book, this section derives a generalised perspective on the role of GUI elements. In particular, as outlined in the introduction, we propose to view GUI elements as a tool for meaningfully structuring an abstract 'space' of input behaviour.

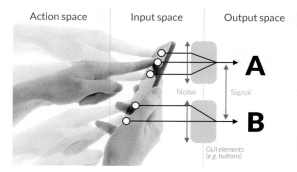

Figure 5.5 Touch interaction conceptualised with three spaces: *action space* (possible user actions, e.g. hand and finger motion), *input space* (possible sensed input, e.g. touchpoints), and *output space* (possible system reaction, e.g. printing a character). In this perspective, the GUI (here: grey buttons) links *input space* and *output space* by mapping the user's input to appropriate output. Thus, GUI elements can be seen as a *tool for structuring this mapping*, regarding what is to be considered 'signal' (here: A vs B) and what is 'noise' (here: varying touch locations on each button).

Specifically, we describe a conceptual framework which examines (touch) interactions and interfaces in three spaces: *action space*, *input space* and *output space*. We then examine the role of GUI elements within this framework to anchor and highlight the probabilistic and Bayesian concepts of *ProbUI* in this generalised view. Finally, we discuss implications of this view in the context of this book.

5.4.1 Three Linked Spaces of Possibilities

A vital aspect of a Bayesian viewpoint is the consideration of *distributions over various possibilities*, or degrees of beliefs, instead of a collapsed, point-like or deterministic view. Such distributions require considering a space of possible values. Thus, here we make explicit the conceptual spaces involved in (touch) interactions to which such distributions might relate. Figure 5.5 provides an overview of the three spaces, described below: *action space*, *input space* and *output space*.

Action Space

As visualised in Figure 5.5, the *action space* (left) conceptually captures the space of possible user actions, that is, (physical) user behaviours, which might be involved in interaction. For the case of mobile touch, for example, the figure hints at the various possibilities of approaching the phone with the hand

and finger, the involved angles, placement of the finger on the screen and so on (cf. [23, 24]). In contrast to the traditional focus on touch as a screen event, considering this action space here contributes to the Bayesian view by acknowledging the broader space of possible user behaviours from which behaviour variations and potential uncertainty in touch interpretations arise.

Input Space

Figure 5.5 (centre) shows the *input space*: In the example of mobile touch, this is the phone's touchscreen. Conceptually, one might say that the (hardware) sensor acts as a filter: As indicated in the figure, the user's rich behaviour in the action space may result in a number of varied yet limited sensor values (e.g. touch locations) in this input space. Again, this view highlights a source of uncertainty, arising from the limited sensing (e.g. 2D touch point) compared to the 'rich' user behaviour (e.g. hand and finger motion in 3D space).

Output Space

Finally, as shown in Figure 5.5 (right), the user input leads to a perceivable reaction in the *output space*. In our example of mobile touch here, this typically involves a GUI change, triggering a functionality (e.g. calling someone, entering text), and so on. As an abstract example in the figure, there are two buttons (screen regions) that trigger either 'A' or 'B' as their output. In contrast to handling deterministic events, this highlights the space of possibilities in *interpreting* and *reacting to* the input sensed in the input space.

5.4.2 A Bayesian Interpretation of the Three Spaces

We now outline a Bayesian interpretation of the three spaces and the way they are involved in touch interaction. To anchor this in a practical example, we further reflect on how this matches the concepts of *ProbUI*.

Generating Actions and Inputs

Viewing users as generators of actions, their preconceptions, legacy bias, expectations, impairments, habits, usage context and so on may be seen as casting a *prior* over the *action space*. The user may also *update* this prior based on *observations* – e.g. of other users, the UI and context – to infer which actions are appropriate to use in said interface. This inference is further conditioned on the user's current, specific intention (e.g. call person X), which we do not further investigate here.

The user's chosen action can then be seen as a 'signal' to the system via the GUI (e.g. touching *here* and not *there*), while the specific execution introduces 'noise' (precise touch location varies even for the same intended finger placement).

As demonstrated with *ProbUI*, the GUI can support a variety of possible signals by providing more than one way of using each element, and it can account for noise by handling input probabilistically, instead of as deterministic events.

Interpreting Actions and Inputs

Fundamentally, the GUI (and system) has to link input space and output space: It has to infer an interpretation of the user's input to map it to appropriate output and/or system (re-)actions. Here, this chapter proposes to view the designed GUI (e.g. choice and placement of elements) as a tool for structuring this mapping between the spaces, regarding what is to be considered 'signal' and what is 'noise'.

For example, in the traditional GUI frameworks with a 1:1 alignment of visuals and function (Section 5.3.1), the placement of a 'login button' provides such structure by splitting the input space into two regions – those pixels that trigger 'login' and those that do not. With this split, the GUI designer has created an opportunity for a behaviour 'signal' (binary: hitting the button or not). At the same time, the designer has implicitly specified varying finger placement across the pixels *on* the button to be treated as 'noise': Functionally, the design does not intend for this variability to matter; the login happens regardless of where the button is hit.

As demonstrated with *ProbUI*, this can be generalised towards much more complex structures (e.g. gesture models) and a probabilistic, Bayesian treatment (e.g. no hard boundaries, multiple parallel hypotheses).

5.4.3 Conceptual Summary

In summary, we propose that GUI elements can be seen as tools for structuring input and interpretation in two ways:

- *Structuring the input space:* The behaviour representations attached to UI elements, as shown in *ProbUI*, can be understood as distributions of expected user behaviour in *input space*. We might thus see UI elements, and their bounding behaviours, as a designer's tool for composing a prior over input behaviour.

- *Structuring the mapping from input space to output space:* UI elements enable UI designers to implicitly structure the space of expected user behaviour with regard to what they consider as (intentional) behavioural signal and as noise in interactions. We might thus consider such a mapping as defining posterior updating, that is, inference, given input behaviour.

Overall, this perspective highlights the value of the probabilistic view: Deterministic GUI elements can only describe the most basic structures in input space and the most basic mappings (bounding boxes). In contrast, probabilistic GUI elements in this view empower GUI designers to explore much richer structures and mappings (or: priors and ways of updating/inference), as demonstrated, for instance, in the generalisations and examples of *ProbUI*.

5.5 Discussion and Implications

5.5.1 Benefits and Limitations of *ProbUI*

As a critical appraisal, we reflect on the specific example of *ProbUI*: As a key benefit for designers/developers, it allows for building probabilistic touch GUIs – meaning GUIs that embed probabilistic models of input behaviour and integrate Bayesian reasoning about user intention (which behaviour and which target). For the end user, concrete benefits (e.g. for usability) mostly depend on how developers make use of these probabilistic capabilities (e.g. implementing useful GUI adaptations).

ProbUI in its current implementation also has limitations. First, the touch models are not directly learned from data, but rather derived from GUI properties (e.g. button sizes; see the paper for more details [10]). This was motivated by allowing developers to still simply 'code' behaviours (as with bounding boxes), instead of having to collect behaviour data first. However, *ProbUI* could be flexibly extended, for example, to allow developers to integrate HMMs fitted on collected data, to use other probabilistic models, or to let models learn from interactions over time (e.g. refitting HMMs after each interaction).

Moreover, in its current use of HMMs, *ProbUI* is limited in the gesture complexity that can be expressed, due to the approach of deriving models from GUI properties without requiring training data. This could be improved by working on more expressive declarative gesture languages (cf. [28, 29]), tools for gesture authoring (e.g. [30, 32, 33]) or a data-driven approach in which (black box) models are fitted on recorded touch gestures.

Another limitation of expressiveness in *ProbUI* is the discrete treatment of time: The HMMs place distributions in space but treat sequences as subsequent discrete events (e.g. touch events). For instance, this makes it challenging to describe behaviours with speed, such as distinguishing between a slow and fast swipe. *ProbUI* addressed this with the option to specify overall interaction times, yet such constraints sit on top of the probabilistic model, and are not an integral part of it. Similar issues exist in related declarative frameworks [28, 29]. Overall, this is an open issue regarding a fully Bayesian treatment to address in future work.

5.5.2 Computational Costs of Probabilistic Touch Interfaces

ProbUI keeps a distribution over multiple hypotheses (e.g. all events are passed to all GUI elements to compute the posterior distribution). This clearly increases the computational costs compared to traditional GUIs with bounding boxes. In particular, both computation and memory costs grow with the number of elements and the number of behaviours defined for each element. This was not a problem for the prototype GUIs in the *ProbUI* experiments [10], and the number of parallel GUI elements seems also limited by usability considerations. Nevertheless, computational costs for such Bayesian approaches in GUIs can be addressed by parallelisation of computations. For example, for *ProbUI*, the likelihoods (i.e. evaluations of the HMMs) could be easily run as separate jobs, to then be merged for computing the posterior.

5.5.3 Implications and Takeaways for Research and Design

The three spaces together *raise awareness of the simplification steps in GUIs,* even for interactions as seemingly simply as a single touch: A touch does not appear out of nowhere, but results from rich behaviour, funnelled through limited sensing. As a takeaway, keeping this simplification in mind might facilitate designing GUIs that respect the 'messiness' (or uncertainty) of real-life contexts and conditions, in particular for mobile and ubicomp devices that involve touch.

Related, the perspective emphasises how the GUI also processes input in a role similar to the sensor: Like a touch sensor, *the GUI also introduces a limited resolution that funnels behaviour interpretation.* As a takeaway, from an interaction point of view, GUI design could be considered as far less detached from hardware sensor choices as currently typical development practices may make it seem. A Bayesian treatment further highlights this and can be expected to make joint design decisions across sensor and UI even more rewarding, in the sense that the Bayesian approach is interested in propagating uncertainty through these steps.

To make this view of GUIs explicit, we introduced the terms signal and noise in this context: Targeting a GUI element vs another (or none at all) allows users to transmit a signal to the system. In contrast, input variations relating to a single element and output mapping are effectively noise. Thus, GUI design implies specification of prior beliefs about user behaviour that is likely, (ir)relevant, to be supported and so on, as well as how related inference will be conducted to trigger system actions. The key takeaway here is that this holds for *any* GUI – probabilistic or not. Therefore, by *explicitly* reflecting on and formulating GUI design in probabilistic and Bayesian terms, we stand to gain richer tools for building GUIs with useful priors and inferences, which, ultimately, facilitate building usable interactive systems.

5.6 Conclusion and Outlook

Today, touch GUIs use bounding boxes to represent user behaviour. These do not account for uncertainty in input and intention, although research has shown that touch input comes with considerable uncertainty due to a range of influencing factors. This chapter presented *ProbUI* as an example of how a probabilistic alternative to bounding boxes could look like. Concretely, *ProbUI* treats touch input as uncertain and decouples the GUI elements' visuals from their internal representation of user behaviour. This opens up three generalisations beyond bounding boxes, namely allowing for probabilistic models, multiple models per element and sequential models. With these capabilities, *ProbUI* opens new opportunities for developers to improve usability and user experience, in particular by building adaptive GUIs that reason about, and react to, ongoing user input behaviour.

More generally, this chapter conceptualised touch interaction with three spaces: *action space* (user actions, e.g. hand and finger motion), *input space* (sensed input, e.g. touchpoints) and *output space* (system reaction, e.g. printing a character). The GUI thus defines a mapping from input space to output space. In this view, GUI elements can be seen as a tool for structuring this mapping. By placing GUI elements and defining their bounding behaviours, designers/developer define what is to be considered 'signal' (e.g. printing A vs B) and what is 'noise' (e.g. varying touch locations on each button).

This view highlights that deterministic GUIs (bounding boxes) represent only the most basic structures and mappings (rectangles in screen space). In contrast, probabilistic GUI elements allow for much richer structures and mappings. This realises a Bayesian approach in both modelling and inference, as shown in *ProbUI*: Instead of being limited to one hard-cut rectangular area per element, GUI designers/developers can account for a *distribution* of expected input behaviours per GUI element, along with a *prior* (e.g. informed by preferred past use, context, etc.). Complementary, instead of one binary decision (touch in bounding box or not), the probabilistic, Bayesian GUI computes a full *posterior* distribution over all behaviours (used how?) and GUI elements (used what?), using probabilities to express uncertain (system) beliefs about the user's intention.

In light of this conceptual perspective, we hope that *ProbUI* and its adaptive GUI widgets serve the reader as an insightful starting point for future research and design efforts on probabilistic interfaces, for touch and beyond.

References

[1] D. Anderson, C. Bailey and M. Skubic. 2004. Hidden Markov model symbol recognition for sketch-based interfaces. Pages 15–21 of: *AAAI Fall Symposium Technical Report* (6). AAAI Press.

[2] M. Annett and Bischof. 2015. Hands, hover, and nibs: understanding stylus accuracy on tablets. Pages 203–210 of: *Proceedings of the 41st Graphics Interface Conference*. GI '15. Canadian Information Processing Society.

[3] G. Apitz, F. Guimbretière and S. Zhai. 2008. Foundations for Designing and Evaluating User Interfaces Based on the Crossing Paradigm. *ACM Transactions on Computer–Human Interaction*, **17**(2), 9:1–9:42.

[4] T. Baldwin and J. Chai. 2012. Towards online adaptation and personalization of key-target resizing for mobile devices. Pages 11–20 of: *Proceedings of the 2012 ACM International Conference on Intelligent User Interfaces*. IUI '12. Association for Computing Machinery.

[5] D. Barber. 2012. *Bayesian Reasoning and Machine Learning*. Cambridge University Press.

[6] F. Bevilacqua, B. Zamborlin, A. Sypniewski, N. Schnell, F. Guédy and N. Rasamimanana. 2010. Continuous realtime gesture following and recognition. Pages 73–84 of: *Proceedings of the 8th International Conference on Gesture in Embodied Communication and Human-Computer Interaction*. GW '09. Springer-Verlag.

[7] X. Bi, Y. Li and S. Zhai. 2013. FFitts law: modeling finger touch with Fitts' law. Pages 1363–1372 of: *Proceedings of the SIGCHI Conference on Human Factors in Computing Systems*. CHI '13. Association for Computing Machinery.

[8] X. Bi and S. Zhai. 2013. Bayesian touch: a statistical criterion of target selection with finger touch. Pages 51–60 of: *Proceedings of the 26th Annual ACM Symposium on User Interface Software and Technology*. UIST '13. Association for Computing Machinery.

[9] D. Buschek and F. Alt. 2015. TouchML: a machine learning toolkit for modelling spatial touch targeting behaviour. Pages 110–114 of: *Proceedings of the 20th International Conference on Intelligent User Interfaces*. IUI '15. Association for Computing Machinery.

[10] D. Buschek and F. Alt. 2017. ProbUI: generalising touch target representations to enable declarative gesture definition for probabilistic GUIs. Page 4640–4653 of: *Proceedings of the 2017 CHI Conference on Human Factors in Computing Systems.* CHI '17. Association for Computing Machinery.

[11] D. Buschek, A. De Luca and F. Alt . 2016. Evaluating the influence of targets and hand postures on touch-based behavioural biometrics. Page 1349–1361 of: *Proceedings of the 2016 CHI Conference on Human Factors in Computing Systems.* CHI '16. Association for Computing Machinery.

[12] D. Buschek, M. Hackenschmied and F. Alt. 2017. Dynamic UI adaptations for one-handed use of large mobile touchscreen devices. Pages 184–201 of: R. Bernhaupt, G. Dalvi, A. Joshi, D. K. Balkrishan, J. O'Neill and M. Winckler, eds., *Human–Computer Interaction – INTERACT 2017.* Lecture Notes in Computer Science. Springer International Publishing.

[13] D. Buschek, J. Kinshofer and F. Alt. 2018. A comparative evaluation of spatial targeting behaviour patterns for finger and stylus tapping on mobile touchscreen devices. *Proceedings of the ACM on Interactive, Mobile, Wearable and Ubiquitous Technologies,* **1**(4), 1–21.

[14] D. Buschek, S. Rogers and R. Murray-Smith. 2013. User-specific touch models in a cross-device context. Pages 382–391 of: *Proceedings of the 15th International Conference on Human–Computer Interaction with Mobile Devices and Services.* MobileHCI '13. Association for Computing Machinery.

[15] D. Buschek, O. Schoenleben and A. Oulasvirta. 2014. Improving accuracy in back-of-device multitouch typing: a clustering-Based approach to keyboard updating. Pages 57–66 of: *Proceedings of the 19th International Conference on Intelligent User Interfaces.* IUI '14. Association for Computing Machinery.

[16] B. Caramiaux, N. Montecchio, A. Tanaka and F. Bevilacqua. 2014. Adaptive gesture recognition with variation estimation for interactive systems. *ACM Transactions on Interactive Intelligent Systems,* **4**(4), 18:1–18:34.

[17] E. K. Choe, K. Shinohara, P. K. Chilana, M. Dixon and J. O. Wobbrock. 2009. Exploring the design of accessible goal crossing desktop widgets. Pages 3733–3738 of: *CHI '09 Extended Abstracts on Human Factors in Computing Systems.* CHI EA '09. Association for Computing Machinery.

[18] R. Eardley, A. Roudaut, S. Gill and S. J. Thompson. 2017. Understanding grip shifts: how form factors impact hand movements on mobile phones. Pages 4680–4691 of: *Proceedings of the 2017 CHI Conference on Human Factors in Computing Systems.* CHI '17. Association for Computing Machinery.

[19] J. Goodman, G. Venolia, K. Steury and C. Parker. 2002. Language modeling for soft keyboards. Pages 194–195 of: *Proceedings of the 7th International Conference on Intelligent User Interfaces.* IUI '02. Association for Computing Machinery.

[20] T. Grossman and R. Balakrishnan. 2005. A probabilistic approach to modeling two-dimensional pointing. *ACM Transactions on Computer–Human Interaction,* **12**(3), 435–459.

[21] A. Gunawardana, T. Paek and C. Meek. 2010. Usability guided key-target resizing for soft keyboards. Pages 111–118 of: *Proceedings of the 15th International*

Conference on Intelligent User Interfaces. IUI '10. Association for Computing Machinery.

[22] N. Henze, E. Rukzio and S. Boll. 2011. 100,000,000 taps: analysis and improvement of touch performance in the large. Page 133–142 of: *Proceedings of the 13th International Conference on Human Computer Interaction with Mobile Devices and Services*. MobileHCI '11. Association for Computing Machinery.

[23] C. Holz and P. Baudisch. 2010. The generalized perceived input point model and how to double touch accuracy by extracting fingerprints. Pages 581–590 of: *Proceedings of the SIGCHI Conference on Human Factors in Computing Systems*. CHI '10. Association for Computing Machinery.

[24] C. Holz and P. Baudisch. 2011. Understanding touch. Pages 2501–2510 of: *Proceedings of the SIGCHI Conference on Human Factors in Computing Systems*. CHI '11. Association for Computing Machinery.

[25] H. W. Ka. 2013. Circling interface: an alternative interaction method for on-screen object manipulation. PhD thesis, University of Pittsburgh.

[26] M. Khamis, D. Buschek, T. Thieron, F. Alt and A. Bulling. 2018. EyePACT: eye-based parallax correction on touch-enabled interactive displays. *Proceedings of the ACM on Interactive, Mobile, Wearable and Ubiquitous Technologies*, **1**(4), 1–18.

[27] S. H. Khandkar and F. Maurer. 2010. A domain specific language to define gestures for multi-touch applications. Pages 2:1–2:6 of: *Proceedings of the 10th Workshop on Domain-Specific Modeling*. DSM '10. Association for Computing Machinery.

[28] K. Kin, B. Hartmann, T. DeRose and M. Agrawala. 2012. Proton: multitouch gestures as regular expressions. Pages 2885–2894 of: *Proceedings of the SIGCHI Conference on Human Factors in Computing Systems*. CHI '12. Association for Computing Machinery.

[29] K. Kin, B. Hartmann, T. DeRose and M. Agrawala. 2012. Proton++: a customizable declarative multitouch framework. Pages 477–486 of: *Proceedings of the 25th Annual ACM Symposium on User Interface Software and Technology*. UIST '12. Association for Computing Machinery.

[30] Y. Li, H. Lu and H. Zhang. 2014. Optimistic programming of touch interaction. *ACM Transactions on Computer–Human Interaction*, **21**(4), 24:1–24:24.

[31] H. Lü and Y. Li. 2012. Gesture coder: a tool for programming multi-Touch gestures by demonstration. Pages 2875–2884 of: *Proceedings of the SIGCHI Conference on Human Factors in Computing Systems*. CHI '12. Association for Computing Machinery.

[32] H. Lü and Y. Li. 2013. Gesture studio: authoring multi-touch interactions through demonstration and declaration. Pages 257–266 of: *Proceedings of the SIGCHI Conference on Human Factors in Computing Systems*. CHI '13. Association for Computing Machinery.

[33] H. Lü, J. A. Fogarty and Y. Li. 2014. Gesture script: recognizing gestures and their structure using rendering scripts and interactively trained parts. Pages 1685–1694 of: *Proceedings of the 32nd Annual ACM Conference on Human Factors in Computing Systems*. CHI '14. Association for Computing Machinery.

[34] T. Moscovich. 2009. Contact area interaction with sliding widgets. Pages 13–22 of: *Proceedings of the 22nd Annual ACM Symposium on User Interface Software and Technology*. UIST '09. Association for Computing Machinery.

[35] J. Musi, D. Weir, R. Murray-Smith and S. Rogers. 2016. Modelling and correcting for the impact of the gait cycle on touch screen typing accuracy. *mUX: The Journal of Mobile User Experience*, **5**(1).

[36] A. Ng, J. Williamson and S. Brewster. 2015. The effects of encumbrance and mobility on touch-based gesture interactions for mobile phones. Pages 536–546 of: *Proceedings of the 17th International Conference on Human-Computer Interaction with Mobile Devices and Services*. MobileHCI '15. Association for Computing Machinery.

[37] A. Oulasvirta and J. Bergstrom-Lehtovirta. 2011. Ease of juggling: studying the effects of manual multitasking. Pages 3103–3112 of: *Proceedings of the SIGCHI Conference on Human Factors in Computing Systems*. CHI '11. Association for Computing Machinery.

[38] C. Perin, P. Dragicevic and J.-D. Fekete. 2015. Crossets: manipulating multiple sliders by crossing. Pages 233–240 of: *Proceedings of the 41st Graphics Interface Conference*. GI '15. Canadian Information Processing Society.

[39] L. Rabiner. 1989. A tutorial on hidden Markov models and selected applications in speech recognition. *Proceedings of the IEEE*, **77**(2), 257–286.

[40] Z. Sarsenbayeva, N. van Berkel, C. Luo, V. Kostakos and J. Goncalves. 2017. Challenges of situational impairments during interaction with mobile devices. Page 477–481 of: *Proceedings of the 29th Australian Conference on Computer-Human Interaction*. OZCHI '17. Association for Computing Machinery.

[41] P. Schmid, S. Malacria, A. Cockburn and M. Nancel. 2020. Interaction interferences: implications of last-instant system state changes. Pages 516–528 of: *Proceedings of the 33rd Annual ACM Symposium on User Interface Software and Technology*. Virtual Event, Association for Computing Machinery.

[42] C. Scholliers, L. Hoste, B. Signer and De Meuter, Wolfgang. 2011. Midas: A Declarative Multi-touch Interaction Framework. Pages 49–56 of: *Proceedings of the Fifth International Conference on Tangible, Embedded, and Embodied Interaction*. TEI '11. Association for Computing Machinery.

[43] J. Schwarz, S. Hudson, J. Mankoff and A. D. Wilson, Andrew D. 2010. A framework for robust and flexible handling of inputs with uncertainty. Pages 47–56 of: *Proceedings of the 23nd Annual ACM Symposium on User Interface Software and Technology*. UIST '10. Association for Computing Machinery.

[44] J. Schwarz, J. Mankoff and S. Hudson. 2011. Monte Carlo methods for managing interactive state, action and feedback under uncertainty. Pages 235–244 of: *Proceedings of the 24th Annual ACM Symposium on User Interface Software and Technology*. UIST '11. Association for Computing Machinery.

[45] J. Schwarz, J. Mankoff and S. E. Hudson, Scott E. 2015. An architecture for generating interactive feedback in probabilistic user interfaces. Pages 2545–2554 of: *Proceedings of the 33rd Annual ACM Conference on Human Factors in Computing Systems*. CHI '15. Association for Computing Machinery.

[46] D. Vogel and R. Balakrishnan. 2010. Occlusion-aware interfaces. Pages 263–272 of: *Proceedings of the SIGCHI Conference on Human Factors in Computing Systems*. CHI '10. Association for Computing Machinery.

[47] D. Vogel and P. Baudisch. 2007. Shift: a technique for operating pen-based interfaces using touch. Pages 657–666 of: *Proceedings of the SIGCHI Conference on Human Factors in Computing Systems*. CHI '07. Association for Computing Machinery.

[48] F. Wang and X. Ren. 2009. Empirical evaluation for finger input properties in multi-Touch interaction. Pages 1063–1072 of: *Proceedings of the SIGCHI Conference on Human Factors in Computing Systems*. CHI '09. Association for Computing Machinery.

[49] D. Weir, S. Rogers, R. Murray-Smith and M. Löchtefeld. 2012. A user-specific machine learning approach for improving touch accuracy on mobile devices. Pages 465–476 of: *Proceedings of the 25th Annual ACM Symposium on User Interface Software and Technology*. UIST '12. Association for Computing Machinery.

[50] Y. Yin, T. Y. Ouyang, K. Partridge and S. Zhai. 2013. Making touchscreen keyboards adaptive to keys, hand postures, and individuals: a hierarchical spatial backoff model approach. Pages 2775–2784 of: *Proceedings of the SIGCHI Conference on Human Factors in Computing Systems*. CHI '13. Association for Computing Machinery.

6

Statistical Keyboard Decoding

Dylan Gaines, John Dudley, Per Ola Kristensson and Keith Vertanen

Abstract

Text entry is a core task in our daily interaction with computers. Entering text using a keyboard remains the de facto standard due to its familiarity and efficiency. However, new interaction settings and devices make conventional text entry using a keyboard more challenging due to higher levels of uncertainty in detected user interaction events. For example, entering text on a smartwatch using a very small keyboard layout naturally results in less accurate touches than can be expected when entering text on a smartphone or physical keyboard. Fortunately, statistical keyboard decoding provides a technique for inferring the user's intended text from their noisy input. The approach leverages Bayes' Rule to help identify the most probable word given a model of the user's uncertain touch interaction and known language regularities. This chapter provides an overview of statistical keyboard decoding and examines the various design parameters which are known to dictate its performance. Two illustrative case studies are also presented which demonstrate how statistical keyboard decoding can enable efficient text entry in challenging interaction settings.

6.1 Introduction

As we delve deeper into the digital age, there are a multitude of devices on which a person might want to enter text, whether to send a message to someone, look up information or jot down a note. However, most mobile devices no longer have keyboards with physical buttons that are distinct keys. When a user cannot feel the boundaries between keys, it becomes less likely that each keystroke will land exactly on the key it was intended to. While incorrect key presses could be corrected using the backspace button, the number of minute errors in everyday text entry could make this a time-consuming task. Instead, statistical keyboard decoding attempts to determine a user's intended word by making use of the location of each key press along with a variety of additional information such as previous key presses for the current word and any surrounding text. This can make text entry much easier on virtual keyboards with a small form factor, such as on a smartwatch, or with noisy sensing, such as a mid-air augmented or virtual reality keyboard.

Statistical keyboard decoding relies on Bayes' rule to determine the most probable intended text given the noisy input provided by the user. It is possible to think of text as a message which the user is trying to convey and the input events as the noisy signal containing this message. The goal in statistical keyboard decoding is to find the most probable intended message given the evidence contained in the signal as well as any prior information available on the types of messages to be expected. In other words, we seek to find the message with the maximum posterior conditional probability given the signal.

From Bayes' rule, we know that this conditional probability is proportional to the product of the likelihood of the signal given the message and the prior probability of the message. A statistical keyboard decoder functions by estimating both these values. The likelihood of the signal given the message is estimated using a probabilistic keyboard model relating touchpoints to the probability of that touch being associated with a given letter. The prior probability of a message is estimated using a model capturing the known regularities of the language.

Formally, let O denote the sequence of noisy observations for which we would like to find the most probable input text T. Commonly, a user is typing a word that adds to some previously written text to the left T_{left}. In some cases (e.g. inserting a word in an existing text passage), there may also be some text to the right of the current location T_{right}. We would like to search for the text hypothesis T_{input} that yields the most probable text T given the input observations and the surrounding text:

$$T = \arg\max_{T_{\text{input}}} P(T_{\text{input}} \mid O, T_{\text{left}}, T_{\text{right}}). \qquad (6.1)$$

This can be rewritten using Bayes' rule as:

$$T = \arg\max_{T_{\text{input}}} \frac{P(O, T_{\text{left}}, T_{\text{right}} \mid T_{\text{input}})P(T_{\text{input}})}{P(O, T_{\text{left}}, T_{\text{right}})}. \qquad (6.2)$$

Assuming O is conditionally independent of T_{left} and T_{right} given T_{input}, and ignoring the denominator which is invariant to the search over T_{input}, this can be written as:

$$T = \arg \max_{T_{\text{input}}} \underbrace{P(O \mid T_{\text{input}})}_{\substack{\text{keyboard} \\ \text{model}}} \underbrace{P(T_{\text{left}}, T_{\text{input}}, T_{\text{right}})}_{\substack{\text{language} \\ \text{model}}} . \qquad (6.3)$$

This general concept is illustrated in Figure 6.1. The user generates a touch event in Figure 6.1(a) which falls between the Q and W keys. The likelihood of this event belonging to Q or W is estimated using the keyboard model which knows the size and location of each key as shown in Figure 6.1(b). Finally, a language model provides the prior probability of the intended letter being a Q or W based on the previous input events and sentence context.

As described, the foundation of statistical keyboard decoding on Bayes' rule is elegant and relatively simple to implement. In practice, however, there are numerous design parameters that govern or mitigate the noise characteristics of the input signal, influence the behaviour of the decoder or impact the user interaction. As a simple example, consider how the size of the keyboard relative to the finger shown in Figure 6.1 is likely to produce touch error characteristics that are radically different from a keyboard where keys are much smaller – say, a fraction of the width of the finger. Other practical considerations encountered include deciding how and when decoding events are triggered.

This chapter provides an introduction to keyboard decoding and reviews several critical design parameters which dictate its performance and behaviour. Two informative case studies will illustrate how thoughtful exploitation of these design parameters can deliver significant performance improvements in challenging text entry scenarios. Finally, we discuss the various challenges and opportunities encountered with statistical keyboard decoding and highlight promising future directions.

6.2 Keyboard Decoding

There are many working parts to a statistical keyboard decoder. The main portion that forms the foundation of text entry and drives the rest of the decoding process is a user's input. On a soft keyboard (one without distinct key boundaries, such as an on-screen smartphone keyboard), we gather user input as a sequence of touch event observations. Each touch event observation has x- and y-coordinates associated with it, as well as a timestamp. Commonly, just the last x- and y-coordinate of a touch event is used to model what key the user intended to hit.

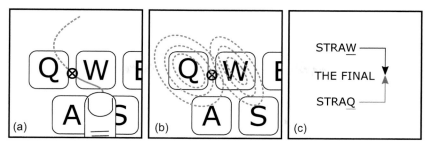

Figure 6.1 An example of a user typing on a mid-air virtual keyboard to illustrate: (a) the generation of a touch event; (b) the estimation of the likelihood given the touch location; and (c) the estimation of the prior probability of the text based on regularities of the language.

The first step in the decoding process is to assess each observation with a keyboard model. The keyboard model has the coordinates of each key centre along with an associated two-dimensional Gaussian distribution for each key. These distributions describe the likelihood of a touch event intended for each particular key landing on the surrounding area. An example was shown previously in Figure 6.1(b). When the keyboard model (sometimes referred to as the touch model) receives an observation, it estimates the likelihood of observing each key given that touch location and outputs a set of key hypotheses along with their associated likelihoods.

We then accumulate the set of key hypotheses from the previous step with prior key hypotheses (since the last full word decode) to produce several observation sequence hypotheses. For each new observation, we also include in this accumulation the possibility that the key was not intended (i.e. insertion error) or is preceded by a key for which no observation was captured (i.e. omission error). This yields a set of key observation sequence hypotheses with associated accumulated likelihoods.

From this point, there are several options to consider. One of these options is to use a character language model, as done by Goodman et al. [10]. The character language model is trained on lots of text in order to learn which character sequences are likely and which are unlikely. An n-gram model refers to a model that considers sequences of length n (e.g. a 3-gram character model considers sequences of 3 characters). A 3-gram character language model can generate a probability distribution over all possible next-character alternatives given the previous two characters. This model promotes English-like key observation sequences in our hypotheses and penalises highly unlikely sequences. For example, in Figure 6.1, W is more likely than Q given the prior text RA. The output of this stage is a re-ranked set of hypotheses (highly unlikely hypotheses can be eliminated for efficiency).

An alternative approach is to use a word language model. This operates similarly to the character language model, but on the word level, taking into account the previous words in the sentence as opposed to the previous characters in the word. Likely words will be promoted in the list, while less likely words will be demoted. Words that are not in the decoder's vocab can still survive as hypotheses. This is important for writing uncommon words or names that may not appear in a dictionary, referred to as out-of-vocabulary (OOV) words. The output of this stage is a re-ranked set of hypotheses based on the word language model.

Our description of keyboard decoding here was high-level. There are numerous details related to how input events are modelled, how the search for hypotheses is implemented, and how free parameters of the decoder are optimised. For a more detailed treatment, see [19].

Many factors can be included in the decoding process to influence the probabilities under the models. We can use varying amounts of left or right context to feed into our n-gram models, but we can also leverage other contextual information that isn't necessarily directly related to the text. Goel et al. [9] factored the accelerometer data from a smartphone device into their keyboard model to help classify touch events while users were walking. Weir et al. [27] used the pressure of each tap to modulate the amount of uncertainty associated with that touch event. Eye tracking could also be used to provide the decoder with additional information on the user's intended tap target.

6.3 Design Parameters

In this section, we review six important design parameters which dictate the performance and behaviour of a statistical keyboard decoder. In the context of text entry, performance is typically evaluated using two main metrics. The first metric is entry rate, which we measure in words per minute (WPM). This is calculated by dividing the number of words typed (assuming a word is five characters, including a space) by the time in minutes. The next metric is character error rate (CER), which is the number of insertions, deletions and substitutions needed to convert the entered text to the reference text divided by the number of characters in the reference text, and then multiplied by 100%. In the following subsections we describe various design parameters and how they can affect both the decoding process and human performance.

6.3.1 Device Size

While statistical keyboard decoding is useful on keyboards of all sizes, it is particularly beneficial on small keyboards. Since small keyboards have such small key targets, it is more likely that any given tap will not fall directly on the intended key. As such, we can use statistical decoding to try to reduce the error rate.

The primary effect of device size on the decoding process lies in the touch, or keyboard, model. As the size of a keyboard shrinks, the size of each key shrinks. Users' fingers, however, remain the same size. This can make it more difficult for users to precisely target specific keys. To accurately model this, we need to adjust our touch model to have larger Gaussians (relative to key size), effectively being less punishing for hypotheses that are further away from a key. An extreme example would be to first consider a keyboard that is the same size as an A4-sized piece of paper. The letters 'Q' and 'D' would be several centimetres apart, and the likelihood that a tap landing on one was intended for the other would be very small. On a smartwatch keyboard, however, this distance would be only a few millimetres. The likelihood of these characters being mixed up is much higher than on the A4-sized keyboard.

6.3.2 Input Length

A decoder can accept varying amounts of information at once. While providing more observations at once can provide additional context and increase the chances of the decoder predicting the correct text, it can also create more possibilities for the decoder to consider. If a decoder accepts only a single character at a time, the number of possibilities are restricted to the 26 letters (assuming we are using English) and any punctuation included in the alphabet such as the apostrophe. However, the decoder can rely only on the location of the tap and previous characters that have been typed as context to determine which character was most likely.

Alternatively, let's say the decoder accepts an entire word at a time. The number of possibilities would be much greater since we can combine characters in many different ways. However, it would give the decoder more information with which to conduct its search. It would know the approximate length of the word and the approximate locations of each character, which would narrow the possibilities greatly. The decoder would also be able to adjust the probabilities of each hypothesis based on its language model and how likely the hypothesised word is to occur after the text to its left. The main downside to a larger input size is that the decoder has to calculate the probabilities for each hypothesis. Since this quickly becomes computationally infeasible, we need to prune which possibilities to fully compute. This creates a trade-off between speed and accuracy in the decoding process, since as we prune more hypotheses we risk eliminating the hypothesis that actually contains the user's intended text.

6.3.3 Delimiter

When performing statistical keyboard decoding, another design parameter that we can change is the delimiter between words. This allows users to denote where one word ends and the next starts. This can signal to the system it is time to decode pending observations into text. In a typical touchscreen keyboard, tapping the space key is treated as a deterministic input event that triggers recognition of the previously typed word.

An alternative design explored by Vertanen et al. [25] was to have users enter an entire sentence of text prior to decoding. They explored three different ways of delimiting word boundaries when typing on a touchscreen keyboard:

- SPACE: The first delimiter was a space key, as one might find on a standard physical or on-screen keyboard. The decoder treated the space character as it did the rest of the characters. There was an associated probability that this space was an insertion error (i.e. the user did not intend to type a space), an omission error (i.e. the user missed typing a space) or a substitution error (i.e. the user intended to type a different key).
- SWIPE: The second delimiter was a right swipe gesture, which the decoder treated deterministically. In this condition, spaces were signified only by this swipe gesture, and the decoder was not able to insert, delete or change spaces into other characters.
- NOSPACE: The final delimiter was no delimiter at all. In this condition, participants flowed from one word directly into the next, and the decoder inferred where the spaces should have been.

In all three conditions, users entered the entire sentence before the observation sequences were sent to the decoder. The entry and error rate results for each of these delimiters are displayed in Figure 6.2. While the SPACE and NOSPACE conditions had similar entry rates, the SWIPE condition was significantly slower. The SWIPE and SPACE conditions had similar error rates, but the NOSPACE condition had a higher and more variable error rate.

This difference in entry rate was likely due to the time it took to perform the swipe action itself, since it is not a gesture most people are used to performing during text entry, and it takes longer than a single tap. The difference in error rate, however, is likely related more to the decoding process. Decoding the

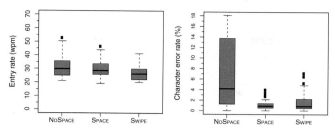

Figure 6.2 Entry rate (left) and error rate (right) using different delimiters to type on a mobile phone virtual keyboard [25].

entire sentence at once leaves a lot of possible hypotheses with not a lot of context to help narrow them down. This effect is magnified when we remove all information about word delimiters, as done in the NoSpace condition. With the presence of delimiters, even probabilistic ones as in the Space condition, the decoder has general guidance on how many words there are in the sentence and how long each one is. Removing delimiters takes away all of this information from the decoder, impeding its ability to accurately decipher the input.

One example of this would be with the phrase 'what a pain'. Without spaces, this becomes 'whatapain'. While the true phrase would be one possible hypothesis, another might be 'what's pain'. Since 'a' and 's' are near each other on a QWERTY keyboard, this could be a common mistake. The decoder would also be able to insert an apostrophe to make the hypothesis better fit the vocabulary and language models. If the spaces were provided deterministically (as in the Swipe condition), this would not be a potential hypothesis since it does not fit the observations. With probabilistic spaces (as in the Space condition), 'what's pain' could still be a hypothesis, but it would likely have a much lower probability. The probability that a user hit space instead of apostrophe is much lower, given the distance between those keys, than a user omitting an apostrophe altogether.

6.3.4 Error Correction and Prevention Features

With any non-deterministic input method there are always sure to be errors, both by the user and the decoder. Correcting these errors after they occur is a necessary part of interface design. Some example correction features include a backspace key and autocorrect algorithms. Autocorrect algorithms are used to correct user mistakes once they complete a word by replacing the typed text with the most likely intended text if the probability exceeds a threshold. However, these algorithms are not perfect and can replace a user's intended text with text the decoder deemed more likely, resulting in the user having to take further corrective action.

Since correcting errors takes additional time and may break the fluidity of text entry, preventing errors is a worthwhile endeavour. Word suggestions are a common type of error prevention feature, since they allow the user to see exactly what will be entered before they select it. There are two types of word suggestions: prefix completions and word corrections. Prefix completions seek to predict the remainder of the user's word based on what they have typed so far (the prefix) and potentially other contexts, depending on the decoder. They can treat the prefix as either deterministic truth, or as noisy input that may be changed. Word corrections, on the other hand, seek to provide likely suggestions on the assumption that the user has entered a full word. This operates similarly to many autocorrect algorithms, but allows the user to see and select potential outcomes before designating the end of a word.

6.3.5 Indication of Users' Uncertainty

When users enter text on any interface, there is always a level of uncertainty. If the user is not looking at the interface, if the interface is very small or if the user is entering text very quickly, their uncertainty may be high. If they can clearly see which character they are typing and are entering text precisely, their uncertainty may be low. It can be useful to have ways for the user to indicate this level of uncertainty to the decoder. The decoder may use this information to incur larger penalties when changing characters the user is more certain of, or vice versa.

Weir et al. [27] developed ForceType, which gave users an opportunity to indicate their uncertainty to the decoder. If the user tapped lightly, the language model would have more weight in the predictions, using surrounding characters and words to decode the text. If the user tapped firmly, the touch model (keyboard model) would have more weight, causing the location of the tap to be used to decode that character. This weighting between models was a gradient, so it was not a matter of light or firm, but rather of how much pressure was placed on the screen. The authors found that this technique increased the overall entry rate of participants and reduced the need for error correction.

Another example of a proactive error prevention feature is the *precision selection mode* used by Dudley et al. [4] in their virtual keyboard deployed on an augmented reality headset. This precision selection mode, illustrated in Figure 6.3, allowed users to explicitly designate particular key selections as certain. Certain selections were not subject to change during decoding. A secondary cursor appeared when the user moved their hand through the

Figure 6.3 Precision key selection sequence as illustrated in Dudley et al. [4]. (1) User starts with their hand above the keyboard plane. (2) User moves their hand inside the keyboard plane. (3) After a short delay, a secondary cursor appears, allowing the user to perform precise selections of desired letters.

augmented reality keyboard. The user could then move the secondary cursor to their desired letter and confirm selection by dwelling for one second. This feature could be kept active to select subsequent letters with certainty as well. In the study performed by Dudley et al. [4], participant error rates were reduced when this feature was enabled, although the difference was not significant. The feature was most frequently used proactively by participants in circumstances where a decoding failure was anticipated (such as for uncommon words) as opposed to usage in response to a previous decode failure for a word.

6.3.6 Text Style and Difficulty

Successfully recognising a user's noisy typing depends crucially on the language model being able to sift through the many possible hypotheses in the decoder's search. Language models operate best when trained on the same style of text that a user is writing. For example, a scientific paper involves different words and phrases from those in a text message. A mismatch here can lead to a marked increase in recognition errors. Vertanen and Kristensson [24] found that on 8254 mobile-like sentences typed on touchscreen keyboards, using a language model trained on newswire text resulted in a CER of 4.6% versus 3.0% for a model trained on web forum posts.

Statistical keyboard decoding can also be important for users of Augmentative and Alternative Communication (AAC) devices. Some AAC users may not be able to speak but instead use a keyboard to communicate. Often AAC users have a slow entry rate and rely heavily on a keyboard's word prediction to accelerate their communication. Vertanen and Kristensson [23] found that optimising a language model for AAC-like text resulted in increasing keystroke savings by 5–11%.

Aside from a mismatch in text style, another thing that can make recognition challenging are rare words such as proper names, slang or abbreviations. These words are often out-of-vocabulary (OOV) with respect to a decoder's word vocabulary. While in principle a decoder using a character language model can still propose an OOV word, in practice, this can be difficult given an OOV word's low frequency in the language model's training data.

Vertanen et al. [21] used OOV words to investigate a number of error avoidance and correction methods. Participants copied sentences that often had a single OOV word. Participants could use a *letter locking* feature to specify letters that should not be subject to change during decoding. Letters were locked by touching a key for at least half a second. Participants locked all the letters of 42.5% of the OOV words compared to only 2.1% of in-vocabulary words. Further, participants selected a button with the literal text typed significantly more in phrases with OOV words. These results show that participants were able to recognise more difficult text and adjust their behaviour accordingly. This can inform future studies on the input of difficult text and feed into the interface design of other error prevention and error correction features.

Gaines et al. [7] explored eliciting difficult text using a composition task where participants invented their own phrases to type rather than the more traditional task of copying a phrase. They found that participants were able to generate phrases that had more frequent OOV words and required more frequent use of error correction and prevention features based on simple instructions. This procedure can be used to test an interface's error correction and prevention features in a more naturalistic composition task.

6.4 Case Studies

We now present two case studies which demonstrate practical applications of statistical keyboard decoding. The first case study illustrates how statistical keyboard decoding can enable the effective use of a full QWERTY keyboard for text entry on a small form factor device such as a smartwatch. The second case study describes the deployment of a statistical keyboard decoder to enable mid-air text entry in the challenging setting of augmented reality with noisy hand tracking.

6.4.1 Smartwatch

One particularly challenging text input scenario is typing on a small form factor device. Here we describe several related studies that were conducted using a smartwatch or similar-sized interface.

Figure 6.4 Different-sized keyboards used in Experiment 3 of [25]. A penny and wristwatch are provided for scale.

Device Size

Vertanen et al. [25] explored using a smaller keyboard, although the authors did so by reducing the size of the keyboard on a smartphone device (Figure 6.4). The authors tested a NORMAL keyboard (60 mm × 40 mm), a SMALL keyboard (40 mm × 26 mm) and a TINY keyboard (25 mm × 16 mm). While there was no significant difference in error rate between the NORMAL and SMALL keyboards, the TINY keyboard had a significantly higher error rate (Figure 6.5, left). As we discussed in the previous section, this is likely due to the keys requiring larger Gaussians relative to their size as their size decreases. This creates more possible characters for each tap and more hypotheses within the decoder's search. There were no significant differences in entry rate between the sizes (Figure 6.5, right). This was the first work to show that acceptable text entry performance was possible by adopting a statistical keyboard decoding approach on smartwatch-sized full QWERTY keyboards. Previous work had focused on approaches that allow precise selection of individual keys (e.g. ZoomBoard [18], Swipeboard [2], SplitBoard [13] and DualKey [12]).

Input Length

In later work, Vertanen et al. [20] developed a keyboard interface for the Sony Smartwatch 3. This keyboard, shown in Figure 6.6, measured only 29 mm × 13 mm on a screen that was 29 mm square. By total area, this keyboard was slightly smaller than the TINY keyboard used in [25]. To save room on the screen and provide deterministic spaces, the space bar was removed in favour of a right swipe gesture that indicated word boundaries. One feature that the

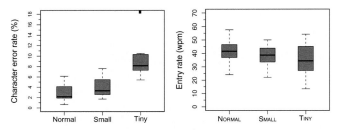

Figure 6.5 Error rate (left) and entry rate (right) in device size experiments in [25].

Figure 6.6 The smartwatch keyboard interface used in [20]. Keys measured approximately 2.9 mm × 4.3 mm.

authors implemented in this interface was to alpha-channel the nearest key over the text area whenever a finger was in contact with the keyboard. This allowed users to have better knowledge of which letters they were typing in a situation where their finger may have obscured a large portion of the keyboard.

Using this interface, Vertanen et al. [20] experimented with how much text the users typed before triggering recognition. In one condition, participants triggered recognition after every word that they typed. In another, they called on the decoder after every other word. In the final condition, participants transcribed the entire phrase before recognition. In each condition, the decoder inferred the spaces between words. As shown in Figure 6.7, sentence-at-a-time enabled participants to enter text significantly faster, while word-at-a-time was significantly slower (two words at a time fell in the middle). There was no significant difference in error rate.

The authors also conducted offline experiments on the data they had collected. They fed the user tap data back into the decoder, but instead of allowing it to infer where the spaces were, the authors fixed the spaces in the input. They found that with known spaces, the larger input length decreased the decoder's

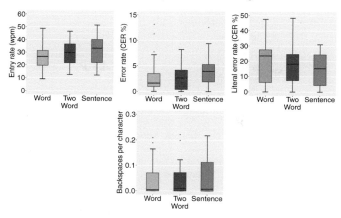

Figure 6.7 Entry rate, error rate (after recognition), literal error rate (before recognition) and backspaces/character in input length experiments [20].

error rate. If instead the decoder had to infer spaces, error rate was similar regardless of the input length.

Error Correction and Prevention

The next iteration of this smartwatch keyboard, VelociWatch, appeared in [21]. This interface added the *letter locking* feature discussed briefly at the end of the previous section. Users were able to press and hold on a letter that they were certain was correct. After a certain time threshold (500 ms), this character would be locked in and the decoder would not be able to change this particular letter during recognition. Users could perform this action for as many characters within a word as they felt necessary. In the first experiment performed by Vertanen et al. [21], participants were given memorable phrases to transcribe using a smartwatch keyboard. This was a within-subjects experiment with two conditions: Lock and NoLock. The letter locking feature was enabled only in the Lock condition.

As shown in Figure 6.8, participants made frequent use of letter locking by long tapping on the keyboard. However, letter locking slowed participants' entry rate from 23.2 wpm to 20.9 wpm. Letter locking also significantly reduced participants' character error rate from 6.2% to 3.3%. To truly measure the effectiveness of letter locking, participants were only able to correct errors prior to recognition; they were not able to change the recognition result via, for example, a backspace key. Because of this, we are able to see that letter locking was effective at preventing recognition errors.

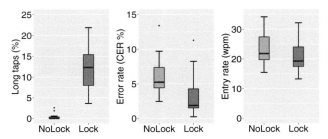

Figure 6.8 Long tap percentage, error rate and entry rate with and without letter locking in the paper by Vertanen et al. [21].

Figure 6.9 The smartwatch keyboard interface used in [21]. The most likely prediction for the current word was shown in the text area, highlighted in black. The upper-left slot contained the literal keys that the user had typed. The remaining slots showed the next most likely word completions or corrections.

Another form of error prevention explored in [21] was word prediction slots. In a follow-up experiment, the QWERTY keyboard remained the same, but the authors added word suggestion slots surrounding the text area, as well as a backspace key on the left side (Figure 6.9). Each slot could be selected by tapping it or by swiping in the diagonal direction of the desired slot, depending on the condition of the study. The upper-left slot contained the literal characters that the user had typed as an additional error prevention feature. The most likely word was placed in the text area and highlighted in black. This slot could be selected by swiping to the right. The remaining slots contained either word completions or corrections, depending on the likelihood of each suggestion, and could be used to either speed up input or correct errors that had occurred in entry.

In this experiment, the authors found that participants had 2.0% CER when typing in-vocabulary phrases and 3.7% CER when typing OOV phrases. They were also slower while typing OOV phrases, at 13.9 wpm compared to 21.3 wpm with in-vocabulary phrases. Participants used the LITERAL slot 16% of the

Figure 6.10 Typing on a virtual keyboard in augmented reality from Dudley et al. [4].

time for OOV phrases and only 3% of the time for in-vocabulary phrases. This shows the literal slot was an effective error prevention feature.

The authors compared this interface to an interface with fewer features that closely resembled the interface designed by Gordon et al. [11]. The alternative keyboard did not have the letter locking or alpha-channelling features, and it only had two word suggestions. Interestingly, participants performed better on the alternative, simpler keyboard than on the VelociWatch interface.

6.4.2 Optical See-Through Augmented Reality

Typing on a mid-air virtual keyboard displayed by an optical see-through (OST) augmented reality (AR) headset represents another challenging text input scenario. Figure 6.10 illustrates a user wearing an AR headset typing on a virtual keyboard. Interaction in this setting is noisy due to the gross amplitude movements of users without any physical reference surface as well as imprecision in the tracking of the hands. Statistical keyboard decoding can mitigate these effects to support effective typing in this challenging setting, as demonstrated by Dudley et al. [4].

The virtual keyboard was developed for use on the first version of the Microsoft HoloLens. The first version of the HoloLens did not provide articulated hand and finger tracking (as is available on the HoloLens 2) and supported tracking of the hand position only, i.e. the position of a point roughly indicating the centre of mass of the back of the hand and without any orientation information. Users controlled a cursor, shown in Figure 6.11, by moving their hand and generating intersections between this cursor and the virtual keyboard plane. This input method approximated a touch-driven interaction paradigm that was hypothesised to be familiar to users despite the unfamiliar setting. This novel keyboard design was christened the virtualised input surface

Figure 6.11 The VISAR* keyboard condition from Dudley et al. [4].

for augmented reality (VISAR) keyboard. By contrast, the system keyboard provided on the first version of the HoloLens was based on a gaze-then-gesture paradigm, requiring users to control a cursor projected based on the head orientation and confirming key selections using a 'tap' gesture.

A series of user studies were conducted to investigate the potential of the touch-driven method supported by the statistical keyboard decoder and explore various relevant design parameters. Several improvements identified through these studies were integrated into the VISAR keyboard, such as adjustment of the keyboard size and orientation, modification of the cursor design as well as the provision of error-tolerant word predictions. The revised and improved VISAR keyboard (referred to as VISAR*) was then evaluated against a baseline derived from the system keyboard using the gaze-then-gesture method (referred to as BASELINE*). The results of this evaluation are summarised in Table 6.1. After eight blocks with 20 phrases per block, the mean entry was significantly higher in the VISAR* condition at 16.76 wpm versus 14.26 wpm in the BASELINE* condition. Error rates were within acceptable levels in both conditions.

A secondary benefit observed by Dudley et al. [4] stemming from the touch-driven paradigm and the integration of the statistical decoder was the ability this afforded users to type with minimal visual keyboard features. A subset of users typing in the VISAR* condition were able to maintain their entry rates within acceptable error bounds when no key labels or key outlines were displayed. This finding is significant in terms of minimising the occlusion of the real world given the limited field of view provided on current OST AR devices.

This case study serves to illustrate how statistical keyboard decoding can mitigate the effects of user and tracking imprecision to support a familiar text entry method in an unfamiliar interaction setting. This has clear benefits in terms

Condition	Entry Rate (wpm)	Error Rate (CER)
BASELINE*	14.26 ± 2.12 [11.22, 18.24]	0.36 ± 0.26 [0.02, 0.85]
VISAR*	16.76 ± 1.67 [14.43, 19.11]	0.63 ± 0.38 [0.26, 1.72]

Table 6.1 Entry rate (wpm) and character error rate (CER%) descriptive statistics from [4]. Results show mean ± 1 standard deviation [min, max].

of supporting walk-up usability and allowing users to leverage their pre-existing motor skills.

6.5 Discussion

The fundamental objective of keyboard decoding is to infer the user's intended text based on observations of user input. Since observations of user input are typically uncertain, it can be challenging to devise a text entry system resilient to the noise intrinsic in the typing process that arises out of the various subcomponents involved: device sensors, the neuromuscular system and the user's cognitive processes. A key to successful inference of the user's text is to use a framework that allows the designer to model the various beliefs of the user's typing process, in particular the text the user is intending to type and the characteristics of any user input, such as the touch distributions over a touchscreen keyboard.

This chapter has reviewed statistical keyboard decoding as a framework for this task. Statistical keyboard decoding allows designers to relatively easily incorporate prior beliefs, notably language models, and likelihood models of user input to generate rich posterior distributions over the hypothesis space of the user's intended text.

Prior beliefs can, for example, be incorporated by using character- and word-level language models suitable for the text the user is likely to type. Performance can be further enhanced by personalising such language models, for example, by mining the user's written text (such as emails sent by the user), or by dynamically adapting the language model to the user's typing (e.g. [5]).

Likelihood models allow the designer to probabilistically model how the system interprets observations of the user's input. As we have reviewed in this chapter, a straightforward approach is to learn a model of the touch distributions over all the keys on a touchscreen keyboard. Such a model can be relatively simple 2D Gaussian distributions [10, 25] or captured by Gaussian Processes [27]. The noisier the user's input is likely to be, the more important the likelihood model will be in capturing the nuances around the uncertainty of the user's input. For example, mid-air keyboards for optical see-through head-mounted displays rely on imprecise hand tracking to infer the user's hand skeleton. In addition, a mid-air keyboard is not supported by a surface, and there is therefore no normal force to halt a user's finger when the finger touches a virtual key. Further, there is no tactile sensation feedback for the user. Due to these factors, an accurate understanding of mid-air keyboard typing behaviour can be incorporated into more sophisticated likelihood models that more accurately reflect all the nuances around mid-air keyboard typing [3, 6].

Posterior distributions provide designers with a model of the hypothesis space of the user's intended text. A common approach is to select the n word candidates with the highest posterior probabilities and present them in a user interface to allow the user to easily and quickly correct errors. However, rich models of posterior distributions also allow for more sophisticated error corrections methods. For example, Vertanen and Kristensson [22] represented such distributions as word-confusion networks and gave users an efficient way to correct errors in a mobile speech interface. A similar approach was employed to correct errors in a VR speech interface [1]. This strategy can also be used for keyboard decoding. Alternatively, word-confusion networks can be used to merge outputs of one or even two separate text entry modalities in order to identify the joint highest probability hypothesis of the user's intended text [17].

The subdivision of prior beliefs, likelihood models and posterior distributions neatly maps into the fundamental Bayesian framework for statistical keyboard decoding which we reviewed earlier in this chapter. However, recent advances in machine learning have also enabled efficient learning of deep neural network-based statistical keyboard decoders, which incorporate such beliefs directly into the decoding model [8].

6.5.1 Future Directions

Statistical keyboard decoding has a wide variety of applications. Its benefit is most acutely seen in interaction scenarios that exhibit high levels of input noise, whether this is due to user or sensor imprecision. In this chapter we have presented compelling examples of its application to small form factor keyboards such as smartwatches and to virtual keyboards presented in augmented reality with noisy hand tracking. Other circumstances in which statistical keyboard decoding has been shown or is likely to show clear benefits is for noisy input caused by user or vehicular motion [9] and noisy input on surfaces with unsighted or unclear reference frames [26, 28]. For such applications, incorporating into the decoder a degree of location invariance or bias learning is likely to be fruitful.

Despite the demonstrated benefits, statistical keyboard decoding does have its limitations. The quality of the word predictions and corrections provided are dependent on the quality of the language models. It is possible to obtain predictions and corrections for words not explicitly captured in these models. However, frequent entry of unmodelled text is likely to yield poor performance and usability. There are likely opportunities to improve performance by incorporating language models that can better adapt to new language constructs as well as adapt to the language use behaviour of particular users.

It also seems that there is a limit to the number of features that can be added to an interface and still improve performance. As we saw in the smartwatch case study, a simpler interface with fewer suggestion slots and less error prevention features outperformed the VelociWatch keyboard. Similarly, the precision key selection mode described in Section 6.3.5 for the AR keyboard did not support improved entry rates and added a potentially confusing interaction experience for only marginal gains in the reduction of error rates. This shows that more is not always better, and it may be wise to carefully select available features so as to not overwhelm users.

One of the major challenges faced when developing and evaluating statistical keyboard decoders is the complex interactions encountered as a consequence of the joint human–machine coupling. For example, keyboard interface and behaviour changes can alter the interaction behaviours of users, frustrating isolated and controlled investigation of design changes. Two potential strategies for addressing this challenge are: (i) systematic design engineering and envelope analysis through simulation; and (ii) evaluation with user models. Both of these strategies have been pursued in the text entry domain [14–16], but there are significant opportunities for advancing the quality and coverage of such methods.

6.6 Conclusions

This chapter has explained the fundamentals of statistical keyboard decoding, which arise directly from a Bayesian formulation of the search the system has to carry out. This search identifies the most probable hypotheses of the user's intended text given prior beliefs of the user's intended text, observations of user input and likelihood model assumptions of such observations. Such a statistical keyboard decoding framework allows a rich exploration of design parameters of the system. We have reviewed several parameters, including the choice of word delimiter, the size of the input device, the length of the user's input, features associated with error correction and prevention, methods of leveraging the user's uncertainty and the difficulty of the user's intended text.

We then reviewed two case studies. First, we presented the design problem of supporting efficient keyboard entry on a very small display, such as a smartwatch. This case study exemplifies that statistical keyboard decoding alleviates the need to invent a new text entry method. Using a statistical keyboard decoding framework in conjunction with a systematic exploration of the most pertinent design parameters enables a design that allows users to type on their smartwatch using a similar keyboard as on their ordinary mobile phones. This is possible because a well-designed statistical keyboard decoder trained on appropriate data is capable of accurately inferring the user's intended text despite the keyboard being so small.

Thereafter we reviewed a case study on supporting a mid-air keyboard in an optical see-through head-mounted display. A statistical keyboard decoder was incorporated to support text entry despite high levels of imprecision and latency in the hand tracking mechanism delivering virtual touch events. Secondary benefits of this approach were also observed with the error-tolerant entry method allowing a portion of users to type without any key labels or outlines shown. This has significant potential benefits in an augmented reality setting by avoiding the unnecessary occlusion of the physical world.

As we increasingly see physical keyboards and keypads replaced by soft or virtual alternatives, there is corresponding growth in demand for more intelligent handling of the uncertainty associated with text input. Underpinned by Bayesian methods, statistical keyboard decoding is an elegant and efficient framework satisfying this need. It helps to translate the noisy signal from the user into their intended text and thereby enables text entry in interaction settings that would be impossible or laborious using conventional input mapping approaches. The power of statistical keyboard decoding has been demonstrated in a range of use cases, and there remain significant opportunities for further extension and enhancement.

References

[1] J. Adhikary and K. Vertanen. 2021. Text entry in virtual environments using speech and a midair keyboard. *IEEE Transactions on Visualization and Computer Graphics*, 27(5), 2648–58.
[2] X. 'A.' Chen, T. Grossman and G. Fitzmaurice. 2014. Swipeboard: a text entry technique for ultra-small interfaces that supports novice to expert transitions. Pages

615–620 of: *Proceedings of the 27th Annual ACM Symposium on User Interface Software and Technology.* UIST '14. Association for Computing Machinery.

[3] J. Dudley, H. Benko, D. Wigdor and P. O. Kristensson. 2019. Performance envelopes of virtual keyboard text input strategies in virtual reality. Pages 289–300 of: *2019 IEEE International Symposium on Mixed and Augmented Reality (ISMAR).* Institute of Electrical and Electronics Engineers.

[4] J. J. Dudley, K. Vertanen and P. O. Kristensson. 2018. Fast and precise touch-based text entry for head-mounted augmented reality with variable occlusion. *ACM Transactions on Computer-Human Interaction (TOCHI),* **25**(6), 1–40.

[5] A. Fowler, K. Partridge, C. Chelba, X. Bi, T. Ouyang and S. Zhai. 2015. Effects of language modeling and its personalization on touchscreen typing performance. Pages 649–658 of: *Proceedings of the 33rd Annual ACM Conference on Human Factors in Computing Systems.* Association for Computing Machinery.

[6] C. R. Foy, J. J. Dudley, A. Gupta, H. Benko and P. O. Kristensson. 2021. Understanding, detecting and mitigating the effects of coactivations in ten-finger mid-air typing in virtual reality. Pages 1–11 of: *Proceedings of the 2021 Annual ACM Conference on Human Factors in Computing Systems.* Association for Computing Machinery.

[7] D. Gaines, P. O. Kristensson and K. Vertanen. 2021. Enhancing the composition task in text entry studies: eliciting difficult text and improving error rate calculation. In: *Proceedings of the SIGCHI Conference on Human Factors in Computing Systems.* CHI '21. Association for Computing Machinery.

[8] S. Ghosh and P. O. Kristensson. 2017. Neural networks for text correction and completion in keyboard decoding. *arXiv preprint arXiv:1709.06429.*

[9] M. Goel, L. Findlater and J. W. Wobbrock. 2012. WalkType: using accelerometer data to accomodate situational impairments in mobile touch screen text entry. Page 2687–2696 of: *Proceedings of the SIGCHI Conference on Human Factors in Computing Systems.* CHI '12. Association for Computing Machinery.

[10] J. Goodman, G. Venolia, K. Steury and C. Parker. 2002. Language modeling for soft keyboards. Pages 194–195 of: *Proceedings of the 7th International Conference on Intelligent User Interfaces.* IUI '02. Association for Computing Machinery.

[11] M. Gordon, T. Ouyang and S. Zhai. 2016. WatchWriter: tap and gesture typing on a smartwatch miniature keyboard with statistical decoding. Pages 3817–3821 of: *Proceedings of the 2016 CHI Conference on Human Factors in Computing Systems.* CHI '16. Association for Computing Machinery.

[12] A. Gupta and R. Balakrishnan. 2016. DualKey: miniature screen text entry via finger identification. Pages 59–70 of: *Proceedings of the SIGCHI Conference on Human Factors in Computing Systems.* CHI '16. Association for Computing Machinery

[13] J. Hong, S. Heo, P. Isokoski and G. Lee. 2015. SplitBoard: a simple split soft keyboard for wristwatch-sized touch screens. Pages 1233–1236 of: *Proceedings of the SIGCHI Conference on Human Factors in Computing Systems.* CHI '15. Association for Computing Machinery.

[14] J. Jokinen, A. Acharya, M. Uzair, X. Jiang and A. Oulasvirta. 2021. Touchscreen typing as optimal supervisory control. Pages 1–14 of: *Proceedings of the 2021 CHI Conference on Human Factors in Computing Systems.* CHI '21. Association for Computing Machinery.

[15] P. O. Kristensson, J. Lilley, R. Black and A. Waller. 2020. A design engineering approach for quantitatively exploring context-aware sentence retrieval for nonspeaking individuals with motor disabilities. Pages 1–11 of: *Proceedings of the 2020 CHI Conference on Human Factors in Computing Systems*. CHI '20. Association for Computing Machinery.

[16] P. O. Kristensson and T. Müllners. 2021. Design and analysis of intelligent text entry systems with function structure models and envelope analysis. In: *Proceedings of the 2021 CHI Conference on Human Factors in Computing Systems*. CHI '21. Association for Computing Machinery.

[17] P. O. Kristensson and K. Vertanen. 2011. Asynchronous multimodal text entry using speech and gesture keyboards. In: *Twelfth Annual Conference of the International Speech Communication Association*.

[18] S. Oney, C. Harrison, A. Ogan and J. Wiese. 2013. ZoomBoard: a diminutive qwerty soft keyboard using iterative zooming for ultra-small devices. Pages 2799–2802 of: *Proceedings of the SIGCHI Conference on Human Factors in Computing Systems*. CHI '13. Association for Computing Machinery.

[19] K. Vertanen. 2021. Intelligent computing for interactive system design: statistics, digital signal processing, and machine learning in practice. Pages 277–320 of: *Probabilistic Text Entry-Case Study 3*. 1st ed. Association for Computing Machinery.

[20] K. Vertanen, C. Fletcher, D. Gaines, J. Gould and P. O. Kristensson, Per Ola. 2018. The impact of word, multiple word, and sentence input on Virtual Keyboard Decoding Performance. In: *Proceedings of the SIGCHI Conference on Human Factors in Computing Systems*. CHI '18. Association for Computing Machinery

[21] K. Vertanen, D. Gaines, C. Fletcher, A. M. Stanage, R. Watling and P. O. Kristensson. 2019. VelociWatch: designing and evaluating a virtual keyboard for the input of challenging text. In: *Proceedings of the SIGCHI Conference on Human Factors in Computing Systems*. CHI '19. Association for Computing Machinery

[22] K. Vertanen and P. O. Kristensson. 2009. Parakeet: a continuous speech recognition system for mobile touch-screen devices. Pages 237–246 of: *Proceedings of the 14th International Conference on Intelligent User Interfaces*. IUI '09. Association for Computing Machinery.

[23] K. Vertanen and P. O. Kristensson. 2011. The imagination of crowds: conversational AAC language modeling using crowdsourcing and large data sources. Pages 700–711 of: *Proceedings of the Conference on Empirical Methods in Natural Language Processing (EMNLP)*. Association for Computational Linguistics.

[24] K. Vertanen and P. O. Kristensson. 2021. Mining, analyzing, and modeling text written on mobile devices. *Natural Language Engineering*, **27**, 1–33.

[25] K. Vertanen, H. Memmi, J. Emge, S. Reyal and P. O. Kristensson. 2015. VelociTap: investigating fast mobile text entry using sentence-based decoding of touchscreen keyboard input. Pages 659–668 of: *Proceedings of the SIGCHI Conference on Human Factors in Computing Systems*. CHI '15. Association for Computing Machinery.

[26] K. Vertanen, H. Memmi and P. O. Kristensson. 2013. The feasibility of eyes-free touchscreen keyboard typing. In: *Proceedings of the ACM SIGACCESS Conference on Computers and Accessibility*. ASSETS '13. Association for Computing Machinery.

[27] D. Weir, H. Pohl, S. Rogers, K. Vertanen and P.O. Kristensson. 2014. Uncertain Text Entry on Mobile Devices. Pages 2307–2316 of: *Proceedings of the SIGCHI Conference on Human Factors in Computing Systems*. CHI '14. Association for Computing Machinery.

[28] S. Zhu, T. Luo, X. Bi and S. Zhai. 2018. Typing on an invisible keyboard. Pages 1–13 of: *Proceedings of the 2018 CHI Conference on Human Factors in Computing Systems*. CHI '18. Association for Computing Machinery.

7

Human–Computer Interaction Design and Inverse Problems

Roderick Murray-Smith, John H. Williamson and Francesco Tonolini

Abstract

We outline the role of forward and inverse modelling approaches in the design of systems to support inference of intention from sensors in human–computer interaction. Inverse problems involve using measurements to infer values of parameters that characterise the system or its inputs, and are key areas of study in many areas of experimental science. Causal, forward models tend to be easier to specify, simulate and gather experimental data for, but the inverse problem is what typically needs to be solved in an interaction context. We need to go from sensor readings on a computer to inferring the intention of a human user.

In this chapter we argue that the design of interfaces can be evaluated by examining how easy they make it to robustly solve the inverse problem of determining human intention from information the computer can access, potentially via intermediate estimates of the state of the human body. It will lay out a theoretical framework for the role of inverse problems in analysis of interaction design, and illustrate that with real-world examples. A simulation model (with available code) is provided for a simplified representation of 3D touch problems, to give readers a worked example to experiment with.

7.1 Introduction

7.1.1 Motivation

Interactive systems must be able to sense and interpret human actions to infer their intentions. Human–computer interaction (HCI) research continually explores novel sensors for novel forms of interaction but lacks a coherent, consistent framework for characterising this process with incrementally improving precision for different sensors and different human behaviours.

Common practice tends to be to handcraft features and associated thresholds for specific use-cases. This can be time-consuming, especially as the dimension of the sensors increases. Furthermore, the thresholds for one application might not be appropriate for another (e.g. touch typing vs continuous gestures). A further issue for the design pipeline is that these handcrafted systems are very sensitive to threshold settings, and different aspects of interaction can only be tested once the full system has been implemented, which can cause problems if performance turns out to be inadequate at a late stage.

We argue that for the field to make consistent, predictable and incremental progress, we need a more general, formal framework for characterisation of the pathway from human intent to sensor state. This pathway can include formal, computational models of human elements such as cognition and physiological processes, as well as purely technical elements such as the characterisation of the physical processes of the sensor. Eventually the forward model could include the anticipated impact of the feedback from the interface on the forward process.

7.1.2 Forward Models and Inverse Problems in HCI

Scientific theories let us make predictions. If we have a complete mathematical model of a physical system, we can predict the outcome of measurements of states of that system. In this chapter we will assume that the parameters are latent variables, which are not observed directly, whereas the sensed measurements are directly observed.

The *forward problem* is this problem of using the models and their latent parameters to predict the results of the observed measurements.[1] The *inverse problem* is the problem of using the observed measurements to infer values of the latent parameters that, given the model structure, characterise the system or its inputs [24]. (Both problems are illustrated in Figure 7.1.) In many cases, where the scientific knowledge is mature, scientists can simulate a system better than they can effectively observe it.

The forward problem for many systems of practical interest often tends to have a unique solution, but the inverse problem does not. For instance, take something as simple as a non-linear saturation effect in the forward mode of a touch sensor, as shown in Figure 7.2. As the finger moves away from the surface, we eventually see no change beyond the range of the sensor. We can predict the forward values with precision, but there are infinitely many possible solutions to the inverse problem in the saturated areas, as shown in Figure 7.3 for a $\tanh()$ function and its inverse $\mathrm{arctanh}()$. This means that solution of

---

[1] This is sometimes called the *measurement model*.

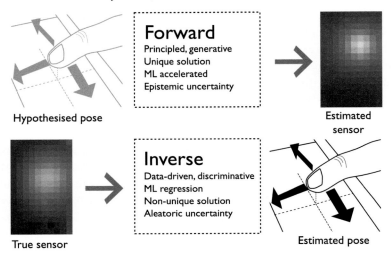

Figure 7.1 Forward and inverse models in a finger-sensing task. The forward model maps from finger pose and position to the sensor readings, and the inverse model maps from sensor readings to an estimated pose and position.

inverse problems requires explicit use of a priori information about the system, and careful consideration of uncertainty in the data.

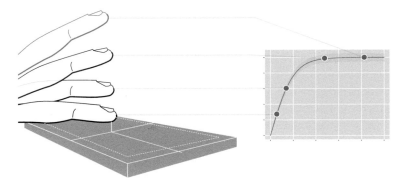

Figure 7.2 A saturation effect is one potential cause of ill-posedness. Distinguished world states (finger poses) are projected to identical sensor states.

The previous presentation was a simplification of many real-world problems. To be more precise, if our model parameters, structures or observations are uncertain, as is typically the case, then we have a distribution of solutions. Figure 7.4 shows the impact of variability in the form of measurement noise,

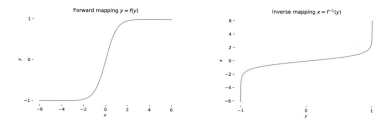

Figure 7.3 Inverse function of a saturation. Note how there is a one-to-one mapping of the forward model, but infinitely many compatible points for the inverse at −1 and 1.

and Figure 7.5 shows the impact of variability of the mapping (e.g. sensor characteristics will have tolerances which lead to variability). Our inversion methods need to be able to robustly cope with such variability.

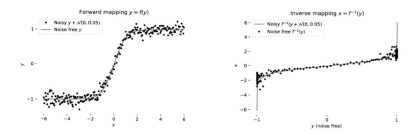

Figure 7.4 Role of additive observation noise. This makes an otherwise unique forward mapping non-unique and leads to increased variability in the inverse mapping, especially visible in low-gradient areas of the forward mapping.

7.1.3 Forward Model Pipeline

We may be considering a forward or measurement model which has no dynamics, or we may partition a complex mapping into a series of simpler transformations via intermediate variables. For the inputs or any of the intermediate states, the forward model may be combined with a *dynamic model*, $p(x_t|x_{t-1})$, which captures the properties of the change in state x over time t – for example, how rapidly can a finger change direction? Alternatively, the associated dynamics can be built into the forward model itself.

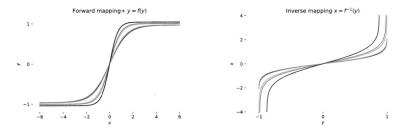

Figure 7.5 Role of variability (such as variations in sensor characteristic curves). This emulates variability in the forward mapping by using $\epsilon \sim \mathcal{N}(0, 0.02)$, and $(1 + \epsilon)\tanh((1 + 10\epsilon)x)$ and shows the variability implications for the inverse.

7.1.4 Proposed Solution

We propose a *dual approach*, where we model both the forward and the inverse problems and fuse them consistently via a probabilistic framework. First-principles models are an attractive way of approaching HCI problems, but it is hard for simple, elegant models to represent messy human behaviour. Data-driven approaches have the advantage that they are precisely tailored to specific real interactions, but they can struggle to generalise robustly and might require large amounts of data to become reliable. Furthermore, as the dimensionality of the sensor system increases, an ad hoc experimentation-based approach to interface design becomes increasingly time-consuming, error-prone and infeasible. We therefore consider an approach which divides up the problem of modelling interaction into two streams:

- **Forward**, first-principles models of interaction derived from physics, physiology and psychology, where parameters are not fully known, with *epistemic* uncertainty and unique solutions, e.g. implementing an executable simulation of what sensor vector we would observe for a given finger pose. The first-principles models can be augmented by machine learning techniques to calibrate or learn the residuals present due to the mismatch of theory and reality, when experimental data are available.
- **Inverse**, data-driven models of interaction, learned from observed interaction with machine learning, with *aleatoric* uncertainty and non-unique solutions – for instance, training a regression model to predict a pose from a touch sensor vector.

This splits the modelling task into two parts with complementary strengths, bringing generalisable, testable simulation models into the forward construction and powerful machine-learned predictive models into the inverse construction.

We show that this is an intellectually appealing way of partitioning the interaction problem and concretely demonstrate that probabilistic fusion of forward and inverse models leads to performance which exceeds either approach alone.

7.2 Bayesian Approaches to Inverse Problems: Inference vs Inversion?

How do *inverse problems* relate to a book on *Bayesian methods*? The question comes down to whether we should frame these problems as *inference problems* or *inversion problems*. Textbooks such as [9] present many practical algorithms for managing the challenges of ill-conditioned inverse approximations to practical forward models. However, the famous Bayesian E.T. Jaynes [12] criticised Tikhonov and Arsenin's [25] foundational work on ill-posed problems as 'A collection of ad hoc mathematical recipes in which the authors try persistently to invert operators which have no inverses. Never perceives that these are problems of *inference*, not *inversion*'.

MacKay [14] highlights that probability calculations are either *forward probabilities* or *inverse probabilities*. Forward probabilities involve a generative model that describes a process that gives rise to some data. Inverse probabilities also involve a generative process, but instead of computing the probability distribution of a quantity produced by the process, we compute the conditional probability of one or more of the unobserved variables, given the observed ones. This requires the use of Bayes' rule, which is a formal way of describing this process of *statistical inversion*.

We assume there is a unknown quantity x, and we observe some noisy measurements y_i. The goal of the statistical inversion is to estimate the unknown quantity x, i.e. compute the conditional *posterior distribution* of the quantity x given the measurements y,

$$p(x|y) = \frac{p(y|x)p(x)}{p(y)}. \tag{7.1}$$

Equation (7.1) includes a probability $p(y|x)$ (the 'likelihood' of y, given x) which represents the 'forward model' or 'measurement model' which describes the causal but inaccurate or noisy relationship between the true parameter x and the observation y. The prior distribution $p(x)$ representing our subjective uncertainty about the value of x before we saw the data y. It can also be presented as $p(x|y) \propto p(y|x)p(x)$, where the normalisation constant $p(y) = \int p(y|x)p(x)dx$.

We can now use the standard computational tools of Bayesian inference from *maximum a posteriori* (MAP) methods to Markov-Chain Monte Carlo (MCMC) numerical integration techniques, e.g. [22, 27]. Traditional Bayesian filtering and smoothing approaches, as described by Särrkä in [22], implicitly solve the inverse problem to infer states from observations in time-series problems.

True inversion requires an invertible forward system, and many interesting real-world systems are not directly invertible and do not have unique solutions (e.g. non-linearities such as the simple saturation effect shown in Figure 7.2 are extremely common). Bayesian approaches therefore provide a more general framework for performing inference of model parameters or input states in inverse problems, and they generate a distribution which gives us insight into the range of possible values, rather than providing a single 'best guess'. The availability of this uncertainty provides us with new degrees of freedom (and associated challenges!) in the design of interactive systems.

Bayes' rule gives us a formal mechanism for managing the uncertainty in our inference. Two types of uncertainty pervade interaction design tasks: *epistemic* uncertainty, where a lack of knowledge means we are unsure as to whether a model of the user, sensor or world is valid; and *aleatoric* uncertainty, where measurements are noisy and subject to random variation [19].

7.3 Related Work/Background

7.3.1 Forward/Inverse Models in HCI

How applicable is this general theory from physical sciences and statistics to the study of human–computer interaction? Humans are highly complex systems with a lot of heterogeneity and context-sensitive behaviour. Can we plausibly apply this approach?

As mentioned earlier, it tends to be more straightforward to design the experiments and acquire the data required for a forward model of human or sensor behaviour. The task can be repeated multiple times, sensor readings made and the model fitted. A frequent challenge is being sure of the 'input', which might be the *intent*; or for sensor systems it might be the human pose, which implies that we require an alternative 'gold standard' sensing system. Often this may be a more expensive, bulky or personally instrumented system which is appropriate for a lab experiment, but not for the application domain. For example, position tracking tabs may need to be attached to a human body while they perform the task, to give a more complete representation of the input x, which led to the sensed data y. Mayer [16] used optical tracking to capture finger state in a capacitive sensing task.

Interface designers, however, who want the computer to be able to respond to the human behaviour need inverse models which can let them determine the intention behind the sensed observations. These inverse problems often have non-unique solutions and are based on incomplete and noisy observations. For instance, we can specify models of human physiology relating to movements of the arm and hand, and gradually improve their fidelity via theoretical insight, a range of experimental techniques and high-fidelity sensors in carefully controlled lab settings.

Advanced sensors like those used in Brain–Computer Interfaces explicitly include forward models of the skull to infer the brain state from EEG sensors, but the same principle can be applied in all interactive systems. The challenge for the interface designer is, however, to infer from some possibly cheap and low-fidelity sensor information which human intentions were associated with movements of their body, which led to the series of sensor readings. Particle filters also use forward and inverse models and have been used in a range of computer vision [4] and HCI applications [5, 21].

7.3.2 Sensor Linearisation

The classical engineering process of linearisation of a sensor (e.g. a pressure sensor) to improve performance can be seen as implicitly addressing this challenge. Experiments characterise the pressure response for a series of known values (forward model), and then a compensating function is applied to the reading to give an effectively linear response when predicting the input pressure (inverse model), which means that the performance of the sensor as an input device can be improved and is not dominated by its physical characteristics.[2] Linearisation of sensors will not eliminate the noise response, and so there can still be problems where the physical inverse problem is ill-posed.

7.3.3 Inverse Problems in Human Behaviour

Collaborative efforts to generate executable computational models of human motor behaviour include [6, 10, 15]. Applications of such motor models in HCI include [2, 3, 20].

Kangasrääsiö et al. [13] introduced the use of computationally efficient Approximate Bayesian Computation (ABC) approaches to solve inverse problems in HCI. Their approach did not specify an explicit forward model a priori, but rather learned a forward model for human cognitive processes which

---

[2] Of course, designers may then take into account other aspects of the system and choose to introduce non-linear mappings which are applied to signals to make a system more easily usable, but that is a separate process from managing the arbitrary properties of the forward model.

would optimise a plausible cost function. The two approaches can be combined as illustrated in human motor control [29].

7.3.4 Machine Learning and Invertible Models

There has been growing interest in invertible neural networks recently in the machine learning community, e.g. [1, 7, 8]. These constrain their architectures and learning algorithms such that they can learn analytically compatible forward and inverse models simultaneously.

7.3.5 Practical Computational Frameworks

One strategic question about the use of such methods is whether they are best suited to *offline* or *online* use. The approach could be used to select and tune relatively simple rules or thresholds, as in current implementations, or it could apply complex inverse inference processes which compute solutions in real time. In some applications there may be issues with the computational viability of full Bayesian inversions, or the associated use of memory. In those cases, we may propose to use the full model in design, and approximations of computationally and memory-efficient algorithms in real-time use.

Algorithmic differentiation is simplifying the application of many optimisations with complex models in machine learning and signal processing, with widely use frameworks such as TensorFlow, pyTorch or JAX. Where forward models were developed in legacy code, it is possible to train flexible ML models as emulators of those systems, which then allows us to create differentiable pipelines of models. The modern frameworks typically support GPU acceleration which can further improve performance.

7.4 Building the Forward Model

7.4.1 Learn a Forward Model

In cases where we understand the properties of the forward model $y = f(x)$ extremely well, we could provide the equations of the system involved. In any case, we will need to verify the accuracy of the associated simulation with measured data. In the common case of complex systems where our understanding is imperfect (especially when they combine with human users), we may need to learn a model from observing input and output data.

The forward model can therefore be a first-principles model, an emulator of such a model, a black-box model, or a combination of any of them. We might also consider models which make point predictions or predictions of distributions.

Typically the data for the forward model is gathered by taking the system concerned through its range of operation. This may be more challenging than it first seems, if humans are required to provide the input states. For high-dimensional inputs, or dynamic inputs which observe changes over time, it may be difficult for humans to sample the space completely or evenly. Techniques such as *Rewarding The Original* [28] can be used to encourage users to explore the input space more completely, and this process may need to be iterated as performance from early models is calibrated. Use of forward models which represent their predictive uncertainty correctly will be useful in pointing out regions which require more data to improve accuracy. Any extra sensing capability to represent the human state will also be used at this point.

7.4.2 Analyse the Forward Model

Is it possible to directly relate the properties of a forward model to their suitability as a sensor for inference of the input to that system before moving on to the inversion stage? For a single-dimensional system it is easy to visually check for monotonicity of the gradient, and for zero-gradient areas. If the sign of the model gradient with respect to input states is changing, it means that there will be multiple possible input x values for a given output y. For zero-gradient areas, then, there will be infinitely many possible x for a given y. Some sensors will have probabilistic properties, so the output is a distribution. Frequently in sensing systems, we will also find that the variability in y may change as a function of x (known as heteroskedastic systems in statistics). For example, the ability to localise the (x, y) coordinates of a finger may become more uncertain as the z parameter increases, as the finger moves further from the sensors. For higher-dimensional systems, it rapidly becomes more difficult to guarantee the uniqueness of solutions by simple inspection, and this is an area with a great deal of scope for exploration.

7.5 Finding the Posterior Distribution of Intention

Given sensor observations, we now need to solve the statistical inverse problem to find the posterior distribution over our parameters of interest, *intention* (or in a pipeline model, precursors of that such as body pose/position).

We can do this with or without an explicit inverse model. Computationally expensive run-time approaches to the inverse model-free approach include the use of MCMC sampling to predict a distribution, or for a point-estimate-based MLE/MAP approach, we iteratively optimise the value of inputs x to the forward model, and use a likelihood based on the mismatch between predictions $f(x)$ and observed sensor reading y in the training data.

However, if we want a computationally more efficient runtime, and to be able to verify performance rigorously, it will often be more appropriate to create a model which represents the inverse mapping. This can be done directly, or via use of a forward model.

7.5.1 Learning a Direct Inverse Model

A simple baseline approach is to learn the inverse model directly from the data. An inverse model $x = g(y)$, where $g(\cdot)$ is the inverse of $f(\cdot)$, can be learned directly from the data, swapping inputs for outputs. This could be a point estimate or a distribution. This is structurally simple, but it can be less robust when responding to cases away from the training data

7.5.2 Use the Forward Model to Learn an Inverse Model

An alternative approach to directly learning it, is to use the forward model to help create an inverse model. We highlight three approaches: invertible forward models, augmenting inverse model training data via forward models, and classical filtering approaches.

Learning Invertible Forward Models

As mentioned earlier, one way of creating an inverse model is to learn the inverse model simultaneously with the forward model by using an appropriately constrained architecture (e.g. [1, 7, 8]).

Using Forward Models to Augment Data for Inverse Model

Others have used forward models to augment the often sparse training data for the inverse problem. In the *Variational Inference for Computational Inverse problems (VICI)* approach, introduced in [26], we used a combination of empirical data, simple physics-based forward models, and Conditional Variational AutoEncoders to be able to generate a large training set for the inverse problem. This was applied to challenges in computational imaging.

Particle Filters

Classical Bayesian filtering incorporates forward and dynamics models jointly to perform inference [22]. Particle filters are well-established Monte Carlo approximations to the solutions of Bayesian filtering equations, and approaches for performing *stateful* tracking; i.e. to track the inferred finger pose over time. The particle filter (or sequential Monte Carlo filter) is a probabilistic predictor-corrector, which maintains an estimate of distribution over possible finger poses $P(\mathbf{y_t})$, $\mathbf{y_t} = [x_t, y_t, z_t, \theta_t, \phi_t]$ as a set of discrete samples. It updates this distribution by weighting samples according to how close their expected sensor state would be to true observations of the sensor $\mathbf{X}$. Heavily weighted samples are propagated forward in time, and low weight samples are discarded. Internal dynamics which model the potential evolution of inferred finger poses allow the filter to predict likely future states when observations are noisy or incomplete.

The approach uses a forward model which predicts $\hat{\mathbf{X}}$ given $\mathbf{y}$ and an inverse model which predicts $\hat{\mathbf{y}}$ from $\mathbf{X}$ in the filter. In each prediction step, the approach maintains a set of samples of possible states for $\mathbf{y}$. A weighting step is applied, first based on the forward model, then a second weighting step based on the inverse model, before performing the importance sampling step. This allows our model to automatically and transparently cope when one of the two models is underdetermined.

7.5.3 Example: Simulation of a 3D Touch Sensing Task

This section will describe a simple simulation of a real-world problem (3D touch sensing), which captures the key aspects of the real problem but allows us to experiment with the properties of the physical system, forward model, inverse solutions and usability.

The ability to sense finger position and pose accurately at a distance from the device screen would allow designers to create novel interaction styles, and researchers to better track, analyse and understand human touch behaviour. Progress in design of capacitive screen technology has led to the ability to sense the user's fingers up to several centimetres above the screen. However, the inference of position and pose is a classic example of an ill-posed inverse problem, given only the readings from the two-dimensional capacitive sensor pads, making the solutions inherently uncertain.

We have chosen to illustrate the role of forward and inverse models in HCI with the finger pose inference problem [17], as shown in Figure 7.1, as it is a realistic, topical problem, where the physical theory of the associated system is well understood, but the sensors used in a practical mobile device have significant limitations, where there are non-unique mappings in the inverse

Inverse Inference Approach	Issues
Forward, principled, causal. Inverted via MCMC (or variational methods, etc.) to a distribution, or via MLE/MAP to point estimates of x.	Needs careful specification and expert input, can be slow and with variable runtime, but presents a 'gold standard', typically well-behaved for all inputs.
Forward, black box. Inverted as above, often as an emulator of a principled model, or from experimental data.	Can be fast but harder to reason about.
Inverse, black box, point. Direct prediction of point estimates of x, learning from data.	Fast, traditional, may have unexpected behaviour outside of training manifold, but risky due to ill-posedness of inversion.
Inverse, black box, distribution. Distribution over x.	May be fast, but requires more advanced ML methods, and hard to be sure that posterior is realistic for the entire operating regime.
Forward + Inverse, black box, distribution. Distribution over x, but augments training data with forward model generated points.	Fast, requires advanced ML methods, but improved performance by joint use of forward and inverse models. Hard to be sure that posterior is realistic for the entire operating regime, but assisted by mutual compatibility tests of forward and inverse predictions.

Table 7.1 Summary of inversion approaches, and associated issues.

problem. Finally, we can also easily augment the sensor model with models of human touch movement such as [20].

Definition of a Toy Problem

For ease of visualisation we will boil the pose problem down to a very simple one-dimensional scenario – inferring the height r of a finger from a noisy sensor reading S. A single capacitive sensor responds to finger presence. The task is to predict the finger's distance from the sensor.

Sensor Characteristics: Forward Model

The strength of response drops off with distance from the finger. For this toy example we simulate this with a simple quadratic drop-off of sensor response with distance:

$$S = 300000 \frac{q_1 q_2}{r^2 + 0.1},$$

where $r = ||x_1 - x_2||$, the distance between the two points, and in this case we have set $q_1 = 1, q_2 = -1$. We show a noise-free response of the sensor as the point lifts up steadily from the surface of the simulated touch screen, in

Figure 7.6(a). When we use our perfect knowledge of the forward model, and directly apply this function to the clean data, we can perfectly infer the position of the finger, and it can compensate for the changing sensitivity to distance $\frac{dS}{dr}$ inherent in this non-linear model.

However, what happens when we have less than perfect knowledge? We show a version with additive sensor observation noise which is normally distributed with a standard deviation 30 times smaller than the signal peak $\pm \mathcal{N}(0, 1e5)$, (saturating at 0), in Figure 7.6(b) (top). While the forward response has the same uncertainty at all distances (homoskedasticity), modulo saturation effects close to $S = 0$, in Figure 7.6(b) (bottom) you can see how a direct application of the inverse function leads to significant heteroskedasticity in the estimated distance, with good accuracy closer to the sensor, but greatly increased variance further away. This highlights that when the forward model has a low gradient $\frac{dS}{dr}$, then when we invert this, $\frac{dr}{dS}$ is very large, so any additive noise on S is amplified by the inverse gradient.

A glance at the centre image in Figure 7.6 also shows what the challenges are for directly learning a machine learning model to map this from the black points, which represent the noisy sensor observations $S \pm \mathcal{N}(0, 1e5)$ via the true distances r. The learned mapping should be good for values of $S > 0.3e6$, but very noisy below that.

What if we have imperfect knowledge of the forward process? For instance, in this case we might have an uncertain estimate of $q_2 = 1 \pm \mathcal{N}(0, 0.1)$. In Figure 7.7 we show samples of the different models, given this uncertainty.

So what else could we do instead of the direct inversion? One straightforward approach is to sample from the model using a MCMC simulation, for example, implementing the forward model with a probabilistic programming language such as pyMC3, conditioned on a noisy observation of S and looking at the distribution of the posterior on r. Figure 7.8 gives an example of such a sampling approach. It shows clearly how the uncertainty on the inferred distance r increases dramatically as the value of S decreases (associated with being further from the sensor). MCMC approaches provide a 'gold standard' on the distribution for the latent variables, but are computationally intensive and hence not immediately applicable for real-time interaction design use, although they can play a role in off-line analysis.

Learning a Neural Network Approximation

One approach to inverting the mapping from sensor S to distance r could be to learn a direct mapping. Conditional Variational Auto-Encoders (CVAEs) are variational methods which allow efficient approximate inference through generative models that scale to the dimensionalities and numbers of examples

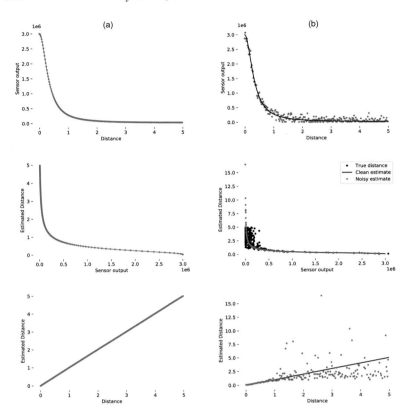

Figure 7.6 Sensor data from a point moving away from the touchscreen. (a) The noise-free forward model and its inverse, with perfect knowledge. The inverse prediction is a perfect match to the real position.
(b) Noisy sensor data from a point moving away from the touch screen. The forward model and its inverse, with perfect knowledge, but noisy sensor data. Note how the relatively small noise level has little impact on the inverse close to the device, but leads to massive variability further away.

typically needed for larger-scale reconstruction tasks while also capturing uncertainty in their recoveries [11, 18, 23]. We use a CVAE of the same complexity, which we will later use for the forward model. In this case, we have a 3-layer MLP with 30 ReLU units per layer, and a bottleneck layer with dimension $z = 3$, but the approach is fairly robust to significantly smaller or larger architectures. This may appear somewhat like overkill for this small one-dimensional problem, but the approach and the code provided is usable for more challenging, higher-dimensional ones.

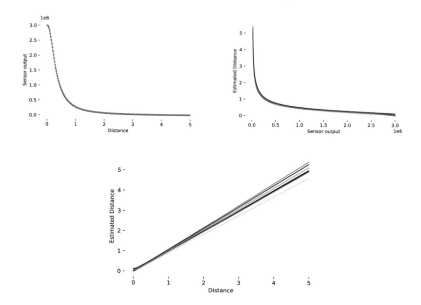

Figure 7.7 Sensor data from a point moving away from the touchscreen. The noise-free forward model and samples of its inverse, with uncertain knowledge of the charge q_2.

In Figure 7.9 we show the result of a trained model capable of a direct mapping from S to r. While in a low-dimensional problem like this one, we can potentially gather enough data, this is often not the case in higher-dimensional problems, so we are simulating that challenge by using a relatively sparse training set.

Using the VICI Neural Network Approach

We now apply the approach proposed in [26] to create an efficient approximation of the MCMC solution. This creates a forward model first. Note how the forward model captures the property of the function well. This can now be used to augment the training set for the inverse model. As you can see from Figure 7.10, the model captures the variability in both the forward and inverse models well. If this were to be used as an input device in an interface, it would mean that we would have an accurate, context-sensitive measure of uncertainty of the finger position. This could be used in the design process to determine cut-off points.

We generate the training data as a mixture of samples from a uniform distribution between 0 and 5.0 and a gamma distribution which generates

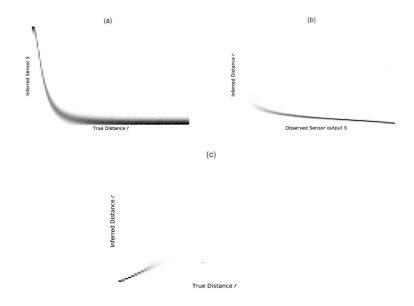

Figure 7.8 MCMC sampling from the model: (a) conditioned on true r, distribution of S; (b) conditioned on an observation of S, giving a distribution on r; (c) conditioned on samples S from true r, what is the distribution of estimated r?

more samples close to zero. This simulates a dataset with a bias towards close-to-device samples, but some systematic experimentation. The distribution is shown in Figure 7.11.

Let us compare the direct and augmented approach for different sizes of training data. We use $N = 150$ and $N = 2000$. For the smaller dataset we see a performance benefit of the forward/inverse approach compared to the direct inverse approach in a reduced root mean squared error (RMSE) for the inverse solutions on the test set (0.0151 vs 0.0158), and especially in lower sensor activations, a significant drop in the standard deviation of predictions, as visible in Figure 7.12.

Some of the problems in finding the solution to the inverse problem can be reduced by gathering larger amounts of training data, but this becomes more difficult in real-world higher-dimensional problems, and where human users need to perform the actions associated with the task. While MCMC-based inference provides a gold standard in inference in complex models, machine learning tools such as neural networks can be used to learn the distributions in a way that can be implemented in real time, even on relatively low-power devices such as

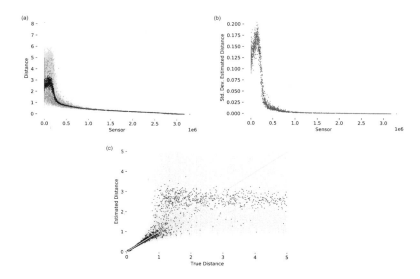

Figure 7.9 Learning a direct CVAE inverse mapping from S to r. $N = 150$ training points. Plot (a) shows the distribution of inverse samples from S to r in light grey, the measured data in medium grey, and the mean prediction in dark grey. Note the high variance in the region of lower sensor output, visible in plot (b), which corresponds to the finger being further from the screen. Plot (c) shows the distribution of actual and predicted distances, showing good performance close to the device but rapidly dispersing from a distance of 1 onwards. Compare these plots to the MCMC samples in Figure 7.8. The RMSE on the test set for reconstructing the distance was 0.0163.

mobile phones. The VICI method provides an approach to approximation of Bayesian inference in a computationally and data-efficient manner, and with the ability to integrate prior physical and physiological models.

As the number of training points increases, the relative benefit of the use of a forward model in the inversion process can decrease. We illustrate that in Figure 7.13, which shows the performance with $N = 2000$ training points, and in this case the VICI approach does not improve on the direct inversion approach. However, in many real-world, high-dimensional problems, acquisition of sufficient data will remain a practical problem.

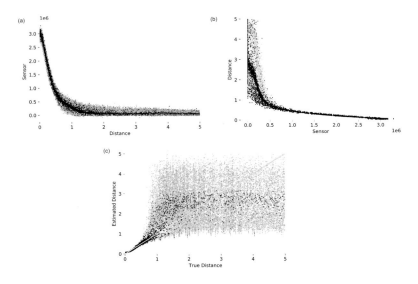

Figure 7.10 Results using the VICI approach. $N = 150$ training points. On the left you see the forward model prediction, on the right the inverse model prediction. Note how the approach can accurately learn to replicate the variability of the real system. Light grey points are predictive samples, dark grey ones means and medium grey ones are real data. The RMSE on the test set was 0.0151, lower than with the direct approach.

7.5.4 Implications for Interaction Design

For interaction design purposes, it is important to relate the uncertainty in solving the inverse problem to the interaction metaphor, so that in contexts in which human intentions are inherently less easily inferred, the human has lower expectations of the precision of possible interactions. Some of these will be characterised in a transparent way to the user by the physics of the situation (e.g. if a proximity sensor becomes less accurate with distance, then above a certain distance, we might design the interaction to not be sensitive to small changes in distance, whereas it might be very tightly coupled when closer to the system). Others may be more complex, highlighting unplanned-for situations where the inference is not robust. For example, the use of combinations of forward and inverse models also allows the system to cross-check the accuracy of the two models for the current observation for mutual compatibility. If it is impossible to find the state from the observations and then correctly predict the observations from that estimate, it gives an indication that we are in a region

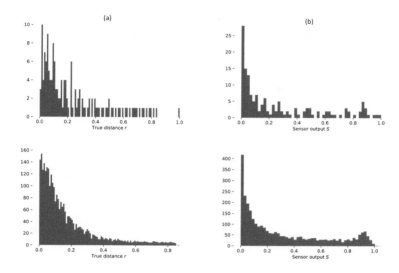

Figure 7.11 Histograms showing the distribution of data in the small and large samples. (Column (a) is r, column (b) is S). Upper figures for $N = 150$ and lower for $N = 2000$.

poorly supported by the model, and that we need to be more cautious in our interpretation of the results, given the uncertainty implied. This availability of uncertainty information is helpful, but the designer still needs to link it to appropriate interaction metaphors, to work well in practice.

7.6 Conclusions

One of the goals of this chapter is to emphasize the importance for designers of thinking about statistical inverse inference when designing sensing systems and their associated interaction metaphors. Progress in machine learning is allowing us to expand the basic approach to more complex, high-dimensional scenarios, but the foundational approaches to statistical inversion are sufficient to understand the broad impact. Almost all the core computational and statistical aspects discussed in this chapter are well known in statistics, applied mathematics, engineering and science, but they are not routinely overtly embedded into the interaction design process.

The recurring questions are: *How can we go from some sensor readings to knowledge of the human physical state?* and *How can we go from the physical state to the associated user intention?* This may then interact with questions

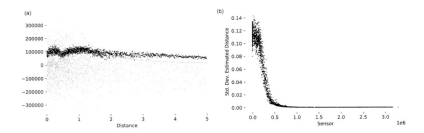

Figure 7.12 Standard deviation of results using the VICI approach. Training on $N = 150$ training points, testing on 2000. In plot (a), dark grey points show standard deviation of predictions, and the light grey points are the actual deviations from the mean in the test data (which have a standard deviation of 1e6, but where you can clearly see the clipping effect of the sensor limiting at zero). The RMSE on the test set was 0.0151, lower than with the direct approach. Compare plot (b) with plot (b) of Figure 7.9 and note the significantly reduced maximum variance.

such as: How the variability among different users, or different performances of the actions maps into variations in physical performance, and hence sensing, and via inversion, back to the inferred intention? In other words, the inversion process may be robust to some variations in the forward process, but very sensitive to others.

If the inverse problem for a particular task and interface combination is difficult to solve, leading to a broad posterior distribution, it means that the interface is likely to become difficult to use, because the system cannot reliably infer intention from sensed data.

We suggest that a key goal of the design process is to computationally design interfaces to make them easy to invert; designing the sensor characteristics, signal processing and interaction metaphors, such that smooth, natural, predictable interactions on the part of a user correspond to efficient tours of the information space, augmented with rich, human-centric feedback. We can design systems such that tools that humans are good at controlling can generate intention signals that are easy to reliably identify, and we can do so in simulation.

When analysing chains of human cognitive, physiological action, coupled with sensing and computational technology, this approach allows us to have controlled analysis and experimentation with a simulation pipeline of models from which we can predict the performance of different physical sensor systems and the associated algorithms for statistical inverse inference of intention from human movements. These models can be a heterogeneous mix

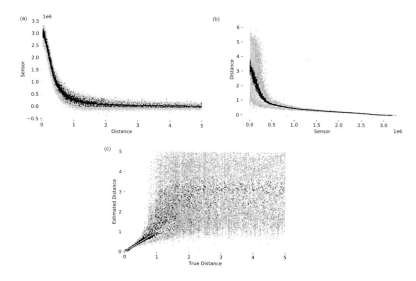

Figure 7.13 Results using the VICI approach with a larger training set ($N = 2000$). (a) The forward model predictions (mean in dark grey, samples in light grey, observed test data in medium grey). (b) Inverse model predictions. (c) Comparison of true distance and inferred distance. In this case there is no benefit of the VICI approach over learning the direct inverse mapping without using a forward model.

of theoretical and empirical models, with associated experimental data for validation and calibration.

This has obvious concrete scientific benefits, but may also be of interest when designing the specifications of future systems. For example, this simulated model can approximate the likely performance for different levels of sensor accuracy, helping the design team specify the appropriate hardware. Coupling the approach with the latest implementation frameworks and data management techniques from machine learning could create a much more systematic approach to validation of proposed model developments and enable a much more constructive, incremental and robust path forward.

Systematic application of probabilistic forward and inverse models has the potential to turn the analysis and design of input systems for human–computer interaction from an art into a science, putting the inference of human intent from sensed signals onto a much more rigorous basis.

Acknowledgements

RM.-S. and J.H.W. acknowledge support from EP/R018634/1 (*Closed-Loop Data Science for Complex, Computationally- and Data-Intensive Analytics*). F.T. and R.M.-S. acknowledge funding from EPSRC grants EP/M01326X/1, EP/T00097X/1 (*QuantIC*, the *UK Quantum Technology Hub in Quantum Enhanced Imaging*) and from Amazon.

References

[1] L. Ardizzone, J. Kruse, D. Rahner, S. Wirkert, E. W. Pellegrini, R. S. Klessen, L. Maier-Hein, C. Rother and U. Köthe. 2019. Analyzing inverse problems with invertible neural Networks. In: *International Conference on Learning Representations (ICLR'19)*.

[2] M. Bachynskyi. 2016. Biomechanical models for human-computer interaction. PhD thesis, Universität des Saarlandes Saarbrücken.

[3] M. Bachynskyi, G. Palmas, A. Oulasvirta, J. Steimle and T. Weinkauf. 2015. Performance and ergonomics of touch surfaces: a comparative study using biomechanical simulation. Pages 1817–1826 of: *Proceedings of the 33rd Annual ACM Conference on Human Factors in Computing Systems*. Association for Computing Machinery.

[4] A. Blake and M. Isard. 1997. The Condensation algorithm-conditional density propagation and applications to visual tracking. Pages 361–367 of: *Advances in Neural Information Processing Systems*. MIT Press.

[5] M. J. Black and A. D. Jepson. 1998. A probabilistic framework for matching temporal trajectories: Condensation-based recognition of gestures and expressions. Pages 909–924 of: *European Conference on Computer Vision*. Springer.

[6] S. L. Delp, F. C. Anderson, A. S. Arnold, P. Loan, A. Habib, C. T. John, E. Guendelman and D. G. Thelen. 2007. OpenSim: open-source software to create and analyze dynamic simulations of movement. *IEEE Transactions on Biomedical Engineering*, **54**(11), 1940–1950.

[7] L. Dinh, J. Sohl-Dickstein and S. Bengio. 2016. Density estimation using Real NVP. *ArXiv e-prints*, May.

[8] W. Grathwohl, R. T. Q. Chen, J. Bettencourt, I. Sutskever and D. Duvenaud. 2018. FFJORD: Free-form continuous dynamics for scalable reversible generative models. *ArXiv e-prints*, October.

[9] P. C. Hansen. 2010. *Discrete Inverse Problems: Insight and algorithms*. SIAM.

[10] R. Hester, A. Brown, L. Husband, R. Iliescu, W. A. Pruett, R. L. Summers and T. Coleman. 2011. HumMod: a modeling environment for the simulation of integrative human physiology. *Frontiers in Physiology*, **2**, 12.

[11] P. Isola, J.-Y. Zhu, T. Zhou and A. A. Efros. 2017. Image-to-image translation with conditional adversarial networks. Pages 1125–1134 of: *Proceedings of the IEEE Conference on Computer Vision and Pattern Recognition*. Institute of Electrical and Electronics Engineers.

[12] E. T. Jaynes. 2003. *Probability Theory: The Logic of Science*. Cambridge University Press.

[13] A. Kangasrääsiö, K. Athukorala, A. Howes, J. Corander, S. Kaski and A. Oulasvirta. 2017. Inferring cognitive models from data using approximate Bayesian computation. Pages 1295–1306 of: *Proceedings of the 2017 CHI Conference on Human Factors in Computing Systems*. CHI '17. Association for Computing Machinery

[14] D. J. C. MacKay. 2003. *Information Theory, Inference and Learning Algorithms*. Cambridge University Press.

[15] M. Mansouri and J. A. Reinbolt. 2012. A platform for dynamic simulation and control of movement based on OpenSim and MATLAB. *Journal of Biomechanics*, **45**(8), 1517–1521.

[16] S. A. Mayer. 2019. *Finger orientation as an additional input dimension for touchscreens*. PhD thesis, University of Stuttgart.

[17] R. Murray-Smith. 2017. Stratified, computational interaction via machine learning. Pages 95–101 of: K. Narendra, ed. *The 18th Yale Workshop on Adaptive and Learning Systems*. Yale University.

[18] A. Nguyen, J. Clune, Y. Bengio, A. Dosovitskiy and J. Yosinski, Jason. 2017. Plug & play generative networks: conditional iterative generation of images in latent space. Pages 4467–77 of: *Proceedings of the IEEE Conference on Computer Vision and Pattern Recognition (CVPR)*. Institute of Electrical and Electronics Engineers.

[19] T. O'Hagan. 2004. Dicing with the unknown. *Significance*, **1**(3), 132–133.

[20] A. Oulasvirta, S. Kim and B. Lee. 2018. Neuromechanics of a button press. Page 4099–4112 of: *Proceedings of the 2018 CHI Conference on Human Factors in Computing Systems*. Association for Computing Machinery.

[21] S. Rogers, J. Williamson, C. Stewart and R. Murray-Smith. 2011. AnglePose: robust, precise capacitive touch tracking via 3D orientation estimation. Pages 2575–84 of: *Proceedings of the SIGCHI Conference on Human Factors in Computing Systems*. Association for Computing Machinery.

[22] S. Särkkä. 2013. *Bayesian Filtering and Smoothing*. Institute of Mathematical Sciences Textbooks, Vol. 3. Cambridge University Press.

[23] K. Sohn, H. Lee and X. Yan. 2015. Learning structured output representation using deep conditional generative models. Pages 3483–491 of: *Advances in Neural Information Processing Systems*. NIPS '15. Neural Information Processing Systems.

[24] A. Tarantola. 2005. *Inverse Problem Theory and Methods for Model Parameter Estimation*. Vol. 89. SIAM.

[25] A. N. Tikhonov and V. Y. Arsenin. 1977. *Solutions of Ill-Posed Problems*. Winston.

[26] F. Tonolini, J. Radford, A. Turpin, D. Faccio and R. Murray-Smith. 2020. Variational inference for computational imaging inverse problems. *Journal of Machine Learning Research*, **21**(179), 1–46.

[27] M. A. A. Turkman, C. D. Paulino and P. Müller. 2019. *Computational Bayesian Statistics: An Introduction*. Institute of Mathematical Sciences Textbooks, Vol. 11. Cambridge University Press.

[28] J. Williamson and R. Murray-Smith. 2012. Rewarding the original: explorations in joint user-sensor motion spaces. Pages 1717–26 of: *Proceedings of the 2012 ACM Annual Conference on Human Factors in Computing Systems*. CHI '12. Association for Computing Machinery.

[29] D. M. Wolpert and M. Kawato. 1998. Multiple paired forward and inverse models for motor control. *Neural Networks*, **11**(7–8), 1317–1329.

Part III

Bayesian Optimisation in Interaction Design

8

Preferential Bayesian Optimisation for Visual Design

Yuki Koyama, Toby Chong and Takeo Igarashi

Abstract

Visual design often involves the task of searching for an optimal parameter set that produces a subjectively preferable design. We can formulate this task as a mathematical optimisation problem with human preference as an objective function. However, we cannot directly apply typical optimisation algorithms to this problem since the system cannot trivially evaluate the objective. The system needs to send queries to a (costly) human evaluator, who only provides relative preference (i.e. which option they like the most). This chapter reviews *preferential Bayesian optimisation* (PBO), a powerful technique to aid this task. PBO is a human-in-the-loop Bayesian optimisation specialising in human preference oracle. This method models the latent preference in a probabilistic manner and generates effective preference queries to either designers or potential audiences based on the preference model. We first describe its mathematical formulation and illustrate its behaviour using a simple pairwise-comparison query. We then provide two practical extensions of PBO: use of a continuous-space query and incorporation of domain-specific knowledge. These two extensions are applied to photo colour enhancement and generative image modelling, respectively, as illustrative examples.

8.1 Motivation for Preferential Bayesian Optimisation

8.1.1 Visual Design as an Optimisation Problem

Visual design often involves *parameter tweaking*, where design software lets the designer manipulate multiple sliders and updates the design preview in accordance with the slider configuration. Some combinations of slider values (i.e. parameter sets) would provide visually preferable design outcomes, and some others would not. Thus, the primary goal of this task is to find the parameter set that produces the most subjectively preferable design outcome. This design process with a parameterised design space is sometimes referred to as *parametric design*.

We can find many parametric design scenarios in computer graphics applications at both casual and professional levels. Photo colour enhancement [10] is one of the most popular scenarios of parametric design, where photo retouch software (e.g. Photoshop[1] and Instagram[2]) provides user-adjustable parameters such as brightness and contrast. Other popular scenarios include animation [15], material appearance [9, 16] and 3D modelling [23, 25]. Recently, many software packages for graphics have node editors to enable *procedural design* for modelling, texturing, composition and so on (e.g. Blender[3] and Houdini[4]), where, once a node tree is constructed, the remaining task is to adjust parameters of each node. *Generative modelling* has become more and more popular recently thanks to deep generative models [5, 6], where a latent vector fed to generative models is the parameter set to be determined. Parametric design scenarios can also be found in architecture design (e.g. Grasshopper[5]), engineering design (e.g. Fusion 360[6]), and more.

Parametric design is, however, not an easy process. It is necessary to generate and compare many possible designs by actively manipulating slider values back and forth. This is because determining appropriate parameter sets is hard without actually seeing the corresponding designs. Thus, this process requires trial and error. When there are only a few sliders, this approach could work; however, when there are many sliders, this task is often unacceptably time-consuming, and it is difficult to reach an appropriate slider configuration. Thus, designers need to have a good strategy to explore possible designs and search for preferable ones, which is usually acquired by domain knowledge and expertise.

This parametric design task can be modelled as a *mathematical optimisation* problem. The *search variables* are the slider values to be adjusted. The *objective function* to be maximised is a function that returns the perceptual preferential score (or the *goodness* score) for a given design parameter set; we call the function the *goodness function*. The *search space* is formed by all possible parameter sets; this is also referred to as the *design space*. The goal of the task is to find the *best* point (i.e. the maximiser of the goodness function) from this space by solving this optimisation problem somehow. Figure 8.1 illustrates the

---

[1] www.adobe.com/products/photoshop.html
[2] www.instagram.com/
[3] www.blender.org/
[4] www.sidefx.com/products/houdini/
[5] www.grasshopper3d.com/
[6] www.autodesk.com/products/fusion-360/overview

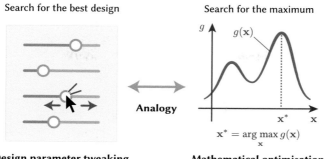

Search for the best design   Search for the maximum

Analogy

Design parameter tweaking   **Mathematical optimisation**

$$\mathbf{x}^* = \arg \max_{\mathbf{x}} g(\mathbf{x})$$

Figure 8.1 Optimisation viewpoint of parametric design process. Design parameter tweaking (usually done by a designer with an ad hoc strategy) and mathematical optimisation (usually done by a computer system with a numerical optimisation algorithm) have many analogous points.

concept. This viewpoint is taken in *computational design* research to devise new ways of utilising computational techniques such as *numerical optimisation* algorithms for solving design problems [8].

This chapter describes a Bayesian approach to effectively solve this optimisation problem and thus facilitate visual parametric design. However, unlike typical optimisation problems we see in textbooks of applied mathematics, this problem needs some special consideration since it involves human preference in its problem definition, as described in the following.

8.1.2 Specific Considerations on Preference Evaluation

One of the most important points that distinguish the above optimisation problem from typical ones is that the objective function is based on humans' *perceptual preference* and thus is not executable on computers. This leads us to think of *human-in-the-loop* techniques. That is, rather than designing an algorithm such that it is executable purely on computers, it would be reasonable to design it to be executed by a hybrid of computers and humans, where computers ask humans to respond to some queries sequentially.

Consequently, we want an algorithm to be very efficient in terms of the number of necessary queries, since the objective function (i.e. human preference) is much more expensive to query than those in typical optimisation problems. For instance, if an objective function can be queried (i.e. its function value can be evaluated) in roughly one millisecond purely on computers, it is feasible for an algorithm to perform 10 000 function evaluations to find a

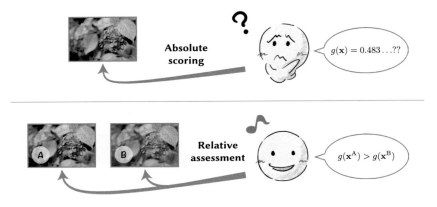

Figure 8.2 Absolute scoring vs relative assessment in terms of perceptual preference on visual designs. Relative assessment is often considered to be more suitable than absolute scoring.

solution; however, since every single query to humans inevitably takes at least a few seconds, it is not feasible for an algorithm to expect 10 000 queries (even 100 queries may be too many).

Another important point is the fact that perceptual function values are not stably observable directly through *absolute* scoring, unlike typical executable objective functions. In other words, supposing that g is a function of a parameter x, we should not expect the function value $g_i = g(x_i)$ for a parameter x_i to be directly observable. This is because absolute scoring (i.e. given a visual design, asking an evaluator to provide its absolute score) would suffer from several critical issues [2, 24], including the *drift effect* (i.e. 'the scale varies over time' [2]), the *anchoring effect* (i.e. 'early experiences dominate the scale' [2]), and the inconsistent scaling among evaluators.

Thus, it has been considered that preference needs to be observed through *relative* assessment [9, 13, 24] instead of absolute scoring, since evaluators can much more stably choose a preferred one from multiple options (see Figure 8.2) than providing absolute scores to them independently. In other words, we should observe which value is larger (i.e. which design is more preferable) among multiple options, instead of directly observing what values they are. The number of options may be two in the simplest form but can be more than two. The important point is that the assessment should be done relatively among multiple options.

Requirements

In summary, we want an optimisation algorithm for solving parametric visual design problems that involve preferential evaluation to have the following properties.

- To involve human evaluators (either designers or audiences) in the algorithmic loop to obtain preferential feedback.
- To be able to find a satisfactory solution with a reasonably small number of queries.
- To use relative assessment as its query form (i.e. preferential query) to human evaluators rather than using absolute scoring.

8.1.3 A Solution: Preferential Bayesian Optimisation

This chapter reviews a powerful Bayesian approach to this problem, which we call *preferential Bayesian optimisation* (PBO) [1, 2, 4, 11, 12, 26]. PBO is a human-in-the-loop extension of *Bayesian optimisation* (BO) [20] designed so as to handle perceptual objective functions. Unlike BO, PBO is specifically formulated based on *preferential query* (i.e. relative assessment of multiple options) and thus does not require absolute scoring. These properties well fit the requirements discussed above.

Another important property of PBO is that it is able to find a good solution with a small number of queries. This property comes from that of BO, which has been explored for solving expensive-to-evaluate problems (e.g. hyperparameter tuning in machine learning [21]). This efficiency in terms of the number of queries is achieved by automatically taking the balance between *exploration* (i.e. visit as many little-explored regions as possible) and *exploitation* (i.e. visit as many high-expectation regions as possible) for determining the next query for each iteration. Likewise, PBO also gains this benefit by taking the exploration–exploitation balance for determining the next preferential query for each iteration. This chapter does not require readers to have prior knowledge of BO, but readers can refer to [20] for a dedicated introduction to BO.

PBO infers posterior distributions of the perceptual objective function from preferential data in a Bayesian manner. Since PBO relies only on preference queries, absolute goodness function values, or *goodness values*, cannot be directly observed. PBO handles these latent values as random variables that follow some prior distribution (e.g. Gaussian process). Using probability models of relative assessment responses [14, 24], given such data, PBO infers the latent goodness values and the posterior distribution of the latent goodness function. PBO then uses the posterior distribution for determining the most worth-observing next preferential query in a way similar to BO. Thus, compared to non-Bayesian approaches to this problem (e.g. simple hill-climbing algorithm), PBO can take full advantage of observed data to minimise the number of queries.

Chapter Organisation

This chapter is organized as follows. We first describe mathematical formulations of PBO and how preferential data are handled in a probabilistic manner (Section 8.2). Then, we provide two practical extensions of PBO with illustrative examples. As for the first extension, we review a preference query form that involves continuous spaces rather than discrete choices, and explain how it can efficiently solve problems such as photo colour enhancement [11] (Section 8.3). As for the second extension, we review a PBO formulation that incorporates domain-specific considerations, and demonstrate its effectiveness in deep generative image modelling scenarios [4] (Section 8.4). Finally, we discuss the relationship to other alternative solutions, the user experience considerations and the opportunities to use PBO as a backend of future creativity support tools (Section 8.5), and then we summarise this chapter (Section 8.6).

8.2 Mathematical Formulation

8.2.1 Problem Definition

Suppose that the target design problem is parameterised by n continuous parameters, $x_1, \ldots, x_n$. Let $\mathbf{x}$ be the concatenation of the design parameter values (or a parameter set), and let $\mathcal{X}$ be the set of all possible parameter sets (or the *design space*). That is,

$$\mathbf{x} = \begin{bmatrix} x_1 & \cdots & x_n \end{bmatrix}^{\mathsf{T}} \in \mathcal{X}. \tag{8.1}$$

Every parameter set is supposed to be associated with a certain visual design. Let $g \colon \mathcal{X} \to \mathbb{R}$ be a *goodness function*, which is defined based on a human's perceptual preference. It takes a parameter set as input and evaluates how good the associated visual design is. A higher goodness value indicates a more preferred design, and vice versa. The goal of the design process is to solve an optimisation problem:

$$\mathbf{x}^* = \arg\max_{\mathbf{x} \in \mathcal{X}} g(\mathbf{x}), \tag{8.2}$$

where $\mathbf{x}^*$ is the maximiser of the goodness function g. In this optimisation problem, the parameter set $\mathbf{x}$ is the search variables, the goodness function g is the objective function to be maximised and the design space $\mathcal{X}$ is the search

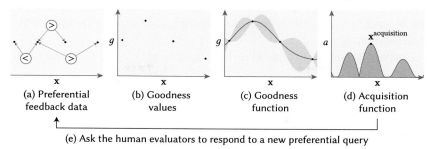

(a) Preferential feedback data

(b) Goodness values

(c) Goodness function

(d) Acquisition function

(e) Ask the human evaluators to respond to a new preferential query

Figure 8.3 Stepwise illustration of a single PBO iteration. The steps (a)–(d) illustrate the data and functions involved in each step. The step (e) involves human evaluation, and the next iteration then begins once this is done.

space. Here, we assume the existence of human evaluators (who can be a single user, multiple crowd workers, etc.) whose preference is consistent and does not change over time.

As mentioned, it is not reasonable to directly observe return values of the objective function g, unlike typical optimisation problems. That is, for a given parameter set $\mathbf{x}$, we cannot directly obtain the value $g(\mathbf{x})$ by asking human evaluators to provide an absolute score. Instead, we can query human evaluators about relative assessment; for example, given parameter sets $\mathbf{x}^A$ and $\mathbf{x}^B$, human evaluators can stably answer which parameter set is better than the other. In the case that the evaluators prefer the visual design corresponding to $\mathbf{x}^A$, we can interpret it as a sample of data representing $g(\mathbf{x}^A) > g(\mathbf{x}^B)$ (see Figure 8.2).

8.2.2 Overview of Preferential Bayesian Optimisation

PBO is an extension of BO and differs from BO mainly in two aspects. First, it involves humans in its loop to incorporate human preference in its computation. This approach is considered as *human computation* [18], which is the concept of solving problems by incorporating humans into computational systems as processing power; human evaluators in PBO are considered a processing module that responds to queries about visual preference. The second aspect is that PBO handles preferential feedback data generated through relative assessment instead of directly handling absolute function values as in BO.

PBO is an iterative algorithm; it iteratively asks the human evaluators to respond to preferential queries to obtain preferential feedback data. We denote by d_t the preferential feedback data sample obtained at the tth iteration, and by $\mathcal{D}_t$ the accumulated preferential data, i.e. $\mathcal{D}_t = \{d_1, \ldots, d_t\}$ (see Figure 8.3(a) for an illustration of a preferential feedback data where $t = 3$). We will explain the details of preferential feedback data representation and its likelihood in the next subsection.

Suppose that the data $\mathcal{D}_t$ involves m data points, $\mathbf{x}^{(1)}, \ldots, \mathbf{x}^{(m)}$, in the target design space (e.g. $m = 4$ in the case of Figure 8.3(a)), and let

$$\mathbf{g} = \begin{bmatrix} g^{(1)} & \cdots & g^{(m)} \end{bmatrix}^{\mathsf{T}} \in \mathbb{R}^m \tag{8.3}$$

be the concatenation of the goodness values on these data points (e.g. $g^{(i)} = g(\mathbf{x}^{(i)})$). Since we cannot directly observe the goodness values $\mathbf{g}$, we need to estimate them from the preferential feedback data $\mathcal{D}_t$. To estimate these unknown goodness values (and to predict goodness values on unseen data points), we here assume the *Gaussian process* (GP) prior [19] to the goodness function (i.e. any finite set of goodness function values is jointly Gaussian distributed), which is a popular choice in BO methods. Refer to the book by Rasmussen and Williams [19] for details of GP.

We now want to estimate the goodness values $\mathbf{g}$ based on the given data $\mathcal{D}_t$ (see Figure 8.3(b)). For this, we perform the *maximum a posteriori* (MAP) estimation:

$$\mathbf{g}_t^{\text{MAP}} = \arg \max_{\mathbf{g}} p(\mathbf{g} \mid \mathcal{D}_t) \tag{8.4}$$

$$= \arg \max_{\mathbf{g}} p(\mathcal{D}_t \mid \mathbf{g}) p(\mathbf{g}) \tag{8.5}$$

$$= \arg \max_{\mathbf{g}} \left\{ \prod_{i=1}^{t} p(d_i \mid \mathbf{g}) \right\} p(\mathbf{g}), \tag{8.6}$$

where $p(d \mid \mathbf{g})$ is the data likelihood, for which several models are available depending on preferential feedback data types as we will explain the details in the next subsection, and $p(\mathbf{g})$ is a multivariate Gaussian distribution since we assume the GP prior.

Once the goodness values are obtained via the MAP estimation, we can predict the underlying goodness function g in the manner of *Gaussian process regression* (GPR) [19] (see Figure 8.3(c)). The GPR technique provides the predictive distribution of the goodness value at an arbitrary data point $\mathbf{x}$ as a Gaussian distribution. That is, we can write

$$g(\mathbf{x}) \sim \mathcal{N}(\mu_t(\mathbf{x}), \sigma_t^2(\mathbf{x})), \tag{8.7}$$

where $\mu_t : \mathcal{X} \to \mathbb{R}$ and $\sigma_t^2 : \mathcal{X} \to \mathbb{R}_{\geq 0}$ are the predicted mean and variance functions respectively.

The next step of PBO is to determine the data point that should be visited in the next query. To evaluate how worth-visiting a point is, BO methods use an *acquisition function* [20] (see Figure 8.3(d)). An acquisition function can be written in the form

$$a_t(\mathbf{x}) = a(\mathbf{x}; \mu_t, \sigma_t^2), \qquad (8.8)$$

where a larger value indicates that the data point is more worth visiting, and vice versa. Roughly speaking, an acquisition function will take the balance between *exploration* (i.e. favour points with large variances) and *exploitation* (i.e. favour points with large means). Using this function, the most worth-visiting point can be determined by

$$\mathbf{x}_t^{\text{acquisition}} = \arg\max_{\mathbf{x} \in \mathcal{X}} a_t(\mathbf{x}). \qquad (8.9)$$

Researchers have been proposed several acquisition function definitions. Among them, *expected improvement* is a popular choice (e.g. [21]) since its performance is often better than others and it does not have hyperparameters that need manual tuning.

The last step in each iteration is to compose a preferential query and ask the human evaluators to respond to it (see Figure 8.3(e)). The preferential query should be about relative assessment. The simplest relative assessment would be pairwise comparison, where two candidates are presented and one of them is selected. In this case, a straightforward way of composing such a query is to choose the most worth-visiting point, $\mathbf{x}_t^{\text{acquisition}}$, and the current-best point,

$$\mathbf{x}_t^+ = \arg\max_{\mathbf{x} \in \{\mathbf{x}^{(1)}, \dots, \mathbf{x}^{(m)}\}} \mu_t(\mathbf{x}), \qquad (8.10)$$

as the candidates to be compared [1].

8.2.3 Preferential Queries and Probability Models

This subsection describes three representative preferential queries: pairwise comparison, top-1 selection, and ranking, and how they can be probabilistically modelled. These probability models are used to calculate the likelihoods of preferential feedback data in the PBO procedure. Refer to technical articles [14, 24] for further details and backgrounds of these probability models, and the documentation of a machine learning library, choix,[7] for recent works on these probability models.

Pairwise Comparison

In this query, two options are given, and the better one is chosen. Let the parameter sets corresponding to the two options be $\mathbf{x}^{(i)}$ and $\mathbf{x}^{(j)}$, and suppose that $\mathbf{x}^{(i)}$ is chosen. The preferential feedback data for this query are denoted by

---

[7] http://choix.lum.li/

$$d = [\mathbf{x}^{(i)} \succ \mathbf{x}^{(j)}].\tag{8.11}$$

The Bradley–Terry model can be used for modelling the probability of this data, and the probability is modelled as

$$p(d \mid \mathbf{g}) = \frac{\exp(g^{(i)})}{\exp(g^{(i)}) + \exp(g^{(j)})} = \sigma(g^{(i)} - g^{(j)}),\tag{8.12}$$

where σ is the standard logistic function.

Top-1 Selection

In this query, n options ($n \geq 2$) are given, and the best one is chosen. Let the parameter sets corresponding to the options be $\mathbf{x}^{(1)}, \ldots, \mathbf{x}^{(n)}$, and suppose that $\mathbf{x}^{(i)}$ is chosen. The preferential feedback data for this query are denoted by

$$d = [\mathbf{x}^{(i)} \succ \{\mathbf{x}^{(1)}, \ldots, \mathbf{x}^{(i-1)}, \mathbf{x}^{(i+1)}, \ldots, \mathbf{x}^{(n)}\}].\tag{8.13}$$

The Bradley–Terry–Luce model can be used for modelling the probability of this data, and the probability is modelled as

$$p(d \mid \mathbf{g}) = \frac{\exp(g^{(i)})}{\exp(g^{(1)}) + \cdots + \exp(g^{(n)})}.\tag{8.14}$$

Note that this model is a generalisation of the Bradley–Terry model; the Bradley–Terry model can be derived from the Bradley–Terry–Luce model by setting $n = 2$.

Ranking

In this query, n options ($n \geq 2$) are given, and the order of these options is answered. Let the parameter sets corresponding to the options be $\mathbf{x}^{(1)}, \ldots, \mathbf{x}^{(n)}$, and suppose that the order is $\mathbf{x}^{(i)}, \mathbf{x}^{(j)}, \ldots, \mathbf{x}^{(k)}$. The preferential feedback data for this query are denoted by

$$d = [\mathbf{x}^{(i)} \succ \mathbf{x}^{(j)} \succ \cdots \succ \mathbf{x}^{(k)}].\tag{8.15}$$

The Plackett–Luce model can be used for modelling the probability of this data, and the probability is modelled as

$$p(d \mid \mathbf{g}) = \frac{\exp(g^{(i)})}{\exp(g^{(i)}) + \exp(g^{(j)}) + \cdots + \exp(g^{(k)})}$$
$$\cdot \frac{\exp(g^{(j)})}{\exp(g^{(j)}) + \cdots + \exp(g^{(k)})} \cdots \cdot \frac{\exp(g^{(k)})}{\exp(g^{(k)})}.\tag{8.16}$$

Algorithm 8.1 Procedure of PBO with pairwise comparison queries.

Result: An optimal parameter set $\mathbf{x}^*$

1 $\mathcal{D} \leftarrow \emptyset$;

2 Set $\mathbf{x}^+$ and $\mathbf{x}^{\text{acquisition}}$ to random points;

3 **repeat**

4   Ask the evaluator to compare $\mathbf{x}^+$ and $\mathbf{x}^{\text{acquisition}}$;

5    $\mathcal{D} \leftarrow \mathcal{D} \cup [\mathbf{x}^{\text{selected}} \succ \mathbf{x}^{\text{not selected}}]$;

6    $\mathbf{g}^{\text{MAP}} \leftarrow \arg\max_{\mathbf{g}} p(\mathbf{g} \mid \mathcal{D})$;   `// Perform MAP estimation`

7   Perform GPR;

8    $\mathbf{x}^{\text{acquisition}} \leftarrow \arg\max_{\mathbf{x} \in \mathcal{X}} a(\mathbf{x})$;   `// Find the next`
     `candidate point`

9    $\mathbf{x}^+ \leftarrow \arg\max_{\mathbf{x} \in \{\mathbf{x}^{(i)}\}_i} \mu(\mathbf{x})$;   `// Find the`
     `current-best point`

10 **until** *The evaluator is satisfied with* $\mathbf{x}^+$;

11 $\mathbf{x}^* \leftarrow \mathbf{x}^+$

Note that this model can be understood as a sequential application of the Bradley–Terry–Luce model; the best option is taken from the n options, then the second-best option is taken from the rest of $n - 1$ options, and so forth.

8.2.4 Implementing Preferential Bayesian Optimisation

To help readers implement PBO, we show an example pseudocode in Algorithm 8.1, where we use the pairwise comparison query for its simplicity. Since there are no feedback data yet at the beginning of the procedure, the current-best point $\mathbf{x}^+$ and $\mathbf{x}^{\text{acquisition}}$ are randomly set in this case (see line 2). A human evaluator is integrated into the loop in line 4. Each iteration involves two maximisation problems (lines 6 and 8), both of which are differentiable and able to be efficiently solved by standard optimisation algorithms such as the limited-memory BFGS method [17]. Note that the latter problem (line 8) often has multiple local optima, so we recommend to solve the problem multiple times with random initialization and take the best one. Once the human evaluator is satisfied with the current-best solution, the iteration ends, and the system returns it as the found optimal solution.

To illustrate how PBO works, we show a sequence of performing the PBO procedure for a one-dimensional toy problem using the pairwise comparison query (see Figure 8.4).

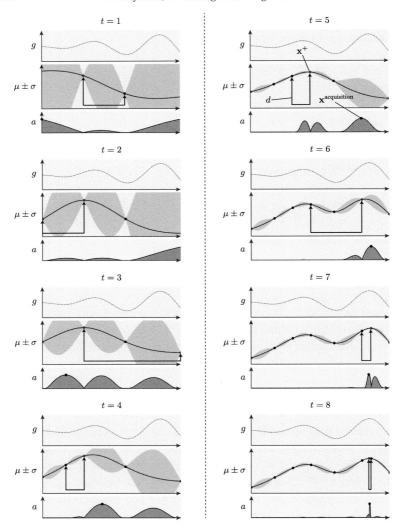

Figure 8.4 How PBO works with pairwise comparison queries. In this example, a one-dimensional synthetic function is used as the objective function to simulate human assessment.

8.3 Extension 1: Optimisation with Continuous-Space Query

This section describes an extension of PBO to improve its efficiency [11]; the key idea is to use a 'continuous-space' query instead of 'discrete-point' queries to obtain richer information from human assessment.

(a) **Task:** Choose the image that looks better	(b) **Task:** Adjust the slider so that the image looks the best

Pairwise comparison	Single-slider manipulation

Figure 8.5 Discrete-point and continuous-space queries. Pairwise comparison (a) involves only two discrete points from the search space. In contrast, single-slider manipulation (b) involves a continuous one-dimensional subspace.

8.3.1 Motivation and Formulation

The pairwise comparison task involves only 'discrete points' in a single query; the preferential information we can obtain in each iteration is limited to only two points in the search space. One useful extension here is to introduce a 'continuous-space' query design, in which the points to be compared are sampled from a continuous subspace of the search space. This continuous-space query design provides much more information than the discrete-point query design since it involves a virtually infinite number of points in a query. Thus, we can expect that it reduces the number of necessary iterations.

Here, we describe *single-slider manipulation* as a representative example of continuous-space queries. The evaluator's task is to manipulate the presented slider and determine the slider tick position that produces the best visual design (see Figure 8.5). Executing this task is interpreted from the mathematical viewpoint as

$$\mathbf{x}_t^{\text{chosen}} = \arg\max_{\mathbf{x} \in \mathcal{S}_t} g(\mathbf{x}), \tag{8.17}$$

where $\mathcal{S}_t \subset \mathcal{X}$ is a one-dimensional subspace of the search space $\mathcal{X}$ for the tth iteration. This subspace is mapped to the slider and thus called a *slider space*. The slider space can be constructed by, for example, connecting $\mathbf{x}_t^+$ and $\mathbf{x}_t^{\text{acquisition}}$.

We can interpret the response to this single-slider manipulation query as

$$\mathbf{x}_t^{\text{chosen}} \succ \{\mathbf{x} \mid \mathbf{x} \in \mathcal{S}_t, \mathbf{x} \neq \mathbf{x}_t^{\text{chosen}}\}, \tag{8.18}$$

where the left-hand side has an infinite number of data points. We can simplify this by using a finite number of representative points from the slider space $\mathcal{S}_t$.

Let $\mathbf{x}_t^A$ and $\mathbf{x}_t^B$ be the two endpoints of the slider space. Using these two points, the query can be approximately interpreted as

$$\mathbf{x}_t^{\text{chosen}} \succ \{\mathbf{x}_t^A, \mathbf{x}_t^B\}. \tag{8.19}$$

This is considered a response that $\mathbf{x}_t^{\text{chosen}}$ is chosen among the three options, $\mathbf{x}_t^{\text{chosen}}$, $\mathbf{x}_t^A$ and $\mathbf{x}_t^B$. Thus we can apply the top-1 selection model to probabilistically model this preferential feedback data.

8.3.2 Experimental Results in Photo Colour Enhancement

We show experimental results of applying PBO with the single-slider manipulation query in one of the most popular parametric design scenarios: photo colour enhancement. In this case, we targeted six parameters to optimise: brightness, contrast, saturation and colour balance for red, green and blue channels. As for the human evaluator, we used microtask-based crowdsourcing to involve multiple individuals in the PBO loop and took the median of the responses to obtain $\mathbf{x}^{\text{chosen}}$ in each iteration. We performed 15 iterations for each case. Figure 8.6 shows the results as well as the original photographs and the results by auto-enhancement in commercial software, Photoshop and Lightroom, for comparison. The numbers shown on each photograph indicate how many times the photograph was selected in crowd voting conducted independently from the PBO procedure. These results suggest that performing 15 iterations was sufficient to reasonably solve these six-dimensional problems, and the PBO approach could produce perceptually preferable solutions.

8.4 Extension 2: Acquisition Function with Domain-Specific Terms

This section demonstrates how to combine domain-specific operations to aid the PBO procedure. In particular, the acquisition function maximisation (Equation (8.9)) is adapted to incorporate domain-specific considerations and user specifications [4].

8.4.1 Motivation

The original PBO formulation is unaware of target domains and users' specific intentions (e.g. editing content locally). While this generality is one of the advantages of PBO, it can be extended for further efficiency by focusing on specific target domains. Here we demonstrate that it is possible to extend

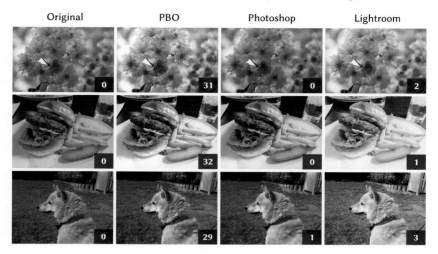

Figure 8.6 Results of applying PBO with a continuous-space query to photo colour enhancement. The first column shows the original input photographs. The second column shows the results, where crowd workers performed single-slider manipulation tasks to indicate their preference. The third and fourth columns show results of applying auto-enhancement of existing software for comparison. The numbers indicate the result of crowd voting conducted independently from the PBO procedure.

the acquisition function by adding some domain-specific terms to incorporate considerations such as local edit or even more specific instruction from the user. To do so, we augment the acquisition function with an additional *content-aware* term, $O(\mathbf{x})$, which injects specific user preference information, such as image edits, to the optimisation. That is,

$$a'_t(\mathbf{x}) = a(\mathbf{x}; \mu_t, \sigma_t^2) + O(\mathbf{x}). \qquad (8.20)$$

This term can contain arbitrary criteria; in the next subsection, we review an example definition specialised for image editing.

8.4.2 Experimental Results in Generative Image Modelling

Generative adversarial networks (GANs) and variational auto-encoders (VAEs) can generate images from a multi-dimensional latent vector (e.g. [6]). Here, choosing a latent vector that produces a desired image can be formulated as a PBO process. However, applying PBO to solve such a problem is challenging since (1) GANs are often trained in a high dimension (512 dimensions in our test case), and (2) a large number of local maxima exist.

For this task, Chong *et al.* [4] developed an interactive image editing system that extends the slider interface described in Section 8.3 and allows users to directly annotate their intention onto the generated image during the PBO process. Let G be a static generator function that generates an image I from a given latent vector $\mathbf{x}$; that is,

$$I = G(\mathbf{x}). \tag{8.21}$$

In this system, in addition to optimising the vector in the slider space, the user can also specify a region to be a specific colour(s) by painting and/or copy-and-pasting image regions from other images onto the system-generated image I. The user-edited image I' contains regions that are edited by the user (i.e. $I'_{x,y} \neq I_{x,y}$) and that are untouched (i.e. $I'_{x,y} = I_{x,y}$). To encourage the PBO engine to produce an image that aligns with the user-edited image I' as a candidate for the next query, the domain-specific term is defined as

$$O(\mathbf{x}) = \sum_x \sum_y \{\{G(\mathbf{x})_{x,y} - I'_{x,y}\} \circ M_{x,y}\}^2, \tag{8.22}$$

where $\circ$ is an element-wise product operator, and M is an image defined as

$$M_{x,y} = \begin{cases} 1.0 & (I'_{x,y} \neq I_{x,y}) \\ 0.2 & (I'_{x,y} = I_{x,y}) \end{cases}. \tag{8.23}$$

We set $M_{x,y} = 1.0$ for regions where the user provides edit, and $M_{x,y} = 0.2$ for the untouched region to represent that the lack of intention to adjust a certain region. We also define an eraser operation as $M_{x,y} = 0.0$ to encourage change. Figure 8.7 shows several examples of image editing by using this approach, where the user could find the desired images by PBO augmented by direct image annotations.

8.5 Discussion

8.5.1 Other Alternative Solutions

This chapter has discussed the parametric visual design problem in which visual designs are assessed by human preference and introduced PBO as a solution. Of course, other alternative solutions exist for this problem.

Interactive evolutionary computation (IEC) [22] is one such solution and had been investigated intensively before PBO emerged. While IEC relies on random serendipity to approach the optimal solution, PBO uses Bayesian formulations to model uncertainty in the search space, by which it determines an as-effective-as-possible query in each iteration. Thus, PBO is likely to require only a small number of iterations.

Initial result   User edits   Final result   Initial result   User edits   Final result

Figure 8.7 Examples of user annotations and candidates suggested by PBO controlling the synthesis results of PGGAN [6]. For each case, the left image shows the initial result generated using a random seed. The middle shows user edits on the initial result, where the user provides annotations by painting and copy-and-pasting regions from other images. The right shows the result of PBO controlled by the user annotations. By providing image annotations, the user could (a) make a man bald, (b) add a beard, (c) make a woman smile, and (d) remove glasses.

Another popular approach is called *design galleries* [15], which provides users with an overview of the possible designs via a user interface. While this approach is useful for understanding the design space and finding an initial solution, it is not designed for the sequential refinement of the solution as in PBO.

It is also possible to devise human-in-the-loop optimisation algorithms by extending *local search* algorithms (e.g. hill climbing) instead of BO (e.g. [3]). While this is an exciting direction to investigate in the future, BO has some advantages over local search algorithms. First, BO considers *all* observed data to determine the most reasonable next query, while local search algorithms consider only the current state. Second, BO can globally search the design space, while local search algorithms search for better solutions only locally around the current solution.

8.5.2 Enhancing User Experience

Additional User Control

While this chapter has focused on the technical aspect of PBO, enhancing user experience is also an important topic. One possible approach is to add more user control during the PBO process so that the user can be more actively involved in the process. For example, a recent study [27] suggested that allowing users to interactively control the balance between exploration and exploitation could improve users' engagement during the user-in-the-loop optimisation process.

Incorporating Direct Parameter Manipulation

The PBO-based workflow does not require users to understand what design parameters are involved and how their values affect the outcome, since users do not interact with raw design parameters during the search process. While this feature can lower the barrier for novices, it can also make the system too black-box. For professional users who are familiar with target design parameters, it would be better to provide the opportunity to directly manipulate the parameters in addition to the PBO-based search. By doing so, the system can have better controllability and transparency, which is often considered necessary in such expert use [7].

Offering a Better Understanding of the Design Space

One of the PBO-based workflow limitations is that users do not have an explicit opportunity to build a mental model of the entire design space. This may affect the confidence in the outcome of the PBO-based workflow; users can be unconfident about the optimality of the outcome without having a global view of the design space. Thus, designing appropriate user interaction to resolve this issue would be important. For example, using a gallery-based interface to provide candidate solutions to users [12] can be a solution to let users effectively understand the design space during the search.

8.5.3 Towards Future Digital Content Creation Tools

Parametric design with high-dimensional search spaces has become popular in various digital content creation scenarios, thanks to recent advances in procedural design tools and deep generative techniques. However, exploring such high-dimensional design spaces remains a challenge, and devising computational strategies for this purpose is an open research topic. We envision that PBO could be one of the solutions, and it would be an important module of digital content creation tools in the next decade.

8.6 Summary

This chapter reviewed PBO, which is an effective solution for parameter searching problems in visual design. PBO is a variant of BO but differs in that PBO involves humans in the loop, and that PBO takes preferential feedback as input. One of the advantages of PBO over other alternatives is that PBO can quickly find satisfactory solutions with only a small number of queries to human evaluators, which is essential to minimise the burden to the evaluators. After reviewing PBO from the mathematical viewpoint, this chapter also described two recent extensions that can make PBO ever more efficient and practical. As indicated by these extensions and their applications, PBO is highly general and extensible. We envision that PBO will play an important role in various design and human–computer interaction scenarios in the near future.

References

[1] E. Brochu, N. de Freitas and A. Ghosh, Abhijeet. 2007. Active preference learning with discrete choice data. Pages 409–416 of: *Proceedings of the 20th International Conference on Neural Information Processing Systems.* NIPS '07. Curran Associates.

[2] E. Brochu, T. Brochu and N. de Freitas. 2010. A Bayesian interactive optimization approach to procedural animation design. Pages 103–12 of: *Proceedings of the 2010 ACM SIGGRAPH/Eurographics Symposium on Computer Animation.* SCA '10. Association for Computing Machinery.

[3] C.-H. Chiu, Y. Koyama, Y.-C. Lai, T. Igarashi and Y. Yue. 2020. Human-in-the-loop differential subspace search in high-Dimensional latent space. *ACM Transactions on Graphics*, **39**(4), 85:1–85:15.

[4] T. Chong, I. Shen, I., Sato and T. Igarashi. 2021. Interactive optimization of generative image modelling using sequential subspace search and content-based guidance. *Computer Graphics Forum*, **40**(1), 279–292.

[5] J. Engel, K. K. Agrawal, S. Chen, I. Gulrajani, C. Donahue and A. Roberts. 2019. GANSynth: Adversarial Neural Audio Synthesis. In: *Proceedings of the 7th International Conference on Learning Representations.* ICLR '19.

[6] T. Karras, T. Aila, S. Laine and J. Lehtinen. 2018. Progressive growing of GANs for improved quality, stability, and variation. In: *Proceedings of the 6th International Conference on Learning Representations.* ICLR '18.

[7] Y. Koyama and M. Goto. 2018. OptiMo: optimization-guided motion editing for keyframe character animation. Pages 161:1–161:12 of: *Proceedings of the 2018 CHI Conference on Human Factors in Computing Systems.* CHI '18. Association for Computing Machinery.

[8] Y. Koyama and T. Igarashi. 2018. Computational design with crowds. Chap. 6, pages 153–184 of: A. Oulasvirta, P. O. Kristensson, X. Bi and A. Howes, eds., *Computational Interaction.* Oxford University Press.

[9] Y. Koyama, D. Sakamoto and T. Igarashi. 2014. Crowd-powered parameter analysis for visual design exploration. Pages 65–74 of: *Proceedings of the 27th Annual ACM Symposium on User Interface Software and Technology.* UIST '14. Association for Computing Machinery.

[10] Y. Koyama, D. Sakamoto and T. Igarashi. 2016. SelPh: progressive learning and support of manual photo color enhancement. Pages 2520–2532 of: *Proceedings of the 2016 CHI Conference on Human Factors in Computing Systems.* CHI '16. Association for Computing Machinery.

[11] Y. Koyama, I. Sato, D. Sakamoto and T. Igarashi. 2017. Sequential line search for efficient visual design optimization by crowds. *ACM Transactions on Graphics*, **36**(4), 48:1–48:11.

[12] Y. Koyama, I. Sato and M. Goto. 2020. Sequential gallery for interactive visual design optimization. *ACM Transactions on Graphics*, **39**(4), 88:1–88:12.

[13] P. Ledda, A. Chalmers, T. Troscianko and H. Seetzen. 2005. Evaluation of tone mapping operators using a high dynamic range display. *ACM Transactions on Graphics*, **24**(3), 640–648.

[14] R. D. Luce. 2008. Luce's choice axiom. *Scholarpedia*, **3**(12), 8077.

[15] J. Marks, B. Andalman, P. A. Beardsley, W. T. Freeman, S. F. Gibson, J. K. Hodgins, T. Kang, B. Mirtich, H. Pfister, W. Ruml, K. Ryall, J. E. Seims and S. M. Shieber. 1997. Design galleries: a general approach to setting parameters for computer graphics and animation. Pages 389–400 of: *Proceedings of the 24th Annual Conference on Computer Graphics and Interactive Techniques*. SIGGRAPH '97. ACM Press/Addison-Wesley.

[16] A. Ngan, F. Durand and W. Matusik. 2006. Image-driven navigation of analytical BRDF models. Pages 399–407 of: *Proceedings of the 17th Eurographics Conference on Rendering Techniques*. EGSR '06. Eurographics Association.

[17] J. Nocedal and S. J. Wright. 2006. *Numerical Optimization*, 2nd ed. Springer Science+Business Media.

[18] A. J. Quinn and B. B. Bederson. 2011. Human computation: a survey and taxonomy of a growing field. Pages 1403–1412 of: *Proceedings of the SIGCHI Conference on Human Factors in Computing Systems*. CHI '11. Association for Computing Machinery.

[19] C. E. Rasmussen and C. K. I. Williams. 2005. *Gaussian Processes for Machine Learning*. MIT Press.

[20] B. Shahriari, K. Swersky, Z. Wang, R. P. Adams and N. de Freitas. 2016. Taking the human out of the loop: A review of Bayesian optimization. *Proceedings of the IEEE*, **104**(1), 148–175.

[21] J. Snoek, H. Larochelle and R. P. Adams. 2012. Practical Bayesian optimization of machine learning algorithms. Pages 2951–2959 of: *Proceedings of the 25th International Conference on Neural Information Processing Systems*. NIPS '12. Curran Associates.

[22] H. Takagi. 2001. Interactive evolutionary computation: fusion of the capabilities of EC optimization and human evaluation. *Proceedings of the IEEE*, **89**(9), 1275–1296.

[23] J. O. Talton, D. Gibson, L. Yang, P. Hanrahan and V. Koltun. 2009. Exploratory modeling with collaborative design spaces. *ACM Transactions on Graphics*, **28**(5), 167:1–167:10.

[24] K. Tsukida and M. R. Gupta. 2011 (May). *How to Analyze Paired Comparison Data*. Tech. rept. UWEETR-2011-0004. University of Washington, Department of Electrical Engineering.

[25] M. E. Yumer, P. Asente, R. Mech and L. B. Kara. 2015. Procedural modeling using autoencoder networks. Pages 109–118 of: *Proceedings of the 28th Annual ACM Symposium on User Interface Software & Technology*. UIST '15. Association for Computer Machinery.

[26] Y. Zhou, Y. Koyama, M. Goto and T. Igarashi. 2020. Generative melody composition with human-in-the-loop Bayesian optimization. Pages 21:1–21:10 of: *Proceedings of the 2020 Joint Conference on AI Music Creativity*. CSMC-MuMe '20. https://arxiv.org/pdf/2010.03190.

[27] Y. Zhou, Y. Koyama, M. Goto and T. Igarashi. 2021. Interactive exploration-exploitation balancing for generative melody composition. Pages 43–47 of: *Proceedings of the 26th International Conference on Intelligent User Interfaces*. IUI '21. Association for Computing Machinery.

9

Bayesian Optimisation of Interface Features

John Dudley and Per Ola Kristensson

Abstract

Designing a novel interface typically involves dealing with a high degree of uncertainty. Without prior related experience it can be very difficult to predict how various design decisions might impact user performance and usability. This chapter describes how Bayesian optimisation can support designers in making design decisions to improve outcomes for the end user. Bayesian optimisation is a machine learning technique that leverages a probabilistic model to guide the process of determining design parameters that optimise some objective. This approach can be formulated as a user-in-the-loop optimisation process wherein interface design alternatives are efficiently explored and evaluated to optimise chosen design objectives for the interface. This chapter offers an accessible introduction to Bayesian optimisation and provides concrete guidance on its application within the HCI domain. To demonstrate the advantages of Bayesian optimisation, we present an illustrative example of its application to an interface design problem in both a conventional 2D setting as well as a novel 3D setting.

9.1 Introduction

Designing a new user interface involves the designer having to make many decisions, such as deciding how user interface elements should appear and how users are meant to interact. For example, consider the design of a single button within a graphical user interface. While such a design is often supported by user interface guidelines, even such a narrow design encompasses many factors in theory, such as its size, placement, appearance and behaviour. Such design decisions tend to be supported based on prior experience, design know-how, prototyping and informal self-evaluations. However, when the design problem is unfamiliar or involves a large number of parameters, such ad hoc approaches are not always effective. Further, it is difficult to argue that parameters configured in this way are truly optimal even if they do yield satisfactory behaviour.

Within the human–computer interaction (HCI) research community, the de facto standard for determining unknown design parameters is mostly through controlled user studies. However, such studies rarely examine more than a handful of parameter operating points, as exploring large parameter spaces in controlled user studies is infeasible. User behaviour also tends to be inconsistent and variable over time. In practice, the qualities of interface features are latent variables that can be inferred only through secondary measures, such as task completion times, error rates, or subjective user ratings.

An alternative strategy to the controlled evaluation of preset operating points is a dynamic selection strategy. *Bayesian optimisation* is a machine learning technique that is well suited for this purpose. It provides a formal procedure for identifying optimal parameters while accommodating the fact that user observations are inherently noisy. At a high level, Bayesian optimisation constructs a model of the performance of the interface with respect to the design parameters and subsequently uses this model to determine which parameter settings to evaluate next. This model is improved with each new observation.

Model-based optimisation methods have been used effectively within the HCI community [7, 23, 26, 29]. In terms of assisting developers in interface design tasks, a range of tools have been proposed in the literature, for example MenuOptimizer [1], DesignScape [22] and Sketchplore [29]. These tools represent a *proactive* approach to interface design optimisation that leverages existing understanding of the users and the tasks to deliver better interfaces. Often this is achieved by encoding such an understanding into an objective function that is subsequently used to drive the optimisation process. These proactive approaches can help to streamline design tasks but do rely on accurate assumptions in the construction of the objective function.

However, for novel interfaces and interactions, limited theory or established analytical models are often available for constructing an effective objective function. An alternative strategy is to use a data-driven approach using a post hoc *refinement* strategy. This encompasses efforts that are typical of traditional evidence-based design [14] as well as more advanced techniques for informing the choice between design alternatives [18, 25, 30]. The refinement of parameters related to game mechanics is a popular application of such methods [19, 20]. The continued investigation of various techniques to assist in the interface design process highlights an appetite for efficient and objective methods. Bayesian optimisation is well suited for this purpose given that it inherently facilitates efficient exploration of the design space and requires minimal assumptions or configuration when deployed on a new design problem. It is slowly gaining traction within the HCI community, with several concrete demonstrations available in the literature (see Section 9.3) of its capability to support HCI design problems.

This chapter provides an introduction to Bayesian optimisation as a tool for supporting interface and interaction design in HCI. We present the formulation of Bayesian optimisation in the context of interface design and outline how its application for user-in-the-loop evaluations in HCI is distinct from more typical applications of the technique. An illustrative example of the use of Bayesian optimisation to facilitate interface feature design is also provided. The aims of this chapter are to introduce researchers in HCI to the value of Bayesian methods for optimisation tasks, and particularly the relevance of Bayesian optimisation.

9.1.1 Chapter Outline

The remainder of this chapter is structured as follows. In Section 9.2, we provide an introduction to Bayesian optimisation in the context of its application to interface design. Section 9.3 highlights important considerations for applying Bayesian optimisation in HCI and presents a generalised procedure for its use. Section 9.4 presents the illustrative case study of refining interface features in two separate experiments. Finally, Section 9.5 discusses the limitations of the approach and identifies key remaining open research questions before concluding remarks in Section 9.6.

9.2 What Is Bayesian Optimisation?

Bayesian optimisation is a machine learning technique that facilitates the exploration of cost functions that are complex or can be estimated only by making noisy observations of a latent function. The technique is well suited to applications in HCI where observations of user performance or behaviour typically involve high levels of noise. For a given user, this noise arises due to natural variation in task performance due to both internal factors (e.g. inattention) and external factors (e.g. variation in task complexity). Between users, the variation in the capabilities of different users can also give rise to noisy observations.

Bayesian optimisation has been used effectively in circumstances in which the system under evaluation is costly (in terms of, for example, money or time) to query. As an example, consider the optimisation of a process where observations of a given performance objective can be obtained only by running a time-intensive simulation or by building a prototype and testing it physically. In such circumstances, there is significant value in determining the ideal operating point with as few samples as possible. The benefit provided by Bayesian optimisation is that it captures the uncertainty of these observations in its model and leverages this to determine where to sample from next.

The model leveraged by the Bayesian optimisation procedure can be thought of as a probabilistic proxy model relating the controllable parameters to the objective that is being optimised. This proxy model is cheap to inspect and evaluate, so we use it to drive decisions on where to evaluate the real objective. Real observations are then fed back to update the model. In theory, as the proxy model receives more observations, it evolves to more accurately capture the relationship between the controllable parameters and the objective. A Gaussian process (see Section 9.2.1) is a common choice for this proxy model.

In this section, we introduce the formulation of Bayesian optimisation. This formulation is presented for an HCI audience and is described with direct reference to the problem of interface design. For a more detailed explanation and formulation, see Snoek [28]. Practical considerations for the implementation and integration of Bayesian optimisation are also presented later in Section 9.2.2.

9.2.1 Formulation

This section provides a brief overview and formulation of the basic principles of Bayesian optimisation. At the expense of completeness, this section provides a simple-to-understand explanation contextualised by the interface design problem.

Bayesian optimisation works by exploiting a probabilistic model that has been fitted to describe some unknown function. In the context of interface design, the goal is to model the function describing how users will perform when presented with a given configuration of the interface defined by an input vector $\mathbf{x}$. This function is *unknown*, as it is often not viable to reliably predict how user performance will be affected by changes to the interface.[1]

The conventional approach in Bayesian optimisation is to model the unknown function as a Gaussian process (GP). A GP describes a distribution over functions with the process $f(\mathbf{x})$ specified by its mean function $m(\mathbf{x})$ and covariance function $k(\mathbf{x}, \mathbf{x}')$, where

---

[1] This is not to say that certain aspects of user performance cannot be predicted or estimated. Techniques such as the Keystroke Level Model and Fitts' law may allow estimating the effects of changes in, for example, element sizes or placement. However, such techniques struggle when applied to simultaneous variation of multiple interface design parameters with nuanced factor interactions.

$$m(\mathbf{x}) = \mathbb{E}\big[f(\mathbf{x})\big], \tag{9.1}$$
$$k(\mathbf{x}, \mathbf{x}') = \mathbb{E}\big[(f(\mathbf{x}) - m(\mathbf{x}))(f(\mathbf{x}') - m(\mathbf{x}'))\big]. \tag{9.2}$$

The Gaussian process is then written as

$$f(\mathbf{x}) \sim GP\big(m(\mathbf{x}), k(\mathbf{x}, \mathbf{x}')\big). \tag{9.3}$$

$m(\mathbf{x})$ and $k(\mathbf{x}, \mathbf{x}')$ are essentially the function parallels of the mean and variance of a random variable. The function $f(\mathbf{x})$ specifies the random variable at location $\mathbf{x}$. The covariance function $k(\mathbf{x}, \mathbf{x}')$ is also known as the *kernel* and loosely describes the similarity between a pair of points $\mathbf{x}$ and $\mathbf{x}'$.

In the interface refinement task, the GP is fitted using data obtained through observations of the chosen objective. One potential choice of objective for interface design problems is task completion time. These observations are in reality noisy transformations of the latent function values $f(\mathbf{x})$. An observation instance, representing a particular design configuration of the interface, has parameter values defined by $\mathbf{x}_i$. A simple but reasonable assumption is that these observations are corrupted by additive Gaussian noise ϵ with variance σ_n^2 and that a real observation y_i at $\mathbf{x}_i$ is defined as

$$y_i = f(\mathbf{x}_i) + \epsilon_i. \tag{9.4}$$

The crux of Bayesian optimisation is to leverage the GP, fitted to a sequence of observations $\{\mathbf{x}_{1:t}, \mathbf{y}_{1:t}\}$ to probabilistically determine what new point – that is, $\mathbf{x}_{t+1}$ – should be evaluated next. The mean and variance of the Gaussian process posterior predictive distribution after t observations are defined by

$$\mu_t(\mathbf{x}_{t+1}) = \mathbf{k}^T(\mathbf{K} + \sigma_n^2 \boldsymbol{I})^{-1}\mathbf{y}_{1:t}, \tag{9.5}$$
$$\sigma_t^2(\mathbf{x}_{t+1}) = k(\mathbf{x}_{t+1}, \mathbf{x}_{t+1}) - \mathbf{k}^T(\mathbf{K} + \sigma_n^2 \boldsymbol{I})^{-1}\mathbf{k}, \tag{9.6}$$

where the kernel matrix $\mathbf{K}$ is given by

$$\mathbf{K} = \begin{bmatrix} k(\mathbf{x}_1, \mathbf{x}_1) & \cdots & k(\mathbf{x}_1, \mathbf{x}_t) \\ \vdots & \ddots & \vdots \\ k(\mathbf{x}_t, \mathbf{x}_1) & \cdots & k(\mathbf{x}_t, \mathbf{x}_t) \end{bmatrix}, \tag{9.7}$$

and $\mathbf{k}$ is given by

$$\mathbf{k}^T = [k(\mathbf{x}_{t+1}, \mathbf{x}_1) \quad k(\mathbf{x}_{t+1}, \mathbf{x}_2) \quad \cdots \quad k(\mathbf{x}_{t+1}, \mathbf{x}_t)]. \tag{9.8}$$

As part of fitting observation data to the GP, a number of subtle assumptions must be made about the target function. One of these relates to how closely nearby points in the space are correlated. The characteristics of the process and observation data dictate the choice of kernel, as detailed in the following section.

Kernel Selection

The kernel itself has parameters, typically referred to as hyperparameters, which can be thought of as describing the general shape of the function space independent of the data points. There are a range of kernels to choose from, with each possessing different properties and expressing different assumptions about the underlying data. Further, different kernels can be combined together to reflect presumed features in the data. An appreciation of the characteristics of the data to be modelled can therefore inform the selection of the most appropriate kernel. For example, the squared exponential (SE) kernel is generally proposed as a good initial selection but assumes a degree of smoothness in the underlying data and therefore may perform poorly in any regions with discontinuities. Another widely used kernel is Matérn, which exhibits other useful properties. Duvenaud ([6], chap. 2) and Rasmussen and Williams ([24], chap. 4) provide helpful overviews of a range of kernels and discuss the kernel selection problem.

The illustrative case study presented in Section 9.4 employs the squared exponential automatic relevance determination (ARD) kernel (see [24], p. 106), which is a special form of the SE kernel where each input dimension has a dedicated hyperparameter. This gives it the useful property of removing irrelevant input. The ARD kernel is selected for its simplicity and to demonstrate that the described approach can perform effectively even in a rudimentary configuration. The ARD kernel with hyperparameters, $\theta = (\sigma_f^2, \sigma_n^2, l_1, ..., l_D)$, where D is the dimensionality, is defined as

$$k(\mathbf{x_p}, \mathbf{x_q}) = \sigma_f^2 \exp\left(-\sum_{d=1}^{D} \frac{(x_{p_d} - x_{q_d})^2}{2l_d^2} \right) + \sigma_n^2 \delta_{pq}, \qquad (9.9)$$

for a pair of points $\mathbf{x_p}$ and $\mathbf{x_q}$ where δ_{pq} is the Kronecker delta. The hyperparameters of Equation (9.9) dictate the general shape of the modelled function. The signal variance σ_f^2 reflects the degree to which the signal varies over the space. The noise variance σ_n^2 reflects the amount of noise added to the underlying signal. The hyperparameters, $l_1, ..., l_D$, 'play the role of characteristic length-scales; loosely speaking, how far do you need to move (along a particular axis) in input space for the function values to become uncorrelated' ([24], p. 106).

Acquisition Function

Once the GP is fitted to the observation points, the next step is to determine which new point to sample based on some probabilistic guidance. This guidance comes from an *acquisition function*: a function that reflects the benefit of sampling a given set of parameter values.

Determining the next sample point is complicated by the need to strike a balance between *exploration* and *exploitation*. The exploration–exploitation trade-off is a commonly faced dilemma when seeking to optimise an objective that requires some form of non-trivial evaluation.

Exploration refers to the evaluation of points in a region about which we have limited information, with the objective of learning more. Exploitation refers to the evaluation of points in a region which we may be knowledgeable about, with the expectation that we can find a new best point.

Exploration is clearly necessary in the initial stages of Bayesian optimisation given that the model has limited awareness of the design space due to the lack of observations. As more observations are collected, it may be preferable to switch to a mode of exploitation in order to concentrate on promising regions of the design space. However, this comes at a cost of potentially missing regions that may in fact yield better outcomes. This tension between exploration and exploitation is difficult to escape, although there are acquisition functions that attempt to manage this trade-off.

The literature provides many choices for an acquisition function. A widely used standard approach is based on expected improvement (EI). The EI acquisition function can be thought of as the potential gain that can be obtained, relative to the current best observation, at a given new observation point. This assessment is based on the current model's mean and variance at that point. The EI acquisition function is defined as

$$EI(\mathbf{x}) = \begin{cases} \Big(\mu(\mathbf{x}) - f(\mathbf{x}^+)\Big)\Phi(Z) + \sigma(\mathbf{x})\varphi(Z) & \text{if } \sigma(\mathbf{x}) > 0, \\ 0 & \text{if } \sigma(\mathbf{x}) = 0, \end{cases} \tag{9.10}$$

where $\mathbf{x}^+$ represents the best observed sample in the sample set, $\Phi(\cdot)$ and $\varphi(\cdot)$ denote the CDF and PDF of the standard normal distribution respectively, and

$$Z = \frac{\mu(\mathbf{x}) - f(\mathbf{x}^+)}{\sigma(\mathbf{x})}. \tag{9.11}$$

Note that the subscripts on μ and σ are omitted for clarity.

The concept of the acquisition function is illustrated in a one-dimensional example in Figure 9.1. The iterative process of updating the model and selecting the next sample point is summarised in Algorithm 9.1.

Algorithm 9.1 Bayesian Optimisation

---

1 **for** $t = 1, 2, ...$ **do**
2 $\quad$ Optimise acquisition function EI given observation set $D_{1:t-1}$ to find new
$\quad\quad$ sample point: $\mathbf{x}_t = \arg\max_x\ EI(\mathbf{x}|D_{1:t-1})$
3 $\quad$ Sample the objective function: $y_t = f(\mathbf{x}_t) + \epsilon_t$
4 $\quad$ Add new sample to dataset: $D_{1:t} = \big(D_{1:t-1}, (\mathbf{x}_t, y_t)\big)$
5 $\quad$ Update the GP.

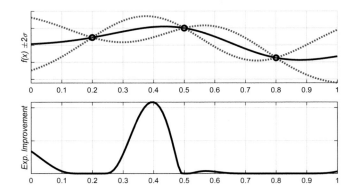

Figure 9.1 Illustration of Bayesian optimisation in 1D. The top plot shows the Gaussian process approximation of the latent function over the design space. Three observations are shown (circled) and the uncertainty around these points is visibly reduced. Below is the Expected Improvement over the design space: the potential that a new observation point has to improve upon the current best observation.

Hyperparameters

As mentioned in the previous sections, there are a range of hyperparameters that dictate the characteristics of the kernel and behaviour of the procedure. Fortunately, these hyperparameters can be tuned by optimising the marginal likelihood.

9.2.2 Implementation and Integration Considerations

The simplicity of Gaussian processes and the Bayesian optimisation procedure make it relative easy to implement. However, for most applications within HCI, it is likely that existing implementations may be suitable. Standard implementations of Bayesian optimisation now exist within scikit-optimize for Python and the Statistics and Machine Learning Toolbox for MATLAB.

Other packaged implementations include BoTorch [2], GPFlowOpt [13] (under active development as Trieste[2]) and MOBOpt [8]. A closely related technique, TS-EMO [3], is available as a MATLAB library.

However, there are some likely data handling activities that are relevant to problems in HCI but which are unlikely to be directly handled in existing tools. For example, it is often useful to ensure the objective being optimised is normally distributed and of unit variance. In some HCI applications, such as those involving completion time, it may be necessary to transform observations by taking the log and scaling.

For the example presented in Section 9.4 later in this chapter, we apply a simple implementation detail based on converting the continuous design space into a discrete set of design candidates. This helps in managing evaluation time but also allows for secondary heuristics to be introduced around resolution of sampling and avoids revisiting previously evaluated candidates.

9.3 Bayesian Optimisation in HCI

Bayesian optimisation is well suited to the task of performing user-in-the-loop optimisation of joint human-machine systems. It has recently been adopted in HCI as a potential tool to support designers. In this section we review compelling uses of Bayesian optimisation in HCI. A more general review of Bayesian optimisation with illustrative examples is provided by Shahriari et al. [27]. In the context of the design of interactive systems, the structure of the Bayesian optimisation procedure may vary depending on the specific goals of the designer and/or task of the end user. We can broadly categorise these different application variants as pursuing either *adaptation* or *refinement*.

Bayesian optimisation can be used to *adapt* a system to perform a particular task through iterative feedback cycles involving an end user. This obviates the need for the designer to be aware of the particular goals of the user and enhances the generalisability of the built system. For example, Brochu et al. [4] leveraged Bayesian optimisation to streamline the process of identifying parameters for the animation of smoke. Users interact with a preference gallery and iteratively train the proxy model to map between animation parameters and subjective objectives of realism and/or aesthetics. Similarly, Koyama et al. have used Bayesian optimisation extensively for image adaptation tasks [16, 17]. The systems demonstrated by Koyama et al. allow users to provide feedback iteratively in order to drive the parameters governing the visual appearance of

---

[2] https://github.com/secondmind-labs/trieste

an image towards some subjective aesthetic. Nielsen et al. [21] use an approach closely related to Bayesian optimisation to calibrate hearing aid parameters with the end user in-the-loop iteratively providing feedback on the degree of preference between two alternative settings. Kadner et al. [10] applied Bayesian optimisation to adapt font parameters to promote legibility for individual readers. The use of Bayesian optimisation for *adaptation* tasks generally implies the involvement of a single user and the need to start afresh when examining the needs of a new user or task.

In other applications of Bayesian optimisation, the goal is to *refine* the joint human-machine system in order to improve its performance for the user population. The designer can use this approach to optimise the performance of the system for broad use, in contrast to adapting settings to a particular task or for a particular user. For example, Khajah et al. [11] used Bayesian optimisation to identify game parameters to maximise user engagement. The illustrative example presented later in Section 9.4 and taken from Dudley et al. [5] aggregated observations of user performance in terms of task completion time in order to identify optimal interface parameters. The challenge for Bayesian optimisation involving *refinement* of an interface is how to manage the integration of observations collected from multiple different users at different times.

The application of Bayesian optimisation within the HCI domain introduces additional considerations over more traditional applications of the technique. These additional considerations relate to three key factors: (1) the aggregation across users; (2) the non-stationary behaviour of users; and (3) the sequencing of human-in-the-loop evaluation.

Compared to, for example, the execution of a complex simulation to make an observation of a given performance objective, in an HCI design task it is typically necessary to capture multiple observations of a given design to obtain an accurate picture of its quality. When sampling from a simulation, it may be reasonable to treat an observation as accurately representing the objective at that operating point. In contrast, when sampling from users, it is essential to aggregate across different users to account for variability. This need for aggregation in part stems from the second factor: the non-stationary behaviour of users. Unlike the mechanical testing of a widget, humans can adjust their behaviour based on experience with an interface and/or may lose interest or motivation over time. These secondary effects give rise to observations that are not accurate representations of the true objective. Finally, the sequencing of human-in-the-loop evaluation necessitates careful consideration of the timing and ordering of tasks. In instances where an individual is recruited to perform multiple evaluations at different operating points, it is ideal that the new design can be selected and presented without significant delay. Again, contrast this

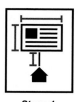 

Stage 1
Identify a meaningful
parameterisation of
the interface

Stage 2
Identify a performance
metric indicative of
interface quality

Stage 3
Perform evaluation
cycles

Stage 4
Inspect the performance
model and update
the design

Figure 9.2 The four stages in the process of designing with Bayesian optimisation.

with the execution of a simulation which does not in itself impose constraints on the timeliness of the Bayesian optimisation procedure.

9.3.1 Generalised Procedure

Bayesian optimisation provides a robust and flexible technique for undertaking objective interface refinement. However, it is important to provide some structure around the application of this technique in order to deliver meaningful outcomes. To this end, this section offers a high-level description of the process for performing interface feature design using Bayesian optimisation. This process can be divided into four key stages, as illustrated in Figure 9.2 and detailed below.

Stage 1: Identify a Meaningful Parameterisation of the Interface

The appearance and behaviour of an interface can be thought of as a product of multiple lower-level design choices. For example, the sizing of textual labels on an interface is one single low-level design choice that ultimately contributes to the appearance and performance of the interface as a whole. Not all low-level design choices are equal in their influence on the resulting performance of the interface. For example, relatively minor deviations in the choice of a font family, font style or size may have an effect on the aesthetics of the interface but are unlikely to directly influence performance.

The application of Bayesian optimisation to interface refinement requires the identification of the subset of design choices that are hypothesised to have the greatest effect on interface performance. This subset of design choices, or *parameters*, represents the *parameterisation* of the interface. Identifying an appropriate parameterisation also involves setting reasonable bounds for a given parameter. For example, font size might reasonably be bounded at one extreme by the size that is too small to read and, at the other extreme, the size that is too large to fit within the display window.

There clearly is a degree of subjectivity involved in the identification of a meaningful parameterisation. This can be alleviated by initial pilot testing and through critical evaluation of the literature and/or related interface implementations.

Stage 2: Identify a Performance Metric Indicative of Interface Quality

The process of Bayesian optimisation necessitates the measurement of a signal of performance. A model is constructed to represent the mapping between a design point (i.e. a particular parameterisation of the interface) and its performance as measured through user evaluations. Identifying a robust and clear signal that reflects the quality and performance of the interface is critical to this process. In the example presented in Section 9.4, this is illustrated using task completion time as the performance metric.

Stage 3: Perform Evaluation Cycles

A range of different interface designs suggested by the Bayesian optimisation technique are then evaluated. In the context of the illustrative example presented in Section 9.4, crowdworkers are employed to efficiently perform this evaluation, but the same outcomes can also be achieved through other means, such as lab-based testing.

This evaluation needs to consider any confounding effects of learning and inter-user variability. In addition, any evaluations performed using crowdsourcing need to be more vigilant to ensure compliance with task instructions.

Stage 4: Inspect the Performance Model and Update the Design

The Bayesian optimisation approach facilitates the efficient exploration of the design space. After sufficient evaluation, the process must switch from exploration to exploitation: identify the parameterisation that yields optimal performance. Determining when to terminate the evaluation cycles requires some judgement but can be informed by the performance improvement trajectory observed, or through subjective user ratings. Finally, the constructed performance model can then be inspected in order to understand both the optimal setting of parameters and the sensitivity of the design parameters.

9.4 Designing with Bayesian Optimisation: An Illustrative Example

In this section we present an illustrative example taken from Dudley et al. [5] of the application of Bayesian optimisation to interface design. In this application of Bayesian optimisation, we show how to parameterise the design space of an interface and how to find effective parameter settings. The procedure in this study leveraged crowdsourcing to construct a rapid human-in-the-loop evaluation cycle.

Two experiments are described: Experiment 1 examined a relatively familiar design problem for a conventional 2D interface, while Experiment 2 examined a more challenging application of Bayesian optimisation to a less familiar 3D interaction setting. The remainder of this section describes the experiments and results obtained and offers generalisable guidance for applying Bayesian optimisation to related problems.

9.4.1 Interface Refinement Experiments

The overarching design problem tackled in this example is the development of an interface to facilitate the exploration of data tooltips associated with locations on a map. The interface refinement activity is made concrete by framing the task around the goal of finding a hotel matching set criteria by reviewing the information contained in the tooltips.

The investigation was split into two separate experiments to illustrate the use of Bayesian optimisation in an initial familiar interaction setting and thereafter in a less-familiar interaction setting. In Experiment 1, the hotel search interface used is shown in Figure 9.3. The user is presented with a search task as shown at the top of Figure 9.3 and reviews the tooltips to locate the corresponding hotel. Only one hotel matches the given criteria. When the correct hotel is found, the user clicks 'select' on the tooltip and then clicks the submit button. If the chosen hotel is incorrect, the user is notified, and the task continues until the correct hotel is submitted.

In Experiment 2, the interface was modified for use on a mobile phone to deliver a low-fidelity virtual reality (VR) experience. The interface for this experiment is shown in Figure 9.4. Rather than moving the mouse cursor to interact with the tooltips, the user adjusts the gaze cursor (shown as a light circle in Figure 9.4) by orienting their mobile phone.

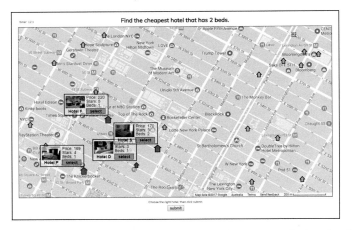

Figure 9.3 Hotel search task interface. The search criteria are displayed at the top of the interface. The tooltip details for four of the hotels are shown at the bottom left.

Figure 9.4 The VR hotel search task in Experiment 2. The mobile device presents a window into the virtual world. The user controls the view of the scene by adjusting the orientation of the device. The gaze cursor (the light circle beneath the Hotel C label) is used to inspect hotel information and locate the hotel that matches the specified criteria.

9.4.2 Parameterising the Interface

As per the procedure introduced in Section 9.3.1, Stage 1 involves determining a meaningful parameterisation of the interface. The parameterisation of the interface used in Experiment 1 is summarised in Table 9.1. This covers attributes of the interface both related to the appearance as well as to the behaviour of interactions. The choice of these parameters in particular relates to their hypothesised impact on the performance and subjective experience of using the interface. For the purpose of presenting an illustrative example of Bayesian optimisation, it is interesting to examine parameters for which there exists some expected trade-off. For example, the *Decay* parameter represents the timeout for hiding a tooltip after it is shown. Setting the *Decay* to be too short may cause the tooltips to vanish before the user has time to read all the information. Setting the *Decay* to be too long may unnecessarily obscure information on the map or in other tooltips.

Table 9.1 Interface parameters examined in Experiment 1.

	PARAMETER	BEHAVIOUR
1	*Distance*	Threshold distance on cursor-to-pin for raising *show tooltip* event.
2	*Delay*	Timeout before responding to *show tooltip* event.
3	*Decay*	Timeout before responding to *hide tooltip* event after cursor exits distance threshold.
4	*Size*	Size of the hotel tooltip.
5	*Opacity*	Transparency of the hotel tooltip.

The parameterisation of the interface used in Experiment 2 is summarised in Table 9.2. The choice of parameters is largely consistent with Experiment 1 except that the *Distance* parameter is now with reference to the view-centre, as controlled by the orientation of the mobile device.

9.4.3 Objective Selection

Stage 2 of the procedure outlined in Section 9.3.1 involves identifying a performance metric indicative of interface quality. It is reasonable to assume that the time it takes to complete a task using an interface provides a proxy measure of its quality. In this study, we therefore use task completion time as the primary objective to minimise. The task completion time is the total time elapsed between the display of the new search task and the submission of the

Table 9.2 Interface parameters examined in Experiment 2.

	PARAMETER	BEHAVIOUR
1	*Distance*	Threshold distance on projected view-centre to pin for raising *show tooltip* event.
2	*Delay*	Timeout before responding to *show tooltip* event.
3	*Decay*	Timeout before responding to *hide tooltip* event after cursor exits distance threshold.
4	*Size*	Size of the hotel tooltip.
5	*Opacity*	Transparency of the hotel tooltip.

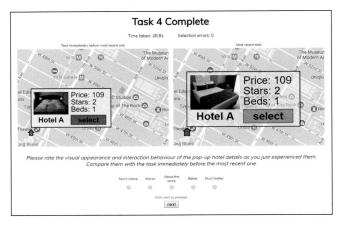

Figure 9.5 The comparative feature rating page. The left thumbnail shows the previous design configuration, while the right shows the most recent configuration.

correct hotel. The elapsed time was displayed in the interface as shown in the top left of Figure 9.3, and above and to the right of the *submit* button in Figure 9.4. If the correct hotel was not submitted within 90 s, the task would auto-advance.

In both experiments, we captured a secondary objective which is the subjective rating of the interface relative to the previously experienced design. The setting of Experiment 1 allowed for this objective to be captured by showing a thumbnail illustrating the current and previous design configuration as shown in Figure 9.5. Given the reduced available screen space in Experiment 2, participants were not provided with thumbnails but were still asked to rate the new interface relative to the previously experienced interface.

In this investigation, the secondary objective is captured as a window into the qualitative experience of participants. It is not directly incorporated into the model or utilised in the Bayesian optimisation procedure.

9.4.4 User Evaluations

With the parameterisation and objective defined, the next step of the procedure described in Section 9.3.1 is to perform evaluation cycles. As described above, we leverage crowdsourcing to rapidly conduct interface evaluations. Crowdsourcing has been used effectively to conduct user studies, and prior work has demonstrated that it can deliver comparable results to lab-based studies [9]. It provides access to a large number of users allowing short tasks to be distributed efficiently and with relatively low cost [12]. There is also

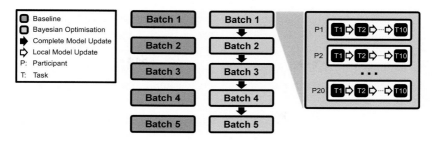

Figure 9.6 Illustration of the batching and model update procedure for the baseline and Bayesian optimisation conditions. In the Bayesian optimisation condition, all task observations collected up to and including the current batch are used to update the complete model for the next batch. Within a given batch, only the individual's prior task performance is used to further update their specific local model.

precedence in using crowdsourcing to evaluate user interfaces, with Komarov et al. [15] demonstrating comparable relative differences between in-lab and crowdsourced evaluations. The study performed by Khajah et al. [11] using Bayesian optimisation to maximise user engagement with a game also employed crowdsourcing to recruit users.

To illustrate the effectiveness of the Bayesian optimisation approach, interface refinement stages were conducted in batches of users, and a baseline user group was also included for comparison. The protocol, summarised in Figure 9.6, involved batching participants into groups of 20. Each participant performed 10 iterations of the task. In the Bayesian optimisation condition, the model leveraged all data from previous batches, as well as prior samples collected for the current individual. Hyperparameters were updated between batches based on all participant data captured up until that point. The baseline condition sampled randomly from the design candidates. The baseline condition can be thought of as a pessimistic control condition representing a naïve designer choosing parameters at random and without the ability to learn from prior outcomes.

9.4.5 Results

The completion time results of Experiment 1 are summarised in Table 9.3 and Figure 9.7. Table 9.3 summarises the median task completion time of each batch and the total number of successful completions (i.e. correct hotel submitted within 90 s). Figure 9.7 shows the boxplots of completion times in each batch for both conditions.

In Batch 1, the aggregate performance of the interface is roughly the same in both conditions. This is expected, since in Batch 1 the model has no data from prior batches and therefore can only leverage the samples collected from the individual. Typical behaviour of the Bayesian optimisation procedure given the dimensionality in this particular case is to sample sparsely over the design space.

Batch 2 sees a 30% reduction in median completion time to 21.5 s relative to Batch 1 in the Bayesian optimisation condition. This indicates that the procedure is leveraging the model to explore regions yielding good interface designs. A more marginal reduction is seen between Batches 2 and 3, and then in Batches 4 and 5, the median completion time is slightly elevated. This shift in aggregate performance in later batches is likely due to wider exploration as the regions of positive design candidates are comprehensively evaluated. Notable, however, is the increase in successful completions in the Bayesian optimisation condition, 95.5% by Batch 5, suggesting that the procedure is effectively avoiding regions of the design space that significantly hinder the execution of the task.

Figure 9.8 shows the preference ratings of participants over batches in both conditions. Note that ratings have been condensed from a five-point scale into *worse*, *same* or *better*. Interesting to note in Figure 9.8 is the increasing proportion of *same* ratings over Batches 1–3, peaking in Batch 3. The peak of *same* ratings coincides with the minimum median completion time, suggesting that the Bayesian optimisation procedure is largely sampling good design candidates with little perceivable difference.

The results of Experiment 2 are summarised in Table 9.4 and Figure 9.9. As in Experiment 1, the completion time results show no significant difference between the two conditions in Batch 1. In subsequent batches, the median completion time reduces to a minimum in Batch 4 before a marginal increase in Batch 5. This result suggests that Bayesian optimisation is effective in helping to

Table 9.3 Median task times and completion counts in Experiment 1.

| Batch | Median Task Time (s) [n] | |
	Baseline	BO
B1	32.9 [165]	30.8 [166]
B2	34.0 [175]	21.5 [170]
B3	31.1 [161]	20.5 [187]
B4	34.1 [172]	21.3 [183]
B5	29.6 [165]	26.1 [191]

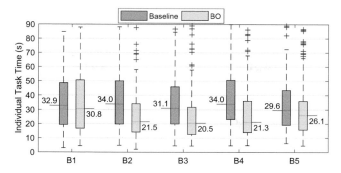

Figure 9.7 Boxplots of task completion time over the five batches for both conditions in Experiment 1. The crosses indicate outliers based on $Q_3 + 1.5 \times (Q_3 - Q_1)$.

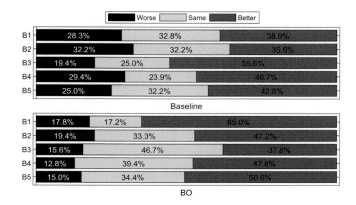

Figure 9.8 Proportion of interfaces rated by users as *worse*, *same* or *better* over the five batches in Experiment 1. The Baseline condition is shown at the top and the Bayesian optimisation condition below. The proportion of *same* user ratings steadily increases over Batches 1–3 in the Bayesian optimisation condition.

locate regions of good design parameters despite the very different deployment setting from Experiment 1.

A similar trend to Experiment 1 was also observed in the preference ratings in Experiment 2. Figure 9.10 plots the preference ratings for Experiment 2 in both conditions. The proportion of *same* ratings increases over Batches 1–3 and peaks in Batch 3. Again, this suggests that the Bayesian optimisation procedure is exploring positive designs with limited noticeable difference. From Table 9.4 we also see that successful completions peaks in Batch 3 at 96%.

Table 9.4 Median task times and completion counts in Experiment 2.

	Median Task Time (s) [n]	
Batch	Baseline	BO
B1	30.7 [170]	32.6 [164]
B2	34.3 [182]	25.5 [187]
B3	30.5 [182]	24.8 [192]
B4	36.3 [180]	24.5 [188]
B5	33.4 [181]	27.1 [186]

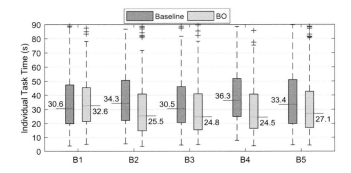

Figure 9.9 Boxplots of task completion time over the five batches for both conditions in Experiment 2. The crosses indicate outliers based on $Q_3 + 1.5 \times (Q_3 - Q_1)$.

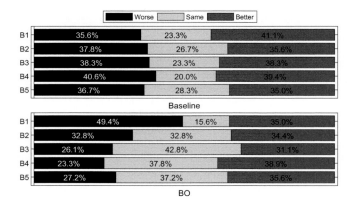

Figure 9.10 Proportion of interfaces rated by users as *worse*, *same* or *better* over the five batches in Experiment 2. The Baseline condition is shown at the top and the Bayesian optimisation condition below. As in Figure 9.8, the proportion of *same* user ratings steadily increases over Batches 1–3 in the Bayesian optimisation condition.

To summarise, these two experiments highlight how Bayesian optimisation can be leveraged to efficiently explore the design space and identify regions of good performance. This example also reveals that it is somewhat difficult to determine when to halt the procedure, especially given the fact that its search behaviour varies over time. The Expected Improvement acquisition function naturally seeks to evaluate at regions with high variance and potential for improvement, as suggested by the performance of nearby design candidates. As design candidates in a region are evaluated, the variance may consequently be reduced, and the procedure will seek to explore less visited regions which may or may not result in performance improvement. This is the trade-off between exploration and exploitation described in Section 9.2.1.

9.4.6 Outcomes

As described previously, Bayesian optimisation leverages a model relating the design space to performance. This model is refined iteratively as more samples are collected. As a consequence, a secondary benefit of the procedure is the ability to directly inspect and query this model. This reflects Stage 4 of the procedure introduced in Section 9.3.1.

Figure 9.11 shows a representation of the performance model obtained in Experiment 1 for each of the design parameters independently. The black circle in Figure 9.11 represents the optimal design candidate found, and each plot shows the effect of varying a single parameter value independently from that point. We can see how this model indicates the sensitivity to the different design parameters. In particular, we can see how varying *Distance*, *Delay* and *Opacity* has limited impact on task completion time, whereas *Decay* and *Size* drive significant changes in task completion time according to the model.

9.5 Discussion

Bayesian optimisation has good applicability to design problems in HCI. The illustrative example presented in Section 9.4 shows how a simple implementation of the procedure can be deployed to both familiar and unfamiliar design problems.

A challenge highlighted in the two experiments presented in Section 9.4 is the difficulty in determining appropriate termination conditions. The capture of subjective preference ratings may provide some assistance for this problem in highlighting the point at which different samples are largely indistinguishable to the users.

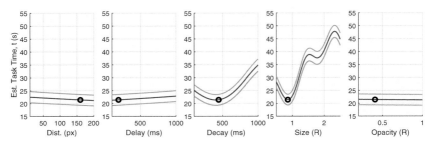

Figure 9.11 Sensitivity around optimal design candidate (circle) as indicated
by the mean (central darker line) and $\pm 2\sigma$ (upper and lower lighter lines) of
the GP. Note that this is the latent function model prediction which does not
reflect the additive signal noise.

Applying Bayesian optimisation to both quantitative and qualitative objectives simultaneously is an obvious extension of this work. There exists modified
acquisition functions to facilitate multi-objective Bayesian optimisation. However, optimising across more than one objective introduces other complications,
such as the need to determine the final design from among a set of Pareto-
optimal candidates.

As described in Section 9.2.2, we make an important simplification for
computational efficiency to discretise the design space into candidate points.
This greatly simplifies the step of determining the new test candidate given the
acquisition function. It is important to consider whether this discretisation is
appropriate for the particular design problem under investigation. There are
opportunities for determining how coarse such a discretisation should be and
whether this might be informed by just-noticeable differences for a given design
parameter.

As articulated in Section 9.3, several factors make the application of Bayesian
optimisation in an HCI context distinct from its more typical use. In HCI,
user performance typically varies over time due to factors such as learning or
fatigue. Such aspects of non-stationary processes are less well explored within
the machine learning community interested in Bayesian optimisation. Further
work is required to examine how these known factors can be accounted for
in collected observations and whether there are some procedural controls that
might be appropriate for the human-in-the-loop setting.

Finally, the illustrative example in Section 9.4 highlights the potential value
of subjective ratings of interface quality. A challenge not addressed, however, is
the fact that subjective ratings of users are typically poorly anchored and drift
based on prior exposure. This is in part the reason for pursuing a pairwise rating

system. However, subsequent evaluations based on a preference gallery may be appropriate, as in work by Brochu et al. [4] and Koyama et al. [16].

9.6 Conclusions

This chapter has provided an introduction to Bayesian optimisation as a tool for facilitating interface design. We have presented an overview of the basic formulation contextualised for understanding by the application to interface design. In Section 9.3, we reviewed compelling uses of the technique in HCI and highlighted the aspects of its application in a human-in-the-loop setting that require special consideration. The illustrative example presented in Section 9.4 highlighted how Bayesian optimisation can be efficiently deployed to familiar and unfamiliar HCI design problems. It is hoped that this chapter will therefore provide a helpful reference for HCI researchers seeking to understand more about Bayesian optimisation and how it can be deployed to their design problems.

References

[1] G. Bailly, A. Oulasvirta, T. Kötzing and S. Hoppe. 2013. MenuOptimizer: interactive optimization of menu systems. Pages 331–342 of: *Proceedings of the 26th Annual ACM Symposium on User Interface Software and Technology.* UIST '13. Association for Computing Machinery.

[2] M. Balandat, B. Karrer, D. R. Jiang, S. Daulton, B. Letham, A. G. Wilson and E. Bakshy. 2020. BoTorch: a framework for efficient Monte-Carlo Bayesian optimization. Pages 21524–21538 of: *Advances in Neural Information Processing Systems 33.* NIPS '20. Neural Information Processing Systems.

[3] E. Bradford, A. M. Schweidtmann and A. Lapkin. 2018. Efficient multiobjective optimization employing Gaussian processes, spectral sampling and a genetic algorithm. *Journal of Global Optimization,* **71**(2), 407–438. Springer.

[4] E. Brochu, T. Brochu and N. de Freitas. 2010. A Bayesian interactive optimization approach to procedural animation design. Pages 103–112 of: *Proceedings of the 2010 ACM SIGGRAPH/Eurographics Symposium on Computer Animation.* Eurographics Association.

[5] J. J. Dudley, J. T Jacques and P. O. Kristensson. 2019. Crowdsourcing interface feature design with Bayesian optimization. Pages 252:1–252:12 of: *Proceedings of the 2019 Conference on Human Factors in Computing Systems.* CHI '19. Association for Computing Machinery.

[6] D. Duvenaud. 2014 (Nov.). Automatic model construction with Gaussian processes. Phd thesis, University of Cambridge.

[7] K. Gajos and D. S. Weld. 2004. SUPPLE: automatically generating user interfaces. Pages 93–100 of: *Proceedings of the 9th International Conference on Intelligent User Interfaces*. IUI '04. Association for Computing Machinery.

[8] P. P. Galuzio, E. H. de V. Segundo, L. dos S. Coelho and V. C. Mariani, Viviana Cocco. 2020. MOBOpt – multi-objective Bayesian optimization. *SoftwareX*, **12**, 100520.

[9] J. Heer and M. Bostock. 2010. Crowdsourcing graphical perception: using Mechanical Turk to assess visualization design. Pages 203–212 of: *Proceedings of the SIGCHI Conference on Human Factors in Computing Systems*. CHI '10. Association for Computing Machinery.

[10] F. Kadner, Y. Keller and C. Rothkopf. 2021. AdaptiFont: increasing individuals' reading speed with a generative font model and Bayesian optimization. In: *Proceedings of the 2021 Conference on Human Factors in Computing Systems*. CHI '21. Association for Computing Machinery.

[11] M. M. Khajah, B. D. Roads, R. V. Lindsey, Y.-E. Liu and M. C. Mozer. 2016. Designing engaging games using Bayesian optimization. Pages 5571–5582 of: *Proceedings of the 2016 CHI Conference on Human Factors in Computing Systems*. CHI '16. Association for Computing Machinery.

[12] A. Kittur, E. H. Chi and B. Suh. 2008. Crowdsourcing user studies with Mechanical Turk. Pages 453–456 of: *Proceedings of the SIGCHI Conference on Human Factors in Computing Systems*. CHI '08. Association for Computing Machinery.

[13] N. Knudde, J. van der Herten, T. Dhaene and I. Couckuyt. 2017. GPflowOpt: a Bayesian optimization library using TensorFlow. *arXiv preprint – arXiv:1711.03845*.

[14] R. Kohavi, R. M. Henne and D. Sommerfield. 2007. Practical guide to controlled experiments on the web: Listen to your customers not to the hippo. Pages 959–967 of: *Proceedings of the 13th ACM SIGKDD International Conference on Knowledge Discovery and Data Mining*. KDD '07. Association for Computing Machinery.

[15] S. Komarov, K. Reinecke and K. Z. Gajos. 2013. Crowdsourcing performance evaluations of user interfaces. Pages 207–216 of: *Proceedings of the SIGCHI Conference on Human Factors in Computing Systems*. CHI '13. Association for Computing Machinery.

[16] Y. Koyama, I. Sato and M. Goto. 2020. Sequential gallery for interactive visual design optimization. *ACM Transactions on Graphics*, **39**(4), 88:1–88.12. Association for Computing Machinery.

[17] Y. Koyama, I. Sato, D. Sakamoto and T. Igarashi. 2017. Sequential line search for efficient visual design optimization by crowds. *ACM Transactions on Graphics*, **36**(4), 48:1–48:11.

[18] Y.-E. Liu, T. Mandel, E. Brunskill and Z. Popović. 2014. Towards automatic experimentation of educational knowledge. Pages 3349–3358 of: *Proceedings of the 32Nd Annual ACM Conference on Human Factors in Computing Systems*. CHI '14. Association for Computing Machinery.

[19] J. D. Lomas, J. Forlizzi, N. Poonwala, N. Patel, S. Shodhan, K. Patel, K. Koedinger and E. Brunskill. 2016. Interface design optimization as a multi-armed bandit

problem. Pages 4142–4153 of: *Proceedings of the 2016 CHI Conference on Human Factors in Computing Systems*. CHI '16. Association for Computing Machinery.

[20] M. M. H. Mahmud, B. Rosman, S. Ramamoorthy and P. Kohli. 2014. Adapting interaction environments to diverse users through online action set selection. In: *Proceedings of the AAAI 2014 Workshop on Machine Learning for Interactive Systems*. Citeseer.

[21] J. B. B. Nielsen, J. Nielsen and J. Larsen. 2015. Perception-based personalization of hearing aids using Gaussian processes and active learning. *IEEE/ACM Transactions on Audio, Speech, and Language Processing*, **23**(1), 162–173.

[22] P. O'Donovan, A. Agarwala and A. Hertzmann. 2015. DesignScape: design with interactive layout suggestions. Pages 1221–1224 of: *Proceedings of the 33rd Annual ACM Conference on Human Factors in Computing Systems*. CHI '15. Association for Computing Machinery.

[23] S. Park, C. Gebhardt, R. Rädle, A. M. Feit, H. Vrzakova, N. R. Dayama, H.-S. Yeo, C. N. Klokmose, A. Quigley, A. Oulasvirta and O. Hilliges. 2018. AdaM: adapting multi-user interfaces for collaborative environments in real-time. Pages 184:1–184:14 of: *Proceedings of the 2018 CHI Conference on Human Factors in Computing Systems*. CHI '18. Association for Computing Machinery.

[24] C. E. Rasmussen and C. K. I. Williams. 2006. *Gaussian Processes for Machine Learning*. MIT Press.

[25] P. Salem. 2017. User interface optimization using genetic programming with an application to landing pages. *Proceedings of the ACM on Human–Computer Interaction*, **1**(EICS), 13:1–13:17.

[26] S. Sarcar, J. Joklnen, A. Oulasvirta, C. Silpasuwanchai, Z. Wang and X. Ren. 2016. Towards ability-based optimization for aging users. Pages 77–86 of: *Proceedings of the International Symposium on Interactive Technology and Ageing Populations*. ITAP '16. Association for Computing Machinery.

[27] B. Shahriari, K. Swersky, Z. Wang, R. P. Adams and N. de. Freitas. 2016. Taking the human out of the loop: a review of Bayesian optimization. *Proceedings of the IEEE*, **104**(1), 148–175.

[28] J. Snoek. 2013. Bayesian optimization and semiparametric models with applications to assistive technology. PhD thesis, University of Toronto, Toronto, Canada.

[29] K. Todi, D. Weir and A. Oulasvirta. 2016. Sketchplore: sketch and explore with a layout optimiser. Pages 543–555 of: *Proceedings of the 2016 ACM Conference on Designing Interactive Systems*. DIS '16. Association for Computing Machinery.

[30] M. Toomim, T. Kriplean, C. Pörtner and J. Landay, James. 2011. Utility of human-computer interactions: toward a science of preference measurement. Pages 2275–2284 of: *Proceedings of the SIGCHI Conference on Human Factors in Computing Systems*. CHI '11. Association for Computing Machinery.

Part IV

Bayesian Cognitive Modelling

10

Cue Integration in Input Performance

Byungjoo Lee

Abstract

When users interact with a computer, they essentially go through a series of input actions (e.g. point-and-click). To perform an input, a user must first accurately and precisely estimate the state of the computer (e.g. the location of the target). From a Bayesian point of view, this can be formulated as a statistical process in which the user estimates the most probable computer state given the sensory signal. Depending on the reliability of the estimate, the input performance of the user – who plans and executes the input based on that estimate – varies greatly. Bayesian decision theory provides a general formulation for the process by which the user estimates the state of a computer and determines the optimal input action. Based on this formulation, this chapter introduces a methodology for modelling user input performance in interaction scenarios where the reliability of the user's computer state estimate is generally low (e.g. real-time video games).

10.1 Introduction

Today, computers mediate many human activities; we perform thousands of input actions every day in various modalities such as touch and voice. Due to this universality and repeatability of input behaviour, even a slight improvement in the user's input performance at the operational level can greatly increase the quality of interaction in the long run. Accordingly, active research has been conducted to improve user input performance in domains such as pointing [4, 6, 7, 21, 25, 40], steering [22], typing [5, 31, 38–40], button pressing [20, 26, 30], and mid-air gesture [11, 23, 34].

To properly perform an input, users must first estimate the state of the computer in relation to input planning and execution. For example, for a point-and-click task using a computer mouse, users must perceive the size of the target and the distance to the target. If such an estimate is unreliable, the input action – which is planned and executed accordingly – will also be unreliable. Therefore, designing the interface such that it is easy for users to accurately and precisely estimate the state of the computer is the most fundamental consideration for successful interaction [29].

There are a number of design factors that can make the user's estimate of a computer state unreliable. The first is an interface design that does not account for the inherent limitations of the user's perceptual system. For example, a target may be displayed in the user's peripheral visual field [18], information may be provided for too short a time (e.g. scrolling through a document too quickly) [27], or there may be a lack of tactile sense when making contact with a target on a touchscreen [7]. The second is the probabilistic determination of the computer state. Examples include the latency of the system's response [9, 41] or the use of artificial intelligence technology to estimate the user's behaviour pattern and provide proactive and probabilistic notifications [2]. To improve user performance in such situations, it is necessary to understand the mechanism by which the interface design affects the reliability of the user's estimate regarding the computer state.

To this end, this chapter introduces a methodology for modelling the reliability of a user's computer state estimate. The reliability model can be derived from the assumption that the user integrates multiple sensory cues, which estimate the computer state, into a single whole in a statistically optimal manner. After estimating the computer state, the user should decide on and properly execute an appropriate input action. Considering additional models for such decision-making and input execution processes, we can finally build a model that predicts the user's input performance. However, in the interest of simplifying the formulation and focusing more on the influence of unreliable estimation on input performance, this chapter primarily assumes the user's optimal decision making and noise-free input execution. These assumptions may seem overly restrictive; however, there are several important input tasks (which will be also introduced in this chapter) that satisfy these assumptions well.

Before describing the user's sensory cue integration process, this chapter first introduces *Bayesian decision theory*, which allows all processes of user input performance – from computer state estimation to decision making and input execution – to be handled together in a single statistical framework. It provides a useful basis for explaining the user's sensory cue integration process and suggests that the ideas presented here may be extended and applied to more general input situations.

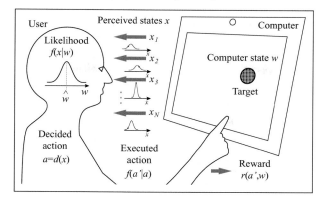

Figure 10.1 The process of the user estimating the computer state and deciding and executing an appropriate input action. This can be formulated by Bayesian decision theory.

10.2 Bayesian Input Performance

Bayesian decision theory is a branch of statistical decision theory and can be generally applied to explain the decision-making process of an intelligent agent. According to this theory, an agent's decision-making process comprises three elements (Figure 10.1). The first is the state of the world w to which the agent belongs. If the agent is a user interacting with the computer, w comprises the state variables of the computer that are related to the task given to the user (e.g. target location or target size in a pointing task).

The second element is the sensory signal x, which the agent obtains from the world it belongs to. For example, in HCI, users are often given a multi-modal sensory signal related to the computer state through display devices, such as screens or speakers. The sensory signal contains information that allows the user to estimate the computer state. From this information, the user's beliefs regarding the computer state can be captured as a likelihood function $f(x|w)$ $(= L(w; x))$

The third element is the action a, which the agent decides upon and executes from the given sensory signal x. In the HCI context, a is an input action that the user decides to perform, given the sensory signal x from the computer. When the agent's decision function is $d()$, the relation of the agent's intended action and the given sensory signal may be expressed as follows: $a = d(x)$. In many cases, the agent's actions cannot be performed as intended due to internal and external noise. Such noisy execution may be captured as the distribution of executed actions a' for the intended action a: $f(a'|a)$.

From this decision-making and action execution process, the agent receives a reward r, which is a function of the executed action a' and the world state w: $r(a', w)$. At this time, for a specific world state w, the expected reward ER_w to be obtained by the agent equipped with the decision function $d(x)$ can be expressed as follows:

$$ER_w(d) = \iint r(a', w)f(a', x|w)da'dx. \tag{10.1}$$

In (10.1), $f(a', x|w)$ is the joint probability function of a' and x at a given world state w. By the chain rule, (10.1) can be further expanded as follows:

$$ER_w(d) = \iint r(a', w)f(a'|x, w)f(x|w)da'dx. \tag{10.2}$$

Here, the probability function of a' depends solely on $a(= d(x))$. Therefore, (10.2) develops into the following:

$$ER_w(d) = \iint r(a', w)f(a'|d(x))f(x|w)da'dx. \tag{10.3}$$

From the formulations so far, we can assume a statistically optimal agent equipped with a decision function $d^*()$ that maximises the expected reward $\bar{r}$. However, according to Bayesian decision theory, the expected reward that is conditional on the world state w enables only partial ordering between decision functions in general. Partial ordering refers to situations in which a single best decision function cannot be found, and several decision functions are incomparable to one another.

To enable the complete ordering of decision functions, and consequently obtain a single optimal decision function, it is necessary to consider the prior probability function of the world state $\pi(w)$ in the formulation of the expected reward as follows:

$$ER = \int ER_w \pi(w)dw$$
$$= \iiint r(a', w)f(a'|d(x))f(x|w)\pi(w)da'dxdw. \tag{10.4}$$

Finally, the decision function $d^*(x)$ that maximises the expected reward in (10.4) is called the Bayes rule:

$$d^*(x) = \arg\max_d ER(d(x)). \tag{10.5}$$

10.2.1 Simplified Input Scenario

Bayesian decision theory provides a general framework for explaining not only the user's input performance in HCI but also all human decision-making and actions. However, for the purposes of this chapter, the original formulation of the theory is overly complex. Therefore, this chapter introduces three additional assumptions regarding the formulation.

The first assumption is that the user's input action is executed without noise ($\therefore a' = a$). In tasks such as pressing a button or performing a short mid-air gesture, for example, the user will execute the input action reliably enough. The second assumption is that the prior probability function of computer states is uniform. This implies that the user does not have a specific prior belief in what the task is to be given, which is sufficient to cover typical interaction scenarios. The third assumption is that rewards are given only when the user's input action exactly matches the computer state, as required by the task (i.e. $a' = w$). For example, in a pointing task, it would be assumed that the reward is given only when the user successfully clicks the exact centre of the target (although, in reality, clicking within the target would suffice). Then the reward function can be assumed to be the Dirac delta function $\delta(a' - w)$ centred on the computer state w.

Based on these three assumptions, (10.4) may be simplified as follows:

$$ER = \iint \delta(a - w)f(x|w)dx\,dw. \tag{10.6}$$

Here, the expected reward is determined solely by the user's input action decision function $d(x)$ and the likelihood function of the computer state $L(w; x)$. If the user already has an optimal decision rule that maximises the expected reward (to be discussed in the following section), the only factor that determines the user's input performance in this simplified interaction scenario is the user's reliability in estimating the computer state. This aligns well with the input situation this chapter originally intended to describe.

10.2.2 User as a Statistically Optimal Observer

In the interaction scenario represented by (10.6), it may be assumed that the user's decision function follows the Bayes rule. This implies that the user is equipped with the decision function $d^*(x)$ that maximises the expected reward ER. This assumption is useful because it allows us to understand the upper bound of the user's performance, even if the user's decision making is in fact not optimal.

In (10.6), the user is rewarded only when an input is equivalent to the computer state (i.e. $a' = w$). Therefore, it can be intuitively understood that the decision function that maximises the expected reward should be a *maximum likelihood estimator*. That is, as a statistically optimal observer, the user must decide to perform an input action on the computer state $\hat{w}$ with the highest likelihood (see Figure 10.1):

$$d^*(x) = \hat{w} = \arg \max_w L(w; x). \tag{10.7}$$

Even if the exact same task is given again, the sensory signal x given to the user is altered for each trial by random noise. Therefore, the user's maximum likelihood estimation $\hat{w}$ also changes for each trial. At this time, the reliability of the estimation can be understood as the probability function of $\hat{w}$, which is conditional on the computer state w: $f(\hat{w}|w)$.

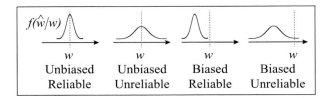

Figure 10.2 Four types of probability function that a user's computer state estimates typically can have. Here, w indicates the computer's true state unknown to the user.

Since we assumed noise-free execution of the input behaviour, the reliability of the user's estimator is the sole determinant of the user's input performance. In particular, it would be preferable to have the mode of estimate distribution be located at the true state (unknown to the user) of the computer. At the same time, the distribution of estimates around the mode should be sufficiently sharp (Figure 10.2). Therefore, building a model that predicts how the distribution of the user's estimate of the computer state would form in an interaction situation would ultimately provide useful insights into the user's input performance. Meanwhile, the distribution of user estimates is determined from the distribution of the user's beliefs regarding the computer state; this distribution is the likelihood function. Therefore, more fundamentally, it is necessary to consider how the likelihood function should be modelled in the process of interaction. However, this is not an easy task due to certain challenges which will be presented in the next section.

10.2.3 Challenges in Likelihood Modelling

The process of estimating and perceiving the state of the external environment has been extensively investigated in psychophysics [16], an academic field that studies the relationship between physical signals and the sensations and perceptions it evokes. Psychophysics studies primarily measure a person's psychometric function for a particular stimulus, quantifying how biased and reliable the person's estimate of that stimulus is.

However, in psychophysics studies, the sensory stimulation given to a person is far more controlled and simpler than the sensory signals provided to the user in a typical HCI process. More specifically, in HCI, as opposed to typical psychophysics experiments, the user is often given multiple sensory cues (i.e. $x_1, x_2, x_3, \ldots, x_N$) regarding a particular state of the computer [11, 30]. This makes the direct application of psychophysics findings to input performance modelling a significant challenge.

Let us take a simple example. When a user wants to execute an application by double-clicking on an icon on the screen, the icon's position may be individually estimated based on either the global display coordinate system (i.e. allocentric) or the user-centred coordinate system (i.e. egocentric). At this time, the likelihood of the target position obtained from each sensory cue $f(x_i|w)$ may be different, and if the user wants to estimate the computer state with the maximum likelihood, he/she will obtain two different point estimates from each likelihood. However, the user must ultimately obtain a single estimate of the target location to complete the task. So, how does the user make a final estimate from different individual estimates?

There are various possibilities for the user to use estimates obtained from multiple sensory cues. The easiest to consider is the so-called winner-takes-it-all (WTA) method, in which the user chooses the estimate with the highest reliability (i.e. distribution of estimates with the narrowest width) among the estimates obtained from each cue [17]. Alternatively, the user may choose the unweighted mean rule (UWM), which simply averages different estimates. However, there seems to be no identifiable reason for the user to choose the UWM method over the WTA method or vice versa.

The next section covers this issue in greater depth. In particular, it will be demonstrated that, given the formulation of Bayesian decision theory and the assumption that the user is the statistically optimal observer, the method by which the user integrates multiple estimates into one is naturally derived.

10.2.4 Sensory Cue Integration

If the sensory signal given to the user consists of N sensory cues, and each sensory cue provides a noisy measurement (x_i) of the computer state (w), the probability function of the user's measurement can be expressed as follows:

$$f(x|w) = f(x_1, x_2, x_3, \ldots, x_N|w). \tag{10.8}$$

If each sensory cue is statistically independent of each other, (10.8) can further be developed as follows:

$$f(x_1, x_2, x_3, \ldots, x_N | w) = \prod_{i=1}^{N} f(x_i | w). \tag{10.9}$$

Assume here that the probability function of each individual sensory cue follows a Gaussian distribution with a mean w_i and standard deviation σ_i:

$$f(x_i | w) = \frac{1}{\sigma_i \sqrt{2\pi}} e^{-\frac{1}{2} \left(\frac{x - w_i}{\sigma_i} \right)^2}. \tag{10.10}$$

Then, as shown in (10.9), the joint probability function $f(x|w)$ is the product of the individual functions; $f(x|w)$ is also a Gaussian distribution with the following mean (w_{integ}) and standard deviation (σ_{integ}):

$$f(x|w) = \frac{1}{\sigma_{\text{integ}} \sqrt{2\pi}} e^{-\frac{1}{2} \left(\frac{x - w_{\text{integ}}}{\sigma_{\text{integ}}} \right)^2},$$

$$w_{\text{integ}} = \sum_{i=1}^{N} k_i w_i \quad \text{and} \quad \sigma_{\text{integ}}^2 = \frac{1}{\sum_{i=1}^{N} 1/\sigma_i^2}. \tag{10.11}$$

Here, k_i is a weight that considers the relative reliability of each sensory cue and is calculated as follows:

$$k_i = \frac{1/\sigma_i^2}{\sum_{j=1}^{N} 1/\sigma_j^2}. \tag{10.12}$$

Both (10.11) and (10.12) predict the process through which the multiple sensory cues given to the user are integrated into a single sensory cue. This process is called human sensory cue integration.

Next, let us consider how the likelihood of the computer state $L(w; x)$ will be expressed in each decision trial. The likelihood of the computer state is equivalent to the probability function $f(x|w)$, but it is a function for which x is fixed for each decision trial, and w_{integ} is considered a variable (or simply it can be rewritten as w). Therefore, the likelihood function is also a Gaussian distribution with a mean x and standard deviation σ_{integ}:

$$L(w; x) = \frac{1}{\sigma_{\text{integ}} \sqrt{2\pi}} e^{-\frac{1}{2} \left(\frac{w - x}{\sigma_{\text{integ}}} \right)^2}. \tag{10.13}$$

Assuming the user is a statistically ideal observer, the user should estimate the computer state as w where the likelihood is maximum. The likelihood

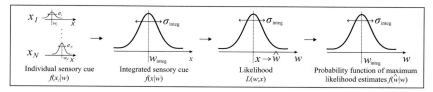

Figure 10.3 Four distributions involved in the sensory cue integration process when statistically independent Gaussian sensory cues are given. Assuming a noise-free execution of the input action, the probability function of the maximum likelihood estimates $f(\hat{w}|w)$ can be regarded as the user's input distribution.

is maximised at the mode of distribution, i.e. when w is x. Thus, the user's maximum likelihood estimate $\hat{w}$ of the computer state is as follows:

$$\hat{w} = x. \tag{10.14}$$

Here, the sensory measurement x is randomly sampled from $f(x|w)$ for each decision trial, so the distribution of the user's estimates $f(\hat{w}|w)$ also follows $f(x|w)$:

$$f(\hat{w}|w) = \frac{1}{\sigma_{\text{integ}}\sqrt{2\pi}} e^{-\frac{1}{2}\left(\frac{\hat{w}-w_{\text{integ}}}{\sigma_{\text{integ}}}\right)^2}. \tag{10.15}$$

Figure 10.3 summarises the four distributions involved in the sensory cue integration process introduced so far. Note that if only a single cue x_i is given, the distribution of the estimates $f(\hat{w}|w)$ from the given cue can also be obtained as a Gaussian with a mean w_i and the standard deviation σ_i. The process here would be identical to that illustrated by Equations (10.13) to (10.15).

Looking more closely at the human sensory cue integration process described by (10.11), (10.12), and (10.3), we discover two important characteristics. First, in the integration process, sensory cues with higher reliability are weighted more heavily. Second, the reliability of the estimate $(1/\sigma_{\text{integ}}^2)$ obtained through integration always has a higher reliability than that of each individual estimate $(1/\sigma_i^2)$.

Finally our assumption of noise-free execution makes the distribution of the estimate equal to the distribution of the user's input response; this is the user's input performance, which is what we want to model and predict! Various experiments have demonstrated that the performance of human perceptual estimation follows the prediction of (10.15) [1, 3, 12, 14, 15, 35, 37].

The following section elaborates in greater detail how the user's input performance can be modelled in real-world HCI tasks, based on the formulations so far. In particular, the modelling process will be demonstrated by taking an input task that is common in real-time games as an example (i.e. moving-target acquisition) [10, 24, 26, 28, 32].

10.3 Modelling Input Performance

There are four steps to modelling the user's input performance following the formulation introduced in this chapter. First, we must identify the sensory cues given to the user; those cues allow the user to estimate the computer states associated with a given task (*sensory cue identification*). Second, we must build mathematical models that explain how the probability function of the computer state measurement, i.e. $f(x_i|w)$, is formed based on each sensory signal (*individual cue modelling*). In this process, existing psychophysics study results may be borrowed; it may also be necessary to construct new models by introducing new assumptions. Furthermore, to simplify modelling, it may be assumed that the probability functions are Gaussian, as demonstrated in the previous section. Third, based on (10.11) and the sensory cue models of the previous step, a model of the computer state's likelihood function $L(w; x)$ is constructed (*cue integration modelling*). Under the assumption of flat prior and noise-free input execution, this model is further developed into the final model for predicting user input performance $f(\hat{w}|w)$. Fourth, since the final input performance model generally has free parameters that represent the user or task-specific factors, the parameters must be determined by fitting the model to the actual user experiment data (*model fitting*).

The most challenging among these steps are sensory cue identification and individual cue modelling. It is difficult to cover all sensory cues users rely on [8, 36] when estimating the specific state of a computer, and the reliability of different sensory cues can dynamically vary [11, 13, 19] depending on the given state of the computer. However, we are approaching this problem from an interaction design perspective. In other words, the goal is to build a workable and practical model that aids in the computational design of an interface. If the model can achieve this desired goal, a certain level of simplification can be justified. The example detailed in the following section will give readers a better sense of the modelling process.

10.3.1 Moving-Target Acquisition

Moving-target acquisition is a basic task in HCI that is often given to users in real-time games. This task requires the user to press a button when a moving target is located within a specific acquisition zone. If the user generates a button input when the target is outside the acquisition zone, the trial is considered a failure, and the user's input performance can be quantified as the failure rate of target acquisition. A model that predicts the failure rate of target acquisition may have a variety of applications, such as the computational design of game difficulty or measuring the cognitive characteristics of game players.

The task requires the user to estimate when to press the button, and the required timing of button input can be regarded as the computer state that the user must estimate based on the given sensory signals. In moving-target acquisition tasks, as opposed to general HCI tasks, it is often difficult for the user to estimate the computer state because the target is usually moving fast. It is also possible to assume noise-free input execution since the user's input action consists solely of pressing a button. These conditions make the task suitable for testing the modelling methodology introduced in this chapter.

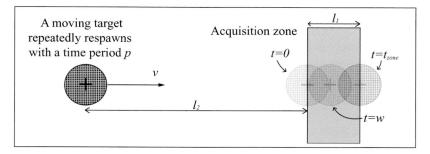

Figure 10.4 Moving target-acquisition task. The user must press a button when the centre of the fast-moving target is located within the acquisition zone. In this chapter, the target is assumed to respawn with a constant time period p and move with a constant velocity v. For this task, the user needs to estimate w, which is the time at which the button should be pressed.

Task Formulation

To simplify the problem, the target is assumed to move in a straight line with a constant velocity towards a fixed acquisition zone. Only one target is on the screen at a time, and it respawns at a specific location in every predetermined time interval (see Figure 10.4). The user must press the button when the centre of the target is located within the acquisition zone. The speed of the target is v; the width of the target acquisition zone is l_1; the distance from the target's appearance to the acquisition zone is l_2; and the time interval at which the target repeatedly appears is p. The goal is to build a model that predicts the failure rate of a user's target acquisition in this task situation. The failure rate y can be expressed as a function of the task variables as follows:

$$y = f(v, l_1, l_2, p). \tag{10.16}$$

In the task, the time duration in which the user is permitted to press the button for each trial is the time it takes for the target to pass through the acquisition zone. This is called t_{zone}, and it can be obtained by dividing the width of the acquisition zone by the speed of the target:

$$t_{\text{zone}} = \frac{l_1}{v}. \tag{10.17}$$

If the moment when the centre of the target first contacts the acquisition zone is defined as $t = 0$, the user must generate a button input between $t = 0$ and $t = t_{\text{zone}}$ for each trial. $t = w$ is the timing of the button input that the user should estimate.

Assumptions

The button input timing w, which the user should estimate, may vary depending on the design variables of the task. Here, to simplify the problem, it is assumed that w is dependent only on t_{zone}:

$$w = c_1 t_{\text{zone}}. \tag{10.18}$$

This indicates that if t_{zone} is longer, w will also move back proportionally. c_1 is a user-specific or task-specific proportionality constant that must be obtained experimentally.

Some additional assumptions are introduced for the user's input process. First, it is assumed that the user is rewarded only when the button is pressed at the input time required for the task ($t = w$), and the prior for the timing at which the button should be pressed is flat (i.e. $\pi(w) \approx \text{Uniform}$). Second, since the user's input action consists only of pressing a button, it is assumed that the user's input action is executed without noise (i.e. $a' \approx a$). Third, it is assumed that the user's decision function follows the Bayes rule. In other words, the user's decision is assumed to maximise the expected reward represented by Equation (10.6). In this case, as described in Section 10.2.2, the user should estimate the button input timing as the value at which the likelihood $L(w; x)$ is maximised.

Sensory Cue Identification

In the process of performing the moving target acquisition task, multiple sensory cues $(x_1, x_2, \ldots, x_N)$ that allow the user to estimate w are given. Of those sensory cues, we consider the two most important in modelling. The first cue (x_t), the temporal structure cue, is obtained from the temporal pattern in which the target repeatedly reaches the acquisition zone at a constant time period p. Like clapping to the beat of the music, the user's internal clock can encode such a repeating pattern [33] to estimate the appropriate timing for the next input. The second cue (x_v), the visually perceivable movement cue, is obtained by visually encoding the target's movement towards the acquisition zone. By perceiving the target speed v and the remaining distance l_2 to the acquisition zone, the user can estimate the appropriate timing for the next input. Both cues are encoded through vision, but to simplify the modelling process, it is assumed that the estimation of w from each cue is statistically independent.

Individual Cue Modelling

Next, it is necessary to model the probability function of the button input timing measured from each sensory cue, i.e. $f(x_t|w)$ and $f(x_v|w)$. To this end, it is assumed that each function follows an unbiased Gaussian with a mean w and standard deviations σ_t and σ_v, respectively:

$$f(x_t|w) = \mathcal{N}(w, \sigma_t^2) = \mathcal{N}(c_1 t_{\text{zone}}, \sigma_t^2),$$
$$f(x_v|w) = \mathcal{N}(w, \sigma_v^2) = \mathcal{N}(c_1 t_{\text{zone}}, \sigma_v^2). \qquad (10.19)$$

Here, σ_t and σ_v represent the reliability of the measurements from each cue and are the only unknown quantities in the model. Each reliability can be expressed as a function of task design variables based on known human perception characteristics.

First, it is known that the precision with which humans encode the time interval between repeated events decreases as the time interval increases [33]. This characteristic of the human internal clock is called the *scalar property*, and we can observe that this is derived from the experience of finding it easier to clap correctly once every second rather than once every five seconds (assuming that dividing the rhythm is forbidden). From this, the reliability of t_{input} measured from the temporal structure cue can be expressed as follows:

$$\sigma_t = c_2 \, p. \qquad (10.20)$$

Here, c_2 is a user-specific or task-specific proportionality constant that must be obtained experimentally.

Second, the reliability of the visually perceivable movement cue (x_v) can be expressed as a function of the cue viewing time (t_{cue}). The cue viewing time is defined as the time between when the target first appears and when it reaches the acquisition zone. It can be calculated as follows:

$$t_{\text{cue}} = \frac{l_2}{v}. \qquad (10.21)$$

Based on this definition, we attempt an *asymptotic analysis* of the reliability of the cue as a function of t_{cue}. Asymptotic analysis is a modelling technique that analyses how the behaviour of a system changes when a particular system variable goes to an extreme value. Here, we analyse two extreme situations: when t_{cue} goes to zero, and when t_{cue} goes to infinity.

First, the case of t_{cue} going to zero is equivalent to the complete lack of a sensory cue, so the corresponding measurement function $f(x_v|w)$ will be flat. σ_v will diverge to infinity in this case. Second, the longer the t_{cue}, the more time the user has to encode the speed of the target and the distance to the acquisition zone. In other words, the longer the t_{cue}, the more reliable the cue will be and the lower the σ_v will be. However, if the cue viewing time is extremely long, will σ_v converge to zero? We know from experience that it will not. No matter how long we observe the target's movement, the target acquisition performance is bounded; σ_v converges to a specific minimum value c_3 as t_{cue} diverges to infinity.

Summarising the asymptotic analysis results, σ_v can finally be expressed as a function of t_{cue} as follows:

$$\sigma_v = c_3 + \frac{1}{e^{(c_4\,t_{cue})}-1}. \tag{10.22}$$

Note that in the above model, σ_v decreases exponentially with the increase of t_{cue}. c_4 represents the rate of exponential decay and, like the lower bound c_3, must be obtained experimentally in a user or task-specific manner.

Cue Integration Modelling

Since the sensory cues were assumed to be statistically independent of each other, the individual sensory cues are integrated into the final cue, as shown in (10.11). The mean (w_{integ}) and standard deviation (σ_{integ}) of the measurement function obtained from the integrated sensory cue are as follows:

$$w_{integ} = \left(\frac{1/\sigma_t^2}{1/\sigma_t^2+1/\sigma_v^2}\right) c_1 t_{zone} + \left(\frac{1/\sigma_v^2}{1/\sigma_t^2+1/\sigma_v^2}\right) c_1 t_{zone} = c_1 t_{zone},$$
$$\sigma_{integ}^2 = \frac{\sigma_t^2\sigma_v^2}{\sigma_t^2+\sigma_v^2}. \tag{10.23}$$

On the other hand, since we assumed that the user's decision function follows the Bayes rule, the probability function of the user's button input timing estimate (i.e. $f(\hat{w}|w)$) is a Gaussian distribution with a mean w_{integ} and standard deviation σ_{integ}, as shown in (10.15):

$$P(\hat{w}|w) = \frac{1}{\sigma_{integ}\sqrt{2\pi}}e^{-\frac{1}{2}\left(\frac{\hat{w}-w_{integ}}{\sigma_{integ}}\right)^2}. \tag{10.24}$$

Finally, since the noise-free execution of the input action is assumed, the observed target acquisition performance of the user is equivalent to the probability function expressed in (10.24).

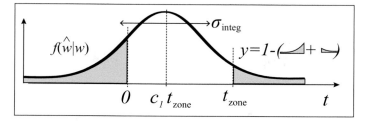

Figure 10.5 The probability function of user button input, as predicted by the model. $t = 0$ is the moment when the target's centre first makes contact with the acquisition zone; $t = t_{\text{zone}}$ is the moment when the target's centre first exits the acquisition zone. If the function is integrated outside the interval between $t = 0$ and $t = t_{\text{zone}}$, it becomes the acquisition failure rate y.

If the function $f(\hat{w}|w)$ is integrated in the interval $[0, t_{\text{zone}}]$, the target acquisition success rate can be predicted, and if the success rate is subtracted from one, the target acquisition failure rate is obtained (see Figure 10.5):

$$y = 1 - \frac{1}{2}\left[\text{erf}\left(\frac{t_{\text{zone}} - w_{\text{integ}}}{\sigma_{\text{integ}}\sqrt{2}}\right) + \text{erf}\left(\frac{w_{\text{integ}}}{\sigma_{\text{integ}}\sqrt{2}}\right)\right]. \tag{10.25}$$

Here, $\text{erf}()$ is the error function.

Model Fitting

The final model derived from the previous section has four free parameters (c_1, c_2, c_3, c_4). These parameters must be obtained by fitting the model to the experimental data; this section demonstrates the process. In particular, the model fitting will be performed for different user groups to test whether the model parameters can reveal differences in individual cognitive characteristics.

A total of 51 paid participants were recruited. Participants were divided into five age groups: 20s to 30s (11 participants), 40s (10), 50s (10), 60s (10) and 70s to 80s (10). The experiment followed a $2 \times 2 \times 2$ within-subjects design with the following independent variables:

- t_{zone}: 0.08 or 0.15 s
- p: 1.25 or 1.8 s
- t_{cue}: 0 or 0.2 s

The experiment was conducted using specially designed hardware with minimal input latency ($\approx$ 1.5 ms) for a one-dimensional moving-target acquisition task.[1] The device included an LED display that could indicate a

[1] https://github.com/SunjunKim/CueIntegrationDevice

moving target and an acquisition zone, and participants performed input actions
by clicking a mouse button connected to the display. The speed of the moving
target was 1.39 m/s, from which l_1 and l_2 were inversely derived according to
each task design. Participants sat 2.8 m away from the LED strip, and the LED
strip was installed horizontally at participant eye level. Participants performed
30 target acquisition trials for each unique task condition. Task conditions were
given to participants in a random order.

After calculating the acquisition failure rate for each unique task condition,
least-squares fitting was performed using Equation (10.25). The fitting was first
performed for each individual participant and then for the aggregated dataset.
The result is shown in Figure 10.6. We can see that the failure rate predicted by
the model agrees well with the aggregated participant failure rate ($R^2 = 0.99$). In
the case of individual fitting, the learning effect was not sufficiently removed due
to an insufficient number of input trials for each condition; therefore, there exists
a variability that the model cannot explain. In particular, the 70s-to-80s group
experienced significant difficulty in performing the task. This resulted in their
average fitting R^2 (M = 0.71, SD = 0.24) being lower than the average fitting
R^2 of the other groups (M = 0.87, SD = 0.073). The parameters obtained from
the aggregated fit are as follows: $c_1 = 0.21$, $c_2 = 0.11$, $c_3 = 0.045$, $c_4 = 450.07$.

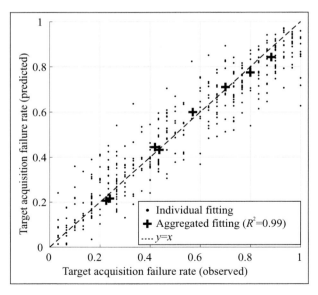

Figure 10.6 Plot of observed failure rates versus predicted failure rates
obtained from the model fitting.

Next, statistical analysis (Kruskal–Wallis test with $\alpha = 0.05$) was performed to observe whether the model parameters varied significantly depending on the age group. Only c_2 showed a statistically significant difference between age groups (H(4) = 20.44, p = 0.004). Figure 10.7 presents a plot of the different c_2 values. The value of c_2 starts to increase from the 50s, and when it reaches the 60s to the 70s, it nearly doubles. If the value of c_2 is higher, the participant experiences greater difficulty in estimating the button input timing from the temporal structure cue (see Equation (10.20)). This result can be interpreted in two ways: the cognitive ability to encode temporal cues may decrease with age, or senior people may be less exposed to tasks that require encoding temporal structure cues (such tasks would include real-time games and music playing). Table 10.1 summarises the mean and standard deviation of all parameters for each age group.

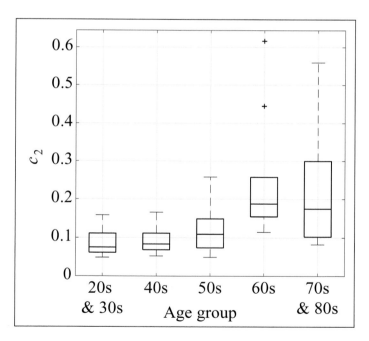

Figure 10.7 Box plot showing the value of c_2 for each age group.

Age group	c_1	c_2*	c_3	c_4
20s & 30s	0.30 (0.16)	0.088 (0.035)	0.042 (0.021)	319.2 (208.7)
40s	0.24 (0.14)	0.097 (0.038)	0.037 (0.018)	242.2 (190.1)
50s	0.30 (0.16)	0.123 (0.066)	0.049 (0.030)	242.2 (198.9)
60s	0.33 (0.17)	0.251 (0.158)	0.053 (0.030)	177.9 (170.8)
70s & 80s	0.27 (0.24)	0.223 (0.151)	0.066 (0.034)	246.9 (213.2)

Note: The number in parentheses indicates the standard deviation, and the asterisk (*) means that the effect of the age group was statistically significant for that parameter.

Table 10.1 Mean and standard deviation of model parameters for each age group.

10.4 Conclusion

This chapter introduced Bayesian methodology that allows us to account for the reliability of a user's computer state estimate. For the methodology, the user's input process is considered a statistical decision-making process. In particular, it is assumed that the user has the optimal decision function that can be formulated according to Bayesian decision theory. From these assumptions, we can build a model that predicts the reliability of the user's computer state estimation in a general input task given multiple sensory cues. This can be developed into a model that predicts the user's input performance based on additional assumptions about the user's input process (flat prior, zero-one reward, and noise-free input execution).

The proposed methodology is useful for modelling input performance in input tasks for which the reliability of user's computer state estimation is generally low. Taking the moving target-acquisition task as an example, this chapter demonstrated the proposed methodology. It was shown that the model built through the proposed methodology can successfully predict the acquisition failure rate of users. Furthermore, the model parameters obtained from the fitting succeeded in revealing the cognitive-behavioural differences between user groups.

Bayesian decision theory, which underlies the formulation of this chapter, can encompass all common input tasks in HCI without any special restrictions (Equations (10.1) to (10.5)). In the end, however, this chapter addressed only simplified input situations, which involved special assumptions about the input process. From this, the input performance model could be derived analytically. This may help readers understand the main idea of the chapter, but it also may not be sufficient for readers who wish to go further. In a more general input task, the user's prior cannot be assumed as uniform, and a more realistic reward function and noisy input execution should be assumed. This implies that computational modelling techniques – rather than the analytic modelling techniques demonstrated in this chapter – must be considered. This is a relatively under-explored area in user performance modelling research, and abundant future studies are expected.

References

[1] D. Alais and D. Burr, David. 2004. The ventriloquist effect results from near-optimal bimodal integration. *Current biology*, **14**(3), 257–262.

[2] N. Banovic, A. Wang, Y. Jin, C. Chang, J. Ramos, A. Dey and J. Mankoff. 2017. Leveraging human routine models to detect and generate human behaviors. Pages 6683–6694 of: *Proceedings of the 2017 CHI Conference on Human Factors in Computing Systems*. CHI '17. Association for Computing Machinery.

[3] P. W. Battaglia, R. A. Jacobs and R. N. Aslin. 2003. Bayesian integration of visual and auditory signals for spatial localization. *Josa a*, **20**(7), 1391–1397.

[4] X. Bi, Y. Li and S. Zhai, Shumin. 2013. FFitts law: modeling finger touch with Fitts' law. Pages 1363–1372 of: *Proceedings of the SIGCHI Conference on Human Factors in Computing Systems*. CHI '13. Association for Computing Machinery.

[5] X. Bi, B. A. Smith and S. Zhai. 2010. Quasi-qwerty soft keyboard optimization. Pages 283–286 of: *Proceedings of the SIGCHI Conference on Human Factors in Computing Systems*. CHI '12. Association for Computing Machinery.

[6] X. Bi and S. Zhai. 2013. Bayesian touch: a statistical criterion of target selection with finger touch. Pages 51–60 of: *Proceedings of the 26th Annual ACM Symposium on User Interface Software and Technology*. UIST '13. Association for Computing Machinery.

[7] X. Bi and S. Zhai. 2016. Predicting finger-touch accuracy based on the dual Gaussian distribution model. Pages 313–319 of: *Proceedings of the 29th Annual Symposium on User Interface Software and Technology*. UIST '13. Association for Computing Machinery.

[8] D. Buckley and J. P. Frisby. 1993. Interaction of stereo, texture and outline cues in the shape perception of three-dimensional ridges. *Vision Research*, **33**(7), 919–933.

[9] G. Casiez, T. Pietrzak, D. Marchal, S. Poulmane, M. Falce and N. Roussel. 2017. Characterizing latency in touch and button-equipped interactive systems. Pages 29–39 of: *Proceedings of the 30th Annual ACM Symposium on User Interface Software and Technology*. UIST '17. Association for Computing Machinery.

[10] S. Do, M. Chang and B. Lee, Byungjoo. 2021. A simulation model of intermittently controlled point-and-click behaviour. In: *Proceedings of the SIGCHI Conference on Human Factors in Computing Systems*. CHI '21. Association for Computing Machinery. https://doi.org/10.1145/3411764.3445514.

[11] S. Do and B. Lee. 2020. Improving reliability of virtual collision responses: a cue integration technique. Pages 1–12 of: *Proceedings of the 2020 CHI Conference on Human Factors in Computing Systems*. CHI '20. Association for Computing Machinery.

[12] M. O. Ernst and M. S. Banks. 2002. Humans integrate visual and haptic information in a statistically optimal fashion. *Nature*, **415**(6870), 429–433.

[13] C. R. Fetsch, A. H. Turner, G. C. DeAngelis and D. E. Angelaki. 2009. Dynamic reweighting of visual and vestibular cues during self-motion perception. *Journal of Neuroscience*, **29**(49), 15601–15612.

[14] S. Gepshtein and M. S. Banks. 2003. Viewing geometry determines how vision and haptics combine in size perception. *Current Biology*, **13**(6), 483–488.

[15] S. Gepshtein, J. Burge, M. O. Ernst and M. S. Banks. 2005. The combination of vision and touch depends on spatial proximity. *Journal of Vision*, **5**(11), 7.

[16] G. A. Gescheider. 2013. *Psychophysics: the Fundamentals*. Psychology Press.

[17] M. Gueguen, N. Vuillerme and B. Isableu. 2012. Does the integration of haptic and visual cues reduce the effect of a biased visual reference frame on the subjective head orientation? *PLoS ONE*, **7**(4), e34380.

[18] C. Gutwin, A. Cockburn and A. Coveney. 2017. Peripheral popout: The influence of visual angle and stimulus intensity on popout effects. Pages 208–219 of: *Proceedings of the 2017 CHI Conference on Human Factors in Computing Systems*. CHI '17. Association for Computing Machinery.

[19] J. M. Hillis, S. J. Watt, M. S. Landy and M. S. Banks. 2004. Slant from texture and disparity cues: Optimal cue combination. *Journal of Vision*, **4**(12), 1.

[20] S. Kim, B. Lee and A. Oulasvirta. 2018. Impact activation improves rapid button pressing. Pages 1–8 of: *Proceedings of the 2018 CHI Conference on Human Factors in Computing Systems*. CHI '18. Association for Computing Machinery.

[21] S. Kim, B. Lee, T. van Gemert and A. Oulasvirta. 2020. Optimal sensor position for a computer mouse. *arXiv preprint arXiv:2001.03352*.

[22] B. Lee and H. Bang. 2015. A mouse with two optical sensors that eliminates coordinate disturbance during skilled strokes. *Human–Computer Interaction*, **30**(2), 122–155.

[23] B. Lee, Q. Deng, E. Hoggan and A. Oulasvirta. 2017. Boxer: a multimodal collision technique for virtual objects. Pages 252–260 of: *Proceedings of the 19th ACM International Conference on Multimodal Interaction*. ICMI '17. Association for Computing Machinery.

[24] B. Lee, S. Kim, A. Oulasvirta, J.-I Lee and E. Park. 2018. Moving target selection: A cue integration model. Pages 1–12 of: *Proceedings of the 2018 CHI Conference on Human Factors in Computing Systems*. CHI '18. Association for Computing Machinery.

[25] B. Lee, M. Nancel, S. Kim and A. Oulasvirta. 2020. AutoGain: gain function adaptation with submovement efficiency optimization. In: *Proceedings of the SIGCHI Conference on Human Factors in Computing Systems*. CHI '20. Association for Computing Machinery. https://doi.org/10.1145/3313831.3376244.

[26] B. Lee and A. Oulasvirta. 2016. Modelling error rates in temporal pointing. Pages 1857–1868 of: *Proceedings of the 2016 CHI Conference on Human Factors in Computing Systems*. CHI '16. Association for Computing Machinery.

[27] B. Lee, O. Savisaari and A. Oulasvirta. 2016. Spotlights: attention-optimized highlights for skim reading. Pages 5203–5214 of: *Proceedings of the 2016 CHI Conference on Human Factors in Computing Systems*. CHI '16. Association for Computing Machinery.

[28] I. Lee, S. Kim and B. Lee. 2019. Geometrically compensating effect of end-to-end latency in moving-target selection games. Pages 1–12 of: *Proceedings of the 2019 CHI Conference on Human Factors in Computing Systems.* CHI '19. Association for Computing Machinery.

[29] C. Lewis and D. A. Norman. 1995. Designing for error. Pages 686–697 of: W. Buxton, S. Greenberg and J. Grudin, eds., *Readings in Human–Computer Interaction.* Elsevier.

[30] A. Oulasvirta, S. Kim and B. Lee. 2018. Neuromechanics of a button press. Pages 1–13 of: *Proceedings of the 2018 CHI Conference on Human Factors in Computing Systems.* CHI '18. Association for Computing Machinery.

[31] A. Oulasvirta, A. Reichel, W. Li, Y. Zhang, M. Bachynskyi, K. Vertanen and P. O. Kristensson. 2013. Improving two-thumb text entry on touchscreen devices. Pages 2765–2774 of: *Proceedings of the SIGCHI Conference on Human Factors in Computing Systems.* CHI '13. Association for Computing Machinery.

[32] E. Park and B. Lee. 2020. An intermittent click planning model. Pages 1–13 of: *Proceedings of the 2020 CHI Conference on Human Factors in Computing Systems.* CHI '20. Association for Computing Machinery.

[33] B. H. Repp. 2005. Sensorimotor synchronization: a review of the tapping literature. *Psychonomic Bulletin & Review*, **12**(6), 969–992.

[34] S. Sridhar, A. M. Feit, C. Theobalt and A. Oulasvirta. 2015. Investigating the dexterity of multi-finger input for mid-air text entry. Pages 3643–3652 of: *Proceedings of the 33rd Annual ACM Conference on Human Factors in Computing Systems.* CHI '15. Association for Computing Machinery.

[35] H. Tassinari, T. E. Hudson and M. S. Landy. 2006. Combining priors and noisy visual cues in a rapid pointing task. *Journal of Neuroscience*, **26**(40), 10154–10163.

[36] J. Trommershauser, K. Kording and M. S. Landy. 2011. *Sensory Cue Integration.* Oxford University Press.

[37] J. Trommershauser, L. T. Maloney and M. S. Landy. 2003. Statistical decision theory and the selection of rapid, goal-directed movements. *JOSA A*, **20**(7), 1419–1433.

[38] K. Vertanen, H. Memmi, J. Emge, S. Reyal and P. O. Kristensson. 2015. VelociTap: investigating fast mobile text entry using sentence-based decoding of touchscreen keyboard input. Pages 659–668 of: *Proceedings of the 33rd Annual ACM Conference on Human Factors in Computing Systems.* CHI '15. Association for Computing Machinery.

[39] D. Weir, H. Pohl, S. Rogers, K. Vertanen and P. O. Kristensson. 2014. Uncertain text entry on mobile devices. Pages 2307–2316 of: *Proceedings of the SIGCHI Conference on Human Factors in Computing Systems.* CHI '12. Association for Computing Machinery.

[40] D. Weir, S. Rogers, R. Murray-Smith and M. Löchtefeld. 2012. A user-specific machine learning approach for improving touch accuracy on mobile devices. Pages 465–476 of: *Proceedings of the 25th Annual ACM Symposium on User Interface Software and Technology.* UIST '12. Association for Computing Machinery.

[41] R. Wimmer, A. Schmid and F. Bockes. 2019. On the latency of USB-connected input devices. Pages 1–12 of: *Proceedings of the 2019 CHI Conference on Human Factors in Computing Systems.* CHI '19. Association for Computing Machinery.

11

Bayesian Parameter Inference for Cognitive Simulators

Jussi P. P. Jokinen, Ulpu Remes, Tuomo Kujala and Jukka Corander

Abstract

This chapter addresses the issue of parameter inference of computational cognitive models that simulate behaviour. Such cognitive simulators play an important role in understanding and predicting human thought and behaviour by implementing hypotheses about the human cognitive processes and modelling these using stepwise simulations. In HCI, these models can be used for a range of applications, such as in UI evaluation and optimisation. However, their usefulness is limited without rigorous parameter fitting procedures, which permit efficient and informative parameter inference that can be used to assess confidence in parameter estimates, and easily replicated across experiments. In the usual case when the simulators are complex, common parameter fitting methods fail in this respect. In this chapter we discuss the feasibility of Bayesian parameter inference for cognitive simulators, presenting practical solutions to Bayesian parameter inference, and demonstrating its usefulness with two cognitive models simulating interactive tasks. Furthermore, we discuss the implications of efficient, informative and robust parameter inference for the future of HCI.

11.1 Introduction

A long-standing objective of human–computer interaction (HCI) and artificial intelligence (AI) research is to facilitate the use of interactive and intelligent systems by developing a better understanding of the users of these systems. This involves taking into account the users' goals, beliefs and abilities in an attempt to align the information ecologies supported by interactive systems with the users' preferences. In this chapter, we consider the hard problem of understanding the user by asking how it can be furthered by inferring parameters of computational cognitive models. These models act as *simulators* that map latent user characteristics to observed behaviour. We use the term 'simulation' to emphasise that these models make step-by-step predictions (in some units of time) of the progress of an interactive task. The validity of these simulators and thus usefulness depends on informative and robust parameter inference. The idea of these models, simply put, is that they implement a series of hypotheses about the human cognitive processes, attempting to predict behaviour based on individual traits and experiences, task description and interactive environment characteristics, which are all represented as parameters in the model.

Given that the structure of a model is psychologically valid and its parameters are specified and interpreted correctly, it is possible to predict what the user would do in different circumstances. This is called *forward modelling*, wherein adjusting the parameters that shape the model's task environment can be used to ask 'what if' questions, thus providing information to decision-making, such as adaptation of user interfaces. For instance, a cognitive model of layout learning can be used to predict visual search performance over different user interfaces (UIs) and for users with different expertise levels, permitting an automated and individualised evaluation of various design choices [18, 19]. In this regard, such models can be used to better adapt technologies for the psychology of users, because they improve our understanding of the latent factors behind users' behaviours. Moreover, they are helpful in developing HCI as a science, permitting theory development and testing by forcing researchers to explicate their theoretical assumptions about users, and allowing simulation of the hypothesised user behaviour.

A major challenge for the development, generalisation and utilisation of cognitive models is that they often encompass a large number of parameters, upon which their psychological validity stands. The existence of these parameters per se is not the problem, but the predictions that the models make are useful only insofar as it is possible to claim that the values of these parameters are set plausibly – which is a hard problem. *Parameter inference* refers to identifying values that are theoretically plausible and lead to realistic predictions. For many parameters of cognitive models used in HCI, parameter inference is fairly straightforward, as the values in question are identified on the basis of existing psychological research or derived from the specifics of the known task environment. For instance, in the aforementioned layout learning model, parameters governing the movement of eyes are psychologically established and not subject to significant variation between tasks or individual users. Similarly, parameters dictating the task environment, such as the size and locations of visual layout elements, are not difficult to set as long as the

forward   inverse

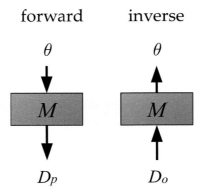

Figure 11.1 In forward modelling, the model M is run with fixed parameter values θ to produce predictions D_p. Conversely, in inverse modelling, observations D_o are used to infer plausible values for θ.

specifics of the UI are fully known to the modeller. However, there are two cases where a parameter cannot be fixed a priori: (1) when the static parameter partially encloses or 'hides' dynamic cognitive mechanisms, therefore requiring recalibration with new tasks; and (2) when variance in the parameter value can be connected to individual differences in behaviour. In both instances, parameter inference becomes an *inverse modelling* problem: given observed behaviour, what are the plausible parameter values? The difference between forward and inverse modelling is illustrated in Figure 11.1.

This chapter focuses on the use of Bayesian parameter estimation for inferring parameters of cognitive simulators based on observed behavioural data. The advantage of the Bayesian approach is in its ability to express prior information and uncertainty about parameter estimates using probability theory. The outcome of parameter estimation is a posterior distribution that expresses probabilities for different parameter values and combinations when the observed behaviour is taken into account. Usually, the reason these simulators are applied and their parameters inferred is to predict and understand user behaviour. This can be accomplished by generating a posterior distribution of predicted behaviours using the inferred parameter distributions. In practice, posterior estimation for parameters of cognitive simulator models is carried out with likelihood-free inference (LFI). LFI methods provide a way to respond to a critical problem with Bayesian inference of parameters of complex simulators: because the models are not closed-form equations, but stepwise simulators involving stochasticity, fit to data under certain parameters can be established only by running the simulator with said parameter values. While Bayesian parameter inference and LFI methods have been received with some interest in cognitive science [9, 21, 40–42], the ultimate goal of this chapter is to facilitate a wider use of these techniques within the computational interaction modelling community.

In what follows, we first define and give examples of computational cognitive models, as used as simulators in HCI to generate predictions of user behaviour. We then discuss the problem of parameter inference for these simulators and review the ways that it can be accomplished. Our focus is on Bayesian parameter inference. We discuss common LFI approaches and demonstrate the use of approximate Bayesian computation (ABC) as an instance of Bayesian parameter inference applicable to cognitive simulators. As we will argue, this approach is appealing for two reasons: (1) because it permits formally incorporating prior knowledge to inform parameter estimation; and (2) because it provides an informative posterior, which can be used to assess the amount of confidence in the parameter estimates. Both of these features increase our capacity to learn about parameters of cognitive models, especially when these parameters are individually determined and critical for predicting task behaviour, and implement interventions for better facilitation of user adaptation.

11.2 Bayesian Parameter Inference for Cognitive Simulator Models

This section formalises Bayesian parameter inference and how it can be used to infer the parameters of cognitive simulator models. We first outline the process of parameter fitting for cognitive simulators (Section 11.2.1) and then discuss how Bayesian parameter inference can be used efficiently and informatively in this process (Section 11.2.2). This is achieved with the likelihood-free methods discussed in Section 11.2.3.

11.2.1 Parameter Inference for Cognitive Simulator Models

In our formal investigation of parameter inference for cognitive simulators, we define a model M with parameters θ. Executing the model maps the input parameters into data that consist of predictions made by the model. Because cognitive models generally involve stochastic elements, the same parameter values do not necessarily generate the same output upon subsequent executions of the model. As a result, it is often necessary to run the model multiple times with the same parameter values, resulting in a more informative distribution of predictions. The prediction data D_p from the model are therefore sampled from the parameterised model $M(\theta)$, instead of representing a deterministic mapping from it.

Compared to testing with human participants, the major benefit of computational cognitive models for HCI is that they are simulators, which can be executed as many times as required. Varying the parameters of the models, especially those pertaining to the task environment, such as the UI, allows researchers and designers to investigate how various UI changes impact behaviour. We present some examples of how cognitive simulators have been used in HCI in Table 11.1. Because these simulators implement hypotheses about how the human cognition processes information and how this process results in behaviour, simulation of human-like behaviour is often possible even for scenarios or interventions for which no existing human data are available. Furthermore, given that a parameter can be posited a role in determining individual behaviour, varying its value permits the prediction of behaviour from various types of users.

However, these simulations are only good insofar as the parameters that govern cognitive processes are set correctly. Where the value or distributions of values of a parameter cannot be deduced from the task or reused from existing research, they must be inferred from observed behaviour. Based on the short review of parameter fitting procedures of cognitive models used in HCI, there is currently no standard and easily replicated inference methodology in place. In case of cognitive models, when parameters have been inferred from observed data, this inference is often either not reported, or it is reported as having been done by adjusting the parameter values by hand until model fit to human data was deemed acceptable [21]. There are some exceptions to this in HCI, such as [33] using genetic optimisation, and [15] using a simplex method, but generally the field lacks a standard for parameter inference. To our knowledge, there are only a few publications in HCI that report using Bayesian parameter estimation [11, 20].

Observing human behaviour, either via psychological experimentation or from observations made during real-life interaction, provides us with data D_o, which can be then used to infer θ. This assumes that the data observed from users and generated by simulating the model are similar in that they describe the same behaviours. For instance, the data can be in terms of aggregate data, such as mean task times or error counts, or more detailed observations, such as logs of user inputs from completing a single task. The most common practice in HCI is to collect data from multiple users, and then create *summary statistics* by aggregating first within and then across individuals, thus abstracting the relevant behavioural aspects of the interaction into few selected point estimates.

Table 11.1 A list of example computational cognitive models in HCI and how their parameters have been set

Ref	Target	Applications	Cog. arch.	Example parameter	Inf.
[14]	Visual search in graphical user interfaces (GUI)	GUI design, predictive tools for testing designs	EPIC	Recoding time for text	L
[10]	Web navigation via hyperlinks	Web design	SNIF-ACT	Attentional weight	F L D
[26]	Information search via search engine	Search engines	ACT-R	Retrieval threshold	D,U
[35]	User multitasking	In-vehicle user interface design and testing	ACT-R	Steering style	F
[2]	Effects of interruptions on user cognition	Interface design for managing interruptions	ACT-R	Time to store a new representation into problem state	L
[33]	Memory-based interaction obstacles	Workload management	CMM	Degree of memory decay	F
[3]	Aviation surface operations and performance	Pilot performance and error prediction	ACT-R	Noise in production utility computation	U
[30]	Decision-making of air traffic controller (ATC)	ATC system design and training	ACT-R	Activation noise	D,U
[6]	Human error	Human reliability analysis	SHERPA	Scale and shape parameters of error probability density function	L
[39]	Human communication	Human-robot communication and interaction	ACT-R/E	Waiting time until switching attention	L
[29]	Impact and use of mobile health applications	Mobile health applications	ACT-R	ACT-R parameters	D
[15]	Safety incident reporting decisions	Mobile crowdsourcing applications	DDM	Response bias	F
[17]	Multitasking in driving	In-vehicle user interface design and testing	CR	Action noise	L

Note: (F = Fit to observation data, L = based on literature, U = Undefined, D = Default values. Cog. arch. = cognitive architecture/theory)

Parameter inference for cognitive simulators can be used to determine user or population-level characteristics based on the observed data. Traditionally, the aim is to estimate parameters $\hat{\theta}$ that maximise a model fit measure. For example, maximum likelihood estimation is based on the idea that parameters θ are supported by the observed data D_o in proportion to the likelihood $P(D_o|\theta)$, which is the probability that the model M with parameters θ generated the observed data D_o, $P(D_p = D_o|\theta)$. Thus, even though the likelihood does not provide direct information about how much a parameter value is supported, this proportionality permits comparing different parameter values according to their likelihood. The maximum likelihood estimate $\hat{\theta}$ is calculated as the parameters θ that maximise $P(D_o|\theta)$. However, when a complex simulation model is used to describe the dependencies between the parameters and simulation outcomes, the observation probabilities $P(D_p = D|\theta)$ can be hard or impossible to determine. This is due to the models being simulators, which cannot be expressed analytically but must be executed in a stepwise fashion, with each step processing information according to complex rules, with potentially multiple sources of added noise. In this case, parameter estimates $\hat{\theta}$ must be determined based on other model fit measures, such as prediction error or discrepancy between summarised D_o and D_p.

While parameter estimation is possible based on model fit measures also when complex simulator models are studied, a problem with point estimates $\hat{\theta}$ is that since the set of observed data is limited in size, the parameters that best match the available observations may not be the ones that best describe the user or make the most accurate predictions about user behaviour in new situations. In addition, a point estimate does not express the amount of confidence that the estimate is correct, and therefore it does not allow researchers and designers to consider how strongly to trust predictions made from a model parameterised in this way. These problems associated with point estimates can be avoided by applying Bayesian parameter inference.

11.2.2 Bayesian Parameter Inference

Bayesian parameter inference is grounded on the fact that we generally cannot know the exact parameter values that best describe the observed data and user(s) behind it. However, it is possible to obtain information about the parameter values, and this information can be represented as a probability distribution over the possible parameter values. Possible information about parameters θ includes both what can be learned based on observations D_o, as discussed in the previous section, and our expectations about plausible parameter values based on what we know about the simulator model. The idea is to express, prior to making observations, what we know about the parameters as a distribution

$P(\theta)$, and then make observations to update this expectation. Given the prior probabilities $P(\theta)$ and observation likelihood $P(D_o|\theta)$, posterior probabilities are defined as

$$P(\theta \mid D_o) = \frac{P(D_o \mid \theta)P(\theta)}{P(D_o)}, \tag{11.1}$$

where $P(D_o)$ is the marginal likelihood $P(D_o) = \int P(D_o|\theta)P(\theta)d\theta$. The posterior $P(\theta|D_o)$ is a probability distribution over parameter values, and it represents what we know about the unknown parameters when we take into account that these parameters produced the observations D_o. Since observations are expected to reduce uncertainty about the parameter values, the posterior distribution is usually more concentrated than the prior. In case where the observations D_o are not informative about the unknown parameters, the posterior will remain close to the prior.

The prior distribution quantifies the modeller's assumptions about plausible parameter values before any comparison between model predictions and observed data are made. It can encode known psychological or physiological constraints, information about known dependencies between parameter values, such that one parameter value cannot exceed another, or information about the most probable values. For example, if previous experiments provide information about how a parameter value varies in a population, this can be used as prior information about what value the parameter takes in a new individual. That such prior information is taken into account in parameter inference is especially important when we wish to make predictions based on a small observation set, because parameter values chosen based on the observations alone could be nonsensical.

Posterior probabilities provide an intuitive way for the modeller to understand which parameter values could describe the observed user. This means that while the posterior can indicate the probable parameter values, it also provides information about uncertainties and allows us to answer questions like what is the probability that the unknown parameter value is below a certain threshold. Moreover, when we want to predict how the observed user behaves in a new situation, the posterior can be used to calculate a *posterior predictive distribution*. In practice, when predictions are generated with a cognitive simulator model, the posterior predictive distribution is sampled by drawing parameter values from the posterior and running the simulator parameterised with these values. With enough samples drawn and simulations run, the predictions from the simulation runs form the posterior predictive distribution. Generating the predictive distribution based on a posterior sample rather than a point estimate allows us to take into account the uncertainties in parameter values and ensure that the predictive distribution variance is not

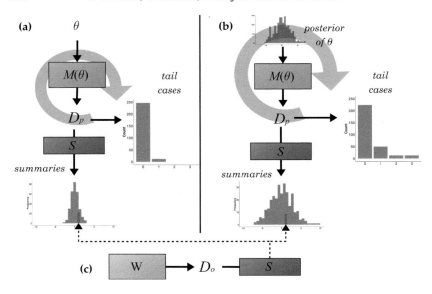

Figure 11.2 (a) A simulator M with fixed parameters θ can be run multiple times to produce a series of predictions D_p, which are each summarised, resulting in a distribution of summaries. (b) When a posterior of parameters θ has been created using Bayesian parameter inference, a posterior predictive distribution can be generated by repeatedly sampling values of θ from the posterior and summarising the resulting predictions D_p. Note that posterior predictive inference may be able to more plausibly estimate the occurrence of tail cases of some model features. Concentrations of observable model features in (a) illustrate that the simulator with fixed parameters can underestimate the amount of tail cases. (c) Observing a process in the world W produces data D_o that can then be summarised using summary statistics S.

underestimated. Figure 11.2 summarises how distributions of summary statistics can be generated with either fixed parameters or by sampling the posterior.

To summarise, posterior probabilities combine prior information with observation likelihoods and provide more information for the modeller than a point estimate. A problem with the posterior is that it can be expensive or impossible to compute. Even when the likelihoods $P(D_o|\theta)$ and prior probabilities $P(\theta)$ can be evaluated, $P(D_o)$ may not be computable in practice. Hence, it is common to work with unnormalised posterior values $P(D_o|\theta)P(\theta)$. The unnormalised posterior does not associate parameter values with actual probabilities, but it can be used much like the likelihood function to compare posterior support to parameter values and to determine maximum a posteriori estimates. It can also be used to sample the posterior distribution, and a sample with N parameter values can be used to calculate descriptors such as posterior distribution mean. Also, running the simulator with the sampled parameter values produces a sample from the posterior predictive distribution.

Finally, a problem with many cognitive simulator models is that the likelihood $P(D_o|\theta)$ cannot be determined based on the model. In this case, posterior estimation has to be carried out with likelihood-free methods that determine approximate posterior probabilities based on prior information encoded in $P(\theta)$ and repeated simulation experiments.

11.2.3 Likelihood-Free Inference

Likelihood-free inference provides means to estimate posterior probabilities over parameter values when it is not possible to calculate the observation likelihood. This section introduces basic ideas in likelihood-free posterior estimation based on approximate Bayesian computation (ABC) and its recent alternatives. ABC methods substitute likelihood evaluations with direct comparisons between observed and simulated data. These classic methods have been reviewed in [23, 37, 41]. The other methods introduced in this section use simulations to learn a distribution model that can be used to compute approximate posterior probabilities based on the observed data. These have been reviewed and discussed in [5].

ABC can be carried out with a rejection sampler that constructs an approximate posterior sample as follows. First, candidate parameter values θ are sampled from the prior distribution $P(\theta)$, and the simulator that predicts user behaviour based on parameters θ is executed with θ to generate simulated user interactions D_p. The simulated data D_p are then compared to the observed data D_o, and the candidate parameter value is accepted in the approximate posterior sample if difference $\Delta(D_o, D_p)$ between the simulated and observed interactions is below a certain threshold ϵ. The process can continue until N candidate parameters have been accepted or until the simulation count exceeds a predetermined maximum.

The above method substitutes likelihood evaluations with direct comparisons between observed and simulated data. In practice, the likelihood $P(D_p = D_o|\theta)$ is approximated as $P(\Delta(D_o, D_p) < \epsilon|\theta)$. This would be exact with $\epsilon = 0$ and $\Delta(D, D')$ that is a distance metric such that $\Delta(D, D') = 0$ when $D = D'$ and $\Delta(D, D') > 0$ otherwise. However since we work with stochastic simulators, innumerable trials could be needed to produce even one simulation outcome D_p that matches the observed data D_o under these conditions. Hence, we must allow some approximation error, and the difference measure $\Delta(D, D')$ and tolerance threshold ϵ are needed to define the conditions under which simulation data are considered an acceptable match with the observed data.

The difference measure $\Delta(D, D')$ formalises what makes observations similar. A common approach is to compress observations into informative features called summary statistics and define $\Delta(D, D')$ as distance between the summaries $S(D)$ and $S(D')$. Summarisation should reduce variation that is not informative about the unknown parameters θ so that the distance between $S(D)$ and $S(D')$ is close to zero when D and D' are data simulated with the same parameters. The summaries are often constructed based on domain information about what features in the observed and simulated data could be sensitive to the unknown parameter values, but it is also possible to derive and choose between candidate statistics based on simulation experiments. For more information on summary statistics selection, we recommend [31].

A problem with the rejection sampler is that the acceptance rate is expected to be low: since posterior distributions tend to be more concentrated than the priors, most candidate parameter values will not be accepted when these are chosen based on their prior probabilities. The tolerance threshold can be used to increase the acceptance rate, but this increases approximation error and makes the posterior distribution wider and closer to the prior distribution. A solution is found in iterative methods that take into account what has been learned about the previous trials when choosing the next candidate parameters. Iterative solutions include methods like ABC population Monte Carlo (ABC PMC), which is discussed and evaluated with cognitive simulator models in [41]. This method starts with the prior distribution and uses the samples that produced the lowest $\Delta(D_o, D_p)$ to determine the next proposal distribution. Since a proposal distribution constructed in this manner is expected to become more and more concentrated around the posterior as iterations proceed, fewer simulations are run with parameters that have low posterior probabilities. The same idea motivates advanced methods like BOLFI [13], which uses sequential model-based optimisation to locate parameter values that minimise expected $\Delta(D_o, D_p)$. BOLFI has been used to estimate cognitive simulator model parameters [11, 20].

Alternatives to the ABC methods that compare simulated and observed data include methods that use simulated data to learn about statistical dependencies between the parameters and simulation outcomes. In practice, the dependencies can be encoded in a distribution model that is fitted to the simulated data and used to determine an approximate posterior model $\hat{P}(\theta|D)$ that can be evaluated at $D = D_o$. Methods based on this principle include the synthetic likelihood and its extensions [32, 43] and methods that utilise kernel density estimation or neural density estimation to model the simulated data distribution. Density estimation has been evaluated with cognitive simulator models [40]. Related methods also include density-ratio estimation, where the approximate posterior estimation problem is converted into a classification problem [8].

Density estimation and other approaches that use simulations to estimate an approximate distribution model operate on the simulated data or summaries and do not require a difference measure or tolerance threshold to be determined. The methods require numerous simulations as training data, but sequential versions exist that utilise the observations D_o to avoid excess simulations with parameters that have low posterior probabilities. These include methods such as sequential neural likelihood [28] and automatic posterior transformation [12]. Moreover, there are applications in HCI wherein the total computation time or total simulation count matters less than the response time between when the user interaction occurs and when the posterior estimate is available for adaptation or other such purposes. These applications could find it valuable that, when observations are not used in the training process, the approximate posterior model can be learned based on simulations offline, and online computations reduce to evaluation at $D = D_o$.

Finally, a concern with the likelihood-free methods is whether posterior estimation can be carried out when the simulator model has many unknown parameters. The standard ABC methods discussed earlier in this section work best with a low-dimensional summary statistic which cannot capture information about numerous parameters. This means that the summaries dimension increases hand in hand with the parameter dimension, and the standard methods are not applicable in problems with more than a few parameters. However, the density and density-ratio estimation methods can be less sensitive to problem dimension, and the standard methods also have variants that decompose difference measure and posterior distribution in order to handle high-dimensional problems. These methods are discussed in [25].

11.3 Using Bayesian Parameter Inference with Cognitive Simulator Models

In this section, we demonstrate the use of Bayesian likelihood-free inference for fitting parameters of computational cognitive models that simulate user behaviour in HCI tasks. Of the two examples provided, the first demonstrates fitting of the model to aggregate data. The second example is then presented to demonstrate how to infer parameter values for individual users. Posterior estimation is carried out with ELFI [24] tools in both examples.

11.3.1 Parameter Estimation of a Menu Search Model

We replicate an experiment presented in previous work [21] where a menu search model was fitted to behavioural data both with methods that optimise a traditional model fit measure and with the ABC method BOLFI [13]. The likelihood-free inference experiments with BOLFI were used to estimate posterior distributions over parameter values based on aggregate and individual observations collected in earlier work [1]. The present demonstration focuses on the population-level posterior distribution that is estimated based on aggregate data. Our aim is to fit the model parameters governing eye movement time and memory recall.

The Task Model

The model studied in this experiment simulates the visual search of menus [4]. The model predicts eye movements in a task where users fixate on the elements of a drop-down menu to find a cued target. Importantly, it predicts how eye movement patterns are a result of adapting to the UI design and cognitive constraints. Therefore, as strategies emerge as adaptations to the UI design, the model permits investigation of how different menu designs impact behaviour. The task and menu environment are described as a Markov decision process, and the simulated user is represented as a computational agent. The agent's actions include fixating on any of the menu items, which causes a saccadic eye movement towards that item, and its subsequent encoding. The task ends upon encoding of the cued target. Additionally, the agent can decide to quit, which is necessary for ending the task in cases where the target is absent. The agent receives negative rewards for time spent on the menu search and a positive reward for finding the item or correctly ending the task, and reinforcement learning is used to discover the optimal search policy.

The menu search model used in the present experiment is based on the version proposed in [20]. Here the task completion times depend on the search path that the model learns to optimise and on two parameters that describe the user: duration associated with each fixation and selection delay that occurs at task completion. The model also takes into account that users sometimes remember the whole menu based on the first item, in which case the optimum behaviour is to directly fixate the target item. This is modelled as menu recall probability. Further model parameters control how shape and semantic relevance can be observed with peripheral vision, and encode properties of the searched menu. These were set to replicate the previous experiment [21].

Finally, the parameters that control learning and data collection were set as follows. The behavioural pattern that is expected to minimise the menu search

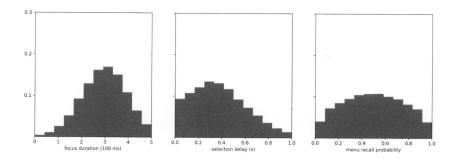

Figure 11.3 Prior distributions over menu search model parameters.

time under given user and menu parameters was learned based on 500,000 training episodes. The limited training episodes mean that the simulator may not learn the exact same behaviour each time even when called with the same parameters. This is one reason we see variation in the simulated task completion times. Another reason is that the simulated data are collected over 100 menu search tasks with random menus and target location. This means that two datasets simulated with the same parameters do not describe task completion times in the exact same tasks. In this experiment, eight items were always present in the menu, with most of the time (90%) the cued target being present, and sometimes (10%) not.

Parameter Estimation

The parameters inferred based on observed behavioural data include focus duration, selection delay and menu recall probability. The focus duration and selection delay parameters are associated with the same prior distributions that were used in previous work [21]: focus duration has a normal distribution prior with mean 300 ms and standard deviation 100 ms truncated to interval [0, 500] ms and selection delay a normal distribution prior with mean 0.3 s and standard deviation 0.3 s truncated to interval [0, 1] s. Menu recall probability is associated with a beta distribution prior with parameters $\alpha = \beta = 1.5$. The prior distributions are visualised in Figure 11.3.

The observation data for this example case come from a study in which human participants conducted the menu search task [1]. The observations used in posterior estimation include the task completion times and whether or not the cued target was present in the menu in each trial. The observed and simulated data are compared based on the summaries and distance proposed in [20]. Task completion times are compressed into mean and standard deviation calculated across trials where the target was present and across trials where the target was not present, and comparison between observed and simulated data is based on squared distance between the means and absolute distance between the standard deviations.

Posterior estimation is carried out with the BOLFI method available in ELFI [24]. BOLFI [13] uses a surrogate model to describe dependencies between parameter values and $\Delta(D_o, D_p)$. Gaussian process regression with a squared exponential kernel is used in the present experiment, and the unknown simulator parameters are each associated with a separate surrogate model parameter to encode how sensitive $\Delta(D_o, D_p)$ is to variation in that parameter. These length scale parameters were also associated with gamma prior distributions with shape $\alpha = 2$ and rate $\beta = 10/(b - a)$, where a and b denote the parameter minimum and maximum value considered in this experiment, to ensure reasonable predictions when the model is fitted based on limited data. The probabilities $P(\Delta(D_o, D_p) < \epsilon)$ that are used as approximate likelihoods can be calculated based on the surrogate model, which means that the surrogate model can substitute the simulator when we sample the approximate posterior. BOLFI initialises the surrogate model with simulations run with candidate parameters sampled from the prior distribution, but runs most simulations with parameter values chosen based on the current model estimate. Fifty parameter combinations were sampled from the prior, and 450 were selected based on the lower confidence bound acquisition rule in the current experiment. Alternative acquisition rules are discussed in [16].

Results and Discussion

We sampled the approximate posterior determined based on the surrogate model learned in BOLFI with $\epsilon = 9$. The sample is used to estimate the approximate posterior mean, which as a parameter estimate minimises the expected squared error between the estimate and true parameter value. The estimated posterior mean is located at parameter values focus duration 250 ms, selection delay 0.29 s, and menu recall probability 0.53.

The marginal distribution over individual parameter values in the posterior sample is visualised in Figure 11.4. We observe that the comparison between observed and simulated data has narrowed down the focus duration and selection delay parameter distributions compared to the prior (Figure 11.3). This means that some parameter values that were considered in the prior distribution have not been able to explain the observed data. The posterior distribution over menu recall probability is close to the prior distribution, which indicates that we were not able to extract much new information about this parameter based on the observed data.

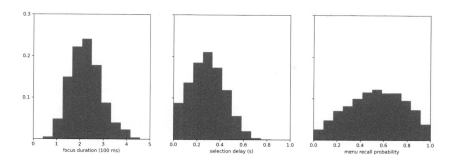

Figure 11.4 Marginal posterior distributions over individual menu search model parameters.

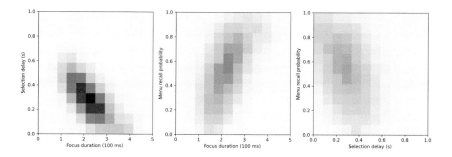

Figure 11.5 Marginal posterior distributions over menu search model parameter pairs.

Figure 11.5 shows the marginal distributions calculated over parameter pairs. Here we can see that the posterior captures a trade-off between the focus duration and selection delay parameters that both contribute to the observed task times. This has been learned based on the observed data, since the prior distributions did not encode correlation between parameters. It means that while we cannot be too certain about the exact parameter values, which is observed as variance in the individual marginal distributions, we can narrow down the most probable combinations for focus duration and selection delay.

11.3.2 Individual Parameter Estimation of a Driving Model

Our second example demonstrates estimation of person-specific parameters to a cognitive simulator. In comparison to the previous example, in which each summary statistic was computed as an aggregate over all participants, the goal of individual parameter estimation is to capture the idiosyncrasies of a single user. A cognitive simulator, if correctly parameterised to an individual, can be used to explore how the user would react to different interfaces or changes in the task circumstances. However, especially when making decisions on an individual basis, it is important to be able to assess the confidence that can be placed on the model's predictions. To that end, we demonstrate here how the posterior produced by Bayesian parameter estimation can be used to investigate how probable certain user behaviours are, as predicted by the model.

The Task Model

We utilise a model of driving that has been used in simulating how drivers share visual attention between the driving and an in-car search task when multitasking [17]. The model is based on a similar idea as the menu search model in the previous example: in-car glancing behaviour is assumed to emerge as an adaptation to task and cognitive constraints. For instance, as the speed of the car increases, in-car glances become shorter because of the increased visual demand of the driving task. Such an adaptive model can be used to predict how circumstances of driving, the design of the in-car interface and the abilities of the user impact driving safety.

The original study did not make any attempts at fitting the parameters of the model to human data; instead, they were set by observing the model's behaviour and determining a parameter value that produced simulations that at face value looked realistic. However, the model includes multiple parameters that the authors discuss might vary between drivers and use cases. Here, we focus on one, action-related noise σ. This parameter dictates how precise the driver's steering movements are, that is, how accurately the car is controlled. Larger parameter values result in more swayed driving, as the driver needs to take small corrective actions to control for the noisy steering. Similarly to the original paper [17], we hypothesise here that the model's driving noise parameter can be varied in order to simulate variance in lateral stability between individual drivers. However, contrary to the original study, we provide empirical support to this evidence by applying Bayesian parameter inference.

Parameter Estimation

We describe our prior expectations about the action-related noise parameter σ as a gamma distribution $P(\sigma) = \Gamma(3, 0.5)$, illustrated in Figure 11.6. The intuition behind this definition is that we assume the following: (1) every individual's action-related noise is greater than 0, due to inherent noise in the human motor system; (2) we expect that this noise is distributed fairly normally around its

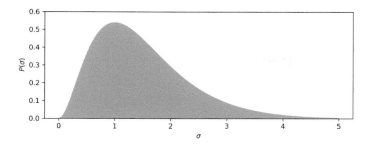

Figure 11.6 The gamma distribution used as a prior in the case example.

mode value, but with a long right tail to accommodate for individuals with a lot of action-related noise, such as elderly drivers or those with motor impairments; (3) we fix the mode of the distribution to be at 1.0, because tests with the driving model indicate that, at face value, the resulting predicted behaviour seems a reasonable approximation of normal driving. It is important to note that none of these points, with the exception of the first one, are strongly grounded in existing research. Regardless, they provide information, even if weak, to the parameter estimation procedure. Furthermore, this process makes explicit our assumptions about the prior, permitting future revisions of it, based on more evidence and reasoning.

The human data used in this example are taken from the original study.[1] The experiment proper had 12 participants conducting in-car visual search while driving the car. In addition, there was a practice session at the start of the experiments, where the participants got comfortable with the controls of the car simulator by driving a slightly curving road. The experiment had two speed conditions, with the car's speed fixed to either 60 km/h or 120 km/h, and so the practice session had these two speeds as well. Here, we use the data from the practice session only, and attempt to fit the driving model's σ parameter to individual drivers based on observing a few minutes of driving with both speeds used.

Both the driving simulator used in the behavioural study and the driving model studied in this experiment generate detailed time series data of the car's lateral position on the road. The data are snapshots of the state of the driving simulator or the model in intervals of 150 ms. Since the behaviour studied in this example is driving stability of individual participants, we use standard deviation of lateral road position to summarise the observations. It is simple to

[1] The data are available at https://gitlab.com/jokinenj/multitasking-driving.

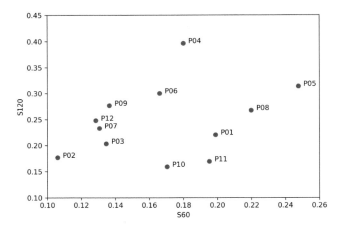

Figure 11.7 Observed individual summary statistics.

compute from both simulated and observed data, and it provides an intuitive measure of the amount of instability in the driving. As the study with human participants included two conditions of fixed speed, we compute the summary statistic twice. The standard deviations of lateral offset calculated based on individual observations ranged between 0.11 and 0.25 in the 60 km/h condition and between 0.16 and 0.40 in the 120 km/m condition. The standard deviations are shown in Figure 11.7.

Fitting parameters on individual basis can be computationally expensive in case there are several individuals to model and the whole inference process is repeated with each observation set. The present experiment uses the LFIRE method [38] available as an ELFI extension, PYLFIRE [22]. This is a density-ratio estimation method that uses classification between simulated datasets to learn the ratio between likelihood and marginal likelihood values. The method calculates approximate posterior probabilities at predetermined parameter values. Here the values were selected at 0.1 interval between 0 and 3. Gaussian process classifiers were trained as the likelihood-ratio model using 100 simulations with each parameter value and 100 simulations with parameters sampled from the prior distribution. The model was then used to calculate approximate posterior probabilities based on all individual observations. This means that while the model training took time, individual posteriors could be calculated based on the model without extra simulation costs.

Results and Discussion

The posterior distributions estimated based on individual observations are each concentrated around mean values between 1.0 and 1.3. The mean values are recorded in Table 11.2. We use each individual posterior distribution to sample $N = 100$ parameter values and run simulation experiments to determine the posterior predictive distribution over driver behaviours. Selected sample distributions over σ and predicted offset in car position are shown in Figure 11.8. The posteriors have clear centres that are at different parameter values. This indicates that the parameter inference procedure was able to capture individual differences in driving behaviour via the action noise parameter σ. We also see that some observations have been more informative about the unknown parameter value than others, as there are differences in the posterior variance. Moreover, individual differences between the participants' action noise values are now visible as differences in the predicted offset in car position.

Table 11.2 Estimated individual posterior mean values.

	P01	P02	P03	P04	P05	P06	P07	P08	P09	P10	P11	P12
$\hat{\sigma}$	1.2	1.0	1.2	1.3	1.3	1.2	1.2	1.2	1.2	1.1	1.1	1.2

The posterior and posterior predictive distributions permit the modeller to consider the plausibility of different parameter values and thus to assess confidence in predictions. For instance, if the interest is in deploying individually tuned driving aids, such as a lane departure warning system, the model can be used to predict on an individual basis when to signal a warning such that the driver has enough time to respond to it. In such an application, it is important that decisions are made based on all the available information and that uncertainties are also taken into account.

11.4 Discussion

Computational cognitive models make it possible for HCI designers and researchers to better understand users by providing psychologically realistic simulations of interactive behaviour. This chapter discussed the role of parameter inference in using such simulators in HCI. Manipulating the parameters of a model makes it flexible, permitting quick prototyping of different interactive scenarios, and predicting behaviour of individuals with

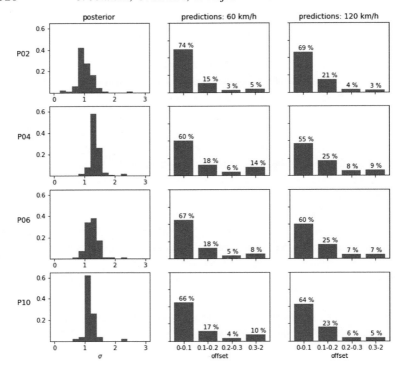

Figure 11.8 Selected posterior and posterior predictive distributions.

various abilities and goals, but only insofar as the parameters are set correctly and informatively. This is especially important in cases where noisy and sparse observations of user-generated data are used in inferring the values of the parameters. Bayesian parameter inference is attractive in this regard, as it allows the modeller to take into account prior information, and it provides a posterior distribution over parameter values.

While the focus of this chapter is on parameter inference, parameters themselves are rarely the final interest of research. The practical purpose of cognitive modelling in HCI is to make predictions based on parameterising these models. How much a certain parameter varies within the user population is therefore not as pertinent a question for UI design as is the range of *actual behaviours* that can be predicted (and observed) based on the distribution of the parameter in question. When these parameters are inferred, it makes sense to provide the whole range of plausible predictions, given what is known about the parameter prior to parameter estimate and after outcomes of simulations with different parameter values are compared to observed data. Bayesian parameter inference facilitates this process by formalising how the posterior parameter distribution is inferred on the basis of a prior and evidence. The posterior can then be sampled for parameter values, which are used to parameterise the simulator to generate a range of predictions called the posterior predictive distribution. For instance, in our example above about inferring the action-related noise parameter of individual drivers, the value of the parameter was only of secondary importance compared to predictions of that driver's behaviour (i.e. variability in lane offset). When such concrete predictions can be made from individual users, it becomes feasible to run the simulator under various task circumstances and thus generate a range of possible future scenarios to inform decision making.

Bayesian parameter inference is also a powerful tool for analysing model flexibility. The problem of overly flexible cognitive models is that if the free parameters of the model can be adjusted such that the model produces any kind of behaviour, then the model's fit to observation data is not a persuasive argument in support of the validity of the model [34]. Solutions to this include determining the predictions of the model over the whole range of the parameter space, accounting for the variability of the data and showing that the model's predictions are restricted in some sense. Bayesian parameter inference allows for all of these in a formalised manner. The posterior predictive distribution is an intuitive way to investigate the whole range of a model's predictions, and because it is generated in light of prior assumptions about the parameter, such as its plausible range, and the observed data, including their variability, the posterior can be used to investigate and demonstrate model flexibility. Especially in cases where the predictions generated by cognitive models are used to make critical decisions, it is important to be able to assess our confidence in the model's predictions and its validity.

Likelihood-free inference provides the practical tools to estimate posterior probabilities over simulator model parameters. The most accessible to new practitioners is the basic ABC sampler. Here, candidate parameters are sampled from the prior distribution and parameters that produce simulated user interactions similar to the observed interactions are accepted in the posterior. This method is not complicated and works when the estimation problem is low-dimensional and the individual simulations are not too expensive to compute. The more advanced methods that use previous simulations to decide the next candidate parameters can reduce the total simulation count by a lot, but they have more parameters that need to be controlled. The same applies to methods that learn a density or density-ratio model based on simulated data. These methods are attractive because the same model can be reused when we want to estimate posterior probabilities based on new observations. But again, there is the need to control more parameters and to evaluate model fit to ensure a reliable estimation outcome. Overall, the various likelihood-free methods make posterior estimation feasible for diverse simulation models and applications, and also provide means to achieve related tasks such as comparison between alternative simulators [7].

The choice of summary statistics is critical for useful parameter inference. In traditional experimental research, where participants conduct well-specified tasks in controlled environments, the choice of dependent variables and their summarisation is largely dependent on the nature of this environment. Often, an individual task is short, and is repeated multiple times by the same participant for the purposes of obtaining reliable estimates of the variable of interest under varying task conditions. Summary statistics, such as mean and standard deviation of the dependent variable, are then used to evaluate how the selected experimental manipulations impact the dependent variables. While this paradigm is useful for research under controlled settings, it is not necessarily applicable for real-life parameter inference, where observation data may be noisy and sparse, and no clear task boundaries can be specified. In our example of inferring individual action-related noise during driving, we used a statistic that describes variability of the car's lateral position over the whole driving episode. In choosing the correct summary statistics for parameter inference, attention must also be paid to the fact that summarisation might hide some important aspects of the interactive process being simulated. For instance, an average number of errors during a particular interaction may hide whether the errors are clustered around some critical moment or spread evenly throughout the episode. Furthermore, the modeller must pay heed to the fact that informative parameter inference is possible only insofar as variation in the parameters inferred causes variation in the summarisation of the simulated predictions.

Many of the elements of parameter inference discussed here, such as efficiency, analysis of model flexibility and selection of summary statistics, are of importance when discussing the future use of cognitive simulators to facilitate adaptation of interactive systems. While computational optimisation of user interfaces is a promising area of research [27], the quality of such optimisation is dependent on a careful specification of an objective function which tells how acceptable a solution is. Predictions made by simulators can provide flexible objective functions, but as we have argued, the quality of this is highly dependent on how the parameters of the simulator model are set. This becomes especially important when optimising interfaces for individual users, with a focus on certain user abilities or idiosyncracies [36]. The ability to pre-train an approximate posterior model and then quickly conduct parameter inference, as showcased in our second example, could offer breakthroughs in online, human-in-the-loop optimisation and adaptation.

References

[1] G. Bailly, A. Oulasvirta, D. P. Brumby and A. Howes. 2014. Model of visual search and selection time in linear menus. Pages 3865–3874 of: *Proceedings of the 32nd Annual ACM Conference on Human Factors in Computing Systems*. CHI '14. Association for Computing Machinery.

[2] J. P. Borst, N. A. Taatgen and H. van Rijn. 2015. What makes interruptions disruptive? A process-model account of the effects of the problem state bottleneck on task interruption and resumption. Pages 2971–2980 of: *Proceedings of the 33rd Annual ACM Conference on Human Factors in Computing Systems*. CHI '15. Association for Computing Machinery.

[3] M. D. Byrne and A. Kirlik. 2005. Using computational cognitive modeling to diagnose possible sources of aviation error. *The International Journal of Aviation Psychology*, **15**(2), 135–155.

[4] X. Chen, G. Bailly, D. P. Brumby, A. Oulasvirta and A. Howes. 2015. The emergence of interactive behavior: a model of rational menu search. Pages 4217–4226 of: *Proceedings of the 33rd Annual ACM Conference on Human Factors in Computing Systems*. CHI '15. Association for Computing Machinery.

[5] K. Cranmer, J. Brehmer and G. Louppe. 2020. The frontier of simulation-based inference. *PNAS*, 117(48), 30055–30062.

[6] V. Di Pasquale, S. Miranda, R. Iannone and S. Riemma. 2015. A simulator for human error probability analysis (sherpa). *Reliability Engineering & System Safety*, **139**, 17–32.

[7] X. Didelot, R. G. Everitt, A. M. Johansen and D. J. Lawson. 2011. Likelihood-free estimation of model evidence. *Bayesian Analysis*, **6**, 49–76.

[8] C. Durkan, I. Murray and G. Papamakarios. 2020. On contrastive learning for likelihood-free inference. *PMLR*, **119**, 2771–2781.

[9] C. R. Fisher, J. W. Houpt and G. Gunzelmann. 2020. Developing memory-based models of ACT-R within a statistical framework. *Journal of Mathematical Psychology*, **98**, 102416.

[10] W.-T. Fu and P. Pirolli. 2007. Snif-act: a cognitive model of user navigation on the World Wide Web. *Human–Computer Interaction*, **22**(4), 355–412.

[11] C. Gebhardt, A. Oulasvirta and O. Hilliges. 2020. Hierarchical reinforcement learning explains task interleaving behavior. *Computational Brain & Behavior*, **4**, 284–304.

[12] D. Greenberg, M. Nonnenmacher and J. Macke. 2019. Automatic posterior transformation for likelihood-free inference. *PMLR*, **97**, 2404–2414.

[13] M. U. Gutmann and J. Corander. 2016. Bayesian optimization for likelihood-free inference of simulator-based statistical models. *Journal of Machine Learning Research*, **17**(125), 1–47.

[14] T. Halverson and A. J. Hornof. 2011. A computational model of "active vision" for visual search in human–computer interaction. *Human–Computer Interaction*, **26**(4), 285–314.

[15] Y. Huang, C. White, H. Xia and Y. Wang. 2017. A computational cognitive modeling approach to understand and design mobile crowdsourcing for campus safety reporting. *International Journal of Human-Computer Studies*, **102**, 27–40.

[16] M. Järvenpää, M. U. Gutmann, A. Pleska, A. Vehtari and P. Marttinen. 2019. Efficient acquisition rules for model-based approximate Bayesian computation. *Bayesian Analysis*, **14**(2), 595–622.

[17] J. P. Jokinen, T. Kujala and A. Oulasvirta. 2020. Multitasking in driving as optimal adaptation under uncertainty. *Human Factors*, article 0018720820927687.

[18] J. P. Jokinen, S. Sarcar, A. Oulasvirta, C. Silpasuwanchai, Z. Wang and X. Ren. Modelling learning of new keyboard layouts. Pages 4203–4215 of: *Proceedings of the 2017 CHI Conference on Human Factors in Computing Systems*. CHI '17. Association for Computing Machinery.

[19] J. P. Jokinen, Z. Wang, S. Sarcar, A. Oulasvirta and X. Ren. 2020. Adaptive feature guidance: modelling visual search with graphical layouts. *International Journal of Human–Computer Studies*, **136**, 102376.

[20] A. Kangasrääsiö, K. Athukorala, A. Howes, J. Corander, S. Kaski and A. Oulasvirta. Inferring cognitive models from data using approximate Bayesian computation. Pages 1295–1306 of: *Proceedings of the 2017 CHI Conference on Human Factors in Computing Systems*. CHI '17. Association for Computing Machinery.

[21] A. Kangasrääsiö, J. P. Jokinen, A. Oulasvirta, A. Howes and S. Kaski. 2019. Parameter inference for computational cognitive models with approximate Bayesian computation. *Cognitive Science*, **43**(6), e12738.

[22] J. Kokko, U. Remes, O. Thomas, H. Pesonen and J. Corander. 2019. PYLFIRE: Python implementation of likelihood-free inference by ratio estimation. *Wellcome Open Research*, **4**, 197.

[23] J. Lintusaari, M. U. Gutmann, R. Dutta, S. Kaski and J. Corander. 2017. Fundamentals and recent developments in approximate Bayesian computation. *Systematic Biology*, **66**(1), e66.

[24] J. Lintusaari, H. Vuollekoski, A. Kangasrääsiö, K. Skytén, M. Järvenpää, P. Marttinen, M. U. Gutmann, A. Vehtari, J. Corander and S. Kaski. 2018. ELFI: Engine for Likelihood-Free Inference. *Journal of Machine Learning Research*, **19**(16), 1–7.

[25] D. J. Nott, V. M.-H. Ong, Y. Fan and S. A. Sisson. 2019. High-dimensional ABC. Pages 211–241 of: S. A. Sisson, Y. Fan, and M. A. Beaumont, eds., *Handbook of Approximate Bayesian Computation*. CRC Press.

[26] M. O'Brien and M. T. Keane. 2007. Modeling user behavior using a search-engine. Pages 357–360 of: *Proceedings of the 12th International Conference on Intelligent User Interfaces*. IUI '07. Association for Computing Machinery.

[27] A. Oulasvirta, N. R. Dayama, M. Shiripour, M. John and A. Karrenbauer. 2020. Combinatorial optimization of graphical user interface designs. *Proceedings of the IEEE*, **108**(3), 434–464.

[28] G. Papamakarios, D. Sterratt and I. Murray. 2019. Sequential neural likelihood: Fast likelihood-free inference with autoregressive flows. *PMLR*, **89**, 837–848.

[29] P. Pirolli, G. M. Youngblood, H. Du, A. Konrad, L. Nelson and A. Springer. 2018. Scaffolding the mastery of healthy behaviors with Fittle+ systems: evidence-based interventions and theory. *Human–Computer Interaction*, 1–34.

[30] C. Pompanon and É. Raufaste. 2009. The intervention trigger model: computational modelling of air traffic control. In *Proceedings of the Annual Meeting of the Cognitive Science Society*, vol. 31.

[31] D. Prangle. Summary statistics. Pages 125–152 of: S. A. Sisson, Y. Fan, and M. A. Beaumont, eds., *Handbook of Approximate Bayesian Computation*. CRC Press, 2019.

[32] L. F. Price, C. C. Drovandi, A. Lee, and D. J. Nott. 2018. Bayesian synthetic likelihood. *Journal of Computational and Graphical Statistics*, **27**, 1–11.

[33] F. Putze, M. Salous and T. Schultz. 2018. Detecting memory-based interaction obstacles with a recurrent neural model of user behavior. Pages 205–209 of: *23rd International Conference on Intelligent User Interfaces*. IUI '18. Association for Computer Machinery.

[34] S. Roberts and H. Pashler. 2000. How persuasive is a good fit? A comment on theory testing. *Psychological Review*, **107**(2), 358.

[35] D. D. Salvucci, M. Zuber, E. Beregovaia and D. Markley. 2005. Distract-r: rapid prototyping and evaluation of in-vehicle interfaces. Pages 581–589 of: *Proceedings of the SIGCHI Conference on Human Factors in Computing Systems*. CHI '06. Association for Computer Machinery.

[36] S. Sarcar, J. P. Jokinen, A. Oulasvirta, Z. Wang, C. Silpasuwanchai and X. Ren. 2018. Ability-based optimization of touchscreen interactions. *IEEE Pervasive Computing*, **17**(1), 15–26.

[37] S. A. Sisson, Y. Fan and M. A. Beaumont, eds. 2019. *Handbook of Approximate Bayesian Computation*. CRC Press.

[38] O. Thomas, R. Dutta, J. Corander, S. Kaski and M. U. Gutmann. 2020. Likelihood-free inference by ratio estimation. *Bayesian Analysis* (advance publication).

[39] J. G. Trafton, M. D. Bugajska, B. R. Fransen and R. M. Ratwani. 2008. Integrating vision and audition within a cognitive architecture to track conversations. Pages 201–208 of: *Proceedings of the 3rd ACM/IEEE International Conference on Human Robot Interaction*. HRI '08. Association for Computer Machinery.

[40] B. M. Turner and P. B. Sederberg. 2014. A generalized, likelihood-free method for posterior estimation. *Psychonomic Bulletin & Review*, **21**(2), 227–250.

[41] B. M. Turner and T. Van Zandt. 2012. A tutorial on approximate Bayesian computation. *Journal of Mathematical Psychology*, **56**(2), 69–85, 2012.

[42] S. Vasishth. 2020. Using approximate Bayesian computation for estimating parameters in the cue-based retrieval model of sentence processing. *MethodsX*, **7**, 100850.

[43] S. N. Wood. 2010. Statistical inference for noisy nonlinear ecological dynamic systems. *Nature*, **466**(7310), 1102–1104.

Appendix: Mathematical Background and Notation

John H. Williamson

Abstract

The mathematical background used in Bayesian approaches can be unfamiliar to interaction designers. This chapter gives a brief introduction to probability theory and standard notation, including conditional probability, expectation and Bayes' Rule. This is followed by a summary of terminology in Bayesian computation with Markov Chain Monte Carlo, and a discussion of common modelling choices including linear models and normal distributions. A brief glossary of terms is provided.

A.1 Introduction

The following section gives a brief introduction to the philosophy, nomenclature and notation common in Bayesian approaches. This is a short summary of the points most relevant to this book, but it is not and cannot be a complete introduction. A very compact outline of the relevant mathematical definitions is given in the *Probability and Statistics Cookbook* by Vallentin.[1]

A.1.1 Probability

We reason about uncertainty by attaching numerical values to how likely configurations of the world are. Probability is represented as a real number, in the range 0 to 1. Probability 0 means impossible, and probability 1 means certain. We talk about the *probability* of things that we do not know, for example, because they happen in the future, or because we do not know them directly.

---

[1] http://statistics.zone

Probability distributions are assignments of probabilities to each configuration within a set of possible configurations.

Philosophy of Probability

The philosophy of probability is a controversial topic. What does probability mean?

In the *frequentist* interpretation of probability, it refers solely to the long-term average occurrence of events from an infinite sequence of identical trials. The probability of a drawing a red king from a shuffled (randomised) deck of standard playing cards is $2/52 = 1/26$; we can keep drawing cards forever, and, on average, we'll see a red king once for every 26 cards drawn. This is a fixed, objective fact.

In the *Bayesian* interpretation, which we are concerned with, probability is purely a numerical quantification of belief. I might have the belief that there is a 20% probability that you understood the previous sentence. This is not a repeatable experiment; reading the sentence again is not the same as reading it the first time. Given that probability, I might naturally expect that if I asked 100 readers, 20 of them *would* have understood the sentence, but that is **not** what the statement says – it is my quantification of belief about *you*, the specific reader, in this specific instance. It is a quantification that I could update to a new value given some new evidence.

In the context of modelling, the Bayesian interpretation of probability leads us to ascribe probabilities not only to random occurrences like the random drawing of a card, but to values which are definite but we do not know. We assign higher probabilities to likely configurations and lower probabilities to less likely configurations. We update these probabilities as evidence is observed to strengthen our belief in configurations compatible with the evidence. In this interpretation, there may be cases where we might reasonably believe there is a true fixed value which we are trying to estimate; our probabilities in this case purely describe our ignorance, not the randomness of the world.

A.1.2 Random Variables and Distributions

We work with **random variables** (RVs), written in capitals, like X. We can treat these as if they were variables (such as a real number, or an integer, or a vector, or any other datatype) whose value we do *not* know, but we do know something about: their distribution – how likely they are to take on certain values. We can imagine a random variable as representing an experiment yet to be performed. We can perform computations with random variables.

Every random variable has a set of possible **outcomes**. For example, these could be the 'heads' or 'tails' for a coin; or the (infinite) set of real numbers in a reaction time problem; or a set of 200 dimensional vectors. The set of possible outcomes is called the **sample space**. Any subset of that sample space is an **event** and has an associated probability. For example, we might have a random variable modelling the number of clicks on a button on a web page. The outcomes would be the click count, with a sample space of non-negative integers $(0, 1, 2, 3, \ldots)$. Possible events might include 'more than 6 clicks', or 'an even number of clicks', or 'zero clicks' (an event covering exactly one outcome), each of which would have an associated probability.

There are two important classes of random variables, that are qualitatively different. A **continuous** random variable has outcomes that range over an (uncountably) infinite set, like the real numbers. A **discrete** random variable has a finite set of distinct outcomes, like the integers one through six, to represent the outcome of a six-faced die.

Outcomes are written lowercase, such as x, and we write the probability of an outcome as $P(X = x)$, the probability that random variable X takes on the specific outcome x; for example $P(\text{touch event} = \text{touchup}) = 0.05$.

Random variables have a **probability distribution** that assigns all outcomes probabilities. This is defined via a function, notated $f_X(x)$, that relates outcomes to probabilities. The sum of probability over all possible outcomes is necessarily one. In the case of a discrete random variable, this is simple: a literal mapping of outcomes to numbers which can be stated as a **probability mass function** (PMF). Each outcome is given a proportion of the total available probability mass (1.0). We can imagine this like a dictionary or hash table mapping outcomes to numbers, which all sum up to one, as in Figure A.1.

```
coin_pmf = {
        "heads": 0.2,
        "tails": 0.8
}

user_emotion_pmf = {"angry":0.1, "calm":0.5,
                    "nervous":0.1, "happy":0.3}
```

For **continuous random variables**, things are a little more complicated. The formal details are out of the scope of this tutorial and require a some background in measure theory. For a continuous RV the probability of any *specific* outcome is zero, but the probability of a value falling into some subset (like a range) is what we are interested in. To get around this issue, we work with **probability density functions** (PDFs), still notated $f_X(x)$. These assign *density*, and not probability, to outcomes. We can get probabilities from density functions by integrating over some subset of the sample space, like a contiguous range.

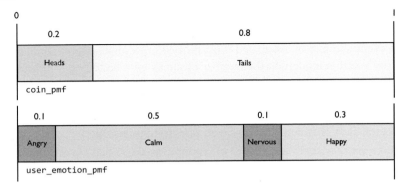

Figure A.1 A probability mass function (PMF) divides up the interval from 0 to 1. Each possible outcome from the sample space gets a proportion of the interval equal to its probability. Here, the upper PMF represents a 'biased coin toss', and the lower represents possible user emotional states.

Many of the tricky parts of probabilistic computation stem from the need to represent and operate on continuous density functions. In modern computational approaches, we normally just sidestep the issue and work with approximations instead. In cases where we do work with density functions, it can be more useful to consider the **cumulative distribution function**, notated $F_X(x)$ (note the capital F) which is the integral of the PDF from $-\infty$ to x for every x (Figure A.2). This gives a probability (not a density) that a value from X would take on a value smaller than x.

$$F_X(x) = \int_{-\infty}^{x} f_x(x)dx. \tag{A.1}$$

Probability density functions are functions, where the specific shape of that function is usually defined by a distribution family (like 'normal' or 'Cauchy') and a vector of parameters, notated θ. When writing the density function $f_X(x)$, we can explicitly indicate that f_X is determined by θ by writing $f_X(x; \theta)$. The density function is configured by a particular setting of θ, and is a function mapping outcomes x to densities. For example, a 'normal distribution' is really a whole family of distributions indexed by two parameters $\theta = [\mu, \sigma]$, the mean and standard deviation.

The **support** of a probability distribution is the region in which it has non-zero density. A normal distribution has non-zero density everywhere and so has **infinite support**; a uniform distribution assigns equal probability inside some range and has zero density outside, and so is said to have **compact** support. This is important for setting priors: a prior distribution with compact support

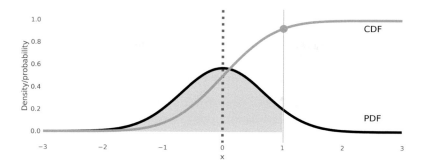

Figure A.2 The probability density function (PDF) and cumulative distribution function (CDF) of a normal distribution. The dot on the CDF is equal to the total area shaded in grey on the PDF.

permanently excludes those hypotheses from consideration. No evidence can ever change the probability from zero. The **tails** of a distribution are elements of the sample set with low probability, extreme values that are far from the bulk of the distribution.

If we have a known probability mass or density function, we can talk about the **likelihood** of an observation given that function, $\mathcal{L}(x; \theta) = f_X(x; \theta)$. This is a quantification of how likely that observation is to have been generated *given* that probability distribution. Typically, we are most interested in how this likelihood changes as θ changes. **Probability** refers to the future, to the observation of unknown values we have yet to encounter; **likelihood** refers to the past, to how compatible observed data are with a distribution. The likelihood of n independent values of x is the product of the likelihoods:

$$\mathcal{L}(x; \theta) = \mathcal{L}(x_1; \theta) \times \mathcal{L}(x_2; \theta) \times \ldots \mathcal{L}(x_n; \theta). \tag{A.2}$$

For numerical reasons (to avoid floating-point underflow), we almost always work with the log-likelihood, which for n independent values is the *sum* of the log-likelihood of each value:

$$\log \mathcal{L}(x_1 \ldots x_n; \theta) = \sum_{i=1}^{n} \log \mathcal{L}(x_i; \theta). \tag{A.3}$$

This computation is numerically stable.

To notate that a random variable has a specific distribution, we write $X \sim D$, to state that X is 'distributed as' D. Usually, this distribution D is specified with the parameters that fully specify it: $X \sim \mathcal{N}(\mu, \sigma^2)$ means that the distribution of X is defined by the probability density function for a normal distribution $\mathcal{N}$ with mean μ and standard deviation σ. When we write this, we associate X with a probability distribution defined by the particular density function.

A.1.3 Distributions over Continuous Variables

When working with continuous random variables, there are many possible choices for the form of the distribution; statisticians have catalogued dozens of distribution types that model certain phenomena or have useful mathematical properties. These distribution classes are the building blocks of probabilistic models. Some probability distributions have very niche application domains, and others are widely used as general-purpose model components. The aforementioned *Probability and Statistics Cookbook* indexes many of these, their properties and their relationships. As concrete examples of widely used continuous distributions, we briefly review the *normal* and *uniform* distributions.

A.1.4 Operations

We can do several important operations with random variables.

- **Likelihood** We can evaluate $f_X(x; \theta)$ at any point to compute $\mathcal{L}(x; \theta) = f_X(x; \theta)$, how likely x is for this specific density/mass function. If the distribution is thought of as a model with a parameter configuration θ, the likelihood tells us how likely x is to be observed under the configuration θ.
- **Sample** We can draw random samples from X. These are definite values whose distribution follows X. Drawing samples is not automatic given a density function and requires specific algorithms for different density functions. In some cases, only approximate samples are feasible.
- **Expectation** We can compute the expectation $E[g(X)]$. This is the sum of some function $g(x)$ evaluated over all possible values of X and weighted by how likely each of the outcomes x are. It is the 'average' of $g(X)$. Often, we have to approximate this by sampling specific x and applying $g(x)$ to the samples, and numerically averaging the result.

A.1.5 Expectations

The **expectation** of a random variable $E[X]$ is the 'average' value it takes on. We can compute by integrating (or summing) over all possible states and multiplying the probability each state with the value of X at that state. For example, if the random variable represented 2D positions (vectors in $\mathbb{R}^2$), the expectation would be an average of all possible vectors weighted by the probability of that vector:

$$E[X] = \int f_X(x)x\,dx. \tag{A.4}$$

Most usefully, given a function $g(x)$ which takes values from X to some other values, we can compute $E[g(X)]$, the expected value of the function of a random variable, again just integrating (or summing) over all possible outcomes from X, x and weighting the value $f(x)$ by the probability of X taking on that value:

$$E[g(X)] = \int f_X(x)g(x)\,dx. \tag{A.5}$$

For example,

$$E[X^2] = \int f_X(x)x^2\,dx. \tag{A.6}$$

Expectations are the lens through which we view probability distributions. We access the results of inference by computing expectations of functions of random variables. For example, the (raw) *moments* of a distribution can be computed as an expectation

$$E[X^n] = \int f_X(x)x^n\,dx, \tag{A.7}$$

from which we can derive the mean and variance of a random variable. Expectations allow us to extract numerical descriptors of distributions which we can then use to make decisions or perform other computations.

The conditional expectation $E[X|Y]$ is the expected value of X given Y, and is

$$E[X|Y] = \int f_{X|Y}(x,y)x\,dx. \tag{A.8}$$

A.1.6 Joint, Marginal and Conditional Probability

If we have two random variables X, Y, then probability $P(X = x, Y = y)$ or $P(X, Y)$ is the probability that X and Y take on the specific values x and y simultaneously. This is the **joint distribution** of X and Y, and is defined by a density function $f_{XY}(x, y)$.

Something that can cause confusion: $P(X > 5)$ is the probability that X takes on values greater than 5, and is a single number such as 0.3. $P(X)$ is a shorthand for $P(X = x)$, and refers to the *whole distribution* over X (i.e. for all x). It is a distribution, not a number! It is defined by the density function $f_X(x)$.

Given a joint distribution over multiple variables, we can always remove a variable from consideration by integrating over all possible values it could take on. This 'integrates out' the variable and is called **marginalisation** (Figure A.3). For example, $P(X)$ is defined by a density function $f_X(x)$ that can be found from $f_{XY}(x, y)$ by integrating over all possible values in the sample space of Y as

$$f_X(x) = \int f_{XY}(x, y) dy. \tag{A.9}$$

$P(X = x | Y = y)$, where | is read as 'given', is the **conditional distribution** of X given Y. It is the probability that X takes on the value x *given that we know* that Y took on the value y. In general, $P(X|Y) \neq P(Y|X)$.

For a continuous random variable, the conditional distribution is defined by a density function:

$$f_{X|Y} = \frac{f_{XY}(x, y)}{f_X(x)} = \frac{f_{XY}(x, y)}{\int f_{XY}(x, y) dy}. \tag{A.10}$$

A.1.7 Bayes' Rule

Bayes' rule is the foundation of Bayesian inference. It simply gives the rule to transpose conditional distributions:

$$P(A|B) = \frac{P(B|A)P(A)}{P(B)}. \tag{A.11}$$

Despite being trivial to state, it is often unintuitive in its implications. Typically, we use Bayes' rule to update our belief about a set of possible *hypotheses H* given some data D, and write

$$P(H|D) = \frac{P(D|H)P(H)}{P(D)}. \tag{A.12}$$

In words: the probability of a hypothesis given data = (probability of seeing this data given that hypothesis) * (probability of that hypothesis set in advance) / (probability of seeing this data given every possible hypothesis).

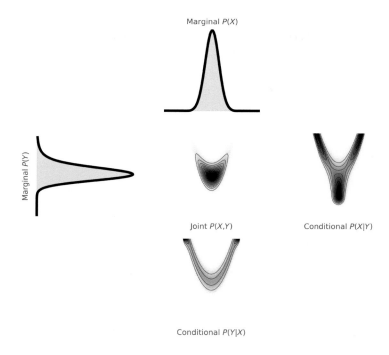

Figure A.3 The density for a joint distribution $P(X, Y)$ (centre, darker indicating higher density) can be integrated over one variable to get the densities of the marginal distributions $P(X)$ or $P(Y)$ (left, top). The density of conditional distributions $P(X|Y)$ and $P(Y|X)$ give the density for one variable *given* that we fix the other.

Prior, Posterior, Likelihood and Marginal Likelihood

Each term has a specific name:

$$\text{posterior} = \frac{\text{likelihood} \times \text{prior}}{\text{evidence}}. \tag{A.13}$$

The *evidence* $P(D)$ is often also called the *marginal likelihood*. Some simple algebra shows that you can always work out $P(D)$:

$$P(D) = \int P(D|H)P(H)dH, \tag{A.14}$$

that is, we integrate (or sum) up over *every possible hypothesis* the product of the likelihood times the prior. This term, the *evidence*, just has the effect of making sure that the probability distribution sums to 1. It is sometimes called the *normalising constant* for this reason. Sometimes we work it out explicitly, as in the worked example below. Often, we only really care about comparing the relative weights of different hypotheses – and for that, we can just ignore the $P(D)$ term. This is the form

$$P(H|D) \propto P(D|H)P(D) \qquad (A.15)$$

that we typically use in most inference. If we are not comparing different models (just different hypotheses *within* some model), then it does not matter what $P(D)$ is; we care only about the relative likelihoods of those hypotheses given the data we actually observed.

A.1.8 Describing Distributions: Quantiles and Credible Intervals

Distributions can be hard to communicate. As well as expectations, **quantiles** are often used as summary statistics to report distributions. Quantiles denote fixed cutpoints in a distribution that split the distribution, such that some quantity of the density lies below a cutpoint. The pth **quantile** of a probability distribution is a number q such that $P(X < q) = p$. For example, the median is the 50% quantile (the value q such that $p = 0.5$) and is the value that splits the distribution of X equally, with an equal probability of a value drawn from the distribution being above or below q. When quantiles are specified in percentages, they are referred to as **percentiles**. The 'inter-quartile range' is the value $IQR = q_3 - q_1$, where q_1 and q_3 are the 25% ($p = 0.25$) and 75% ($p = 0.75$) quantiles. Quantiles can be a more robust way to report distributions; the median, for example, is little affected by changes in extreme values in the tails of a distribution.

A **credible interval** is an interval that covers a particular quantity of density. It is particularly common in Bayesian analyses to describe the posterior distribution of parameters. For example, a 90% credible interval (CI) is *any* interval such that $P(l < X < h) = 0.9$, for some values l and h. For any given distribution, there are an infinite number of credible intervals, since the only requirement is that the interval $[l, h]$ 'cover' a certain amount of density. The two most commonly used intervals to summarise distributions are the **centred** or **equal-tailed** credible interval, where the probability of being above or below the interval is equal, and the **highest (posterior) density interval** (HPDI), which is the *shortest* interval that covers the given range ($P(l < X < h) = c$

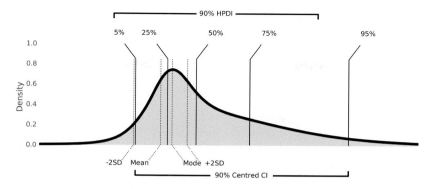

Figure A.4 The 5%, 25%, 50%, 75% and 95% percentiles of a distribution, along with the centred and highest density credible intervals (upper and lower brackets). Compare with the mean, the mean +/− two standard deviations (+/−2 SD) and the mode of the distribution (labelled below).

such that $h - l$ is minimised). These are both useful ways of summarising distributions, and are often used in reporting of posterior distributions.

Figure A.4 illustrates the percentiles and credible intervals for an asymmetric distribution, alongside summary statistics like the mean and standard deviation.

A.1.9 Entropy

Entropy measures the uncertainty of a distribution. We can define entropy for distributions over discrete values as:

$$H(X) = -\sum_x P(X = x) \log_2 P(X = x), \qquad (A.16)$$

which is just the (negative) expected log probability of X.

Entropy is a measure of the surprise, uncertainty or information content of a distribution; it is larger when distributions imply a wider diversity of effective possibilities. Entropy is zero if all the probability mass is concentrated on a single outcome and all others are impossible. Entropy is measured in bits when using a log base of 2, or *nats* when using base e.

It does not make sense to discuss the absolute entropy of continuous distributions. However, we can instead measure the Kullback–Leibler (KL) divergence (relative entropy) between two continuous distributions P and Q, assuming both distributions are defined over the same sample space, such as the real numbers. This KL divergence is defined as:

$$D_{KL}(P||Q) = \int \log_2 \frac{f_Q(x)}{f_P(x)} dx, \qquad (A.17)$$

writing $f_P(x)$ as the density function for P and likewise $f_Q(x)$ for Q, where the integral ranges over the whole sample space of P and Q. This is not a symmetric measure: $D_{KL}(P||Q) \neq D_{KL}(Q||P)$ in general. The relative entropy tells us how much information is required to transform from one distribution to another. In Bayesian inference, this may be used to measure the change from the prior distribution to the posterior distribution. A large KL-divergence indicates that a substantial amount of information has been learned, and the posterior is more concentrated than the prior was.

A.2 Sample-Based Inference

One of the most important practical ways of working with distributions – and thus doing Bayesian inference – is to work with *samples* instead of distributions. We cannot easily manipulate continuous density functions with computer programs. We can, however, work with ensembles of random samples – *definite* values which we can draw from a probability distribution. If we then want to do computations, such as compute the product or sum of random variables, we can perform the operations on the samples instead. This can often be done in parallel and accelerated with SIMD computation, or with GPU compute.

This makes it trivial to do approximate computations with random variables. Say we wanted to compute the distribution of the square of a normally distributed number. It is hard to write down the associated probability density function via algebra, but trivial to write code that samples from it, given a function that can draw samples from a normal distribution:

```
def squared_normal(mean, std, n):
        return np.random.normal(mean, std, n) ** 2
```

This gives us n samples from the resulting 'squared normal' distribution. Most relevantly, we can approximate any expectation $E[f(X)]$ from these samples. Using the notation $x^{(i)}$ to mean 'the ith random sample drawn from the distribution of random variable X', we can write:

$$E[f(X)] \approx \frac{1}{N} \sum_i f(x^{(i)}) \qquad (A.18)$$

```
def sample_expect(sample_x, f, n):
        return 1/n * sum(f(sample_x()) for i in range(n))
```

This approximation converges to $E[f(x)]$ with an error that decreases as $O(\sqrt{n})$.

Importantly for interaction, if we have a simulator of some kind that can take definite inputs, we can 'pump' random samples into it. Imagine a simulation of a UI that takes touch events and outputs UI component events. We can draw samples from some simple distribution representing touch events, like a normal distribution, feed them to the simulator and collect the distribution of activated UI components. No complicated integrals are required.

Sample-based algorithms which use random samples drawn from distributions are called **Monte Carlo** algorithms (and quasi-Monte Carlo (QMC) if the samples are not random but chosen in a more systematic way). Monte Carlo approaches are critical to modern inference. Techniques such as Markov Chain Monte Carlo use simple sample-based algorithms to approximate intractable Bayesian inference; in particular to compute $P(A|B) \propto P(B|A)P(A)$, the product of a prior and a likelihood, without computing the marginal likelihood $P(B)$. In 'online' settings, such as tracking a hand from a video stream, techniques like particle filters (sequential Monte Carlo approaches) use simulators to propagate samples forward (to predict what is happening 'behind the scenes') and then compare each of the sampled predictions with reality (to refine the belief). This predict-correct model is a startlingly powerful approach to solve many problems in interaction where information flows over time.

A.2.1 Markov Chain Monte Carlo

Markov chain Monte Carlo (MCMC) is probably the most common method for performing Bayesian inference at present, and certainly the best supported by software libraries. This class of methods draws approximate samples from a posterior probability distribution, given a prior, likelihood and observations. MCMC avoids the problem of computing the marginal likelihood $P(D)$ and instead is concerned with computing the relative probabilities of different hypotheses $P(H|D) \propto P(D|H)P(H)$. The details of MCMC are beyond the scope of this tutorial. Although there exist sophisticated algorithms, the

Figure A.5 A Markov Chain Monte Carlo process sampling from a two-parameter probability density with a very awkward form (density shown as contour lines). Despite the complex form, the corresponding density function $f_X(x)$ can be evaluated anywhere, giving the density at that particular point. An MCMC sampler progressively wanders through the space, eventually collecting samples that tend to random samples from the entire distribution. The three panels show samples (black dots) drawn by the MCMC sampling process after 100, 500 and 1500 samples (left to right). The process gradually explores the density function, drawing more samples in denser regions.

principle is simple: define a process that wanders through the sample space in such a way that the points visited end up as if they were drawn at random from a distribution. This can be done with nothing other than the ability to sample the density function at any given point. Figure A.5 shows an example of an MCMC sampler applied to a two-dimensional distribution.

The basic algorithms for MCMC are very simple but have strong theoretical guarantees that they will *eventually* correctly approximate the posterior distribution. There are many sophistications that can accelerate this approach. In particular, if it is possible to obtain the derivatives of the probability densities involved with respect to the parameters, Hamiltonian Monte Carlo (HMC) can very efficiently sample posteriors. The advent of automatic differentiation packages like Theano, Tensorflow, PyTorch and JAX has made it straightforward to obtain derivatives directly from code. This approach allows models to be written as programs, which can be much more flexible than traditional statistical models (e.g. flexibly combining continuous and discrete variables, dropping in a neural network or even using recursion or other flow control).

In practice, given a finite computation budget, using MCMC approaches still requires care. This involves performing *diagnostics* to establish that the sampling process is doing something sensible; *tuning* the sampling process to make sampling more effective; and sometimes *reparameterising* models to make them sample more cleanly. For example, for numerical reasons, it can often be easier to sample from a model with standardised parameters (re-scaled to have mean 0, standard deviation 1) rather than in the original units, even though the probability distributions are theoretically unchanged by this normalisation step.

> The 'folk theorem of statistical computing' states:
> *'When you have computational problems, often there's a problem with your model.'* – Andrew Gelman[2]
> In other words, an MCMC sampler (or other approximation approach) that fails to deliver results in reasonable time is an indication that the model itself might be problematic.

Traces

When applied to Bayesian inference problems, MCMC approaches produce **traces** as output; sequences of samples giving definite settings for all parameters in a model, rather than the functional form of a distribution. To answer questions, we can use descriptive statistics of the traces. For example, the arithmetic mean of the trace of one parameter can be used as an approximation of the expectation of the posterior distribution of that parameter, $E[\hat{X}] = \frac{1}{N}\sum_{i=1} N x_i$. Credible intervals can be approximated by percentiles of the trace samples (e.g. sort N trace samples and take the values in indices at $0.25N$ and $0.75N$ as the 50% credible interval). The approximate distribution of the posterior can be visualised using a histogram of the trace, a kernel density estimate or a box plot.

Traces are the output of most probabilistic programming systems. In their raw form, they can be seen as very large tables. Each row represents an independent value drawn. Each column corresponds to one parameter, as in the example in Figure A.6.

The trace time series shown above is often used as a crude debugging tool. A sampler that works well should produce traces that 'bounce around' pretty much randomly, leading to a thick, noisy time series when plotted. A sampler that gets stuck or oscillates between a few distinct values is probably not sampling well. More sophisticated diagnostics can be run to numerically evaluate the quality of an MCMC trace, but no measure can diagnose all possible sampling problems.

Posteriors and Posterior Predictives

When sampling from a model, the trace is a sequence of samples, each of which specifies a parameter configuration. These are samples (approximately) from the *posterior* distribution of the model. These parameter configurations can be

---

[2] https://statmodeling.stat.columbia.edu/2008/05/13/the_folk_theore/

J. H. Williamson

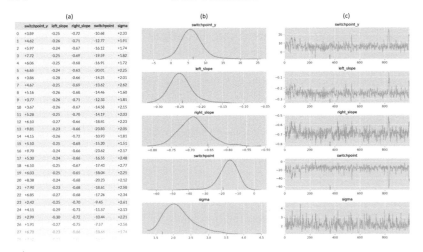

(a)				
switchpoint_y	left_slope	right_slope	switchpoint	sigma
0	+3.89	-0.25	-0.72	-10.68	+2.33
1	+4.62	-0.26	-0.71	-12.77	+1.91
2	+5.97	-0.24	-0.67	-16.12	+1.74
3	+2.72	-0.25	-0.69	-19.59	+1.82
4	+6.06	-0.25	-0.68	-16.91	+1.72
5	+6.65	-0.24	-0.63	-20.01	+2.25
6	+3.86	-0.28	-0.66	-14.25	+2.01
7	+4.67	-0.25	-0.69	-13.62	+2.62
8	+5.16	-0.26	-0.68	-14.46	+1.60
9	+3.77	-0.26	-0.71	-12.33	+1.81
10	+3.67	-0.26	-0.67	-14.58	+2.15
11	+5.28	-0.25	-0.70	-14.19	+2.03
12	+6.10	-0.27	-0.66	-18.81	+2.23
13	+9.81	-0.23	-0.66	-23.83	+2.05
14	+4.15	-0.26	-0.72	-10.93	+1.81
15	+5.10	-0.25	-0.68	-15.20	+1.51
16	+9.70	-0.24	-0.66	-23.62	+2.17
17	+5.30	-0.24	-0.66	-16.55	+2.48
18	+6.10	-0.25	-0.67	-17.43	+2.77
19	+6.03	-0.25	-0.65	-18.04	+2.25
20	+8.38	-0.24	-0.68	-20.23	+2.12
21	+7.90	-0.23	-0.68	-18.61	+2.58
22	+6.85	-0.27	-0.68	-17.26	+2.34
23	+2.42	-0.25	-0.70	-9.45	+2.61
24	+4.11	-0.29	-0.73	-11.57	+2.13
25	+2.99	-0.30	-0.72	-10.44	+2.21
26	+1.91	-0.27	-0.75	-7.57	+2.56
27	+6.70	-0.23	-0.66	-18.66	+1.74

Figure A.6 An MCMC trace from a simple probabilistic model. The raw output of the sampler is simply a table (a); each row is a sample and each column is a parameter in the model. These are typically summarised for presentation, in this case using kernel density estimates to summarise the distribution of each parameter (b) and a time series of the parameter values during sampling (c).

fed back into the original model and used to compute synthetic samples from the *observation* distribution. These are samples from the *posterior predictive*, and they are samples in the same space as the original observed data.

In cases in which we care about explaining the causes of a phenomenon, the posterior is typically of interest. In cases we care about making predictions about what an inference implies, the posterior predictive is typically of greatest interest. For example, if we were modelling the reaction time of a user as a function of their age, samples from the posterior distribution might capture possible values of a parameter relating reaction time and age (e.g. +1 year increases reaction time by 2 ms). The posterior predictive distribution samples would be a sequence of simulated reaction times given the fitted model and a set of ages (either from the original data or from some new dataset).

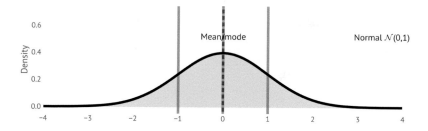

Figure A.7 The standard normal distribution $\mathcal{N}(0, 1)$.

A.3 Common Distributions and Models in Bayesian Inference

A.3.1 Distributions

The Normal Distribution

The **normal distribution** (or Gaussian distribution) is a particularly common distribution in modelling, and notated $X \sim \mathcal{N}(\mu, \sigma^2)$, meaning '$X$ is distributed as a normal distribution with mean μ and variance σ^2'. The density function that defines **standard normal distribution** $\mathcal{N}(0, 1)$ (Figure A.7) has a very simple form:

$$f_X(x) = \frac{1}{Z} e^{-\frac{1}{2}x^2}, \tag{A.19}$$

where Z is a normalising constant.

If we were to write the density function for $\mathcal{N}(\mu, \sigma^2)$ in Python, it would be defined as:

```python
def normal(mu, sigma):
    Z = sigma * np.sqrt(2*np.pi)
    # the specific density function
    # is created with the parameters
    # set when `normal` is called
    def f_x(x):
        y = (x - mu) / sigma
        return 1/Z * np.exp(-0.5 * y ** 2)
    return f_x

# create a mu=3, sigma=12
# density function
n = normal(3, 12)

# get the likelihood (density) at 1.5
# under those parameters
n(1.5)
```

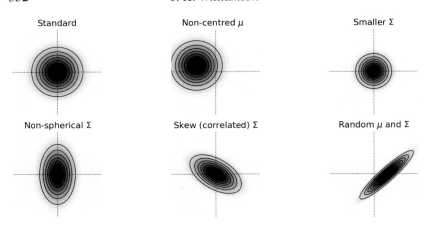

Figure A.8 Six different 2D multivariate normal distributions, shown as filled contour plots; darker grey indicates higher density. The parameter μ specifies the mode of the distribution, and Σ specify the scaling and skewing of the distribution.

The normal distribution has many special qualities, and its convenience and simplicity mean that it is often used to model or approximate the results of computations even when it is not a perfect representation. The subsection 'When Normal Distributions Do Not Make Sense' within Section A.3.1 discusses some of these issues in modelling.

Multivariate normal The normal distribution generalises easily to distributions over vector spaces, the **multivariate normal distribution**. This is often useful in problems in interaction (e.g. representing a distribution of possible points on a 2D screen that a user might be pointing at). This distribution captures a 'location' with a **mean vector** μ and a 'scale' with a covariance matrix Σ; as in $X \sim \mathcal{N}(\mu, \Sigma)$. The density is highest at the point μ and falls away around this point. The covariance matrix captures both how stretched the distribution is in each dimension and *also the correlation between dimensions* (see Figure A.8 for examples). This is a simple and flexible way to represent distributions over variables that have a correlation structure.

The Uniform Distribution

Another concrete example of a continuous distribution, the **uniform distribution** $U(a, b)$ simply assigns equal density to every value in the interval from a to b, and zero elsewhere. A definition like $X \sim u\,(0, 1)$ corresponds to a belief that an X *definitely* is bounded within this interval, but all possibilities within that bound are equal. It has a density function equal to the constant function $f_X(x) = \frac{1}{b-a}$ for all values in the range $[a, b]$ and otherwise zero, and therefore has compact support. As a prior in Bayesian inference, it makes weak assumptions, but the assignment of zero probability to some hypotheses can either be essential (to enforce known constraints) or a danger (if incorrect, no amount of evidence will ever overwhelm the initial assumption that certain states are impossible).

Other Distributions

There are many distribution families used in statistical modelling: the gamma distribution, useful for modelling strictly positive values; the beta distribution, useful for modelling values bounded from 0 to 1; the Dirichlet distribution, useful for modelling collections of variables who sum to 1; the Cauchy distribution, useful for modelling problems with extreme values. Some of these distributions are highly specialised and useful only in niche contexts, while others are general building blocks in probabilistic modelling. The aforementioned *Probability and Statistics Cookbook* has a concise summary of major distribution families, both continuous and discrete, and their inter-relations.

When Normal Distributions Make Sense

There are many reasons why the normal distribution, sometimes called a Gaussian distribution, is often a natural choice for probabilistic modelling and occurs frequently in Bayesian models:

- Many natural phenomena are normally distributed. This is partly explained by the *central limit theorem* which states that the *sum* of many independent random variations will tend to a stable distribution, (almost) *regardless* of what the distribution of those variations is. In virtually all cases we are interested in, this stable distribution is the normal distribution. For example, the length of a user's arm is likely to be approximately normally distributed, because many independent random factors contribute to arm growth (genetics, nutrition, etc.).
- Normal distributions extend easily from a density over real numbers (a number line) to vector spaces (a multi-dimensional space). In the multi-dimensional case, they are parameterised by a mean vector μ and a covariance matrix Σ giving the spread over space. This makes it easy to model multi-dimensional problems. Every slice of a normal distribution is also a normal distribution. Imagine projecting a 2D normal distribution onto a line, or a 3D distribution onto a plane – the result is always another normal distribution. This is not the case for other distribution families.

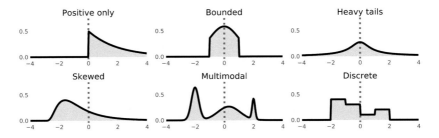

Figure A.9 Six distribution shapes that are unsuitable for modelling with a normal distribution.

- Normal distributions are linear in their parameters. This means that samples from an $\mathcal{N}(\mu, \sigma)$ distribution are exactly the same as samples drawn from $\mu + \sigma * \mathcal{N}(0, 1)$, which can make many computations easier to work with.
- If all we know is the mean and standard deviation of a variable, the normal distribution is the distribution that assumes the least – the maximum entropy choice. This makes it the natural choice for priors when those parameters encode our knowledge.
- The normal distribution is trivial to draw samples from. It is so easy to do so that drawing samples from other distribution families is often implemented by transforming normally distributed samples. Given we need to be able to draw samples to use methods like MCMC, this is a practical motivation to use normal distributions.
- In some cases, Bayesian inference can be computed *exactly* for normal distributions, if we have particular forms of prior on the mean and standard deviation (or covariance matrix). When this is possible, it is extremely efficient and has no approximation error.

When Normal Distributions Do Not Make Sense

For these reasons, much Bayesian modelling extensively uses normal distributions. However, they can be unsuitable in some modelling problems relevant to interaction design, illustrated in Figure A.9:

- Normal distributions have exactly one mode (one 'peak' in the distribution). This makes them poor at representing problems where two or more very distinct hypotheses are likely.
- Normal distributions are perfectly symmetric, and they assign exactly equal probability to a value being some distance greater than the mean as to the

same distance less than the mean. This can be problematic when modelling values such as reaction times, which are often skewed towards larger values.

- They represent distributions over continuous values. They cannot be correctly used to represent values from a discrete set (e.g. ordinal values from 1 to 10, such as from a subjective response questionnaire).
- Normal distributions have infinite support and do not assign zero density to *any* value: anything is possible. This means that they cannot, for example, represent values that are strictly positive, or which are bounded within a specific range.
- They have 'light tails'. The probability of a value being far from the mean becomes very small very quickly. This makes normal distributions inappropriate when occasional extreme values are possible. Other distributions, such as *t* distributions, can be much better models when extreme events are possible.

Maximum Entropy

The **principle of maximum entropy** is a guiding rule in building Bayesian models. It is simply a restatement of Occam's Razor: in the absence of other evidence, believe in the simplest explanation. **Entropy** is a measure of how uncertain a distribution is. A wider distribution has higher entropy than one that concentrates over fewer values. Maximum entropy implies we should choose prior distributions which are as *uncertain as possible* while remaining compatible with what we know. For example, if we *know* that a distribution should have a specific mean and standard deviation, and that is *all* we know, then the correct way to encode that prior belief is as a normal distribution. This distribution shape encodes the least possible knowledge beyond the mean and standard deviation. Figure A.10 shows several possible maximum entropy distributions for different starting assumptions.

A.3.2 Modelling Choices

Bayesian modelling is extremely flexible, and we can build and infer models with complex structures and exotic probability distributions. For many ordinary modelling tasks, there are two modelling choices that are common and computationally convenient:

- The use of normal distributions, either in prior distributions over parameters, or in the likelihood functions defining how likely data is to be observed under those parameters.
- Linear models, that relate parameters and observations via only weighted sums, such as linear regression.

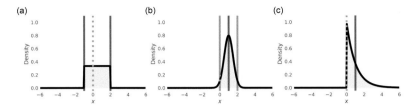

Figure A.10 Which distribution is the maximum entropy choice? It depends on what we know. For example, if we know a mean and a standard deviation, the normal distribution (b) maximises entropy (assumes the least). If we know an upper and lower bound, a uniform distribution (a) maximises entropy. If we know a mean and that a distribution is always positive, an exponential distribution (c) maximises entropy.

Linear models with normal distributions can do a huge amount; most standard frequentist testing models (ANOVA, t-test) are linear normal models.[3] Because of their ubiquity in modelling, particularly in human–computer interaction, the following section discusses the relative benefits and drawbacks of these modelling assumptions.

Linear Models

In the simplest linear models, with one set of observed input x and one set of observed outputs y, we infer a distribution over parameters (a, b) that define a line. In models with more parameters, a linear model would describe a (hyper-)plane. Such models are ubiquitous across disciplines. One reason is that in traditional statistical operations which required hand computations, linear models were all that was feasible. It is the easiest option from a computational point of view.

The other reason is that for any smooth function, basic calculus tells us that a linear approximation is good *for some small region around a point*. If the phenomena we are interested in are concentrated in a sufficiently small region, then a linear model is a reasonable way to capture effects like y gets bigger when x gets bigger, even if the underlying phenomenon is clearly not linear. However, in many problems we encounter in interaction design, a linear model is weak if extended beyond this small-variation realm. Real world processes often saturate, shoot off to asymptotes, have maxima or minima, or are only defined within some bounded range (Figure A.11). In these cases, a linear approximation can be a very misleading modelling choice. A linear model is often a good 'first cut' when we know little else, but we should be wary that

---

[3] https://lindeloev.github.io/tests-as-linear/

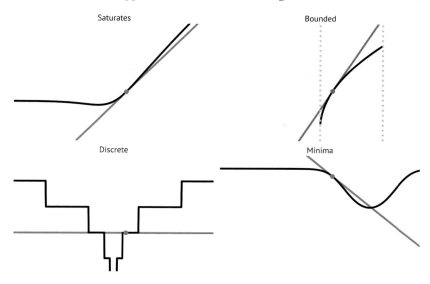

Figure A.11 Illustrations of common cases where a linear model works poorly. True function in black, linear approximation in grey. Linear approximations can break down in the presence of saturation effects; where values are only defined within some limited range; where the function being modelled is not smooth or continuous; or where there are turning points, like maxima or minima in the true function.

a linear model might be evidence of modelling which tries to explain the data observed, rather than modelling which tries to explain the underlying process.

A.4 Glossary of Mathematical Terms

- **argmax/argmin** $\operatorname{argmax}_x f(x)$ is the value x that makes $f(x)$ largest (smallest for argmin).
- **conditional expectation** $E[X|Y]$ the expected value of X, using the weighting $P(X = x|Y = y)$ instead of $P(X = x)$.
- **conditional probability** $P(X|Y)$ the probability $P(X = x|Y = y)$ of X taking on the value x *given that we know* that random variable Y takes on the value y. Equal to $P(X = x)P(Y = y)$ if and only if X and Y are independent.
- **configuration** a specific collection of parameter values that indexes one specific model state.
- **covariance matrix** the generalisation of variance to multi-dimensional spaces, where a distribution can be spread differently across different directions in a vector space.
- **credible interval** A range of values which contains a certain proportion of probability density. A 90% credible interval, for example, is any interval that contains exactly 90% of the density, and we can correctly say that we believe the value to lie inside those bounds with 90% certainty, $P(a < X < b) = 0.9$.
- **cumulative distribution function** $F_x(x)$ is the integral $\int_{-\infty}^{x} f_X(x)dx$ and is equal to the probability $P(X <= x)$.
- **entropy** a measure of surprise or dispersion in a distribution. For discrete distributions, it is the quantity of information required to exactly specify a specific outcome given knowledge of the distribution.
- **event** a subset of outcomes from a sample space that can have a probability associated with it. For example, a distribution capturing the age of users A has outcomes that range over positive integers. An event would be a subset of outcomes, like 'all users over 30', which could have an associated probability ($P(A \geq 30) = 0.1$, for example). Given a probability mass function $f_A(a)$, $P(A \geq 30) = \sum_{30}^{\infty} f_A(a)$.
- **evidence** or **marginal likelihood** $P(D)$ the probability assigned to each possible observation, typically either ignored or computed by the rule $P(D) = \int P(D|H)P(D)dH$.
- **expectation** $E[X]$ the expected or 'average' value of the random variable X; the sum of each outcome weighted by its probability; $E[f(X)]$ the expected value of a function applied to the outcomes (not the probabilities) of a random variable X, weighted by their probabilities.

- **forward model** a model that describes the world reasoning from observations to internal states.

- **inverse model** a model that describes the world reasoning from internal states to observations.

- **inference** the process of reasoning about unknowns given evidence. In Bayesian inference, this is a change in probability distribution from a prior to a posterior distribution.

- **joint distribution** $P(X, Y)$ the distribution of two or more random variables, giving the probability of each possible combination of all outcomes.

- **linear model** a model that uses only weighted sums, such as $y = a_1 x + a_0$ (a_1 and a_0 being the weights).

- **likelihood** $L(x; \theta)$ how likely an observation x is to have been generated under a statistical model with parameters θ, or written as $P(D|H)$; how likely an observation (data) D is to have been generated under the parameters (hypothesis) H.

- **log-likelihood** $\log L(x; \theta)$ normally used in place of likelihood in computations to make numerical calculations easier by avoiding underflow.

- **marginal distribution** a distribution over a subset of random variables (often just one), derived from a joint distribution by marginalisation.

- **marginalisation** computing the marginal distribution of a subset of random variables in a joint distribution by summing/integrating over all the *other* variables in their joint distribution; for example, computing $f_X(x)$ from $f_{XY}(x, y)$ by summing over all possible values of y.

- **mean** the average value of a random variable, equal to the expectation $E[X]$.

- **median** the value that divides a probability density function into upper and lower portions of equal mass.

- **mode** the maximum value of a probability density function (if it exists), or sometimes the *local* maximum of a density function.

- **Monte Carlo methods** approximate methods based on drawing random samples from probability distributions and doing computations upon those.

- **MCMC** or **Markov Chain Monte Carlo**, a flexible class of algorithms used to draw approximate samples from intractable probability distributions by creating a random walk that eventually converges to unbiased random sampling.

- **normal distribution (or Gaussian distribution)** a probability distribution over real numbers (and real vector spaces), specified by a mean and (co-)variance. It has many convenient properties and is the *maximum entropy* distribution where only the mean and variance are known.

- **parameter** a value that defines part of a model. Parameters are typically notated as part of a parameter vector, written as θ, that collects all relevant parameters in a model.
- **percentile** the quantile specified in percentage units (e.g. 50% for $q = 0.5$).
- **posterior predictive** the distribution over *observations* after inference.
- **posterior** $P(H|D)$ the probability assigned to each hypothesis (parameter setting) after inference; the result of applying Bayes' rule.
- **prior** $P(H)$ the probability assigned to each hypothesis (parameter setting) before inference.
- **probability mass/density function, PDF/PMF** a function $f_X(x)$ that maps every outcome x to a mass (probability) or density.
- **probability**, a number between 0 and 1 indicating (in the Bayesian viewpoint) a degree of belief. Probability is notated in different ways in different texts, and its usage is context dependent:
  - $P(A)$ the probability of an *event* A, where an event is a subset of possible outcomes from a sample space, such as the probability that a six-sided die comes up with an even number.
  - $P(X = x)$ the probability that a random variable X takes on an outcome x.
- **quantile** a value q such that the pth proportion of probability mass/density lies below q; e.g. the median is value q such that $P(X < q) = 0.5$.
- **random variable** X, a variable whose value is not known but whose probability distribution is known.
- **sample** a specific definite value drawn from a probability distribution, usually at random.
- **standard deviation** the square root of the variance.
- **support** the set of values for which a probability density function is non-zero; typically compact (bounded range), infinite (unbounded) or semi-infinite (bounded on one side).
- **tails** regions of a probability distribution which have low probability; extreme values.
- **trace** a sequence of samples drawn from a probability distribution by MCMC; the typical output of inference on a probabilistic program.
- **uniform** a probability distribution that assigns equal density to all outcomes in a contiguous interval.
- **utility function** A function $u(x)$ mapping each outcome x to some measure of 'goodness' – the utility of that outcome.
- **variance** a measure of the spread or dispersion of a random variable, equal to the expectation $E[(X - E[X])^2]$.

Printed in the United States
by Baker & Taylor Publisher Services